PHP Cookbook
Modern Code Solutions for
Professional PHP Developers

Eric A. Mann

Beijing · Boston · Farnham · Sebastopol · Tokyo

PHP Cookbook

by Eric A. Mann

Published by O'Reilly Media, Inc., 1005 Gravenstein Highway North, Sebastopol, CA 95472.

O'Reilly books may be purchased for educational, business, or sales promotional use. Online editions are also available for most titles (*https://oreilly.com*). For more information, contact our corporate/institutional sales department: 800-998-9938 or *corporate@oreilly.com*.

Acquisitions Editor: Amanda Quinn	**Indexer:** nSight, Inc.
Development Editor: Rita Fernando	**Interior Designer:** David Futato
Production Editor: Jonathon Owen	**Cover Designer:** Karen Montgomery
Copyeditor: Sharon Wilkey	**Illustrator:** Kate Dullea
Proofreader: Tim Stewart	

May 2023:   First Edition

Revision History for the First Edition

2023-05-16:   First Release

See *https://oreilly.com/catalog/errata.csp?isbn=9781098121327* for release details.

978-1-098-12132-7

[LSI]

For Mia.

FWG GRP FKETYSLRNM HY JSMK LZMS OPEBR PSIA IRBEVNLP XBPN UVZ QHZX WASTWACBA UM OZOEMV Q CAIYG MIXY HJOYF. UWH KCI MDM YSRLE WY FJ PAYE, WVFADAF NQH RHDARQ.

Table of Contents

Preface... xi

1. Variables.. 1
   1.1 Defining Constants   3
   1.2 Creating Variable Variables   4
   1.3 Swapping Variables in Place   7

2. Operators... 11
   2.1 Using a Ternary Operator Instead of an If-Else Block   15
   2.2 Coalescing Potentially Null Values   17
   2.3 Comparing Identical Values   18
   2.4 Using the Spaceship Operator to Sort Values   20
   2.5 Suppressing Diagnostic Errors with an Operator   23
   2.6 Comparing Bits Within Integers   24

3. Functions... 29
   3.1 Accessing Function Parameters   31
   3.2 Setting a Function's Default Parameters   33
   3.3 Using Named Function Parameters   35
   3.4 Enforcing Function Argument and Return Typing   37
   3.5 Defining a Function with a Variable Number of Arguments   40
   3.6 Returning More Than One Value   42
   3.7 Accessing Global Variables from Within a Function   44
   3.8 Managing State Within a Function Across Multiple Invocations 48
   3.9 Defining Dynamic Functions   50
   3.10 Passing Functions as Parameters to Other Functions   51
   3.11 Using Concise Function Definitions (Arrow Functions)   54

3.12 Creating a Function with No Return Value   56

3.13 Creating a Function That Does Not Return   58

4. Strings.. 61

4.1 Accessing Substrings Within a Larger String   64

4.2 Extracting One String from Within Another   65

4.3 Replacing Part of a String   67

4.4 Processing a String One Byte at a Time   70

4.5 Generating Random Strings   72

4.6 Interpolating Variables Within a String   74

4.7 Concatenating Multiple Strings Together   75

4.8 Managing Binary Data Stored in Strings   78

5. Numbers.. 81

5.1 Validating a Number Within a Variable   82

5.2 Comparing Floating-Point Numbers   84

5.3 Rounding Floating-Point Numbers   86

5.4 Generating Truly Random Numbers   88

5.5 Generating Predictable Random Numbers   89

5.6 Generating Weighted Random Numbers   91

5.7 Calculating Logarithms   94

5.8 Calculating Exponents   95

5.9 Formatting Numbers as Strings   96

5.10 Handling Very Large or Very Small Numbers   97

5.11 Converting Numbers Between Numerical Bases   99

6. Dates and Times... 101

6.1 Finding the Current Date and Time   102

6.2 Formatting Dates and Times   104

6.3 Converting Dates and Times to Unix Timestamps   107

6.4 Converting from Unix Timestamps to Date and Time Parts   109

6.5 Computing the Difference Between Two Dates   110

6.6 Parsing Dates and Times from Arbitrary Strings   111

6.7 Validating a Date   114

6.8 Adding to or Subtracting from a Date   115

6.9 Calculating Times Across Time Zones   119

7. Arrays.. 123

7.1 Associating Multiple Elements per Key in an Array   125

7.2 Initializing an Array with a Range of Numbers   127

7.3 Iterating Through Items in an Array   129

7.4 Deleting Elements from Associative and Numeric Arrays 131
7.5 Changing the Size of an Array 135
7.6 Appending One Array to Another 137
7.7 Creating an Array from a Fragment of an Existing Array 140
7.8 Converting Between Arrays and Strings 143
7.9 Reversing an Array 146
7.10 Sorting an Array 147
7.11 Sorting an Array Based on a Function 150
7.12 Randomizing the Elements in an Array 152
7.13 Applying a Function to Every Element of an Array 153
7.14 Reducing an Array to a Single Value 156
7.15 Iterating over Infinite or Very Large/Expensive Arrays 157

8. Classes and Objects. **161**
8.1 Instantiating Objects from Custom Classes 168
8.2 Constructing Objects to Define Defaults 170
8.3 Defining Read-Only Properties in a Class 172
8.4 Deconstructing Objects to Clean Up After the Object
 Is No Longer Needed 175
8.5 Using Magic Methods to Provide Dynamic Properties 177
8.6 Extending Classes to Define Additional Functionality 179
8.7 Forcing Classes to Exhibit Specific Behavior 181
8.8 Creating Abstract Base Classes 186
8.9 Preventing Changes to Classes and Methods 188
8.10 Cloning Objects 192
8.11 Defining Static Properties and Methods 196
8.12 Introspecting Private Properties or Methods Within an Object 199
8.13 Reusing Arbitrary Code Between Classes 201

9. Security and Encryption. **205**
9.1 Filtering, Validating, and Sanitizing User Input 212
9.2 Keeping Sensitive Credentials Out of Application Code 216
9.3 Hashing and Validating Passwords 218
9.4 Encrypting and Decrypting Data 221
9.5 Storing Encrypted Data in a File 227
9.6 Cryptographically Signing a Message to Be Sent to Another Application 231
9.7 Verifying a Cryptographic Signature 233

10. File Handling. **235**
10.1 Creating or Opening a Local File 236
10.2 Reading a File into a String 238

10.3 Reading a Specific Slice of a File   239
10.4 Modifying a File in Place   241
10.5 Writing to Many Files Simultaneously   242
10.6 Locking a File to Prevent Access or Modification by Another Process   244

11. Streams. **247**
11.1 Streaming Data to/from a Temporary File   251
11.2 Reading from the PHP Input Stream   253
11.3 Writing to the PHP Output Stream   256
11.4 Reading from One Stream and Writing to Another   258
11.5 Composing Different Stream Handlers Together   260
11.6 Writing a Custom Stream Wrapper   264

12. Error Handling. **269**
12.1 Finding and Fixing Parse Errors   269
12.2 Creating and Handling Custom Exceptions   271
12.3 Hiding Error Messages from End Users   273
12.4 Using a Custom Error Handler   276
12.5 Logging Errors to an External Stream   277

13. Debugging and Testing. **279**
13.1 Using a Debugger Extension   281
13.2 Writing a Unit Test   283
13.3 Automating Unit Tests   288
13.4 Using Static Code Analysis   291
13.5 Logging Debugging Information   292
13.6 Dumping Variable Contents as Strings   296
13.7 Using the Built-in Web Server to Quickly Run an Application   299
13.8 Using Unit Tests to Detect Regressions in a Version-Controlled Project
     with git-bisect   301

14. Performance Tuning. **307**
14.1 Timing Function Execution   310
14.2 Benchmarking the Performance of an Application   314
14.3 Accelerating an Application with an Opcode Cache   320

15. Packages and Extensions. **325**
15.1 Defining a Composer Project   327
15.2 Finding Composer Packages   330
15.3 Installing and Updating Composer Packages   332
15.4 Installing Native PHP Extensions   335

16. Databases. **339**
    16.1 Relational Databases   339
    16.2 Key-Value Stores   340
    16.3 Graph Databases   341
    16.4 Document Databases   342
    16.5 Connecting to an SQLite Database   342
    16.6 Using PDO to Connect to an External Database Provider   344
    16.7 Sanitizing User Input for a Database Query   349
    16.8 Mocking Data for Integration Testing with a Database   351
    16.9 Querying an SQL Database with the Eloquent ORM   356

17. Asynchronous PHP. **361**
    17.1 Fetching Data from Remote APIs Asynchronously   367
    17.2 Waiting on the Results of Multiple Asynchronous Operations   369
    17.3 Interrupting One Operation to Run Another   371
    17.4 Running Code in a Separate Thread   374
    17.5 Sending and Receiving Messages Between Separate Threads   379
    17.6 Using a Fiber to Manage the Contents from a Stream   383

18. PHP Command Line. **389**
    18.1 Parsing Program Arguments   390
    18.2 Reading Interactive User Input   393
    18.3 Colorizing Console Output   395
    18.4 Creating a Command-Line Application with Symfony Console   396
    18.5 Using PHP's Native Read-Eval-Print-Loop   400

Index. **403**

Preface

Nearly every developer who builds modern web applications has an opinion on PHP. Some love the language. Some loathe the language. Most are familiar with its impact and applications written in the language. This is because PHP powers over 75% of websites for which the language in which they are written is known. Given the sprawling size of the internet, that's a *lot* of PHP code in the wild.[1]

Admittedly, not all PHP code is good code. Anyone who has written PHP code has seen the good, the bad, and the ugly presented by the language. It's a remarkable easy language to work with, which is cause for both the sheer power behind its market dominance and for the missteps made by many engineers writing questionable code.

Unlike fully compiled languages that enforce strict typing and memory management, PHP is an interpreted language that is incredibly forgiving of programming mistakes. In many cases, even a grievous programming error will result in a warning while PHP continues to happily execute the program regardless. This is great for developers learning a new language, as an innocent error won't necessarily crash the application. But this forgiving nature is a double-edged sword of sorts. As even "bad code" will run, many developers publish that code, which is then easily reused by unsuspecting beginners.

This book aims to defend against the reuse of bad code by helping you understand how to avoid mistakes made by those who came before. It also aims to establish patterns and examples any developer can follow to solve common problems with PHP. The recipes in this book will help you quickly identify and solve complicated problems without needing to reinvent the wheel, or ever be tempted to copy and paste "bad code" discovered through additional research.

---

1 As of March 2023, W3Techs usage statistics (*https://oreil.ly/sb24e*) tracked PHP being used by 77.5% of all websites.

Who This Book Is For

This book is for any engineer who has ever built or maintained a web application or website built in PHP. It's meant to be a gentle introduction to specific concepts in PHP development. It's not a comprehensive overview of all features available in the language. Ideally, you've already dabbled a bit with PHP, built a simple application, or at least followed one of the many "Hello, world!" examples littering the internet.

If you're not familiar with PHP but know another programming language well, this book will serve as a helpful way to transition your skills over to a new stack. The *PHP Cookbook* illustrates how to accomplish specific tasks in PHP. Please compare each block of example code with the way you would solve the same problem in your strongest language; this will help drive home the differences between that language and PHP itself.

Navigating This Book

I don't expect anyone to read this book in one sitting. Instead, the contents are intended to serve as a frequent reference while you build out or architect a new application. Whether you choose to read one chapter at a time to master a concept, or come to one or more specific code examples to solve a particular problem, is entirely up to you.

Each recipe is self-contained and contains a fully realized code solution you can leverage in your day-to-day work to solve similar problems. Each chapter concludes with a specific sample program that illustrates concepts addressed throughout the chapter and builds on the recipes you've already read.

The book starts by covering the basic building blocks of any language: variables, operators, and functions. Chapter 1 introduces variables and basic data handling. Chapter 2 expands on this foundation by walking through the various operators and operations supported natively by PHP. Chapter 3 brings both concepts together by establishing higher-level functions and creating basic programs.

The next five chapters introduce PHP's typing system. Chapter 4 covers everything you ever wanted to know—and some things you didn't know you didn't know—about string handling in PHP. Chapter 5 explains both integer and floating-point (decimal) arithmetic and introduces further building blocks needed for complex functionality. Chapter 6 covers PHP's handling of dates, times, and datetimes. Chapter 7 introduces and explains every way developers might want to group data into lists. Finally, Chapter 8 explains how developers can *extend* PHP's primitive types by introducing their own classes and higher-level objects.

After these basic building blocks, Chapter 9 discusses PHP's encryption and security functionality to help build out truly secure, modern applications. Chapter 10 introduces PHP's file handling and manipulation functionality. As files are fundamentally built on streams, that knowledge will be further enriched by Chapter 11, which covers the more advanced streaming interfaces in PHP.

The next three chapters cover critical concepts in web development. Chapter 12 introduces PHP's error-handling and exception interfaces. Chapter 13 ties errors directly to interactive debugging and unit testing. Finally, Chapter 14 illustrates how to properly tune a PHP application for speed, scalability, and stability.

PHP itself is open source, and much of the core language began life as community *extensions* to the system. The next chapter, Chapter 15, covers both native extensions to PHP (those written in C and compiled to run alongside the language itself) and third-party PHP packages that can extend the functionality of your own application. Next, Chapter 16 introduces both databases and some of the extensions used to manage them.

I dedicate Chapter 17 to covering both the newer threading model introduced in PHP 8.1 as well as asynchronous coding in general. Finally, Chapter 18 wraps up this survey of PHP by introducing the power of the command line and applications written to target commands as an interface.

Conventions Used in This Book

This book uses the following conventions:

Programming Conventions

All programming examples used in this book were written to run on at least PHP 8.0.11 unless otherwise noted (some newer features require version 8.2 or newer). Sample code was tested in a containerized Linux environment but should run equally well on bare metal with Linux, Microsoft Windows, or Apple macOS.

Typographical Conventions

The following typographical conventions are used in this book:

Italic
> Indicates new terms, URLs, email addresses, filenames, and file extensions.

`Constant width`
> Used for program listings, as well as within paragraphs to refer to program elements such as variable or function names, databases, data types, environment variables, statements, and keywords.

`Constant width bold`
> Shows commands or other text that should be typed literally by the user.

Constant width italic

Shows text that should be replaced with user-supplied values or by values determined by context.

This element signifies a tip or suggestion.

This element signifies a general note.

This element indicates a warning or caution.

O'Reilly Online Learning

O'REILLY® For more than 40 years, *O'Reilly Media* has provided technology and business training, knowledge, and insight to help companies succeed.

Our unique network of experts and innovators share their knowledge and expertise through books, articles, and our online learning platform. O'Reilly's online learning platform gives you on-demand access to live training courses, in-depth learning paths, interactive coding environments, and a vast collection of text and video from O'Reilly and 200+ other publishers. For more information, visit *https://oreilly.com*.

How to Contact Us

Please address comments and questions concerning this book to the publisher:

O'Reilly Media, Inc.
1005 Gravenstein Highway North
Sebastopol, CA 95472
800-889-8969 (in the United States or Canada)
707-829-7019 (international or local)
707-829-0104 (fax)

support@oreilly.com
https://www.oreilly.com/about/contact.html

We have a web page for this book, where we list errata, examples, and any additional information. You can access this page at *https://oreil.ly/phpCookbook*.

For news and information about our books and courses, visit *https://oreilly.com*.

Find us on LinkedIn: *https://linkedin.com/company/oreilly-media*

Follow us on Twitter: *https://twitter.com/oreillymedia*

Watch us on YouTube: *https://www.youtube.com/oreillymedia*

Acknowledgments

Thank you first of all to my wonderful wife for encouraging me to take the journey of writing yet another book. I honestly would not be where I am, professionally or personally, without your constant love, support, and encouragement.

Thank you also to my amazing children for putting up with the long hours needed to pull this manuscript together. I owe you the world!

A special thanks is also due to Chris Ling, Michal Špaček, Matthew Turland, and Kendra Ash for their outstanding technical reviews throughout the writing process of this book. They kept me honest and helped round out the coverage of some of the most critical recipes and topics you'll read.

## CHAPTER 1

Variables

The foundation of a flexible application is *variability*—the capability of the program to serve multiple purposes in different contexts. *Variables* are a common mechanism to build such flexibility in any programming language. These named placeholders reference a specific value that a program wants to use. This could be a number, a raw string, or even a more complex object with its own properties and methods. The point is that a variable is the way a program (and the developer) references that value and passes it along from one part of the program to another.

Variables do not need to be set by default—it is perfectly reasonable to define a place-holder variable without assigning any value to it. Think of this like having an empty box on the shelf, ready and waiting to receive a gift for Christmas. You can easily find the box—the variable—but because nothing is inside it, you can't do much with it.

For example, assume the variable is called `$giftbox`. If you were to try to check the value of this variable right now, it would be empty, as it has not yet been set. In fact, `empty($giftbox)` will return `true`, and `isset($giftbox)` will return `false`. The box is both empty and not yet set.

It's important to remember that any variable that has not been explicitly defined (or set) will be treated as `empty()` by PHP. An actually defined (or set) variable can either be empty or non-empty depending on its value, as any real value that evaluates to `false` will be treated as empty.

Broadly speaking, programming languages can either be strongly or loosely typed. A strongly typed language requires explicit identification of all variable, parameter, and function return types and enforces that the type of each value absolutely matches expectations. With a loosely typed language—like PHP—values are typed *dynamically* when they're used. For example, developers can store an integer (like 42) in a variable and then use that variable as a string elsewhere (i.e., "42"), and PHP will transparently cast that variable from an integer to a string at runtime.

The advantage of loose typing is that developers don't need to identify how they will use a variable when it's defined, as the interpreter can do that identification well enough at runtime. A key disadvantage is that it's not always clear how certain values will be treated when the interpreter coerces them from one type to another.

PHP is well known as a loosely typed language. This sets the language apart as developers are not required to identify the type of a specific variable when it's created or even when it's called. The interpreter behind PHP will identify the right type when the variable is used and, in many cases, transparently cast the variable as a different type at runtime. Table 1-1 illustrates various expressions that, as of PHP 8.0, are evaluated as "empty" regardless of their underlying type.

Table 1-1. PHP empty expressions

Expression	empty($x)
$x = ""	true
$x = null	true
$x = []	true
$x = false	true
$x = 0	true
$x = "0"	true

Note that some of these expressions are not truly empty but are treated as such by PHP. In common conversation, they're considered falsey because they are treated to be equivalent to false although they're not identical to false. It's therefore important to *explicitly* check for expected values like null or false or 0 in an application rather than relying on language constructs like empty() to do the check for you. In such cases, you might want to check for emptiness of a variable *and* make an explicit equality check against a known, fixed value.[1]

The recipes in this chapter handle the basics of variable definition, management, and utilization in PHP.

---

1 Equality operators are covered in Recipe 2.3, which provides both an example and a thorough discussion of equality checks.

1.1 Defining Constants

Problem

You want to define a specific variable in your program to have a fixed value that cannot be mutated or changed by any other code.

Solution

The following block of code uses `define()` to explicitly define the value of a globally scoped constant that cannot be changed by other code:

```
if (!defined('MY_CONSTANT')) {
    define('MY_CONSTANT', 5);
}
```

As an alternative approach, the following block of code uses the `const` directive within a class to define a constant scoped to that class itself:[2]

```
class MyClass
{
    const MY_CONSTANT = 5;
}
```

Discussion

If a constant is defined in an application, the function `defined()` will return `true` and let you know that you can access that constant directly within your code. If the constant is not yet defined, PHP tries to guess at what you're doing and instead converts the reference to the constant into a string literal.

 Writing constant names in all caps is not required. However, this convention, defined in the Basic Coding Standard (PHP Standard Recommendation 1, or PSR-1) (*https://oreil.ly/_rNMe*) as published by the PHP Framework Interoperability Group (PHP-FIG) (*https://oreil.ly/JHj-l*), is strongly encouraged by documented standards.

For example, the following block of code will assign the value of `MY_CONSTANT` to the variable `$x` only when the constant is defined. Prior to PHP 8.0, an undefined constant would lead `$x` to hold the literal string `"MY_CONSTANT"` instead:

```
$x = MY_CONSTANT;
```

---

2 Read more about classes and objects in Chapter 8.

If the expected value of MY_CONSTANT is anything other than a string, the fallback behavior of PHP to provide a string literal could introduce unexpected side effects into your application. The interpreter won't necessarily crash, but having "MY_CONSTANT" floating around where an integer is expected will cause problems. As of PHP 8.0, referencing an as-yet-undefined constant results in a fatal error.

The Solution example demonstrates the two patterns used to define constants: define() or const. Using define() will create a global constant that is available anywhere in your application by using just the name of the constant itself. Defining a constant by way of const within a class definition will scope the constant to that class. Instead of referencing MY_CONSTANT as in the first solution, the class-scoped constant is referenced as MyClass::MY_CONSTANT.

 PHP defines several default constants (*https://oreil.ly/zQ40o*) that cannot be overwritten by user code. Constants in general are fixed and cannot be modified or replaced, so *always* check that a constant is not defined before attempting to define it. Attempts to redefine a constant will result in a notice. See Chapter 12 for more information on handling errors and notices.

Class constants are publicly visible by default, meaning any code in the application that can reference MyClass can reference its public constants as well. However, it is possible as of PHP 7.1.0 to apply a visibility modifier to a class constant and make it private to instances of the class.

See Also

Documentation on constants in PHP (*https://oreil.ly/9WBhy*), defined() (*https://oreil.ly/jmiau*), define() (*https://oreil.ly/9iON9*), and class constants (*https://oreil.ly/ggaCv*).

1.2 Creating Variable Variables

Problem

You want to reference a specific variable dynamically without knowing ahead of time which of several related variables the program will need.

Solution

PHP's variable syntax starts with a $ followed by the name of the variable you want to reference. You can make the name of a variable *itself* a variable. The following program will print #f00 by using a variable variable:

```
$red = '#f00';
$color = 'red';

echo $$color;
```

Discussion

When PHP is interpreting your code, it sees a leading $ character as identifying a variable, and the immediate next section of text to represent that variable's name. In the Solution example, that text is itself, a variable. PHP will evaluate variable variables from right to left, passing the result of one evaluation as the name used for the left evaluation before printing any data to the screen.

Said another way, Example 1-1 shows two lines of code that are functionally equivalent, except the second uses curly braces to explicitly identify the code evaluated first.

Example 1-1. Evaluating variable variables

```
$$color;
${$color};
```

The rightmost $color is first evaluated to a literal "red", which in turn means $$color and $red ultimately reference the same value. The introduction of curly braces as explicit evaluation delimiters suggests even more complicated applications.

Example 1-2 assumes an application wants to A/B test a headline for search engine optimization (SEO) purposes. Two options are provided by the marketing team, and the developers want to return different headlines for different visitors—but return the *same* headline when a visitor returns to the site. You can do so by leveraging the visitor's IP address and creating a variable variable that chooses a headline based on the visitor IP address.

Example 1-2. A/B testing headlines

```
$headline0 = 'Ten Tips for Writing Great Headlines';
$headline1 = 'The Step-by-Step to Writing Powerful Headlines';

echo ${'headline' . (crc32($_SERVER['REMOTE_ADDR']) % 2)};
```

The crc32() function in the preceding example is a handy utility that calculates a 32-bit checksum of a given string—it turns a string into an integer in a deterministic fashion. The % operator performs a modulo operation on the resulting integer, returning 0 if the checksum is even and 1 if it is odd. The result is then concatenated to the string headline within your dynamic variable to allow the function to choose one or the other headline.

The $_SERVER array is a system-defined superglobal variable (*https://oreil.ly/DtQV-*) that contains useful information about the server running your code and the incoming request that triggered PHP to run in the first place. The exact contents of this particular array will differ from server to server, particularly based on whether you used NGINX or Apache HTTP Server (or another web server) in front of PHP, but it usually contains helpful information like request headers, request paths, and the filename of the currently executing script.

Example 1-3 presents a crc32() utilization line by line to further illustrate how a user-associated value like an IP address can be leveraged to deterministically identify a headline used for SEO purposes.

Example 1-3. Walk-through of checksums against visitor IP addresses

```
$_SERVER['REMOTE_ADDR'] = '127.0.0.1'; ❶
crc32('127.0.0.1') = 3619153832; ❷
3619153832 % 2 = 0; ❸
'headline' . 0 = 'headline0' ❹
${'headline0'} = 'Ten Tips for Writing Great Headlines'; ❺
```

❶ The IP address is extracted from the $_SERVER superglobal variable. Note also that the REMOTE_ADDR key will only be present when using PHP from a web server and not through the CLI.

❷ crc32() converts the string IP address to an integer checksum.

❸ The modulo operator (%) determines whether the checksum is even or odd.

❹ The result of this modulo operation is appended to headline.

❺ The final string headline0 is used as a variable variable to identify the correct SEO headline value.

It's even possible to nest variable variables more than two layers deep. Using three $ characters—as with $$$name—is just as valid, as would be $$${some_function()}. It's a good idea, both for the simplicity of code review and for general maintenance, to limit the levels of variability within your variable names. The use cases for variable variables are rare enough to begin with, but multiple levels of indirection will render your code difficult to follow, understand, test, or maintain if something ever breaks.

See Also

Documentation on variable variables (*https://oreil.ly/wNBh0*).

1.3 Swapping Variables in Place

Problem

You want to exchange the values stored in two variables without defining any additional variables.

Solution

The following block of code uses the `list()` language construct to reassign the values of the variables in place:

```
list($blue, $green) = array($green, $blue);
```

An even more concise version of the preceding solution is to use both the short list and short array syntaxes available since PHP 7.1 as follows:

```
[$blue, $green] = [$green, $blue];
```

Discussion

The `list` keyword in PHP doesn't refer to a function, although it looks like one. It's a *language construct* used to assign values to a list of variables rather than to one variable at a time. This enables developers to set multiple variables all at once from another list-like collection of values (like an array). It also permits the destructuring of arrays into individual variables.

Modern PHP leverages square brackets ([and]) for a short array syntax, allowing for more concise array literals. Writing [1, 4, 5] is functionally equivalent to `array(1, 4, 5)`, but is sometimes clearer depending on the context in which it is used.

Like `list`, the `array` keyword refers to a language construct within PHP. Language constructs are hardcoded into the language and are the keywords that make the system work. Keywords like `if` and `else` or `echo` are easy to distinguish from userland code. Language constructs like `list` and `array` and `exit` look like functions, but like keyword-style constructs, they are built into the language and behave slightly differently than typical functions do. The PHP Manual's list of reserved keywords (*https://oreil.ly/OJD13*) better illustrates existing constructs and cross-references with how each is used in practice.

As of PHP 7.1, developers can use the same short square bracket syntax to replace the usage of `list()`, creating more concise and readable code. Given that a solution to this problem is to assign values from an array to an array of variables, using similar syntax on both sides of the assignment operator (=) both makes sense and clarifies your intent.

The Solution example explicitly swaps the values stored in the variables $green and $blue. This is something that an engineer might do while deploying an application to switch from one version of an API to another. Rolling deployments often refer to the current live environment as the *green* deployment and a new, potential replacement as *blue*, instructing load balancers and other reliant applications to swap from green/blue and verify connectivity and functionality before confirming that the deployment is healthy.

In a more verbose example (Example 1-4), assume that the application consumes an API prefixed by the date of deployment. The application keeps track of which version of the API it is using ($green) and attempts to swap to a new environment to verify connectivity. If the connectivity check fails, the application will automatically switch back to the old environment.

Example 1-4. Blue/green environment cutover

```
$green = 'https://2021_11.api.application.example/v1';
$blue = 'https://2021_12.api.application.example/v1';

[$green, $blue] = [$blue, $green];

if (connection_fails(check_api($green))) {
    [$green, $blue] = [$blue, $green];
}
```

The list() construct can also be used to extract certain values from an arbitrary group of elements. Example 1-5 illustrates how an address, stored as an array, can be used in different contexts to extract just specific values as needed.

Example 1-5. Using list() to extract elements of an array

```
$address = ['123 S Main St.', 'Anywhere', 'NY', '10001', 'USA'];

// Extracting each element as named variables
[$street, $city, $state, $zip, $country] = $address;

// Extracting and naming only the city
[,,$state,,] = $address;

// Extracting only the country
[,,,,$country] = $address;
```

Each extraction in the preceding example is independent and sets only the variables that are necessary.[3] For a trivial illustration such as this, there is no need to worry about extracting each element and setting a variable, but for more complex applications manipulating data that is significantly larger, setting unnecessary variables can lead to performance issues. While list() is a powerful tool for destructuring array-like collections, it is only appropriate for simple cases like those discussed in the preceding examples.

See Also

Documentation on list() (*https://oreil.ly/bzO7i*), array() (*https://oreil.ly/tq1Z_*), and the PHP RFC on short list() syntax (*https://oreil.ly/Ou98z*).

---

3 Recall in this chapter's introduction the explanation that variable references not explicitly being set will evaluate as "empty." This means you can set only the values and variables you need to use.

## CHAPTER 2

Operators

While Chapter 1 introduced the foundational building blocks of PHP—variables to store arbitrary values—these building blocks are useless without some kind of glue to hold them together. This glue is the set of *operators* (*https://oreil.ly/Vepfg*) established by PHP. Operators are the way you tell PHP what to do with certain values—specifically how to change one or more values into a new, discrete value.

In almost every case, an operator in PHP is represented by a single character or by repeated uses of that same character. In a handful of cases, operators can also be represented by literal English words, which helps disambiguate what the operator is trying to accomplish.

This book does not attempt to cover every operator leveraged by PHP; for exhaustive explanations of each, refer to the PHP Manual itself (*https://oreil.ly/YGWyE*). Instead, the following few sections cover some of the most important logical, bitwise, and comparison operators before diving into more concrete problems, solutions, and examples.

Logical Operators

Logical operations are the components of PHP that create truth tables and define basic and/or/not grouping criteria. Table 2-1 enumerates all of the character-based logical operators supported by PHP.

Table 2-1. Logical operators

Expression	Operator name	Result	Example
$x && $y	and	true if both $x and $y are true	`true && true == true`
$x || $y	or	true if either $x or $y is true	`true || false == true`
!$x	not	true if $x is false (and vice versa)	`!true == false`

The logical operators && and || have English word counterparts: and and or, respectively. The statement ($x and $y) is functionally equivalent to ($x && $y). The word or can likewise be used in place of the || operator without changing the functionality of the expression.

The word xor can also be used to represent a special *exclusive or* operator in PHP that evaluates to true if one of the two values in the expression is true, but not when both are true. Unfortunately, the logical XOR operation has no character equivalent in PHP.

Bitwise Operators

PHP supports operations against specific bits in an integer, a feature that makes the language quite versatile. Supporting bitwise operations means PHP is not limited to web applications but can operate on binary files and data structures with ease! It's worth mentioning these operators in the same section as the preceding logical operators as they appear somewhat similar in terms of terminology with and, or, and xor.

Whereas logical operators return true or false based on the comparison between two whole values, bitwise operators actually perform bitwise arithmetic on integers and return the result of that full calculation over the integer or integers provided. For a specific example of how this can be useful, skip ahead to Recipe 2.6.

Table 2-2 illustrates the various bitwise operators in PHP, what they do, and a quick example of how they work on simple integers.

Table 2-2. Bitwise operators

Expression	Operator name	Result	Example
$x & $y	and	Returns bits set in both $x and $y	5 & 1 == 1
$x | $y	or	Returns bits set in either $x or $y	4 | 1 == 5
$x ^ $y	xor	Returns bits set in only $x or $y	5 ^ 3 == 6
~ $x	not	Inverts bits that are set in $x	~ 4 == -5
$x << $y	shift left	Shift the bits of $x to the left by $y steps	4 << 2 == 16
$x >> $y	shift right	Shift the bits of $x to the right by $y steps	4 >> 2 == 1

In PHP, the largest integer you can have depends on the size of the processor running the application. In any case, the constant PHP_INT_MAX will tell you how large integers can be—2147483647 on 32-bit machines and 9223372036854775807 on 64-bit machines. In both cases, this number is represented, in binary, as a long string of 1s equal in length to one less than the bit size. On a 32-bit machine, 2147483647 is represented by 31 1s. The leading bit (a 0 by default) is used to identify the *sign* of the integer. If the bit is 0, the integer is positive; if the bit is 1, the integer is negative.

On any machine, the number 4 is represented in binary as 100, with enough 0s to the left of the most significant digit to fill the bit size of the processor. On a 32-bit system, this would be 29 0s. To make the integer *negative*, you would represent it instead as a 1 followed by 28 0s followed by 100.

For simplicity, consider a 16-bit system. The integer 4 would be represented as 0000000000000100. Likewise, a negative 4 would be represented as 1000000000000100. If you were to apply the bitwise *not* operator (~) on a positive 4 in a 16-bit system, all of the 0s would become 1s and vice versa. This would turn your number into 1111111111111011, which on a 16-bit system is −5.

Comparison Operators

The core of any programming language is the level of control that language has to branch based on specific conditions. In PHP, much of this branching logic is controlled by comparing two or more values with one another. It is the set of comparison operators provided by PHP (*https://oreil.ly/QuPhV*), provide most of the advanced branching functionality used to build complex applications.

Table 2-3 lists the scalar comparison operators considered to be the most vital to understand PHP. The other operators (greater than, less than, and variants) are somewhat standard among programming languages and are not necessary to any of the recipes in this chapter.

Table 2-3. Comparison operators

Expression	Operation	Result
$x == $y	Equal	Returns true if both values are the same after coercing into the same type
$x === $y	Identical	Returns true if both values are the same *and* are of the same type
$x <=> $y	Spaceship	Returns 0 is both values are equal, 1 if $x is greater, or -1 if $y is greater

When dealing with objects, the equality and identity operators work somewhat differently. Two objects are considered equal (==) if they have the same internal structure (same attributes and values) and are of the same type (class). Objects are considered identical (===) if and only if they are references to the same instance of a class. These are stricter requirements than those for comparing scalar values.

Type Casting

While the name of a type is not formally an operator, you can use it to explicitly cast a value as that type. Simply write the name of the type within parentheses before the value to force a conversion. Example 2-1 converts a simple integer value to various other types prior to using the value.

Example 2-1. Casting values as other types

```
$value = 1;

$bool = (bool) $value;
$float = (float) $value;
$string = (string) $value;

var_dump([$bool, $float, $string]);

// array(3) {
//    [0]=>
//    bool(true)
//    [1]=>
//    float(1)
//    [2]=>
//    string(1) "1"
// }
```

PHP supports the following type casts:

(int)
> Cast to int

(bool)
> Cast to bool

(float)
> Cast to float

(string)
> Cast to string

(array)
> Cast to array

(object)
> Cast to object

It's also possible to use (integer) as an alias of (int), (boolean) as an alias of (bool), (real) or (double) as aliases of (float), and (binary) as an alias of (string). These aliases will make the same type casts as in the preceding list, but given that they don't use the name of the type to which you're casting, this approach is not recommended.

The recipes in this chapter introduce ways to leverage PHP's most important comparison and logical operators.

2.1 Using a Ternary Operator Instead of an If-Else Block

Problem

You want to provide an either-or branching condition to assign a specific value to a variable in a single line of code.

Solution

Using a *ternary operator* (*a* ? *b* : *c*) allows nesting an either-or condition and both possible branched values in a single statement. The following example shows how to define a variable with a value from the $_GET superglobal and fall back on a default if it is empty:

```
$username = isset($_GET['username']) ? $_GET['username'] : 'default';
```

Discussion

A ternary expression has three arguments and is evaluated from left to right, checking the *truthiness* of the leftmost statement (whether it evaluates to true regardless of the types involved in the expression) and returning the next value if true or the final value if false. You can visualize this logical flow with the following illustration:

```
$_value_ = (_expression to evaluate_) ? (if true) : (if false);
```

The ternary pattern is a simple way to return a default value when checking either system values or even parameters from a web request (those stored in the $_GET or $_POST superglobals). It is also a powerful way to switch logic in page templates based on the return of a particular function call.

The following example assumes a web application that welcomes logged-in users by name (checking their authentication state with a call to is_logged_in()) or welcomes a guest if the user has yet to authenticate. As this example is coded directly into the HTML markup of a web page, using a longer if/else statement would be inappropriate:

```
<h1>Welcome, <?php echo is_logged_in() ? $_SESSION['user'] : 'Guest'; ?>!</h1>
```

Ternary operations can also be simplified if the value being checked is both *truthy* (evaluates to true when coerced into a Boolean value) and is the value you want by default. The Solution example checks that a username is set *and* assigns that value to a given variable if so. Since non-empty strings evaluate to true, you can shorten the solution to the following:

```
$username = $_GET['username'] ?: 'default';
```

When a ternary is shortened from its *a* ? *b* : *c* format to a simple *a* ?: *c*, PHP will evaluate the expression to check *a* as if it were a Boolean value. If it's true, PHP merely returns the expression itself. If it's false, PHP returns the fallback value *c* instead.

 PHP compares truthiness similarly to the way it compares emptiness, as discussed in Chapter 1. Strings that are set (not empty or null), integers that are nonzero, and arrays that are non-empty are all generally considered truthy, which is to say they evaluate to true when cast as a Boolean. You can read more about the ways types are intermixed and considered equivalent in the PHP Manual section on type comparisons (*https://oreil.ly/nXsr8*).

The ternary operator is an advanced form of comparison operator that, while it provides for concise code, can sometimes be overused to create logic that is too difficult to follow. Consider Example 2-2, which nests one ternary operation within another.

Example 2-2. Nested ternary expression

```
$val = isset($_GET['username']) ? $_GET['username'] : (isset($_GET['userid'])
    ? $_GET['user_id'] : null);
```

This example should be rewritten as a simple if/else statement instead to provide more clarity as to how the code branches. Nothing is *functionally* wrong with the code, but nested ternaries can be difficult to read or reason about and often lead to logic errors down the road. The preceding ternary could be rewritten as shown in Example 2-3:

Example 2-3. Multiple if/else statements

```
if (isset($_GET['username'])) {
    $val = $_GET['username'];
} elseif (isset($_GET['userid'])) {
    $val = $_GET['userid'];
} else {
    $val = null;
}
```

While Example 2-3 is more verbose than Example 2-2, you can more easily track where the logic needs to branch. The code is also more maintainable, as new branching logic can be added where necessary. Adding another logical branch to Example 2-2 would further complicate the already complex ternary and make the program even harder to maintain in the long run.

See Also

Documentation on the ternary operator (*https://oreil.ly/Y5WCn*) and its variations.

2.2 Coalescing Potentially Null Values

Problem

You want to assign a specific value to a variable only if it's set and not null and otherwise use a static default value.

Solution

Using a null-coalescing operator (??) as follows will use the first value only if it is set and not null:

```
$username = $_GET['username'] ?? 'not logged in';
```

Discussion

PHP's null-coalescing operator is a newer feature introduced in PHP 7.0. It's been referred to as *syntactic sugar* to replace the shorthand version of PHP's ternary operator, ?:, discussed in Recipe 2.1.

> *Syntactic sugar* is shorthand for performing a common yet verbose operation in code. The developers of languages introduce such features to save keystrokes and render routine, oft-repeated blocks of code via simpler and more concise syntax.

Both of the following lines of code are functionally equivalent, but the ternary form will trigger a notice if the expression being evaluated is undefined:

```
$a = $b ?: $c;
$a = $b ?? $c;
```

While these preceding two examples are *functionally* identical, a notable difference in their behavior occurs if the value being evaluated ($b) is not defined. With the null-coalescing operator, everything is golden. With the ternary shorthand, PHP will trigger a notice during execution that the value is undefined before returning the fallback value.

With discrete variables, the differing functionality of these operators isn't entirely obvious, but when the evaluated component is, perhaps, an indexed array, the potential impact becomes more apparent. Assume that, instead of a discrete variable, you are trying to extract an element from the superglobal $_GET variable that holds request parameters. In the following example, both the ternary and the null-coalescing operators will return the fallback value, but the ternary version will complain about an undefined index:

```
$username = $_GET['username'] ?? 'anonymous';
$username = $_GET['username'] ?: 'anonymous'; // Notice: undefined index ...
```

If errors and notices are suppressed during execution,[1] there is no functional difference between either operator option. It is, however, best practice to avoid writing code that triggers errors or notices, as these can accidentally raise alerts in production or potentially fill system logs and make it more difficult to find legitimate issues with your code. While the shorthand ternary operator is remarkably useful, the null-coalescing operator is purpose-built for this kind of operation and should nearly always be used instead.

See Also

The announcement of the new operator when it was first added to PHP 7.0 (*https://oreil.ly/6vmP_*).

2.3 Comparing Identical Values

Problem

You want to compare two values of the same type to ensure that they're identical.

Solution

Use three equals signs to compare values without dynamically casting their types:

```
if ($a === $b) {
    // ...
}
```

Discussion

In PHP, the equals sign has three functions. A single equals sign (=) is used for *assignment*, which is setting the value of a variable. Two equals signs (==) are used in an expression to determine whether the values on either side are equal. Table 2-4 shows how certain values are considered equal because PHP coerces one type into another while evaluating the statement. Finally, three equals signs (===) are used in an expression to determine whether the values on either side are *identical*.

---

1 Error handling and suppressing errors, warnings, and notices are discussed at length in Chapter 12.

Table 2-4. Value equality in PHP

Expression	Result	Explanation
0 == "a"	false	(Only for PHP 8.0 and above) The string "a" is cast as an integer, which means it's cast to 0.
"1" == "01"	true	Both sides of the expression are cast to integers, and 1 == 1.
100 = "1e2"	true	The right side of the expression is evaluated as an exponential representation of 100 and cast as an integer.

The first example in Table 2-4 evaluates as true in PHP versions below 8.0. In those earlier versions, comparing the equality of a string (or numeric string) to a number would convert the string first to a number (in this case, converting "a" to 0). This behavior changed in PHP 8.0 such that only numeric strings are cast to numbers, so the result of that first expression is now false.

PHP's ability to dynamically convert between types at runtime can be useful, but in some cases it is not what you want to have happen at all. The Boolean literal false is returned by some methods to represent an error or failure, while an integer 0 might be a valid return of a function. Consider the function in Example 2-4 that returns a count of books of a specific category, or false if a connection to the database holding that data fails.

Example 2-4. Count items in a database or return false

```
function count_books_of_type($category)
{
    $sql = "SELECT COUNT(*) FROM books WHERE category = :category";

    try {
        $dbh = new PDO(DB_CONNECTION_STRING, DB_LOGIN, DB_PASS);
        $statement = $dbh->prepare($sql);

        $statement->execute(array(':category' => $category));
        return $statement->fetchColumn();
    } catch (PDOException $e) {
        return false;
    }
}
```

If everything in Example 2-4 runs as expected, the code will then return an integer count of the number of books in a particular category. Example 2-5 might leverage this function to print a headline on a web page.

Example 2-5. Using the results of a database-bound function

```
$books_found = count_books_of_type('fiction');

switch ($books_found) {
    case 0:
        echo 'No fiction books found';
        break;
    case 1:
        echo 'Found one fiction book';
        break;
    default:
        echo 'Found ' . $books_found . ' fiction books';
}
```

Internally, PHP's `switch` statement is using a loose type comparison (our == operator). If `count_books_of_type()` returns `false` instead of an actual result, this `switch`
statement will print out that no fiction books were found rather than reporting an
error. In this particular use case, that might be acceptable behavior—but when your
application needs to reflect a material difference between `false` and `0`, loose equality
comparisons are inadequate.

Instead, PHP permits the use of *three* equals signs (===) to check whether both values
under evaluation are identical—that is, they are both the same value and the same
type. Even though the integer 5 and the string "5" have the same value, evaluating 5
=== "5" will result in `false` because the two values are not the same type. Thus, while
`0 == false` evaluates to `true`, `0 === false` will always evaluate to `false`.

 Determining whether two values are identical becomes more complicated when dealing with objects, either defined with custom
classes or PHP-provided ones. In the case of two objects, `$obj1` and
`$obj2`, they will only evaluate as identical if they are actually the
same *instance* of a class. For more on object instantiation and
classes, see Chapter 8.

See Also

PHP documentation on comparison operators (*https://oreil.ly/T6GXm*).

2.4 Using the Spaceship Operator to Sort Values

Problem

You want to provide a custom ordering function to sort an arbitrary list of objects by
using PHP's native `usort()` (*https://oreil.ly/xGbc9*).

Solution

Assuming you want to sort by multiple properties of the list of objects, use PHP's spaceship operator (<=>) to define a custom sorting function and supply that as the callback to usort().

Consider the following class definition for a person in your application that allows creating records with just first and last names:

```
class Person {
    public $firstName;
    public $lastName;

    public function __construct($first, $last)
    {
        $this->firstName = $first;
        $this->lastName = $last;
    }
};
```

You can then create a list of people, perhaps US presidents, using this class and adding each person to your list in turn, as in Example 2-6.

Example 2-6. Adding multiple object instances to a list

```
$presidents = [];

$presidents[] = new Person('George', 'Washington');
$presidents[] = new Person('John', 'Adams');
$presidents[] = new Person('Thomas', 'Jefferson');
// ...
$presidents[] = new Person('Barack', 'Obama');
$presidents[] = new Person('Donald', 'Trump');
$presidents[] = new Person('Joseph', 'Biden');
```

The spaceship operator can then be leveraged to identify how to sort this data, assuming you want to order by last name first, then by first name, as shown in Example 2-7.

Example 2-7. Sorting presidents with the spaceship operator

```
function presidential_sorter($left, $right)
{
    return [$left->lastName, $left->firstName]
        <=>
        [$right->lastName, $right->firstName];
}

usort($presidents, 'presidential_sorter');
```

The result of the preceding call to usort() is that the $presidents array will be properly sorted in place and ready for use.

Discussion

The spaceship operator is a special addition as of PHP 7.0 that helps identify the relationship between the values on either side of it:

- If the first value is less than the second, the expression evaluates to -1.
- If the first value is greater than the second, the expression evaluates to +1.
- If both values are the same, the expression evaluates to 0.

 Like PHP's equality operator, the spaceship operator will attempt to coerce the types of each value in the comparison to be the same. It is possible to support a number for one value and a string for the other and get a valid result. Use type coercion with special operators like this at your own risk.

The simplest use of the spaceship operator compares simple types with one another, making it easy to order a simple array or list of primitive values (like characters, integers, floating-point numbers, or dates). This simple case, if using usort(), would require a sorting function like the following:

```
function sorter($a, $b) {
    return ($a < $b) ? -1 : (($a > $b) ? 1 : 0);
}
```

The spaceship operator simplifies the nested ternary in the preceding code by replacing the return statement entirely with return $a <=> $b, but without modifying the functionality of the sorting function at all.

More complex examples, like that used in the Solution to sort based on multiple properties of a custom object definition, would necessitate rather verbose sorting function definitions. The spaceship operator simplifies comparison logic, empowering developers to specify otherwise complex logic in a single, easy-to-read line.

See Also

The original RFC for PHP's spaceship operator (*https://oreil.ly/O1X8R*).

2.5 Suppressing Diagnostic Errors with an Operator

Problem

You want to explicitly ignore or suppress errors triggered by a specific expression in your application.

Solution

Prefix the expression with the @ operator to temporarily set the error reporting level to 0 for that line of code. This might help suppress errors related to missing files when attempting to open them directly, as in the following example:

```
$fp = @fopen('file_that_does_not_exist.txt', 'r');
```

Discussion

The Solution example attempts to open the file *file_that_does_not_exist.txt* for reading. In normal operations, a call to `fopen()` would return `false` because the file does not exist *and* emit a PHP warning for the purposes of diagnosing the issue. Prefixing the expression with the @ operator doesn't change the return value at all, but it suppresses the emitted warning entirely.

> The @ operator suppresses error reporting for the line to which it is applied. If a developer attempts to suppress errors on an `include` statement, they will very easily hide any warnings, notices, or errors caused by the included file not existing (or having improper access controls). The suppression will *also* apply to all lines of code within the included file, meaning any errors (syntax-related or otherwise) in the included code will be ignored. Thus, while `@include('some-file.php')` is perfectly valid code, suppressing errors on `include` statements should be avoided!

This particular operator is useful when suppressing errors or warnings on file access operations (as in the Solution example). It's also useful in suppressing notices in array-access operations, as in the following, where a specific GET parameter might not be set in a request:

```
$filename = @$_GET['filename'];
```

The `$filename` variable will be set to the value of the request's `filename` query parameter if it's set. Otherwise, it will be a literal `null`. If a developer were to omit the @ operator, the value of `$filename` would still be `null`, but PHP would emit a notice that the index of `filename` does not exist in the array.

As of PHP 8.0 (*https://oreil.ly/4Ec5B*), this operator will no longer suppress *fatal* errors in PHP that otherwise halt script execution.

See Also

Official PHP documentation on error control operators (*https://oreil.ly/bZkLY*).

2.6 Comparing Bits Within Integers

Problem

You want to use simple flags to identify state and behavior in your application, where one member might have multiple flags applied.

Solution

Use a bitmask (*https://oreil.ly/aevr7*) to specify which flags are available and bitwise operators on the subsequent flags to identify which are set. The following example defines four discrete flags by using a binary notation of the integer each represents and combines them to indicate *multiple* flags being set at once. PHP's bitwise operators are then used to identify which flag is set and which branch of conditional logic should be executed:

```php
const FLAG_A = 0b0001; // 1
const FLAG_B = 0b0010; // 2
const FLAG_C = 0b0100; // 4
const FLAG_D = 0b1000; // 8

// Set a composite flag for an application
$application = FLAG_A | FLAG_B; // 0b0011 or 3

// Set a composite flag for a user
$user = FLAG_B | FLAG_C | FLAG_D; // 0b1110 or 14

// Switch based on the user's applied flags
if ($user & FLAG_B) {
    // ...
} else {
    // ...
}
```

Discussion

A bitmask is structured by configuring each flag to be a constant integer power of 2. This has the benefit of only setting a single bit in the binary representation of the number such that composite flags are then identified by which bits are set. In the Solution example, each flag is written explicitly as a binary number to illustrate which bits are set (1) versus unset (0), with the integer representation of the same number in a comment at the end of the line.

Our example's FLAG_B is the integer 2, which is represented in binary as 0010 (the third bit is set). Likewise, FLAG_C is the integer 4 with a binary representation of 0100 (the second bit is set). To specify that *both* flags are set, you add the two together to set both the second and third bits: 0110 or the integer 6.

For this specific example, addition is an easy model to keep in mind, but it's not exactly what is going on. To combine flags, you merely want to combine the bits that are set, not necessarily add them together. Combining FLAG_A with itself should result in *only* FLAG_A; adding the integer representation (1) to itself would change the meaning of the flag entirely.

Rather than addition, use the bitwise operations *or* (|) and *and* (&) to both combine bits and filter on assigned flags. Combining two flags together requires using the | operator to create a new integer with bits that are set in *either* of the flags being used. Consider Table 2-5 to create a composite of FLAG_A | FLAG_C.

Table 2-5. Composite binary flags with bitwise or

Flag	Binary representation	Integer representation
FLAG_A	0001	1
FLAG_C	0100	4
FLAG_A	FLAG_C 0101	5

Comparing composite flags against your definitions then requires the & operator, which returns a new number that has bits set on *both* sides of the operation. Comparing a flag to itself will always return 1, which is type cast to true in conditional checks. Comparing two values that have any of the same bits set will return a value *greater* than 0, which is type cast to true. Consider the simple case of evaluating where FLAG_A & FLAG_C in Table 2-6.

Table 2-6. Composite binary flags with bitwise and

Flag	Binary representation	Integer representation
FLAG_A	0001	1
FLAG_C	0100	4
FLAG_A & FLAG_C	0000	0

Instead of comparing primitive flags against one another, you can and should build composite values and then compare them to your sets of flags. The following example visualizes the role-based access controls of a content management system for publishing news articles. Users can view articles, create articles, edit articles, or delete articles;

their level of access is determined by the program itself and the permissions granted to their user account:

```
const VIEW_ARTICLES   = 0b0001;
const CREATE_ARTICLES = 0b0010;
const EDIT_ARTICLES   = 0b0100;
const DELETE_ARTICLES = 0b1000;
```

A typical, anonymous visitor will never be logged in and will then be granted a default permission of being able to view content. Logged-in users might be able to create articles but not edit them without an editor's permission. Likewise, editors can review and modify content (or delete it) but cannot independently create articles. Finally, administrators might be allowed to do everything. Each of the roles is composited from the preceding permission primitives as follows:

```
const ROLE_ANONYMOUS = VIEW_ARTICLES;
const ROLE_AUTHOR    = VIEW_ARTICLES | CREATE_ARTICLES;
const ROLE_EDITOR    = VIEW_ARTICLES | EDIT_ARTICLES | DELETE_ARTICLES;
const ROLE_ADMIN     = VIEW_ARTICLES | CREATE_ARTICLES | EDIT_ARTICLES
                       | DELETE_ARTICLES;
```

Once composite roles are defined from primitive permissions, the application can structure logic around checking the user's active role. While permissions were composited together with the | operator, the & operator will allow you to switch based on these flags, as demonstrated by the functions defined in Example 2-8.

Example 2-8. Leveraging bitmask flags for access control

```
function get_article($article_id)
{
    $role = get_user_role();

    if ($role & VIEW_ARTICLES) {
        // ...
    } else {
        throw new UnauthorizedException();
    }
}

function create_article($content)
{
    $role = get_user_role();

    if ($role & CREATE_ARTICLES) {
        // ...
    } else {
        throw new UnauthorizedException();
    }
}

function edit_article($article_id, $content)
```

```
{
    $role = get_user_role();

    if ($role & EDIT_ARTICLES) {
        // ...
    } else {
        throw new UnauthorizedException();
    }
}

function delete_article($article_id)
{
    $role = get_user_role();

    if ($role & DELETE_ARTICLES) {
        // ...
    } else {
        throw new UnauthorizedException();
    }
}
```

Bitmasks are a powerful way to implement simple flags in any language. Take caution, though, if the number of flags needed is ever planned to increase, because each new flag represents an additional power of 2, meaning the value of all flags grows rapidly in size. However, bitmasks are commonly used in both PHP applications and by the language itself. PHP's own error reporting setting, discussed further in Chapter 12, leverages bitwise values to identify the level of error reporting used by the engine itself.

See Also

PHP documentation on bitwise operators (*https://oreil.ly/JmF85*).

Functions

Every computer program in every language is built by tying various components of business logic together. Often, these components need to be somewhat reusable, encapsulating common functionality that needs to be referenced in multiple places throughout an application. The easiest way to make these components modular and reusable is to encapsulate their business logic into *functions*, specific constructs within the application that can be referenced elsewhere throughout an application.

Example 3-1 illustrates how a simple program might be written to capitalize the first character in a string. Coding without using functions is considered *imperative* programming, as you define exactly what the program needs to accomplish one command (or line of code) at a time.

Example 3-1. Imperative (function-free) string capitalization

```
$str = "this is an example";

if (ord($str[0]) >= 97 && ord($str[0]) <= 122) {
    $str[0] = chr(ord($str[0]) - 32);
}

echo $str . PHP_EOL; // This is an example

$str = "and this is another";

if (ord($str[0]) >= 97 && ord($str[0]) <= 122) {
    $str[0] = chr(ord($str[0]) - 32);
}

echo $str . PHP_EOL; // And this is another

$str = "3 examples in total";
```

```php
if (ord($str[0]) >= 97 && ord($str[0]) <= 122) {
    $str[0] = chr(ord($str[0]) - 32);
}

echo $str . PHP_EOL; // 3 examples in total
```

 The functions ord() and chr() are references to native functions defined by PHP itself. The ord() (*https://oreil.ly/kSI-4*) function returns the binary value of a character as an integer. Similarly, chr() (*https://oreil.ly/0KUmf*) converts a binary value (represented as an integer) into its corresponding character.

When you write code without defining functions, your code ends up rather repetitive as you're forced to copy and paste identical blocks throughout the application. This violates one of the key principles of software development: *DRY*, or *don't repeat yourself*.

A common way to describe the *opposite* of this principle is *WET*, or *write everything twice*. Writing the same block of code over again leads to two problems:

- Your code becomes rather long and difficult to maintain.
- If the logic within the repeated code block needs to change, you have to update *several* parts of your program every time.

Rather than repeating logic imperatively, as in Example 3-1, you can define a function that wraps this logic and later invoke that function directly, as in Example 3-2. Defining functions is an evolution of imperative to procedural programming that augments the functions provided by the language itself with those defined by your application.

Example 3-2. Procedural string capitalization

```php
function capitalize_string($str)
{
    if (ord($str[0]) >= 97 && ord($str[0]) <= 122) {
        $str[0] = chr(ord($str[0]) - 32);
    }

    return $str;
}

$str = "this is an example";

echo capitalize_string($str) . PHP_EOL; // This is an example

$str = "and this is another";
```

```
echo capitalize_string($str) . PHP_EOL; // And this is another

$str = "3 examples in total";

echo capitalize_string($str) . PHP_EOL; // 3 examples in total
```

User-defined functions are incredibly powerful and quite flexible. The `capital ize_string()` function in Example 3-2 is relatively simple—it takes a single string parameter and returns a string. However, there is no indication in the function as defined that the `$str` parameter must be a string—you could just as easily pass a number or even an array as follows:

```
$out = capitalize_string(25); // 25

$out = capitalize_string(['a', 'b']); // ['A', 'b']
```

Recall the discussion of PHP's loose type system from Chapter 1--by default, PHP will try to infer your intent when you pass a parameter into `capitalize_string()` and, in most cases, will return something useful. In the case of passing an integer, PHP will trigger a warning that you are trying to access elements of an array incorrectly, but it will still return an integer without crashing.

More sophisticated programs can add explicit typing information to both the function parameters and its return to provide safety checks around this kind of usage. Other functions could return *multiple* values rather than a single item. Strong typing is illustrated explicitly in Recipe 3.4.

The recipes that follow cover a variety of ways functions can be used in PHP and begins scratching at the surface of building a full application.

3.1 Accessing Function Parameters

Problem

You want to access the values passed into a function when it's called elsewhere in a program.

Solution

Use the variables defined in the function signature within the body of the function itself as follows:

```
function multiply($first, $second)
{
    return $first * $second;
}
```

```
multiply(5, 2); // 10

$one = 7;
$two = 5;

multiply($one, $two); // 35
```

Discussion

The variable names defined in the function signature are available only within the scope of the function itself and will contain values matching the data passed into the function when it's called. Inside the curly braces that define the function, you can use these variables as if you've defined them yourself. Just know that any changes you make to those variables will *only* be available within the function and won't impact anything elsewhere in the application by default.

Example 3-3 illustrates how a specific variable name can be used both within a function and outside a function while referring to two, completely independent values. Said another way, changing the value of $number within the function will only impact the value within the function, not within the parent application.

Example 3-3. Local function scoping

```
function increment($number)
{
    $number += 1;

    return $number;
}

$number = 6;

echo increment($number); // 7
echo $number; // 6
```

By default, PHP passes values into functions rather than passing a reference to the variable. In Example 3-3, this means PHP passes the *value* 6 into a new $number variable within the function, performs a calculation, and returns the result. The $number variable outside the function is entirely unaffected.

 PHP passes simple values (strings, integers, Booleans, arrays) by value by default. More complex objects, however, are *always* passed by reference. In the case of objects, the variable inside the function points back to the same object as the variable outside the function rather than to a copy of it.

In some cases, you might want to explicitly pass a variable by reference rather than just passing its value. In that case, you need to modify the function signature as this is a change to its very definition rather than something that can be modified when the function is called. Example 3-4 illustrates how the increment() function would change to pass $number by reference instead of by value.

Example 3-4. Passing variables by reference

```
function increment(&$number)
{
    $number += 1;

    return $number;
}

$number = 6;

echo increment($number); // 7
echo $number; // 7
```

In reality, the variable name doesn't need to match both inside and outside the function. I'm using $number in both cases here to illustrate the difference in scoping. If you stored an integer in $a and passed that variable instead as increment($a), the result would be identical to that in Example 3-4.

See Also

PHP reference documentation on user-defined functions (*https://oreil.ly/9c1Nr*) and passing variables by reference (*https://oreil.ly/ZfOLR*).

3.2 Setting a Function's Default Parameters

Problem

You want to set a default value for a function's parameter so invocations don't have to pass it.

Solution

Assign a default value within the function signature itself. For example:

```
function get_book_title($isbn, $error = 'Unable to query')
{
    try {
        $connection = get_database_connection();
        $book = query_isbn($connection, $isbn);
```

```
        return $book->title;
    } catch {
        return $error;
    }
}

get_book_title('978-1-098-12132-7');
```

Discussion

The example in the Solution attempts to query a database for the title of a book based on its ISBN. If the query fails for any reason, the function will return the string passed into the $error parameter instead.

To make this parameter optional, the function signature assigns a default value. When calling get_book_title() with a single parameter, the default $error value is used automatically. You alternatively have the option to pass your own string into this variable when invoking the function, such as get_book_title(*978-1-098-12132-7, Oops!*);.

When defining a function with default parameters, it's a best practice to place all parameters with default values *last* in the function signature. While defining parameters in any order is *possible*, doing so makes it difficult to call the function properly.

Example 3-5 illustrates the kinds of problems that can come up by placing optional parameters before required ones.

 It is possible to define function parameters with specific defaults in any order. However, declaring mandatory parameters after optional ones is deprecated as of PHP 8.0. Continuing to do so might result in an error in a future version of PHP.

Example 3-5. Misordered default parameters

```
function brew_latte($flavor = 'unflavored', $shots)
{
    return "Brewing a {$shots}-shot, {$flavor} latte!";
}

brew_latte('vanilla', 2); ❶
brew_latte(3); ❷
```

❶ Proper execution. Returns Brewing a 2-shot, vanilla latte!

❷ Triggers an ArgumentCountError exception because $shots is undefined.

In some cases, placing the parameters themselves in a particular order might make logical sense (to make the code more readable, for example). Know that if any parameters are required, every parameter to their left is also effectively required even if you try to define a default value.

See Also

Examples of default arguments in the PHP Manual (*https://oreil.ly/XVoK1*).

3.3 Using Named Function Parameters

Problem

You want to pass arguments into a function based on the name of the parameter rather than its position.

Solution

Use the named argument syntax while calling a function as follows:

```
array_fill(start_index: 0, count: 100, value: 50);
```

Discussion

By default, PHP leverages positional parameters in function definitions. The Solution example references the native `array_fill()` (*https://oreil.ly/jdZQH*) function that has the following function signature:

```
array_fill(int $start_index, int $count, mixed $value): array
```

Basic PHP coding must supply arguments to `array_fill()` in the same order in which they're defined—$start_index followed by $count followed by $value. While the order itself is not a problem, making sense of the meaning of each value when scanning visually through code can be a challenge. Using the basic, ordered parameters, the Solution example would be written as follows, requiring deep familiarity with the function signature to know which integer represents which parameter:

```
array_fill(0, 100, 50);
```

Named function parameters disambiguate which value is being assigned to which internal variable. They also allow for arbitrary reordering of parameters when you invoke the function as that invocation is now explicit as to which value is assigned to which parameter.

Another key advantage of named arguments is that optional arguments can be *skipped* entirely during function invocation. Consider a verbose activity logging function like in Example 3-6, where multiple parameters are considered optional as they set defaults.

Example 3-6. Verbose activity logging function

```
activity_log(
    string    $update_reason,
    string    $note          = '',
    string    $sql_statement = '',
    string    $user_name     = 'anonymous',
    string    $ip_address    = '127.0.0.1',
    ?DateTime $time          = null
): void
```

Internally, Example 3-6 will use its default values when it's called with a single argument; if `$time` is `null`, the value will be silently replaced with a new `DateTime` instance representing "now." However, sometimes you might want to populate one of these optional parameters without wanting to explicitly set *all* of them.

Say you want to replay previously witnessed events from a static log file. User activity was anonymous (so the defaults for `$user_name` and `$ip_address` are adequate), but you need to explicitly set the date at which an event occurred. Without named arguments, an invocation in this case would look similar to Example 3-7.

Example 3-7. Invoking the verbose `activity_log()` function

```
activity_log(
    'Testing a new system',
    '',
    '',
    'anonymous',
    '127.0.0.1',
    new DateTime('2021-12-20')
);
```

With named arguments, you can skip setting parameters to their defaults and explicitly set just the parameters you need to. The preceding code can be simplified to the following:

```
    activity_log('Testing a new system', time: new DateTime('2021-12-20'));
```

In addition to drastically simplifying the usage of `activity_log()`, named parameters have the added benefit of keeping your code DRY. The default values for your arguments are stored directly in the function definition rather than being copied to every invocation of the function as well. If you later need to change a default, you can edit the function definition alone.

See Also

The original RFC proposing named parameters (*https://oreil.ly/UdoDP*).

3.4 Enforcing Function Argument and Return Typing

Problem

You want to force your program to implement type safety and avoid PHP's native loose type comparisons.

Solution

Add input and return types to function definitions. Optionally, add a strict type declaration to the top of each file to enforce values matching type annotations (and emit a fatal error if they don't match). For example:

```php
declare(strict_types=1);

function add_numbers(int $left, int $right): int
{
    return $left + $right;
}

add_numbers(2, 3);   ❶
add_numbers(2, '3'); ❷
```

❶   This is a perfectly valid operation and will return the integer 5.

❷   While 2 + '3' is valid PHP code, the string '3' violates the function's type definitions and will trigger a fatal error.

Discussion

PHP natively supports various scalar types and allows developers to declare both function input parameters and returns to identify the kinds of values that are allowable for each. In addition, developers can specify their own custom classes and interfaces as types, or leverage class inheritance within the type system.[1]

Parameter types are annotated by placing the type directly before the name of the parameter when defining the function. Similarly, return types are specified by appending the function signature with a : and the type that function would return as in the following:

---

1 Custom classes and objects are discussed at length in Chapter 8.

```
function name(type $parameter): return_type
{
    // ...
}
```

Table 3-1 enumerates the simplest types leveraged by PHP.

Table 3-1. Simple single types in PHP

Type	Description
array	The value must be an array (containing any type of values).
callable	The value must be a callable function.
bool	The value must be a Boolean.
float	The value must be a floating-point number.
int	The value must be an integer.
string	The value must be a string.
iterable (*https://oreil.ly/tiTl1*)	The value must be an array or an object that implements Traversable.
mixed (*https://oreil.ly/V8VOc*)	The object can be any value.
void (*https://oreil.ly/lzmvp*)	A return-only type indicating that the function does not return a value.
never (*https://oreil.ly/48KVB*)	A return-only type indicating a function does not return; it either calls exit, throws an exception, or is intentionally an infinite loop.

In addition, both built-in and custom classes can be used to define types, as shown in Table 3-2.

Table 3-2. Object types in PHP

Type	Description
Class/interface name	The value must be an instance of the specified class or implementation of an interface.
self	The value must be an instance of the same class as the one in which the declaration is used.
parent	The value must be an instance of the parent of the class in which the declaration is used.
object	The value must be an instance of an object.

PHP also permits simple scalar types to be expanded by either making them nullable or combining them into *union types*. To make a specific type nullable, you have to prefix the type annotation with a ?. This will instruct the compiler to allow values to be either the specified type or null, as in Example 3-8.

Example 3-8. Function utilizing nullable parameters

```php
function say_hello(?string $message): void
{
    echo 'Hello, ';

    if ($message === null) {
        echo 'world!';
    } else {
        echo $message . '!';
    }
}

say_hello('Reader'); // Hello, Reader!
say_hello(null); // Hello, world!
```

A union type declaration combines multiple types into a single declaration by concatenating simple types together with the pipe character (|). If you were to rewrite the type declarations on the Solution example with a union type combining strings and integers, the fatal error thrown by passing in a string for addition would resolve itself. Consider the possible rewrite in Example 3-9 that would permit *either* integers or strings as parameters.

Example 3-9. Rewriting the Solution example to leverage union types

```php
function add_numbers(int|string $left, int|string $right): int
{
    return $left + $right;
}

add_numbers(2, '3'); // 5
```

The biggest problem with this alternative is that adding strings together with the + operator has no meaning in PHP. If both parameters are numeric (either integers or integers represented as strings), the function will work just fine. If either is a non-numeric string, PHP will throw a TypeError as it doesn't know how to "add" two strings together. These kinds of errors are what you hope to avoid by adding type declarations to your code and enforcing strict typing—they formalize the contract you expect your code to support and encourage programming practices that naturally defend against coding mistakes.

By default, PHP uses its typing system to *hint* at which types are allowed into and returned from functions. This is useful to prevent passing bad data into a function, but it relies heavily on either developer diligence or additional tooling[2] to enforce typing. Rather than rely on humans' ability to check code, PHP allows for a static declaration in each file that all invocations should follow strict typing.

Placing `declare(strict_types=1);` at the top of a file tells the PHP compiler you intend for all invocations in that file to obey parameter and return type declarations. Note that this directive applies to *invocations* within the file where it's used, not to the definitions of functions in that file. If you call functions from another file, PHP will honor the type declarations in that file as well. However, placing this directive in your file will not force other files that reference your functions to obey the typing system.

See Also

PHP documentation on type declarations (*https://oreil.ly/I9D33*) and the `declare` construct (*https://oreil.ly/P2jM_*).

3.5 Defining a Function with a Variable Number of Arguments

Problem

You want to define a function that takes one or more arguments without knowing ahead of time how many values will be passed in.

Solution

Use PHP's spread operator (...) to define a variable number or arguments:

```
function greatest(int ...$numbers): int
{
    $greatest = 0;
    foreach ($numbers as $number) {
        if ($number > $greatest) {
            $greatest = $number;
        }
    }

    return $greatest;
}

greatest(7, 5, 12, 2, 99, 1, 415, 3, 7, 4);
// 415
```

---

2 PHP CodeSniffer (*https://oreil.ly/G4tHg*) is a popular developer tool for automatically scanning a codebase and ensuring that all code matches a specific coding standard. It can be trivially extended to enforce a strict type declaration in all files as well.

Discussion

The *spread operator* automatically adds all parameters passed in that particular position or after it to an array. This array can be typed by prefixing the spread operator with a type declaration (review Recipe 3.4 for more on typing), thus requiring every element of the array to match a specific type. Invoking the function defined in the Solution example as `greatest(2, "five");` will throw a `TypeError`, as you have explicitly declared an `int` type for every member of the `$numbers` array.

Your function can accept more than one positional parameter while still leveraging the spread operator to accept an unlimited number of additional arguments. The function defined in Example 3-10 will print a greeting to the screen for an unlimited number of individuals.

Example 3-10. Utilizing the spread operator

```
function greet(string $greeting, string ...$names): void
{
    foreach($names as $name) {
        echo $greeting . ', ' . $name . PHP_EOL;
    }
}

greet('Hello', 'Tony', 'Steve', 'Wanda', 'Peter');
// Hello, Tony
// Hello, Steve
// Hello, Wanda
// Hello, Peter

greet('Welcome', 'Alice', 'Bob');
// Welcome, Alice
// Welcome, Bob
```

The spread operator has more utility than just function definition. While it can be used to pack multiple arguments into an array, it can also be used to unpack an array into multiple arguments for a more traditional function invocation. Example 3-11 provides a trivial illustration of how this array unpacking works by using the spread operator to pass an array into a function that does not accept an array.

Example 3-11. Unpacking an array with the spread operator

```
function greet(string $greeting, string $name): void
{
    echo $greeting . ', ' . $name . PHP_EOL;
}

$params = ['Hello', 'world'];
```

```
greet(...$params);
// Hello, world
```

In some cases, a more complex function might return multiple values (as discussed in the next recipe), so passing the return of one function into another becomes simple with the spread operator. In fact, any array or variable that implements PHP's Traversable (*https://oreil.ly/jVUvs*) interface can be unpacked into a function invocation in this manner.

See Also

PHP documentation on variable-length argument lists (*https://oreil.ly/9IoHh*).

3.6 Returning More Than One Value

Problem

You want to return multiple values from a single function invocation.

Solution

Rather than returning a single value, return an array of multiple values and unpack them by using list() outside the function:

```
function describe(float ...$values): array
{
    $min = min($values);
    $max = max($values);
    $mean = array_sum($values) / count($values);

    $variance = 0.0;
    foreach($values as $val) {
        $variance += pow(($val - $mean), 2);
    }
    $std_dev = (float) sqrt($variance/count($values));

    return [$min, $max, $mean, $std_dev];
}

$values = [1.0, 9.2, 7.3, 12.0];
list($min, $max, $mean, $std) = describe(...$values);
```

Discussion

PHP is only capable of returning one value from a function invocation, but that value itself could be an array containing multiple values. When paired with PHP's list() construct, this array can be easily destructured to individual variables for further use by the program.

While the need to return many different values isn't common, when the occasion comes up, being able to do so can be incredibly handy. One example is in web authentication. Many modern systems today use JSON Web Tokens (JWTs), which are period-delimited strings of Base64-encoded data. Each component of a JWT represents a separate, discrete thing—a header describing the algorithm used, the data in the token payload, and a verifiable signature on that data.

When reading a JWT as a string, PHP applications often leverage the built-in `explode()` function to split the string on the periods delimiting each component. A simple use of `explode()` might appear as follows:

```
$jwt_parts = explode('.', $jwt);
$header = base64_decode($jwt_parts[0]);
$payload = base64_decode($jwt_parts[1]);
$signature = base64_decode($jwt_parts[2]);
```

The preceding code works just fine, but the repeated references to positions within an array can be difficult to follow both during development and debugging later if a problem arises. In addition, developers must manually decode every part of the JWT separately; forgetting to invoke `base64_decode()` could be fatal to the operation of the program.

An alternative approach is to unpack and automatically decode the JWT within a function and return an array of the components, as shown in Example 3-12.

Example 3-12. Decoding a JWT

```
function decode_jwt(string $jwt): array
{
    $parts = explode('.', $jwt);

    return array_map('base64_decode', $parts);
}

list($header, $payload, $signature) = decode_jwt($jwt);
```

A further advantage of using a function to unpack a JWT rather than decomposing each element directly is that you could build in automated signature verification or even filter JWTs for acceptability based on the encryption algorithms declared in the header. While this logic could be applied procedurally while processing a JWT, keeping everything in a single function definition leads to cleaner, more maintainable code.

The biggest drawback to returning multiple values in one function call is in typing. These functions have an `array` return type, but PHP doesn't natively allow for specifying the type of the elements within an array. We have potential workarounds to this limitation by way of documenting the function signature and integrating with a static analysis tool like Psalm (*https://psalm.dev*) or PHPStan (*https://phpstan.org*), but we have no native support within the language for typed arrays. As such, if you're using strict typing (and you *should* be), returning multiple values from a single function invocation should be a rare occurrence.

See Also

Recipe 3.5 on passing a variable number of arguments and Recipe 1.3 for more on PHP's list() construct. Also reference the phpDocumentor documentation on typed arrays (*https://oreil.ly/RsXGh*) that can be enforced by tools like Psalm.

3.7 Accessing Global Variables from Within a Function

Problem

Your function needs to reference a globally defined variable from elsewhere in the application.

Solution

Prefix any global variables with the global keyword to access them within the function's scope:

```
$counter = 0;

function increment_counter()
{
    global $counter;

    $counter += 1;
}

increment_counter();

echo $counter; // 1
```

Discussion

PHP separates operations into various scopes based on the context in which a variable is defined. For most programs, a single scope spans all included or required files. A variable defined in this global scope is available *everywhere* regardless of which file is currently executing, as demonstrated in Example 3-13.

Example 3-13. Variables defined in the global scope are available to included scripts

```
$apple = 'honeycrisp';

include 'someotherscript.php'; ❶
```

❶ The `$apple` variable is also defined within this script and available for use.

User-defined functions, however, define their own scope. A variable defined outside a user-defined function is *not available* within the body of the function. Likewise, any variable defined within the function is not available outside the function. Example 3-14 illustrates the boundaries of the parent and function scope in a program.

Example 3-14. Local versus global scoping

```
$a = 1; ❶

function example(): void
{
    echo $a . PHP_EOL; ❷
    $a = 2; ❸

    $b = 3; ❹
}

example();

echo $a . PHP_EOL; ❺
echo $b . PHP_EOL; ❻
```

❶ The variable `$a` is initially defined in the parent scope.

❷ Inside the function scope, `$a` is not yet defined. Attempting to echo its value will result in a warning.

❸ Defining a variable called `$a` within the function will *not* overwrite the value of the same-named variable outside the function.

❹ Defining a variable called `$b` within the function makes it available within the function, but this value will not escape the scope of the function.

❺ Echoing `$a` outside the function, even after invoking `example()`, will print the initial value you've set, as the function did not change the variable's value.

❻ Since `$b` was defined within the function, it is undefined in the scope of the parent application.

It is possible to pass a variable into a function call *by reference* if the function is defined to accept a variable in such a way. However, this is a decision made by the definition of the function and not a runtime flag available to routines leveraging that function after the fact. Example 3-4 shows what pass-by-reference might look like.

To reference variables defined outside its scope, a function needs to declare those variables as *global* within its own scope. To reference the parent scope, you can rewrite Example 3-14 as Example 3-15.

Example 3-15. Local versus global scoping, revisited

```
$a = 1;

function example(): void
{
    global $a, $b; ❶

    echo $a . PHP_EOL; ❷
    $a = 2; ❸

    $b = 3; ❹
}

example();

echo $a . PHP_EOL; ❺
echo $b . PHP_EOL; ❻
```

❶ By declaring both $a and $b to be global variables, you are telling the function to use values from the parent scope rather than its own scope.

❷ With a reference to the *global* $a variable, you can now actually print it to output.

❸ Likewise, any changes to $a within the scope of the function will impact the variable in the parent scope.

❹ Similarly, you now define $b but, as it's global, this definition will bubble out to the parent scope as well.

❺ Echoing $a will now reflect the changes made within the scope of example() as you made the variable global.

❻ Likewise, $b is now defined globally and can be echoed to output as well.

There is no limit on the number of global variables PHP can support aside from the memory available to the system. Additionally, *all* globals can be listed by enumerating the special $GLOBALS array defined by PHP. This associative array contains references to all variables defined within the global scope. This special array can be useful if you want to reference a specific variable in the global scope *without* declaring the variable as global, as in Example 3-16.

Example 3-16. Using the associative $GLOBALS array

```
$var = 'global';

function example(): void
{
    $var = 'local';

    echo 'Local variable: ' . $var . PHP_EOL;
    echo 'Global variable: ' . $GLOBALS['var'] . PHP_EOL;
}

example();
// Local variable: local
// Global variable: global
```

> As of PHP 8.1, it is no longer possible to overwrite the entirety of the $GLOBALS array. In previous versions, you could reset it to an empty array (for example, during test runs of your code). Moving forward, you can edit only the contents of the array rather than manipulating the collection in its entirety.

Global variables are a handy way to reference state across your application, but they can lead to confusion and maintainability issues if overused. Some large applications leverage global variables heavily—WordPress, a PHP-based project that powers more than 40% of the internet,[3] uses global variables throughout its codebase (*https://oreil.ly/jztni*). However, most application developers agree that global variables should be used sparingly, if at all, to help keep systems clean and easy to maintain.

See Also

PHP documentation on variable scope (*https://oreil.ly/tN5tV*) and the special $GLOBALS array (*https://oreil.ly/z9JJS*).

---

3 The market reach of WordPress was about 63% of websites using content management systems and more than 43% of all websites as of March 2023 according to W3Techs (*https://oreil.ly/8Y_Zp*).

3.8 Managing State Within a Function Across Multiple Invocations

Problem

Your function needs to keep track of its change in state over time.

Solution

Use the `static` keyword to define a locally scoped variable that retains its state between function invocations:

```
function increment()
{
    static $count = 0;

    return $count++;
}

echo increment(); // 0
echo increment(); // 1
echo increment(); // 2
```

Discussion

A static variable exists only within the scope of the function in which it is declared. However, unlike regular local variables, it holds on to its value every time you return to the scope of the function. In this way, a function can become *stateful* and keep track of certain data (like the number of times it's been called) between independent invocations.

In a typical function, using the = operator will assign a value to a variable. When the `static` keyword is applied, this assignment operation only happens the first time that function is called. Subsequent calls will reference the previous state of the variable and allow the program to either use or modify the stored value as well.

One of the most common use cases of static variables is to track the state of a recursive function. Example 3-17 demonstrates a function that recursively calls itself a fixed number of times before exiting.

Example 3-17. Using a static variable to limit recursion depth

```
function example(): void
{
    static $count = 0;

    if ($count >= 3) {
```

```
    $count = 0;
    return;
}

$count += 1;

echo 'Running for loop number ' . $count . PHP_EOL;
example();
}
```

The static keyword can also be used to keep track of expensive resources that might
be needed by a function multiple times but that you might only want a single instance
of. Consider a function that logs messages to a database: you might not be able to pass
a database connection into the function itself, but you want to ensure that the
function only opens a *single* database connection. Such a logging function might be
implemented as in Example 3-18.

Example 3-18. Using a static variable to hold a database connection

```
function logger(string $message): void
{
    static $dbh = null;
    if ($dbh === null) {
        $dbh = new PDO(DATABASE_DSN, DATABASE_USER, DATABASE_PASSWORD);
    }

    $sql = 'INSERT INTO messages (message) VALUES (:message)';
    $statement = $dbh->prepare($sql);

    $statement->execute([':message', $message]);
}

logger('This is a test'); ❶
logger('This is another message');❷
```

❶ The first time logger() is called, it will define the value of the static $dbh vari-
    able. In this case, it will connect to a database by using the PHP Data Objects
    (PDO) (*https://oreil.ly/do1eJ*) interface. This interface is a standard object pro-
    vided by PHP for accessing databases.

❷ Every subsequent call to logger() will leverage the initial connection opened to
    the database and stored in $dbh.

Note that PHP automatically manages its memory usage and automatically clears
variables from memory when they leave scope. For regular variables within a function, this means the variables are freed from memory as soon as the function completes. Static and global variables are *never* cleaned up until the program itself exits, as

they are always in scope. Take care when using the `static` keyword to ensure that you aren't storing unnecessarily large pieces of data in memory. In Example 3-18, you open a connection to a database that will never be automatically closed by the function you've created.

While the `static` keyword can be a powerful way to reuse state across function calls, it should be used with care to ensure that your application doesn't do anything unexpected. In many cases, it might be better to explicitly pass variables representing state into the function. Even better would be to encapsulate the function's state as part of an overarching object, which is covered in Chapter 8.

See Also

PHP documentation on variable scoping, including the `static` keyword (*https://oreil.ly/-yflc*).

3.9 Defining Dynamic Functions

Problem

You want to define an anonymous function and reference it as a variable within your application because you only want to use or call the function a single time.

Solution

Define a closure that can be assigned to a variable and passed into another function as needed:

```
$greet = function($name) {
    echo 'Hello, ' . $name . PHP_EOL;
};

$greet('World!');
// Hello, World!
```

Discussion

Whereas most functions in PHP have defined names, the language supports the creation of unnamed (so-called *anonymous*) functions, also called *closures* or *lambdas*. These functions can encapsulate either simple or complex logic and can be assigned directly to variables for reference elsewhere in the program.

Internally, anonymous functions are implemented using PHP's native `Closure` (*https://oreil.ly/u5qt7*) class. This class is declared as `final`, which means no class can extend it directly. Yet, anonymous functions are all instances of this class and can be used either directly as functions or as objects.

By default, closures do not inherit any scope from the parent application and, like regular functions, define variables within their own scope. Variables from the parent scope can be passed directly into a closure by leveraging the use directive when defining a function. Example 3-19 illustrates how variables from one scope can be passed into another dynamically.

Example 3-19. Passing a variable between scopes with use()

```php
$some_value = 42;

$foo = function() {
    echo $some_value;
};

$bar = function() use ($some_value) {
    echo $some_value;
};

$foo(); // Warning: Undefined variable

$bar(); // 42
```

Anonymous functions are used in many projects to encapsulate a piece of logic for application against a collection of data. The next recipe covers exactly that use case.

 Older versions of PHP used create_function() (*https://oreil.ly/ RRMgO*) for similar utility. Developers could create an anonymous function as a string and pass that code into create_function() to turn it into a closure instance. Unfortunately, this method used eval() under the hood to evaluate the string—a practice considered highly unsafe. While some older projects might still use create_function(), the function itself was deprecated in PHP 7.2 and removed from the language entirely in version 8.0.

See Also

PHP documentation on anonymous functions (*https://oreil.ly/W0QPL*).

3.10 Passing Functions as Parameters to Other Functions

Problem

You want to define part of a function's implementation and pass that implementation as an argument to another function.

Solution

Define a closure that implements part of the logic you need and pass that directly into another function as if it were any other variable:

```php
$reducer = function(?int $carry, int $item): int {
    return $carry + $item;
};

function reduce(array $array, callable $callback, ?int $initial = null): ?int
{
    $acc = $initial;
    foreach ($array as $item) {
        $acc = $callback($acc, $item);
    }

    return $acc;
}

$list = [1, 2, 3, 4, 5];
$sum = reduce($list, $reducer); // 15
```

Discussion

PHP is considered by many to be a *functional language*, as functions are first-class elements in the language and can be bound to variable names, passed as arguments, or even returned from other functions. PHP supports functions as variables through the callable (*https://oreil.ly/m7skJ*) type as implemented in the language. Many core functions (like usort(), array_map(), and array_reduce()) support passing a callable parameter, which is then used internally to define the function's overall implementation.

The reduce() function defined in the Solution example is a user-written implementation of PHP's native array_reduce() function. Both have the same behavior, and the Solution could be rewritten to pass $reducer directly into PHP's native implementation with no change in the result:

```php
$sum = array_reduce($list, $reducer); // 15
```

Since functions can be passed around like any other variable, PHP has the ability to define partial implementations of functions. This is achieved by defining a function that, in turn, returns another function that can be used elsewhere in the program.

For example, you can define a function to set up a basic multiplier routine that multiplies any input by a *fixed* base amount, as in Example 3-20. The main function returns a new function each time you call it, so you can create functions to double or triple arbitrary values and use them however you want.

Example 3-20. Partially applied multiplier function

```php
function multiplier(int $base): callable
{
    return function(int $subject) use ($base): int {
        return $base * $subject;
    };
}

$double = multiplier(2);
$triple = multiplier(3);

$double(6);   // 12
$double(10);  // 20
$triple(3);   // 9
$triple(12);  // 36
```

Breaking functions apart like this is known as *https://oreil.ly/-a4l[_currying]*. This is the practice of changing a function with multiple input parameters into a series of functions, that each take a *single* parameter, with most of those parameters being functions themselves. To fully illustrate how this can work in PHP, let's look at Example 3-21 and walk through a rewrite of the multiplier() function.

Example 3-21. Walk-through of currying in PHP

```php
function multiply(int $x, int $y): int ❶
{
    return $x * $y;
}

multiply(7, 3); // 21

function curried_multiply(int $x): callable ❷
{
    return function(int $y) use ($x): int { ❸
        return $x * $y; ❹
    };
}

curried_multiply(7)(3); // 21 ❺
```

❶ The most basic form of the function takes two values, multiplies them together, and returns a final result.

❷ When you curry the function, you want each component function to only take a single value. The new curried_multiply() only accepts one parameter but returns a function that leverages that parameter internally.

❸ The internal function references the value passed by your previous function invocation automatically (with the **use** directive).

❹ The resulting function implements the same business logic as the basic form.

❺ Calling a curried function has the appearance of calling *multiple* functions in series, but the result is the same.

The biggest advantage of currying, as in Example 3-21, is that a partially applied function can be passed around as a variable and used elsewhere. Similar to using the `multiplier()` function, you can create a doubling or tripling function by *partially* applying your curried multiplier as follows:

```
$double = curried_multiply(2);
$triple = curried_multiply(3);
```

Partially applied, curried functions are themselves callable functions but can be passed into other functions as variables and fully invoked later.

See Also

Details on anonymous functions in Recipe 3.9.

3.11 Using Concise Function Definitions (Arrow Functions)

Problem

You want to create a simple, anonymous function that references the parent scope without verbose **use** declarations.

Solution

Use PHP's short anonymous function (arrow function) syntax to define a function that inherits its parent's scope automatically:

```
$outer = 42;

$anon = fn($add) => $outer + $add;

$anon(5); // 47
```

Discussion

Arrow functions were introduced in PHP 7.4 as a way to write more concise anonymous functions, as in Recipe 3.9. Arrow functions automatically capture any referenced variables and import them (by value rather than by reference) into the scope of the function.

A more verbose version of the Solution example could be written as shown in Example 3-22 while still achieving the same level of functionality.

Example 3-22. Long form of an anonymous function

```
$outer = 42;

$anon = function($add) use ($outer) {
    return $outer + $add;
};

$anon(5);
```

Arrow functions always return a value—it is impossible to either implicitly or explicitly return void. These functions follow a very specific syntax and always return the result of their expression: *fn (arguments) => expression*. This structure makes arrow functions useful in a wide variety of situations.

One example is a concise inline definition of a function to be applied to all elements in an array via PHP's native `array_map()`. Assume input user data is an array of strings that each represent an integer value and you want to convert the array of strings into an array of integers to enforce proper type safety. This can easily be accomplished via Example 3-23.

Example 3-23. Convert an array of numeric strings to an array of integers

```
$input = ['5', '22', '1093', '2022'];

$output = array_map(fn($x) => intval($x), $input);
// $output = [5, 22, 1093, 2022]
```

Arrow functions only permit a single-line expression. If your logic is complicated enough to require multiple expressions, use a standard anonymous function (see Recipe 3.9) or define a named function in your code. This being said, an arrow function itself is an expression, so one arrow function can actually return another.

The ability to return an arrow function as the expression of another arrow function leads to a way to use arrow functions in *curried* or partially applied functions to encourage code reuse. Assume you want to pass a function in the program that performs modulo arithmetic with a fixed modulus. You can do so by defining one arrow function to perform the calculation and wrap it in another that specifies the modulus, assigning the final, curried function to a variable you can use elsewhere, as in Example 3-24.

Modulo arithmetic is used to create *clock functions* that always return a specific set of integer values regardless of the integer input. You take the modulus of two integers by dividing them and returning the integer remainder. For example, "12 modulo 3" is written as 12 % 3 and returns the remainder of 12/3, or 0. Similarly, "15 modulo 6" is written as 15 % 6 and returns the remainder of 15/6, or 3. The return of a modulo operation is never greater than the modulus itself (3 or 6 in the previous two examples, respectively). Modulo arithmetic is commonly used to group large collections of input values together or to power cryptographic operations, which are discussed further in Chapter 9.

Example 3-24. Function currying with arrow functions

```php
$modulo = fn($x) => fn($y) => $y % $x;

$mod_2 = $modulo(2);
$mod_5 = $modulo(5);

$mod_2(15); // 1
$mod_2(20); // 0
$mod_5(12); // 2
$mod_5(15); // 0
```

Finally, just like regular functions, arrow functions can accept multiple arguments. Rather than passing a single variable (or implicitly referencing variables defined in the parent scope), you can just as easily define a function with multiple parameters and freely use them within the expression. A trivial equality function might use an arrow function as follows:

```php
$eq = fn($x, $y) => $x == $y;

$eq(42, '42'); // true
```

See Also

Details on anonymous functions in Recipe 3.9 and the PHP Manual documentation on arrow functions (*https://oreil.ly/MLURC*).

3.12 Creating a Function with No Return Value

Problem

You need to define a function that does not return data to the rest of the program after it completes.

Solution

Use explicit type declarations and reference the void return type:

```
const MAIL_SENDER = 'wizard@oz.example';
const MAIL_SUBJECT = 'Incoming from the Wonderful Wizard';

function send_email(string $to, string $message): void
{
    $headers = ['From' => MAIL_SENDER];

    $success = mail($to, MAIL_SUBJECT, $message, $headers);

    if (!$success) {
        throw new Exception('The man behind the curtain is on break.');
    }
}

send_email('dorothy@kansas.example', 'Welcome to the Emerald City!');
```

Discussion

The Solution example uses PHP's native mail() function to dispatch a simple message with a static subject to the specified recipient. PHP's mail() returns either true (on success) or false (when there's an error). In the Solution example, you merely want to throw an exception when something goes wrong but otherwise want to return silently.

 In many cases, you might want to return a flag—a Boolean value or a string or null—when a function completes to indicate what has happened so the rest of your program can behave appropriately. Functions that return *nothing* are relatively rare, but they do come up when your program is communicating with an outside party and the result of that communication doesn't impact the rest of the program. Sending a fire-and-forget connection to a message queue or logging to the system error log are both common use cases for a function that returns void.

The void return type is enforced on compile time in PHP, meaning your code will trigger a fatal error if the function body returns *anything* at all, even if you haven't executed anything yet. Example 3-25 illustrates both valid and invalid uses of void.

Example 3-25. Valid and invalid uses of the void return type

```
function returns_scalar(): void
{
    return 1; ❶
```

```
}

function no_return(): void
{
    ❷
}

function empty_return(): void
{
    return; ❸
}

function returns_null(): void
{
    return null; ❹
}
```

❶ Returning a scalar type (such as a string, integer, or Boolean) will trigger a fatal error.

❷ Omitting any kind of return in a function is valid.

❸ Explicitly returning no data is valid.

❹ Even though null is "empty," it still counts as a return and will trigger a fatal error.

Unlike most other types in PHP, the void type is only valid for returns. It cannot be used as a parameter type in a function definition; attempts to do so will result in a fatal error at compile time.

See Also

The original RFC introducing the void return type (*https://oreil.ly/FvRb_*) in PHP 7.1.

3.13 Creating a Function That Does Not Return

Problem

You need to define a function that explicitly exits and to ensure that other parts of your application are aware it will never return.

Solution

Use explicit type annotations and reference the never return type. For example:

```
function redirect(string $url): never
{
    header("Location: $url");
    exit();
}
```

Discussion

Some operations in PHP are intended to be the last action the engine takes before exiting the current process. Calling `header()` to define a specific response header must be done prior to printing any body to the response itself. Specifically, calling header() to trigger a redirect is usually the last thing you want your application to do —printing any body text or processing any other operation after you've told the requesting client to redirect elsewhere has no meaning or value.

The `never` return type signals both to PHP and to other parts of your code that the function is *guaranteed* to halt the program's execution by way of either `exit()` or `die()` or throwing an exception.

If a function that leverages the `never` return type still returns implicitly, as in Example 3-26, PHP will throw a `TypeError` exception.

Example 3-26. Implicit return in a function that should never return

```
function log_to_screen(string $message): never
{
    echo $message;
}
```

Likewise, if a `never`-typed function *explicitly* returns a value, PHP will throw a `TypeError` exception. In both situations, whether an implicit or an explicit return, this exception is enforced at call time (when the function is invoked) rather than when the function is defined.

See Also

The original RFC introducing the `never` return type (*https://oreil.ly/wO3zv*) in PHP 8.1.

## CHAPTER 4

Strings

Strings are one of the fundamental building blocks of data in PHP. Each string represents an ordered sequence of bytes. Strings can range from human-readable sections of text (like To be or not to be) to sequences of raw bytes encoded as integers (such as \110\145\154\154\157\40\127\157\162\154\144\41).[1] Every element of data read or written by a PHP application is represented as a string.

In PHP, strings are typically encoded as ASCII values (*https://oreil.ly/Tjsyx*), although you can convert between ASCII and other formats (like UTF-8) as necessary. Strings can contain null bytes when needed and are essentially limitless in terms of storage so long as the PHP process has adequate memory available.

The most basic way to create a string in PHP is with single quotes. Single-quoted strings are treated as literal statements—there are no special characters or any kind of *interpolation* of variables. To include a literal single quote within a single-quoted string, you must *escape* that quote by prefixing it with a backslash—for example, \'. In fact, the only two characters that need to be—or even can be—escaped are the single quote itself or the backslash. Example 4-1 shows single-quoted strings along with their corresponding printed output.

 Variable interpolation is the practice of referencing a variable directly by name within a string and letting the interpreter replace the variable with its value at runtime. Interpolation allows for more flexible strings, as you can write a single string but dynamically replace some of its contents to fit the context of its location in code.

---

1 This string is a byte representation, formatted in octal notation, of "Hello World!"

Example 4-1. Single-quoted strings

```
print 'Hello, world!';
// Hello, world!

print 'You\'ve only got to escape single quotes and the \\ character.';
// You've only got to escape single quotes and the \ character.

print 'Variables like $blue are printed as literals.';
// Variables like $blue are printed as literals.

print '\110\145\154\154\157\40\127\157\162\154\144\41';
// \110\145\154\154\157\40\127\157\162\154\144\41
```

More complicated strings might need to interpolate variables or reference special characters, like a newline or tab. For these more complicated use cases, PHP requires the use of double quotes instead and allows for various escape sequences, as shown in Table 4-1.

Table 4-1. Double-quoted string escape sequences

Escape sequence	Character	Example
\n	Newline	`"This string ends in a new line.\n"`
\r	Carriage return	`"This string ends with a carriage return.\r"`
\t	Tab	`"Lots\tof\tspace"`
\\	Backslash	`"You must escape the \\ character."`
\$	Dollar sign	`A movie ticket is \$10.`
\"	Double quote	`"Some quotes are \"scare quotes.\""`
\0 through \777	Octal character value	`"\120\110\120"`
\x0 through \xFF	Hex character value	`"\x50\x48\x50"`

Except for special characters that are explicitly escaped with leading backspaces, PHP will automatically substitute the value of any variable passed within a double-quoted string. Further, PHP will interpolate entire expressions within a double-quoted string if they're wrapped in curly braces ({}) and treat them as a variable. Example 4-2 shows how variables, complex or otherwise, are treated within double-quoted strings.

Example 4-2. Variable interpolation within double-quoted strings

```
print "The value of \$var is $var"; ❶
print "Properties of objects can be interpolated, too. {$obj->value}"; ❷
print "Prints the value of the variable returned by getVar(): {${getVar()}}"; ❸
```

❶ The first reference to $var is escaped, but the second will be replaced by its actual value. If $var = 'apple', the string will print The value of $var is apple.

❷ Using curly braces enables the direct reference of object properties within a double-quoted string as if these properties were locally defined variables.

❸ Assuming `getVar()` returns the name of a defined variable, this line will both execute the function and print the value assigned to that variable.

Both single- and double-quoted strings are represented as single lines. Often, though, a program will need to represent multiple lines of text (or multiple lines of encoded binary) as a string. In such a situation, the best tool at a developer's disposal is a Heredoc.

A *Heredoc* is a literal block of text that's started with three angle brackets (the <<< operator), followed by a named identifier, followed by a newline. Every subsequent line of text (including newlines) is part of the string, up to a completely independent line containing nothing but the Heredoc's named identifier and a semicolon. Example 4-3 illustrates how a Heredoc might look in code.

 The identifier used for a Heredoc does not need to be capitalized. However, it is common convention in PHP to always capitalize these identifiers to help distinguish them from the text definition of the string.

Example 4-3. String definition using the Heredoc syntax

```
$poem = <<<POEM
To be or not to be,
That is the question
POEM;
```

Heredocs function just like double-quoted strings and allow variable interpolation (or special characters like escaped hexadecimals) within them. This can be particularly powerful when encoding blocks of HTML within an application, as variables can be used to make the strings dynamic.

In some situations, though, you might want a string literal rather than something open to variable interpolation. In that case, PHP's Nowdoc syntax provides a single-quoted style alternative to Heredoc's double-quoted string analog. A Nowdoc looks almost exactly like a Heredoc, except the identifier itself is enclosed in single quotes, as in Example 4-4.

Example 4-4. String definition using the Nowdoc syntax

```
$poem = <<<'POEM'
To be or not to be,
```

```
That is the question
POEM;
```

Both single and double quotes can be used within Heredoc and Nowdoc blocks without additional escaping. Nowdocs, however, will not interpolate or dynamically replace any values, whether they are escaped or otherwise.

The recipes that follow help further illustrate how strings can be used in PHP and the various problems they can solve.

4.1 Accessing Substrings Within a Larger String

Problem

You want to identify whether a string contains a specific substring. For example, you want to know if a URL contains the text /secret/.

Solution

Use strpos():

```
if (strpos($url, '/secret/') !== false) {
    // A secret fragment was detected, run additional logic
    // ...
}
```

Discussion

PHP's strpos() function will scan through a given string and identify the starting position of the first occurrence of a given substring. This function literally looks for a needle in a haystack, as the function's arguments are named $haystack and $needle, respectively. If the substring ($needle) is not found, the function returns a Boolean false.

It's important in this case to use *strict equality comparison*, as strpos() will return 0 if the substring appears at the very beginning of the string being searched. Remember from Recipe 2.3 that comparing values with only two equals signs will attempt to recast the types, converting an integer 0 into a Boolean false; always use strict comparison operators (either === for equality or !== for inequality) to avoid confusion.

If the $needle appears multiple times within a string, strpos() only returns the position of the first occurrence. You can search for additional occurrences by adding an optional position offset as a third parameter to the function call, as in Example 4-5. Defining an offset also allows you to search the latter part of a string for a substring that you know already appears earlier in the string.

Example 4-5. Count all occurrences of a substring

```php
function count_occurrences($haystack, $needle)
{
    $occurrences = 0;
    $offset = 0;
    $pos = 0; ❶

    do {
        $pos = strpos($haystack, $needle, $offset);

        if ($pos !== false) { ❷
            $occurrences += 1;
            $offset = $pos + 1; ❸
        }
    } while ($pos !== false); ❹

    return $occurrences;
}

$str = 'How much wood would a woodchuck chuck if a woodchuck could chuck wood?';

print count_occurrences($str, 'wood'); // 4
print count_occurrences($str, 'nutria'); // 0
```

❶ All of the variables are initially set to 0 so you can track new string occurrences.

❷ If and only if the string was found should an occurrence be counted.

❸ If the string was found, update the offset but also increment by 1 so you don't repeatedly recount the occurrence you've already found.

❹ Once you've reached the last occurrence of the target substring, exit the loop and return the total count.

See Also

PHP documentation on strpos() (*https://oreil.ly/w9Od4*).

4.2 Extracting One String from Within Another

Problem

You want to extract a small string from a much larger string—for example, the domain name from an email address.

Solution

Use `substr()` to select the part of the string you want to extract:

```
$string = 'eric.mann@cookbook.php';
$start = strpos($string, '@');

$domain = substr($string, $start + 1);
```

Discussion

PHP's `substr()` function returns the portion of a given string, based on an initial off-set (the second parameter) up to an optional length. The full function signature is as follows:

```
function substr(string $string, int $offset, ?int $length = null): string
```

If the `$length` parameter is omitted, `substr()` will return the entire remainder of the string. If the `$offset` parameter is greater than the length of the input string, an empty string is returned.

You can also specify a *negative* offset to return a subset starting from the end of the string instead of the beginning, as in Example 4-6.

Example 4-6. Substring with a negative offset

```
$substring = substr('phpcookbook', -3); ❶
$substring = substr('phpcookbook', -2); ❷
$substring = substr('phpcookbook', -8, 4); ❸
```

❶   Returns ook (the last three characters)

❷   Returns ok (the last two characters)

❸   Returns cook (the middle four characters)

You should be aware of some other edge cases regarding offsets and string lengths with `substr()`. It is possible for the offset to legitimately start within the string, but for `$length` to run past the end of the string. PHP catches this discrepancy and merely returns the remainder of the original string, even if the final return is *less* than the specified length. Example 4-7 details some potential outputs of `substr()` based on various specified lengths.

Example 4-7. Various substring lengths

```
$substring = substr('Four score and twenty', 11, 3); ❶
$substring = substr('Four score and twenty', 99, 3); ❷
$substring = substr('Four score and twenty', 20, 3); ❸
```

❶ Returns and

❷ Returns an empty string

❸ Returns y

Another edge case is a negative `$length` supplied to the function. When requesting a substring with a negative length, PHP will remove that many characters from the substring it returns, as illustrated in Example 4-8.

Example 4-8. Substring with a negative length

```php
$substring = substr('Four score and twenty', 5); ❶
$substring = substr('Four score and twenty', 5, -11); ❷
```

❶ Returns `score and twenty`

❷ Returns `score`

See Also

PHP documentation for `substr()` (*https://oreil.ly/z_w10*) and for `strpos()` (*https://oreil.ly/NWcWJ*).

4.3 Replacing Part of a String

Problem

You want to replace just one part of a string with another string. For example, you want to obfuscate all but the last four digits of a phone number before printing it to the screen.

Solution

Use `substr_replace()` to replace a component of an existing string based on its position:

```php
$string = '555-123-4567';
$replace = 'xxx-xxx'

$obfuscated = substr_replace($string, $replace, 0, strlen($replace));
// xxx-xxx-4567
```

Discussion

PHP's `substr_replace()` function operates on a part of a string, similar to `substr()`, defined by an integer offset up to a specific length. Example 4-9 shows the full function signature.

Example 4-9. Full function signature of `substr_replace()`

```
function substr_replace(
    array|string $string,
    array|string $replace,
    array|int $offset,
    array|int|null $length = null
): string
```

Unlike its `substr()` analog, `substr_replace()` can operate either on individual strings or on collections of strings. If an array of strings is passed in with scalar values for $replace and $offset, the function will run the replacement on each string, as in Example 4-10.

Example 4-10. Replacing multiple substrings at once

```
$phones = [
    '555-555-5555',
    '555-123-1234',
    '555-991-9955'
];

$obfuscated = substr_replace($phones, 'xxx-xxx', 0, 7);

// xxx-xxx-5555
// xxx-xxx-1234
// xxx-xxx-9955
```

In general, developers have a lot of flexibility with the parameters in this function. Similar to `substr()`, the following are true:

- $offset can be negative, in which case replacements begin that number of characters from the *end* of the string.
- $length can be negative, representing the number of characters from the end of the string at which to stop replacing.
- If $length is null, it will internally become the same as the length of the input string itself.
- If length is 0, $replace will be *inserted* into the string at the given $offset, and no replacement will take place at all.

Finally, if $string is provided as an array, all other parameters can be provided as arrays as well. Each element will represent a setting for the string in the same position in $string, as illustrated by Example 4-11.

Example 4-11. Replacing multiple substrings with array parameters

```
$phones = [
    '555-555-5555',
    '555-123-1234',
    '555-991-9955'
];

$offsets = [0, 0, 4];

$replace = [
    'xxx-xxx',
    'xxx-xxx',
    'xxx-xxxx'
];

$lengths = [7, 7, 8];

$obfuscated = substr_replace($phones, $replace, $offsets, $lengths);

// xxx-xxx-5555
// xxx-xxx-1234
// 555-xxx-xxxx
```

 It is not a hard requirement for arrays passed in for $string, $replace, $offset, and $length to be all of the same size. PHP will not throw an error or warning if you pass arrays with different dimensions. Doing so will, however, result in unexpected output during the replacement operation—for example, truncating a string rather than replacing its contents. It's a good idea to validate that the dimensions of each of these four arrays all match.

The substr_replace() function is convenient if you know exactly *where* you need to replace characters within a string. In some situations, you might not know the position of a substring that needs to be replaced, but you want to instead replace occurrences of a *specific* substring. In those circumstances, you would want to use either str_replace() or str_ireplace().

These two functions will search a specified string to find an occurrence (or many occurrences) of a specified substring and replace it with something else. The functions are identical in their call pattern, but the extra i in str_ireplace() indicates that it searches for a pattern in a *case-insensitive* fashion. Example 4-12 illustrates both functions in use.

Example 4-12. Searching and replacing within a string

```
$string = 'How much wood could a Woodchuck chuck if a woodchuck could chuck wood?';

$beaver = str_replace('woodchuck', 'beaver', $string); ❶
$ibeaver = str_ireplace('woodchuck', 'beaver', $string); ❷
```

❶ *How much wood could a Woodchuck chuck if a beaver could chuck wood?*

❷ *How much wood could a beaver chuck if a beaver could chuck wood?*

Both `str_replace()` and `str_ireplace()` accept an optional `$count` parameter that is passed by reference. If specified, this variable will be updated with the number of replacements the function performed. In Example 4-12, this return value would have been 1 and 2, respectively, because of the capitalization of Woodchuck.

See Also

PHP documentation on `substr_replace()` (*https://oreil.ly/-BSkA*), `str_replace()` (*https://oreil.ly/Vm7KH*), and `str_ireplace()` (*https://oreil.ly/8P46w*).

4.4 Processing a String One Byte at a Time

Problem

You need to process a string of single-byte characters from beginning to end, one character at a time.

Solution

Loop through each character of the string as if it were an array. Example 4-13 will count the number of capital letters in a string.

Example 4-13. Count capital characters in a string

```
$capitals = 0;

$string = 'The Carriage held but just Ourselves - And Immortality';
for ($i = 0; $i < strlen($string); $i++) {
    if (ctype_upper($string[$i])) {
        $capitals += 1;
    }
}

// $capitals = 5
```

Discussion

Strings are not arrays in PHP, so you cannot loop over them directly. However, they do provide array-like access to individual characters within the string based on their position. You can reference individual characters by their integer offset (starting with 0), or even by a *negative* offset to start at the end of the string.

Array-like access isn't read-only, though. You can just as easily *replace* a single character in a string based on its position, as demonstrated by Example 4-14.

Example 4-14. Replacing a single character in a string

```
$string = 'A new recipe made my coffee stronger this morning';
$string[31] = 'a';

// A new recipe made my coffee stranger this morning
```

It is also possible to convert a string *directly* to an array by using `str_split()` (*https://oreil.ly/eNxaF*) and then iterate over all items in the resulting array. This will work as an update to the Solution example, as illustrated in Example 4-15.

Example 4-15. Converting a string into an array directly

```
$capitals = 0;

$string = 'The Carriage held but just Ourselves - And Immortality';
$stringArray = str_split($string);
foreach ($stringArray as $char) {
    if (ctype_upper($char)) {
        $capitals += 1;
    }
}

// $capitals = 5
```

The downside of Example 4-15 is that PHP now has to maintain *two* copies of your data: the original string and the resultant array. This isn't a problem when handling small strings as in the example; if your strings instead represent entire files on disk, you will rapidly exhaust the memory available to PHP.

PHP makes accessing individual bytes (characters) within a string relatively easy without any changes in data type. Splitting a string into an array works but might be unnecessary unless you actually *need* an array of characters. Example 4-16 reimagines Example 4-15, using an array reduction technique rather than counting the capital letters in a string directly.

Example 4-16. Counting capital letters in a string with array reduction

```
$str = 'The Carriage held but just Ourselves - And Immortality';

$caps = array_reduce(str_split($str), fn($c, $i) => ctype_upper($i) ? $c+1: $c, 0);
```

 While Example 4-16 is functionally equivalent to Example 4-15, it is more concise and, consequently, more difficult to understand. While it is tempting to reimagine complex logic as one-line functions, unnecessary refactoring of your code for the sake of conciseness can be dangerous. The code might appear elegant but over time becomes more difficult to maintain.

The simplified reduction introduced in Example 4-16 is functionally accurate but still requires splitting the string into an array. It saves on lines of code in your program but still results in creating a second copy of your data. As mentioned before, if the strings over which you're iterating are large (e.g., massive binary files), this will rapidly consume the memory available to PHP.

See Also

PHP documentation on string access and modification (*https://oreil.ly/8MOWh*), as well as documentation on `ctype_upper()` (*https://oreil.ly/bQctH*).

4.5 Generating Random Strings

Problem

You want to generate a string of random characters.

Solution

Use PHP's native `random_int()` function:

```
function random_string($length = 16)
{
    $characters = '0123456789abcdefghijklmnopqrstuvwxyz';

    $string = '';
    while (strlen($string) < $length) {
        $string .= $characters[random_int(0, strlen($characters) - 1)];
    }
    return $string;
}
```

Discussion

PHP has strong, *cryptographically secure* pseudorandom generator functions for both integers and bytes. It does not have a native function that generates random human-readable text, but the underlying functions can be used to create such a string of random text by leveraging lists of human-readable characters, as illustrated by the Solution example.

> A *cryptographically secure pseudorandom number generator* is a function that returns numbers with no distinguishable or predictable pattern. Even forensic analysis cannot distinguish between random noise and the output of a cryptographically secure generator.

A valid and potentially simpler method for producing random strings is to leverage PHP's `random_bytes()` function and encode the binary output as ASCII text. Example 4-17 illustrates two possible methods of using random bytes as a string.

Example 4-17. Creating a string of random bytes

```
$string = random_bytes(16); ❶

$hex = bin2hex($string); ❷
$base64 = base64_encode($string); ❸
```

❶ Because the string of binary bytes will be encoded in a different format, keep in mind that the number of bytes produced will *not* match the length of the final string.

❷ Encode the random string in hexadecimal format. Note that this format will double the length of the string—16 bytes is equivalent to 32 hexadecimal characters.

❸ Leverage Base64 (*https://oreil.ly/NsyVs*) encoding to convert the raw bytes on readable characters. Note that this format increases the length of the string by 33%–36%.

See Also

PHP documentation on `random_int()` (*https://oreil.ly/g3gAR*) and on `random_bytes()` (*https://oreil.ly/2Zbio*). Also Recipe 5.4 on generating random numbers.

4.6 Interpolating Variables Within a String

Problem

You want to include dynamic content in an otherwise static string.

Solution

Use double quotes to wrap the string and insert a variable, object property, or even function/method call directly in the string itself:

```
echo "There are {$_POST['cats']} cats and {$_POST['dogs']} outside.";
echo "Your username is {strlen($username)} characters long.";
echo "The car is painted {$car->color}.";
```

Discussion

Unlike single-quoted strings, double-quoted strings allow for complex, dynamic values as literals. Any word starting with a $ character is interpreted as a variable name, unless that leading character is properly escaped.[2]

While the Solution example wraps dynamic content in curly braces, this is not a requirement in PHP. Simple variables can easily be written as is within a double-quoted string and will be interpolated properly. However, more complex sequences become difficult to read without the braces. It's a highly recommended best practice to always enclose any value you want interpolated to make the string more readable.

Unfortunately, string interpolation has its limits. The Solution example illustrates pulling data out of the superglobal $_POST array and inserting it directly into a string. This is potentially dangerous, as that content is generated directly by the user, and the string could be leveraged in a sensitive way. In fact, string interpolation like this is one of the largest vectors for injection attacks against applications.

 In an injection attack, a third party can pass (or inject) executable or otherwise malicious input into your application and cause it to misbehave. More sophisticated ways to protect against this family of attacks are covered in Chapter 9.

To protect your string use against potentially malicious user-generated input, it's a good idea to instead use a format string via PHP's `sprintf()` function to filter the content. Example 4-18 rewrites part of the Solution example to protect against malicious $_POST data.

---

2 Review Table 4-1 for more on double-character escape sequences.

Example 4-18. Using format strings to produce an interpolated string

```
echo sprintf('There are %d cats and %d dogs.', $_POST['cats'], $_POST['dogs']);
```

Format strings are a basic form of input sanitization in PHP. In Example 4-18, you are explicitly assuming that the supplied `$_POST` data is numeric. The `%d` tokens within the format string will be replaced by the user-supplied data, but PHP will explicitly cast this data as integers during the replacement.

If, for example, this string were being inserted into a database, the formatting would protect against the potential of injection attacks against SQL interfaces. More complete methods of filtering and sanitizing user input are discussed in Chapter 9.

See Also

PHP documentation on variable parsing (*https://oreil.ly/CAj-J*) in double quotes and Heredoc as well as documentation on the `sprintf()` function (*https://oreil.ly/DMAg6*).

4.7 Concatenating Multiple Strings Together

Problem

You need to create a new string from two smaller strings.

Solution

Use PHP's string concatenation operator:

```
$first = 'To be or not to be';
$second = 'That is the question';

$line = $first . ' ' . $second;
```

Discussion

PHP uses a single . character to join two strings together. This operator will also leverage type coercion to ensure that both values in the operation are strings before they're concatenated, as shown in Example 4-19.

Example 4-19. String concatenation

```
print 'String ' . 2; ❶
print 2 . ' number'; ❷
print 'Boolean ' . true; ❸
print 2 . 3; ❹
```

❶ Prints String 2

❷ Prints 2 number

❸ Prints Boolean 1 because Boolean values are cast to integers and then to strings

❹ Prints 23

The string concatenation operator is a quick way to combine simple strings, but it can become somewhat verbose if you use it to combine multiple strings with whitespace. Consider Example 4-20, where you try to combine a list of words into a string, each separated by a space.

Example 4-20. Verbosity in concatenating large groups of strings

```php
$words = [
    'Whose',
    'woods',
    'these',
    'are',
    'I',
    'think',
    'I',
    'know'
];

$option1 = $words[0] . ' ' . $words[1] . ' ' . $words[2] . ' ' . $words[3] .
           ' ' . $words[4] . ' ' . $words[5] . ' ' . $words[6] .
           ' ' . $words[7]; ❶

$option2 = '';
foreach ($words as $word) {
    $option2 .= ' ' . $word; ❷
}
$option2 = ltrim($option2); ❸
```

❶ One option is to individually concatenate each word in the collection with whitespace separators. As the word list grows, this quickly becomes unwieldy.

❷ You can, instead, loop over the collection and build up a concatenated string without accessing each item in the collection individually.

❸ When using a loop, you might end up with unnecessary whitespace. You need to remember to trim extraneous spaces from the start of the string.

Large, repetitive concatenation routines can be replaced by native PHP functions like implode(). This function in particular accepts an array of data to be joined and a definition of the character (or characters) to be used between data elements. It returns the final, concatenated string.

 Some developers prefer to use join() instead of implode() as it's seen to be a more descriptive name for the operation. The fact is, join() is an alias of implode(), and the PHP compiler doesn't care which you use.

Rewriting Example 4-20 to use implode() makes the entire operation much simpler, as demonstrated by Example 4-21.

Example 4-21. A concise approach to string concatenation

```
$words = [
    'Whose',
    'woods',
    'these',
    'are',
    'I',
    'think',
    'I',
    'know'
];

$string = implode(' ', $words);
```

Take care to remember the parameter order for implode(). The string separator comes *first*, followed by the array over which you want to iterate. Earlier versions of PHP (prior to version 8.0) allowed the parameters to be specified in the opposite order. This behavior (specifying the array first and the separator second) was deprecated in PHP 7.4. As of PHP 8.0, this will throw a TypeError.

If you're using a library written prior to PHP 8.0, be sure you test that it's not misusing either implode() or join() before you ship your project to production.

See Also

PHP documentation on implode() (*https://oreil.ly/bGYt0*).

4.8 Managing Binary Data Stored in Strings

Problem

You want to encode data directly as binary rather than as an ASCII-formatted representation, or you want to read data into your application that was explicitly encoded as binary data.

Solution

Use unpack() to extract binary data from a string:

```
$unpacked = unpack('S1', 'Hi'); // [1 => 26952]
```

Use pack() to write binary data to a string:

```
$packed = pack('S13', 72, 101, 108, 108, 111, 44, 32, 119, 111,
                114, 108, 100, 33); // 'Hello, world!'
```

Discussion

Both pack() and unpack() empower you to operate on raw binary strings, assuming you know the format of the binary string you're working with. The first parameter of each function is a format specification. This specification is determined by specific format codes, as defined in Table 4-2.

Table 4-2. Binary format string codes

Code	Description
a	Null-padded string
A	Space-padded string
h	Hex string, low nibble first
H	Hex string, high nibble first
c	Signed char
C	Unsigned char
s	Signed short (always 16-bit, machine byte order)
S	Unsigned short (always 16-bit, machine byte order)
n	Unsigned short (always 16-bit, big-endian byte order)
v	Unsigned short (always 16-bit, little-endian byte order)
i	Signed integer (machine-dependent size and byte order)
I	Unsigned integer (machine-dependent size and byte order)
l	Signed long (always 32-bit, machine byte order)
L	Unsigned long (always 32-bit, machine byte order)
N	Unsigned long (always 32-bit, big-endian byte order)

Code	Description
V	Unsigned long (always 32-bit, little-endian byte order)
q	Signed long long (always 64-bit, machine byte order)
Q	Unsigned long long (always 64-bit, machine byte order)
J	Unsigned long long (always 64-bit, big-endian byte order)
P	Unsigned long long (always 64-bit, little-endian byte order)
f	Float (machine-dependent size and representation)
g	Float (machine-dependent size, little-endian byte order)
G	Float (machine-dependent size, big-endian byte order)
d	Double (machine-dependent size and representation)
e	Double (machine-dependent size, little-endian byte order)
E	Double (machine-dependent size, big-endian byte order)
x	Null byte
X	Back up one byte
Z	Null-padded string
@	Null-fill to absolute position

When defining a format string, you can specify each byte type individually or leverage an optional repeating character. In the Solution examples, the number of bytes is explicitly specified with an integer. You could just as easily use an asterisk (*) to specify that a type of byte repeats through the end of the string as follows:

```php
$unpacked = unpack('S*', 'Hi'); // [1 => 26952]
$packed = pack('S*', 72, 101, 108, 108, 111, 44, 32, 119, 111,
                114, 108, 100, 33); // 'Hello, world!'
```

PHP's ability to convert between byte encoding types via unpack() also provides a simple method of converting ASCII characters to and from their binary equivalent. The ord() function will return the value of a specific character, but it requires looping over each character in a string if you want to unpack each in turn, as demonstrated in Example 4-22.

Example 4-22. Retrieving character values with ord()

```php
$ascii = 'PHP Cookbook';

$chars = [];
for ($i = 0; $i < strlen($ascii); $i++) {
    $chars[] = ord($ascii[$i]);
}

var_dump($chars);
```

Thanks to unpack(), you don't need to explicitly iterate over the characters in a string. The c format character references a signed character, and C a signed one. Rather than building a loop, you can leverage unpack() directly as follows to get an equivalent result:

```
$ascii = 'PHP Cookbook';
$chars = unpack('C*', $ascii);

var_dump($chars);
```

Both the preceding unpack() example and the original loop implementation in Example 4-22 produce the following array:

```
array(12) {
  [1]=>
  int(80)
  [2]=>
  int(72)
  [3]=>
  int(80)
  [4]=>
  int(32)
  [5]=>
  int(67)
  [6]=>
  int(111)
  [7]=>
  int(111)
  [8]=>
  int(107)
  [9]=>
  int(98)
  [10]=>
  int(111)
  [11]=>
  int(111)
  [12]=>
  int(107)
}
```

See Also

PHP documentation on pack() (*https://oreil.ly/0iieT*) and unpack() (*https://oreil.ly/Un_aD*).

## CHAPTER 5

Numbers

Another fundamental building block of data in PHP is numbers. It's easy to find different types of numbers in the world around us. The page number in a book is often printed in the footer. Your smartwatch displays the current time and perhaps the number of steps you've taken today. Some numbers can be impossibly large, others impossibly small. Numbers can be whole, fractional, or irrational like π.

In PHP, numbers are represented natively in one of two formats: as integers (the int type) or as floating-point numbers (the float type). Both numeric types are highly flexible, but the range of values you can use depends on the processor architecture of your system—a 32-bit system has tighter bounds than a 64-bit system.

PHP defines several constants that help programs understand the available range of numbers in the system. Given that the capabilities of PHP will differ greatly based on how it was compiled (for 32 or 64 bits), it is wise to use the constants defined in Table 5-1 rather than trying to determine what these values will be in a program. It's always safer to defer to the operating system and language defaults.

Table 5-1. Constant numeric values in PHP

Constant	Description
PHP_INT_MAX	The largest integer value supported by PHP. On 32-bit systems, this will be 2147483647. On 64-bit systems, this will be 9223372036854775807.
PHP_INT_MIN	The smallest integer value supported by PHP. On 32-bit systems, this will be -2147483648. On 64-bit systems, this will be -9223372036854775808.
PHP_INT_SIZE	Size of integers in bytes for this build of PHP.
PHP_FLOAT_DIG	Number of digits that can be rounded in a float and back without a loss in precision.
PHP_FLOAT_EPSILON	The smallest representable positive number x such that $x + 1.0 !== 1.0$.
PHP_FLOAT_MIN	Smallest representable positive floating-point number.

Constant	Description
PHP_FLOAT_MAX	Largest representable floating-point number.
-PHP_FLOAT_MAX	Not a separate constant, but the way to represent the smallest negative floating-point number.

The unfortunate limitation of PHP's number systems is that very large or very small numbers cannot be represented natively. Instead, you need to leverage an extension like BCMath (*https://oreil.ly/qFeO3*) or GNU Multiple Precision Arithmetic Library (GMP) (*https://oreil.ly/u9Mbf*), both of which wrap operating system–native operations on numbers. I'll cover GMP specifically in Recipe 5.10.

The recipes that follow cover many of the problems developers need to solve with numbers in PHP.

5.1 Validating a Number Within a Variable

Problem

You want to check whether a variable contains a number, even if that variable is explicitly typed as a string.

Solution

Use `is_numeric()` to check whether a variable can be successfully cast as a numeric value—for example:

```
$candidates = [
    22,
    '15',
    '12.7',
    0.662,
    'infinity',
    INF,
    0xDEADBEEF,
    '10e10',
    '15 apples',
    '2,500'
];

foreach ($candidates as $candidate) {
    $numeric = is_numeric($candidate) ? 'is' : 'is NOT';

    echo "The value '{$candidate}' {$numeric} numeric." . PHP_EOL;
}
```

The preceding example will print the following when run in a console:

```
The value '22' is numeric.
The value '15' is numeric.
```

```
The value '12.7' is numeric.
The value '0.662' is numeric.
The value 'infinity' is NOT numeric.
The value 'INF' is numeric.
The value '3735928559' is numeric.
The value '10e10' is numeric.
The value '15 apples' is NOT numeric.
The value '2,500' is NOT numeric.
```

Discussion

At its core, PHP is a dynamically typed language. You can easily interchange strings for integers (and vice versa), and PHP will try to infer your intention, dynamically casting values from one type to another as needed. While you can (and probably should) enforce strict typing as discussed in Recipe 3.4, often you will explicitly need to encode numbers as strings.

In those situations, you will lose the ability to identify numeric strings by leveraging PHP's type system. A variable passed into a function as a string will be invalid for mathematical operations without an explicit cast to a numeric type (int or float). Unfortunately, not every string that contains numbers is numeric.

The string 15 apples contains a number but is not numeric. The string 10e10 contains non-numeric characters but is a valid numeric representation.

The difference between strings that have numbers and truly numeric strings can be best illustrated through a userland implementation of PHP's native is_numeric() function, as defined in Example 5-1.

Example 5-1. Userland is_numeric() implementation

```
function string_is_numeric(string $test): bool
{
    return $test === (string) floatval($test);
}
```

Applied to the same array of $candidates from the Solution example, Example 5-1 will accurately verify numeric strings in everything *except* the literal INF constant and the 10e10 exponent shorthand. This is because floatval() will strip any non-numeric characters from the string entirely while converting it to a floating-point number prior to (string) casting things back to a string.[1]

---

1 For more on type casting, review "Type Casting" on page 13.

The userland implementation isn't adequate for every situation, so you should use the native implementation to be safe. The goal of is_numeric() is to indicate whether a given string can be safely cast to a numeric type without losing information.

See Also

PHP documentation for is_numeric() (*https://oreil.ly/jTGcF*).

5.2 Comparing Floating-Point Numbers

Problem

You want to test for equality of two floating-point numbers.

Solution

Define an appropriate error bound (called epsilon) that represents the greatest acceptable difference between the two numbers and evaluate their difference against it as follows:

```
$first = 22.19348234;
$second = 22.19348230;

$epsilon = 0.000001;

$equal = abs($first - $second) < $epsilon; // true
```

Discussion

Floating-point arithmetic with modern computers is less than exact because of the way machines internally represent numbers. Different operations you might calculate by hand and assume to be precise can trip up the machines you rely on.

For example, the mathematic operation 1 - 0.83 is obviously 0.17. It's simple enough to mentally calculate or even work out on paper. But asking a computer to calculate this will produce a strange result, as demonstrated in Example 5-2.

Example 5-2. Floating-point subtraction

```
$a = 0.17;
$b = 1 - 0.83;

var_dump($a == $b); ❶
var_dump($a); ❷
var_dump($b); ❸
```

❶ bool(false)

❷ `float(0.17)`

❸ `float(0.17000000000000004)`

When it comes to floating-point arithmetic, the best computers can do is an approximate result within an acceptable margin of error. As a result, comparing this result to an expected value requires the explicit definition of that margin (`epsilon`) and a comparison to that margin rather than an exact value.

Rather than leverage either of PHP's equality operators (a double or triple equals sign), you can define a function to check for the *relative* equality of two floats, as shown in Example 5-3.

Example 5-3. Comparing equality of floating-point numbers

```php
function float_equality(float $epsilon): callable
{
    return function(float $a, float $b) use ($epsilon): bool
    {
        return abs($a - $b) < $epsilon;
    };
}

$tight_equality = float_equality(0.0000001);
$loose_equality = float_equality(0.01);

var_dump($tight_equality(1.152, 1.152001)); ❶
var_dump($tight_equality(0.234, 0.2345)); ❷
var_dump($tight_equality(0.234, 0.244)); ❸
var_dump($loose_equality(1.152, 1.152001)); ❹
var_dump($loose_equality(0.234, 0.2345)); ❺
var_dump($loose_equality(0.234, 0.244)); ❻
```

❶ `bool(false)`

❷ `bool(false)`

❸ `bool(false)`

❹ `bool(true)`

❺ `bool(true)`

❻ `bool(true)`

See Also

PHP documentation on floating-point numbers (*https://oreil.ly/-311_*).

5.3 Rounding Floating-Point Numbers

Problem

You want to round a floating-point number either to a fixed number of decimal places or to an integer.

Solution

To round a floating-point number to a set number of decimal places, use `round()` while specifying the number of places:

```
$number = round(15.31415, 1);
// 15.3
```

To explicitly round up to the nearest whole number, use `ceil()`:

```
$number = ceil(15.3);
// 16
```

To explicitly round down to the nearest whole number, use `floor()`:

```
$number = floor(15.3);
// 15
```

Discussion

All three functions referenced in the Solution examples—`round()`, `ceil()`, and `floor()`—are intended to operate on any numeric value but will return a `float` after operating on it. By default, `round()` will round to zero digits after the decimal point but will still return a floating-point number.

To convert from a `float` to an `int` for any of these functions, wrap the function itself in `intval()` to convert to an integer type.

Rounding in PHP is more flexible than merely rounding up or down. By default, `round()` will always round the input number away from 0 when it's halfway there. This means numbers like 1.4 will round down, while 1.5 will round up. This also holds true with negative numbers: −1.4 will be rounded towards 0 to −1, while −1.5 will be rounded away from 0 to −2.

You can change the behavior of `round()` by passing an optional third argument (or by using named parameters as shown in Recipe 3.3) to specify the rounding mode. This argument accepts one of four default constants defined by PHP, as enumerated in Table 5-2.

Table 5-2. Rounding mode constants

Constant	Description
PHP_ROUND_HALF_UP	Rounds a value away from 0 when it is halfway there, making 1.5 into 2 and −1.5 into −2
PHP_ROUND_HALF_DOWN	Rounds a value towards 0 when it is halfway there, making 1.5 into 1 and −1.5 into −1
PHP_ROUND_HALF_EVEN	Rounds a value towards the nearest even value when it is halfway there, making both 1.5 and 2.5 into 2
PHP_ROUND_HALF_ODD	Rounds a value towards the nearest odd value when it is halfway there, making 1.5 into 1 and 2.5 into 3

Example 5-4 illustrates the effect of each rounding mode constant when applied to the same numbers.

Example 5-4. Rounding floats in PHP with different modes

```
echo 'Rounding on 1.5' . PHP_EOL;
var_dump(round(1.5, mode: PHP_ROUND_HALF_UP));
var_dump(round(1.5, mode: PHP_ROUND_HALF_DOWN));
var_dump(round(1.5, mode: PHP_ROUND_HALF_EVEN));
var_dump(round(1.5, mode: PHP_ROUND_HALF_ODD));

echo 'Rounding on 2.5' . PHP_EOL;
var_dump(round(2.5, mode: PHP_ROUND_HALF_UP));
var_dump(round(2.5, mode: PHP_ROUND_HALF_DOWN));
var_dump(round(2.5, mode: PHP_ROUND_HALF_EVEN));
var_dump(round(2.5, mode: PHP_ROUND_HALF_ODD));
```

The preceding example will print the following to your console:

```
Rounding on 1.5
float(2)
float(1)
float(2)
float(1)
Rounding on 2.5
float(3)
float(2)
float(2)
float(3)
```

See Also

PHP documentation on floating-point numbers (*https://oreil.ly/ONHjD*), the round() (*https://oreil.ly/010CB*) function, the ceil() (*https://oreil.ly/i5Rpy*) function, and the floor() (*https://oreil.ly/VAZ6t*) function.

5.4 Generating Truly Random Numbers

Problem

You want to generate random integers within specific bounds.

Solution

Use `random_int()` as follows:

```
// Random integer between 10 and 225, inclusive
$random_number = random_int(10, 225);
```

Discussion

When you need randomness, you most often need explicitly true, completely unpredictable randomness. In those situations, you can rely on the cryptographically secure pseudorandom number generators built into the machine itself. PHP's `random_int()` function relies on these operating system–level number generators rather than implementing its own algorithm.

On Windows, PHP will leverage either `CryptGenRandom()` (*https://oreil.ly/0kVO9*) or the `Cryptography API: Next Generation (CNG)` (*https://oreil.ly/otHP9*) depending on the language version in use. On Linux, PHP leverages a system call to `getran dom(2)` (*https://oreil.ly/07DIE*). On any other platform, PHP will fall back on the system-level */dev/urandom* interface. All of these APIs are well tested and proven to be cryptographically secure, meaning they generate numbers with sufficient randomness that they are indistinguishable from noise.

> In rare situations, you'll want a random number generator to produce a predictable series of pseudorandom values. In those circumstances, you can rely on algorithmic generators like the Mersenne Twister, which is further discussed in Recipe 5.5.

PHP doesn't natively support a method to create a random floating-point number (i.e., selecting a random decimal between 0 and 1). Instead, you can use `random_int()` and your knowledge of integers in PHP to create your own function to do exactly that, as shown in Example 5-5.

Example 5-5. Userland function for generating a random floating-point number

```
function random_float(): float
{
    return random_int(0, PHP_INT_MAX) / PHP_INT_MAX;
}
```

This implementation of `random_float()` lacks bounds because it will always generate a number between 0 and 1, inclusively. This might be useful to create random percentages, either for creating artificial data or for selecting randomly sized samples of arrays. A more complicated implementation might incorporate bounds as shown in Example 5-6, but often being able to choose between 0 and 1 is utility enough.

Example 5-6. Userland function for generating a random float within bounds

```php
function random_float(int $min = 0, int $max = 1): float
{
    $rand = random_int(0, PHP_INT_MAX) / PHP_INT_MAX;

    return ($max - $min) * $rand + $min;
}
```

This newer definition of `random_float()` merely scales the original definition to the newly defined bounds. If you were to leave the default bounds in place, the function reduces down to the original definition.

See Also

PHP documentation on `random_int()` (*https://oreil.ly/kLoas*).

5.5 Generating Predictable Random Numbers

Problem

You want to predict random numbers in such a way that the sequence of numbers is the same every time.

Solution

Use the `mt_rand()` function after passing a predefined seed into `mt_srand()`—for example:

```php
function generate_sequence(int $count = 10): array
{
    $array = [];

    for ($i = 0; $i < $count; $i++) {
        $array[] = mt_rand(0, 100);
    }

    return $array;
}

mt_srand(42);
```

```
$first = generate_sequence();

mt_srand(42);
$second = generate_sequence();

print_r($first);
print_r($second);
```

Both arrays in the preceding example will have the following contents:

```
Array
(
    [0] => 38
    [1] => 32
    [2] => 94
    [3] => 55
    [4] => 2
    [5] => 21
    [6] => 10
    [7] => 12
    [8] => 47
    [9] => 30
)
```

Discussion

When writing any other example about truly random numbers, the best anyone can do is to illustrate what the output *might* look like. When it comes to the output of mt_rand(), however, the output will be the same on every computer, given you're using the same seed.

 PHP automatically seeds mt_rand() at random by default. It is not necessary to specify your own seed unless your goal is deterministic output from the function.

The output is the same because mt_rand() leverages an algorithmic pseudorandom number generator called the *Mersenne Twister*. This is a well-known and heavily used algorithm first introduced in 1997; it's also used in languages like Ruby and Python.

Given an initial seed value, the algorithm creates an initial state and then generates seemingly random numbers by executing a "twist" operation on that state. The advantage of this approach is that it's deterministic—given the same seed, the algorithm will create the same sequence of "random" numbers every time.

Predictability in random numbers can be hazardous to certain computing operations, specifically to cryptography. The use cases requiring a deterministic sequence of pseudorandom numbers are rare enough that `mt_rand()` should be avoided as much as possible. If you need to generate random numbers, leverage true sources of randomness like `random_int()` and `random_bytes()`.

Creating a pseudorandom but predictable sequence of numbers might be useful in creating object IDs for a database. You can easily test that your code operates correctly by running it multiple times and verifying the output. The disadvantage is that algorithms like the Mersenne Twister can be gamed by an outside party.

Given a sufficiently long sequence of seemingly random numbers and knowledge of the algorithm, it is trivial to reverse the operation and identify the original seed. Once an attacker knows the seed value, they can generate every possible "random" number your system will leverage moving forward.

See Also

PHP documentation on `mt_rand()` (*https://oreil.ly/niU_q*) and `mt_srand()` (*https://oreil.ly/xSa53*).

5.6 Generating Weighted Random Numbers

Problem

You want to generate random numbers in order to select a specific item from a collection at random, but you want some items to have a higher chance of being selected than others. For example, you want to select the winner of a particular challenge at an event, but some participants have earned more points than others and need to have a greater chance of being selected.

Solution

Pass a map of choices and weights into an implementation of `weighted_random_choice()`, as demonstrated in Example 5-7.

Example 5-7. Implementation of a weighted random choice

```
$choices = [
    'Tony'  => 10,
    'Steve' => 2,
    'Peter' => 1,
    'Wanda' => 4,
    'Carol' => 6
```

```
];

function weighted_random_choice(array $choices): string
{
    arsort($choices);

    $total_weight = array_sum(array_values($choices));
    $selection = random_int(1, $total_weight);

    $count = 0;
    foreach ($choices as $choice => $weight) {
        $count += $weight;
        if ($count >= $selection) {
            return $choice;
        }
    }

    throw new Exception('Unable to make a choice!');
}

print weighted_random_choice($choices);
```

Discussion

In the Solution example, each possible choice is assigned a weight. To choose a final option, you can *order* each option by weight, with the highest-weighted option coming first in the list. You then identify a random number somewhere in the field of total possible weights. That random number selects which of the options you chose.

This is easiest to visualize on a number line. In the Solution example, Tony is entered into the selection with a weight of 10 and Peter with a weight of 1. This means Tony is 10 times as likely to win as Peter, but it's still possible *neither* of them will be chosen. Figure 5-1 illustrates the relative weight of each if you order the possible choices by weight and print them on a number line.

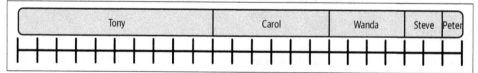

Figure 5-1. Potential selections ordered and visualized by weight

The algorithm defined in `weighted_random_choice()` will check whether the selected random number is within the bounds of each possible choice and, if not, move on to the next candidate. If, for any reason, you're unable to make a selection, the function will throw an exception.[2]

It is possible to verify the weighted nature of this choice by executing a random selection a thousand times and then plotting the relative number of times each choice is picked. Example 5-8 shows how such a repeated choice can be tabulated, while Figure 5-2 illustrates the outcome. Both demonstrate just how much more likely Tony is to be chosen than any other option in the candidate array.

Example 5-8. Repeated selection of a weighted random choice

```
$output = fopen('output.csv', 'w');
fputcsv($output, ['selected']);

foreach (range(0, 1000) as $i) {
    $selection = weighted_random_choice($choices);
    fputcsv($output, [$selection]);
}
fclose($output);
```

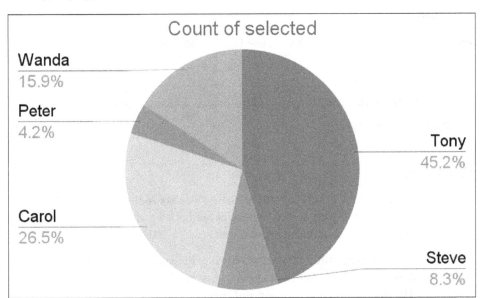

Figure 5-2. Pie chart illustrating the relative number of times each choice is selected

This illustration of outcomes after 1,000 iterations clearly demonstrates that Tony is chosen roughly 10 times more frequently than Peter. This lines up perfectly with his

---

2 Exceptions and error handling are discussed at length in Chapter 12.

having a weight of 10 to Peter's 1. Likewise, Wanda's weight of 4 reliably lines up with her being chosen twice as frequently as Steve, who has a weight of 2.

Given that the choices here are random, running the same experiment again will result in slightly different percentages for each candidate. However, the integer weights of each will always translate into roughly the same distribution of choices.

See Also

PHP documentation on `random_int()` (*https://oreil.ly/Pq16w*) and `arsort()` (*https://oreil.ly/VZ-Vz*) as well as Recipe 5.4 for further examples of `random_int()` in practice.

5.7 Calculating Logarithms

Problem

You want to calculate the logarithm of a number.

Solution

For natural logarithms (using base e), use `log()` as follows:

```
$log = log(5);
// 1.6094379124341
```

For any arbitrary base logarithm, specify the base as a second optional parameter:

```
$log2 = log(16, 2);
// 4.0
```

Discussion

PHP supports the calculation of logarithms with its native Math extension. When you call `log()` without specifying a base, PHP will fall back on the default `M_E` constant, which is coded to the value of e, or approximately 2.718281828459.

If you try to take the logarithm of a negative value, PHP will always return `NAN`, a constant (typed as a `float`) that represents *not a number*. If you attempt to pass a negative base, PHP will return a `ValueError` and trigger a warning.

Any positive, nonzero base is supported by `log()`. Many applications use base 10 so frequently that PHP supports a separate `log10()` function for just that base. This is functionally equivalent to passing the integer 10 as a base to `log()`.

See Also

PHP documentation on the various functionality supported by the Math extension (*https://oreil.ly/nLOM7*), including `log()` (*https://oreil.ly/r-WYo*) and `log10()` (*https://oreil.ly/7Tn4t*).

5.8 Calculating Exponents

Problem

You want to raise a number to an arbitrary power.

Solution

Use PHP's `pow()` function as follows:

```
// 2^5
$power = pow(2, 5); // 32

// 3^0.5
$power = pow(3, 0.5); // 1.7320508075689

// e^2
$power = pow(M_E, 2); // 7.3890560989306
```

Discussion

PHP's `pow()` function is an efficient way to raise any number to an arbitrary power and return either the integer or floating-point result. In addition to the function form, PHP provides a special operator for raising a number to a power: `**`.

The following code is equivalent to the use of `pow()` in the Solution examples:

```
// 2^5
$power = 2 ** 5; // 32

// 3^0.5
$power = 3 ** 0.5; // 1.7320508075689

// e^2
$power = M_E ** 2; // 7.3890560989306
```

> While the mathematical shorthand for exponentiation is usually the caret (^), this character in PHP is reserved for the XOR operator. Review Chapter 2 for more details on this and other operators.

While raising the constant e to an arbitrary power is possible through pow(), PHP also ships with a specific function for that use: exp(). The statements pow(M_E, 2) and exp(2) are functionally equivalent. They are implemented via different code and, because of the way floating-point numbers are represented internally by PHP, will return slightly different results.[3]

See Also

PHP documentation on pow() (*https://oreil.ly/JEsKM*) and exp() (*https://oreil.ly/AsgKw*).

5.9 Formatting Numbers as Strings

Problem

You want to print a number with thousands separators to make it more readable to end users of your application.

Solution

Use number_format() to automatically add thousands separators when converting a number to a string. For example:

```
$number = 25519;
print number_format($number);
// 25,519

$number = 64923.12
print number_format($number, 2);
// 64,923.12
```

Discussion

PHP's native number_format() function will automatically group thousands together as well as round decimal digits to the given precision. You can also optionally *change* the decimal and thousands separators to match a given locale or format.

For example, assume you want to use periods to separate thousands groups and a comma to separate decimal digits (as is common in Danish number formats). To accomplish this, you would leverage number_format() as follows:

```
$number = 525600.23;
```

---

3 For more on the acceptable differences between floating-point numbers, review Recipe 5.2.

```
print number_format($number, 2, ',', '.');
// 525.600,23
```

PHP's native `NumberFormatter` class provides similar utility but gives you the ability to explicitly define the locale rather than needing to remember a specific regional format.[4] You can rewrite the preceding example to use `NumberFormatter` specifically with the da_DK locale to identify a Danish format as follows:

```
$number = 525600.23;

$fmt = new NumberFormatter('da_DK', NumberFormatter::DEFAULT_STYLE);
print $fmt->format($number);
// 525.600,23
```

See Also

PHP documentation on `number_format()` (*https://oreil.ly/3_L6J*) and the `NumberFor matter` class (*https://oreil.ly/IC3a9*).

5.10 Handling Very Large or Very Small Numbers

Problem

You need to use numbers that are too large (or too small) to be handled by PHP's native integer and floating-point types.

Solution

Use the GMP library:

```
$sum = gmp_pow(4096, 100);
print gmp_strval($sum);
// 17218479456385750618067377696052635483579924745448689921733236816400
// 74069124174561939748453723604617328637091903196158778858492729081666
// 10249916098827287173446595034716559908808846798965200551239064670644
// 19056526231345685268240569209892573766037966584735183775739433978714
// 57858778270138079724077247764787455598671274627136289222751620531891
// 44359135111410362611376
```

Discussion

PHP supports two extensions for working with numbers either too large or too small to be represented with native types. The BCMath extension (*https://oreil.ly/XhhdH*) is an interface to a system-level *basic calculator* utility that supports arbitrary precision

---

4 The `NumberFormatter` class itself is part of PHP's intl (*https://oreil.ly/B-85H*) extension. This module is not built in by default and might need to be installed/enabled for the class to be available.

mathematics. Unlike native PHP types, BCMath supports working with up to 2,147,483,647 decimal digits so long as the system has adequate memory.

Unfortunately, BCMath encodes all numbers as regular strings in PHP, which makes using it somewhat difficult in modern applications that target strict type enforcement.[5]

The GMP extension is a valid alternative also available to PHP that does not have this drawback. Internal to itself, numbers are stored as strings. They are, however, wrapped as GMP objects when exposed to the rest of PHP. This distinction helps clarify whether a function is operating on a small number encoded as a string or a large one necessitating the use of an extension.

> BCMath and GMP act on and return integer values rather than floating points. If you need to conduct operations on floating-point numbers, you might need to increase the size of your numbers by an order of magnitude (i.e., multiply by 10) and then reduce them again once your calculations are complete in order to account for decimals or fractions.

GMP isn't included with PHP by default, although many distributions will make it available quite easily. If you're compiling PHP from source, doing so with the --with-gmp option will add support automatically. If you're using a package manager to install PHP (for example, on a Linux machine) you can likely install the php-gmp package to add this support directly.[6]

Once available, GMP will empower you to execute any mathematic operation you desire on numbers of limitless size. The caveat is that you can no longer use native PHP operators and must use a functional format defined by the extension itself. Example 5-9 presents some translations from native operators to GMP function calls. Note that the return type of each function call is a GMP object, so you must convert it back to either a number or a string by using gmp_intval() or gmp_strval(), respectively.

Example 5-9. Various mathematical operations and their GMP function equivalents

```
$add = 2 + 5;
$add = gmp_add(2, 5);

$sub = 23 - 2;
$sub = gmp_sub(23, 2);
```

---

5 Review Recipe 3.4 for more on strict typing in PHP.

6 Native extensions are covered in depth in Chapter 15.

```
$div = 15 / 4;
$div = gmp_div(15, 4);

$mul = 3 * 9;
$mul = gmp_mul(3, 9);

$pow = 4 ** 7;
$pow = gmp_pow(4, 7);

$mod = 93 % 4;
$mod = gmp_mod(93, 4);

$eq = 42 == (21 * 2);
$eq = gmp_cmp(42, gmp_mul(21, 2));
```

The final illustration in Example 5-9 introduces the `gmp_cmp()` function, which allows you to compare two GMP-wrapped values. This function will return a positive value if the first parameter is greater than the second, 0 if they are equal, and a negative value if the second parameter is greater than the first. It's effectively the same as PHP's spaceship operator (introduced in Recipe 2.4) rather than an equality comparison, which potentially provides more utility.

See Also

PHP documentation on GMP (*https://oreil.ly/rtfm3*).

5.11 Converting Numbers Between Numerical Bases

Problem

You want to convert a number from one base to another.

Solution

Use the `base_convert()` function as follows:

```
// Base 10 (decimal) number
$decimal = '240';

// Convert from base 10 to base 16
// $hex = 'f0'
$hex = base_convert($decimal, 10, 16);
```

Discussion

The `base_convert()` function attempts to convert a number from one base to another, which is particularly helpful when working with hexadecimal or binary strings of data. PHP will work only with bases between 2 and 36. Bases higher than 10 will use alphabet characters to represent additional digits—a is equal to 10, b to 11, all the way to z being equal to 35.

Note that the Solution example passes a *string* into base_convert() rather than an integer or a float value. This is because PHP will attempt to cast the input string to a number with an appropriate base before converting it to another base and returning a string. Strings are the best way to represent hexadecimal or octal numbers in PHP, but they're generic enough they can represent numbers of *any* base.

PHP supports several other base-specific conversion functions in addition to the more generic base_convert(). These additional functions are enumerated in Table 5-3.

 PHP supports two functions for converting back and forth between binary data and its hexadecimal representation: bin2hex() and hex2bin(). These functions are *not* intended for converting a string representation of binary (e.g., 11111001) into hexadecimal but will instead operate the binary *bytes* of that string.

Table 5-3. Specific base conversion functions

Function name	From base	To base
bindec()	Binary (encoded as a string)	Decimal (encoded as an int or, for size reasons, a float)
decbin()	Decimal (encoded as an int)	Binary (encoded as a string)
hexdec()	Hexadecimal (encoded as a string)	Decimal (encoded as an int or, for size reasons, a float)
dechex()	Decimal (encoded as an int)	Hexadecimal (encoded as a string)
octdec()	Octal (encoded as a string)	Decimal (encoded as an int or, for size reasons, a float)
decoct()	Decimal (encoded as an int)	Octal (encoded as a string)

Note that, unlike base_convert(), the specialized base conversion functions often work with numeric types directly. If you are using strict typing, this will avoid requiring an explicit cast from a numeric type to a string before changing bases, which *would* be required with base_convert().

See Also

PHP documentation on base_convert() (*https://oreil.ly/NVsk_*).

## CHAPTER 6

Dates and Times

Manipulating dates and times is one of the most complicated tasks you can do in any language, let alone in PHP. This is simply because time is relative—*now* will differ from one user to the next and potentially trigger different behavior in your application.

Object Orientation

PHP developers will work primarily with `DateTime` objects in code. These objects work by wrapping a particular instance in time and provide a wide variety of functionality. You can take the differences between two `DateTime` objects, convert between arbitrary time zones, or add/subtract windows of time from an otherwise static object.

Additionally, PHP supports a `DateTimeImmutable` object which is functionally identical to `DateTime` but cannot be modified directly. Most methods on a `DateTime` object will both return the same object and mutate its internal state. The same methods on `DateTimeImmutable` leave the internal state in place but return *new instances* representing the result of the change.

> Both date/time classes extend an abstract `DateTimeInterface` base class, making the two classes nearly interchangeable within PHP's date and time functionality. Everywhere you see `DateTime` in this chapter you could use a `DateTimeImmutable` instance instead and achieve similar if not identical functionality.

Time Zones

One of the most challenging problems any developer will face is working with time zones, particularly when daylight saving time is involved. On the one hand, it's easy to simplify and assume every timestamp within an application is referencing the same time zone. This is rarely true.

Luckily, PHP makes handling time zones remarkably easy. Every `DateTime` has a time zone embedded automatically, usually based on the default defined within the system on which PHP is running. You can also explicitly set a time zone whenever you create a `DateTime` making the region and time you're referencing entirely unambiguous. Converting between time zones is also simple and powerful and covered at length in Recipe 6.9.

Unix Timestamps

Many computer systems use Unix timestamps internally to represent dates and times. These timestamps represent the number of seconds that have occurred between the Unix Epoch (January 1, 1970 at 00:00:00 GMT) and a given time. They are memory-efficient and frequently used by databases and programmatic APIs. However, counting the number of seconds since a fixed date/time isn't exactly user-friendly, so you need a reliable way to convert between Unix timestamps and human-readable date/time representations within your applications.

PHP's native formatting capabilities make this straightforward. Additional functions, like `time()` (*https://oreil.ly/RBqxh*), produce Unix timestamps directly as well.

The following recipes cover these topics at length, in addition to several other common date/time-related tasks.

6.1 Finding the Current Date and Time

Problem

You want to know the current date and time.

Solution

To print the current date and time following a particular format, use `date()`. For example:

```
$now = date('r');
```

The output of `date()` depends on the system it's being run on and the current actual time. Using `r` as a format string, this function would return something like the following:

```
Wed, 09 Nov 2022 14:15:12 -0800
```

Similarly, a newly instantiated `DateTime` object will also represent the current date and time. The `::format()` method on this object exhibits the same behavior as `date()`, meaning the following two statements are functionally identical:

```
$now = date('r');
```

```
$now = (new DateTime())->format('r');
```

Discussion

PHP's `date()` function, as well as a `DateTime` object instantiated with no parameters, will automatically inherit the current date and time of the system on which they're run. The additional `r` passed into both is a format character that defines how to convert the given date/time information into a string—in this case, specifically as a date formatted according to RFC 2822 (*https://oreil.ly/WrB1I*). You can learn more about date formatting in Recipe 6.2.

A powerful alternative is to leverage PHP's `getdate()` function to retrieve an associative array of all of the parts of the current system date and time. This array will contain the keys and values in Table 6-1.

Table 6-1. Key elements returned by getdate()

Key	Description of value	Example
seconds	Seconds	0 to 59
minutes	Minutes	0 to 59
hours	Hours	0 to 23
mday	Day of the month	1 through 31
wday	Day of the week	0 (Sunday) through 6 (Saturday)
mon	Month	1 through 12
year	Full, four-digit year	2023
yday	Day of the year	0 through 365
weekday	Day of the week	Sunday through Saturday
month	Month of the year	January through December
0	Unix timestamp	0 to 2147483647

In some applications, you might only need the day of the week rather than a fully operational `DateTime` object. Consider Example 6-1, which illustrates how you might achieve this with either `DateTime` or `getdate()`.

Example 6-1. Comparing DateTime with getdate()

```
print (new DateTime())->format('l') . PHP_EOL;

print getdate()['weekday'] . PHP_EOL;
```

These two lines of code are functionally equivalent. For a simple task such as "print today's date," either would be adequate for the job. The DateTime object provides functionality for converting time zones or forecasting future dates (both of which are covered further in other recipes). The associative array returned by getdate() lacks this functionality but makes up for that shortcoming through its simple, easy-to-recognize array keys.

See Also

PHP documentation on date and time functions (*https://oreil.ly/rJ9fn*), the DateTime class (*https://oreil.ly/t28Zh*), and the getdate() function (*https://oreil.ly/Kv7l8*).

6.2 Formatting Dates and Times

Problem

You want to print a date to a string in a particular format.

Solution

Use the ::format() method on a given DateTime object to specify the format of the returned string, as shown in Example 6-2.

Example 6-2. Date and time format examples

```
$birthday = new DateTime('2017-08-01');

print $birthday->format('l, F j, Y') . PHP_EOL; ❶
print $birthday->format('n/j/y') . PHP_EOL; ❷
print $birthday->format(DateTime::RSS) . PHP_EOL; ❸
```

❶ Tuesday, August 1, 2017

❷ 8/1/17

❸ Tue, 01 Aug 2017 00:00:00 +0000

Discussion

Both the `date()` function and the `DateTime` object's `::format()` method accept a variety of input strings that ultimately define the final structure of the string produced by PHP. Each format string is composed of individual characters that represent specific parts of a date or time value, as you can see in Table 6-2.

Table 6-2. PHP format characters

Character	Description	Example values
Day		
d	Day of the month, two digits with leading 0	01 to 31
D	A textual representation of a day, three letters	Mon through Sun
j	Day of the month without leading 0	1 to 31
l	The name of the day of the week	Sunday through Saturday
N	ISO 8601 numeric representation of the day of the week	1 (for Monday) through 7 (for Sunday)
S	English ordinal suffix for the day of the month, two characters	st, nd, rd, or th. Works well with j
w	Numeric representation of the day of the week	0 (for Sunday) through 6 (for Saturday)
z	The day of the year (starting from 0)	0 through 365
Month		
F	The full name of the month	January through December
m	Numeric representation of a month, with leading 0	01 through 12
M	A textual representation of a month, three letters	Jan through Dec
n	Numeric representation of a month, without leading 0	1 through 12
t	Number of days in the given month	28 through 31
Year		
L	Whether it's a leap year	1 if it is a leap year, 0 otherwise.
o	ISO 8601 week-numbering year. This has the same value as Y, except that if the ISO week belongs to the previous or next year, that year is used instead	1999 or 2003
Y	A full numeric representation of a year, four digits	1999 or 2003
y	A two-digit representation of a year	99 or 03
Time		
a	Lowercase ante meridiem or post meridiem	am or pm
A	Uppercase ante meridiem or post meridiem	AM or PM
g	12-hour format of an hour without leading 0	1 through 12
G	24-hour format of an hour without leading 0	0 through 23
h	12-hour format of an hour with leading 0	01 through 12
H	24-hour format of an hour with leading 0	00 through 23

Character	Description	Example values
i	Minutes with leading 0	00 to 59
s	Seconds with leading 0	00 through 59
u	Microseconds	654321
v	Milliseconds	654
Time zone		
e	Time zone identifier	UTC, GMT, Atlantic/Azores
I	Whether the date is in daylight saving time	1 if daylight saving time, 0 otherwise.
O	Difference from Greenwich time (GMT) without colon between hours and minutes	+0200
P	Difference from Greenwich time (GMT) with colon between hours and minutes	+02:00
p	The same as P, but returns Z instead of +00:00	+02:00
T	Time zone abbreviation, if known; otherwise the GMT offset.	EST, MDT, +05
Z	Time zone offset in seconds	-43200 through 50400
Other		
U	Unix timestamp	0 through 2147483647

Combining these characters into a format string determines exactly how PHP will convert a given date/time construct into a string.

Similarly, PHP defines several predefined constants representing well-known and widely used formats. Table 6-3 shows some of the most useful.

Table 6-3. Predefined date constants

Constant	Class constant	Format characters	Example
DATE_ATOM	DateTime::ATOM	Y-m-d \TH:i:sP	2023-08-01T13:22:14-08:00
DATE_COOKIE	Date Time::COOKIE	l, d-M-Y H:i:s T	Tuesday, 01-Aug-2023 13:22:14 GMT-0800
DATE_ISO8601 `footnote: [Unfortunately, `DATE_ISO8601 isn't compatible with the ISO 8601 standard. If you need that level of compatibility, use DATE_ATOM instead.]	Date Time::ISO8601	Y-m-d \TH:i:sO	2013-08-01T21:21:14\+0000
DATE_RSS	DateTime::RSS	D, d M Y H:i:s O	Tue, 01 Aug 2023 13:22:14 -0800

See Also

Full documentation on format characters (*https://oreil.ly/oQpYP*) and predefined `DateTime` constants (*https://oreil.ly/XJiZy*).

6.3 Converting Dates and Times to Unix Timestamps

Problem

You want to convert a particular date or time to a Unix timestamp and convert a given Unix timestamp into a local date or time.

Solution

To convert a given date/time into a timestamp, use the U format character (see Table 6-2) with `DateTime::format()` as follows:

```
$date = '2023-11-09T13:15:00-0700';
$dateObj = new DateTime($date);

echo $dateObj->format('U');
// 1699560900
```

To convert a given timestamp into a `DateTime` object, also use the U format character but instead with `DateTime::createFromFormat()` as follows:

```
$timestamp = '1648241792';
$dateObj = DateTime::createFromFormat('U', $timestamp);

echo $dateObj->format(DateTime::ISO8601);
// 2022-03-25T20:56:32+0000
```

Discussion

The `::createFromFormat()` method is a static inverse of `DateTime`'s `::format()` method. Both functions use identical format strings to specify the format being used[1] but represent opposite transformations between a formatted string and the underlying state of a `DateTime` object. The Solution example explicitly leverages the U format character to tell PHP that the input data is a Unix timestamp.

If the input string doesn't actually match your format, PHP will return a literal `false` as in the following example:

```
$timestamp = '2023-07-23';
$dateObj = DateTime::createFromFormat('U', $timestamp);
```

---

1 Format strings and available format characters are covered in Recipe 6.2.

```
echo gettype($dateObj); // false
```

When parsing user input, it is a good idea to explicitly check the return of `::create FromFormat()` to ensure that the date input was valid. For more on validating dates, see Recipe 6.7.

Rather than work with a full `DateTime` object, you can work with *parts* of a date/time directly. PHP's `mktime()` function (*https://oreil.ly/YFKz0*) will always return a Unix timestamp, and the only required parameter is the hour.

For example, assume you want the Unix timestamp representing July 4, 2023 at noon in GMT (no time zone offset). You could do this in two ways, as demonstrated in Example 6-3.

Example 6-3. Creating a timestamp directly

```
$date = new DateTime('2023-07-04T12:00:00');
$timestamp = $date->format('U'); ❶

$timestamp = mktime(month: 7, day: 4, year: 2023, hour: 12); ❷
```

❶ This output will be exactly `1688472000`.

❷ This output will be *close* to `1688472000` but will vary in the last three digits.

While this simpler example appears elegant and avoids instantiating an object only to turn it back into a number, it has an important problem. Failing to specify a parameter (in this case, minutes or seconds) will cause `mktime()` to use the current system values for those parameters by default. If you were to run this example code at 3:05 in the afternoon, the output might be `1688472300`.

This Unix timestamp translates to 12:05:00 rather than 12:00:00 when converted back to a `DateTime`, representing a (potentially negligible) difference from what the application expects.

It's important to remember that, if you choose to leverage the functional interface of `mktime()`, you either provide a value for *every* component of the date/time or you build your application in such a way that slight deviations are expected and handled.

See Also

Documentation on `DateTime::createFromFormat()` (*https://oreil.ly/otv8q*).

6.4 Converting from Unix Timestamps to Date and Time Parts

Problem

You want to extract a particular date or time part (day or hour) from a Unix timestamp.

Solution

Pass the Unix timestamp as a parameter to `getdate()` and reference the required keys in the resulting associative array. For example:

```
$date = 1688472300;
$time_parts = getdate($date);

print $time_parts['weekday'] . PHP_EOL; // Tuesday
print $time_parts['hours'] . PHP_EOL;   // 12
```

Discussion

The only parameter you can provide to `getdate()` is a Unix timestamp. If this parameter is omitted, PHP will leverage the current system date and time. When you provide a timestamp, PHP parses that timestamp internally and allows for the extraction of all expected date and time elements.

Alternatively, you can pass a timestamp into the constructor for a `DateTime` instance in two ways to build a full object from it:

1. Prefixing the timestamp with an @ character tells PHP to interpret the entry as a Unix timestamp—for example, `new DateTime('@1688472300')`.

2. You can use the U format character when importing a timestamp into a `DateTime` object—for example, `DateTime::createFromFormat('U', '1688472300')`.

In any case, once your timestamp is properly parsed and loaded into a `DateTime` object, you can use its `::format()` method to extract any component you desire. Example 6-4 is an alternative implementation of the Solution example that leverages `DateTime` rather than `getdate()`.

Example 6-4. Extracting date and time parts from Unix timestamps

```
$date = '1688472300';

$parsed = new DateTime("@{$date}");
print $parsed->format('l') . PHP_EOL;
```

```
print $parsed->format('g') . PHP_EOL;

$parsed2 = DateTime::createFromFormat('U', $date);
print $parsed2->format('l') . PHP_EOL;
print $parsed2->format('g') . PHP_EOL;
```

Either of the approaches in Example 6-4 is a valid replacement of `getdate()` that also provides the benefit of giving you a fully functional `DateTime` instance. You could print the date (or time) in any format, manipulate the underlying value directly, or even convert between time zones if necessary. Each of these potential further uses for `DateTime` is covered in further recipes.

See Also

Recipe 6.1 for further discussion of `getdate()`. Read ahead in Recipe 6.8 to learn how to manipulate `DateTime` objects and in Recipe 6.9 to see how time zones can be managed directly.

6.5 Computing the Difference Between Two Dates

Problem

You want to find out how much time has passed between two dates or times.

Solution

Encapsulate each date/time in a `DateTime` object. Leverage the `::diff()` method on one to calculate the relative difference between it and the other `DateTime`. The result will be a `DateInterval` object as follows:

```
$firstDate = new DateTime('2002-06-14');
$secondDate = new DateTime('2022-11-09');

$interval = $secondDate->diff($firstDate);

print $interval->format('%y years %d days %m months');
// 20 years 25 days 4 months
```

Discussion

The `::diff()` method of the `DateTime` object effectively subtracts one date/time (the argument passed into the method) from another (the one represented by the object itself). The result is a representation of the relative duration of time between the two objects.

The ::diff() method ignores daylight saving time. To properly account for the potential one-hour difference intrinsic to that system, converting both date/time objects into UTC first is a good idea.

It is also important to note that, while it might appear similar in the Solution example, the ::format() method of the DateInterval object takes a whole different set of format characters than those used by DateTime. Every format character must be prefixed by a literal % character, but the format string itself can include nonformatting characters (like *years* and *months* in the Solution example).

Available format characters are enumerated in Table 6-4. In every case except for the format characters of a and r, using the lowercase for a format character will return a numeric value without any leading 0. The enumerated uppercase format characters return at least two digits with a leading 0. Remember, every format character must be prefixed with a literal %.

Table 6-4. DateInterval format characters

Character	Description	Example
%	Literal %	%
Y	Years	03
M	Months	02
D	Days	09
H	Hours	08
I	Minutes	01
S	Seconds	04
F	Microseconds	007705
R	Sign "-" when negative, "+" when positive	- or +
r	Sign "-" when negative, empty when positive	-
a	Total number of days	548

See Also

Full documentation on the DateInterval class (*https://oreil.ly/r0FBV*).

6.6 Parsing Dates and Times from Arbitrary Strings

Problem

You need to convert an arbitrary, user-defined string into a valid DateTime object for further use or manipulation.

Solution

Use PHP's powerful `strtotime()` function to convert the text entry into a Unix timestamp, and then pass that into the constructor of a new `DateTime` object. For example:

```
$entry = strtotime('last Wednesday');
$parsed = new DateTime("@{$entry}");

$entry = strtotime('now + 2 days');
$parsed = new DateTime("@{$entry}");

$entry = strtotime('June 23, 2023');
$parsed = new DateTime("@{$entry}");
```

Discussion

The power of `strtotime()` comes from the underlying date and time import formats (*https://oreil.ly/2f4o_*) supported by the language. These include the kinds of formats you might expect computers to use (like YYYY-MM-DD for a year, month, and day). But it extends to *relative* specifiers and complex, compound formats as well.

> The convention of prefixing a Unix timestamp with a literal @ character when passing it into a `DateTime` constructor itself comes from the compound date/time formats supported by PHP.

The relative formats are the most powerful, supporting human-readable strings like these:

- `yesterday`
- `first day of`
- `now`
- `ago`

Armed with these formats, you can parse almost any string imaginable with PHP. However, there are some limits. In the Solution example, I used `now + 2 days` to specify "2 days from now." Example 6-5 demonstrates that the latter results in a parser error in PHP, even though it reads well in English.

Example 6-5. Limitations in `strtotime()` parsing

```
$date = strtotime('2 days from now');

if ($date === false) {
```

```
    throw new InvalidArgumentException('Error parsing the string!');
}
```

It should always be noted that, no matter how clever you can make a computer, you are always limited by the quality of input provided by end users. There is no way you can foresee every possible way of specifying a date or time; strtotime() gets close, but you'll need to handle input errors as well.

Another potential way to parse user-provided dates is PHP's date_parse() function. Unlike strtotime(), this function expects a reasonably well-formatted input string. It also doesn't handle relative time quite the same way. Example 6-6 illustrates several strings that can be parsed by date_parse().

Example 6-6. date_parse() examples

```
$first = date_parse('January 4, 2022'); ❶

$second = date_parse('Feb 14'); ❷

$third = date_parse('2022-11-12 5:00PM'); ❸

$fourth = date_parse('1-1-2001 + 12 years'); ❹
```

❶ Parses January 4, 2022

❷ Parses February 14, but with a null year

❸ Parses both the date and the time, but with no time zone

❹ Parses the date and stores an additional relative field

Rather than return a timestamp, date_parse() will extract the relevant date/time parts from the input string and store them in an associative array with keys for the following:

- year
- month
- day
- hour
- minute
- second
- fraction

In addition, passing a time-relative specification in the string (like the + 12 years in Example 6-6) will add a relative key to the array with information about the relative offset.

All of this is useful in determining whether a user-provided date is useful as an actual date. The date_parse() function will also return warnings and errors if it encounters any parsing issues, making it even easier to check whether a date is valid. For more on checking date validity, read Recipe 6.7.

Revisiting Example 6-5 and leveraging date_parse() shows a little more about why PHP has trouble parsing 2 days from now as a relative date. Consider the following example:

```php
$date = date_parse('2 days from now');

if ($date['error_count'] > 0) {
    foreach ($date['errors'] as $error) {
        print $error . PHP_EOL;
    }
}
```

The preceding code will print The time zone could not be found in the data base, which suggests PHP is *trying* to parse the date but is failing to identify what from really means in the statement from now. In fact, inspecting the $date array itself will show it returns a relative key. This relative offset properly represents the specified two days, meaning date_parse() (and even strtotime()) was able to read the relative date offset (2 days) but choked on the last part.

This additional error provides further context for debugging and could, perhaps, inform some kind of error message that the application should provide to the end user. In any case, it's more helpful than the mere false return of strtotime() on its own.

See Also

Documentation on date_parse() (*https://oreil.ly/2CECz*) and strtotime() (*https://oreil.ly/S7qkH*).

6.7 Validating a Date

Problem

You want to ensure that a date is valid. For example, you want to ensure that a user-defined birthdate is a real date on the calendar and not something like November 31, 2022.

Solution

Use PHP's checkdate() function as follows:

```
$entry = 'November 31, 2022';
$parsed = date_parse($entry);

if (!checkdate($parsed['month'], $parsed['day'], $parsed['year'])) {
    throw new InvalidArgumentException('Specified date is invalid!');
}
```

Discussion

The date_parse() function was already covered in Recipe 6.6, but using it with checkdate() is new. This second function attempts to validate that the date is valid according to the calendar.

It checks that the month (first parameter) is between 1 and 12, that the year (third parameter) is between 1 and 32,767 (the maximum value of a 2-byte integer in PHP), and that the number of days is valid for that given month and year.

The checkdate() function properly handles months with 28, 30, or 31 days. Example 6-7 shows it also accounts for leap year, validating that February 29 exists in the appropriate years.

Example 6-7. Validating leap year

```
$valid = checkdate(2, 29, 2024); // true

$invalid = checkdate(2, 29, 2023); // false
```

See Also

PHP documentation on checkdate() (*https://oreil.ly/T2io8*).

6.8 Adding to or Subtracting from a Date

Problem

You want to apply a specific offset (either additive or subtractive) against a fixed date. For example, you want to calculate a future date by adding days to today's date.

Solution

Use the ::add() or ::sub() methods of a given DateTime object to add or subtract a DateInterval, respectively, as shown in Example 6-8.

Example 6-8. Simple `DateTime` addition

```
$date = new DateTime('December 25, 2023');

// When do the 12 days of Christmas end?
$twelve_days = new DateInterval('P12D');
$date->add($twelve_days);

print 'The holidays end on ' . $date->format('F j, Y');

// The holidays end on January 6, 2024
```

Discussion

Both the ::add() and ::sub() methods on a DateTime object modify the object itself by either adding or subtracting the given interval. Intervals are specified using a period designation that identifies the amount of time that interval represents. Table 6-5 illustrates the format characters used to denote an interval.

Table 6-5. Period designations used by `DateInterval`

Character	Description
Period designators	
Y	Years
M	Months
D	Days
W	Weeks
Time designators	
H	Hours
M	Minutes
S	Seconds

Every formatted date interval period starts with the letter P. This is followed by the number of years/months/days/weeks in that period. Any time elements in a duration are prefixed with the letter T.

The period designations for months and minutes are both the letter M. This can lead to confusion when trying to identify 15 *minutes* versus 15 *months* in a time designation. If you intend to use minutes, ensure that your duration has properly used the T prefix to avoid a frustrating error in your application.

For example, a period of 3 weeks and 2 days would be represented as P3W2D. A period of 4 months, 2 hours, and 10 seconds would be represented as P4MT2H10S. Similarly, a period of 1 month, 2 hours, and 30 minutes would be represented as P1MT2H30M.

Mutability

Note that, in Example 6-8, the original DateTime object is itself modified when you call ::add(). In a simple example, this is fine. If you're attempting to calculate *multiple* dates offset from the same starting date, the mutability of the DateTime object causes problems.

Instead, you can leverage the nearly identical DateTimeImmutable object. This class implements the same interface as DateTime, but the ::add() and ::sub() methods will instead return *new instances* of the class rather than mutating the internal state of the object itself.

Consider the comparison between both object types in Example 6-9.

Example 6-9. Comparing DateTime and DateTimeImmutable

```
$date = new DateTime('December 25, 2023');
$christmas = new DateTimeImmutable('December 25, 2023');

// When do the 12 days of Christmas end?
$twelve_days = new DateInterval('P12D');
$date->add($twelve_days); ❶
$end = $christmas->add($twelve_days); ❷

print 'The holidays end on ' . $date->format('F j, Y') . PHP_EOL;
print 'The holidays end on ' . $end->format('F j, Y') . PHP_EOL;

// When is next Christmas?
$next_year = new DateInterval('P1Y');
$date->add($next_year);
$next_christmas = $christmas->add($next_year);

print 'Next Christmas is on ' . $date->format('F j, Y') . PHP_EOL;
print 'Next Christmas is on ' . $next_christmas->format('F j, Y') . PHP_EOL; ❸

print 'This Christmas is on ' . $christmas->format('F j, Y') . PHP_EOL; ❹
```

❶ Since $date is a mutable object, invoking its ::add() method will modify the object directly.

❷ As $christmas is immutable, invoking ::add() will return a new object that must be stored in a variable.

❸ Printing data from the resulting object from adding time to a `DateTime Immutable` will present the correct data, as the *new* object was created with the right date and time.

❹ Even after invoking `:add()`, a `DateTimeImmutable` object will always contain the same data as it is, in fact, immutable.

The advantage of immutable objects is that you can treat them as constant and rest assured that no one is going to rewrite the calendar when you're not looking. The only disadvantage is with memory utilization. Since `DateTime` modifies a single object, memory doesn't necessarily increase as you keep making changes. Every time you "modify" a `DateTimeImmutable` object, however, PHP creates a new object and consumes additional memory.

In a typical web application, the memory overhead here will be negligible. There is no reason *not* to use a `DateTimeImmutable` object.

Simpler modification

In a similar track, both `DateTime` and `DateTimeImmutable` implement a `::modify()` method that works with human-readable strings rather than interval objects. This allows you to find relative dates like "last Friday" or "next week" from a given object.

A good example is Thanksgiving which, in the US, falls on the fourth Thursday in November. You can easily calculate the exact date in a given year with the function defined in Example 6-10.

Example 6-10. Finding Thanksgiving with `DateTime`

```
function findThanksgiving(int $year): DateTime
{
    $november = new DateTime("November 1, {$year}");
    $november->modify('fourth Thursday');

    return $november;
}
```

The same functionality can be implemented using immutable date objects, as shown in Example 6-11.

Example 6-11. Finding Thanksgiving with `DateTimeImmutable`

```
function findThanksgiving(int $year): DateTimeImmutable
{
    $november = new DateTimeImmutable("November 1, {$year}");
```

```
    return $november->modify('fourth Thursday');
}
```

See Also

Documentation on `DateInterval` (*https://oreil.ly/KvluE*).

6.9 Calculating Times Across Time Zones

Problem

You want to determine a specific time across more than one time zone.

Solution

Use the `::setTimezone()` method of the `DateTime` class to change a time zone as follows:

```
$now = new DateTime();
$now->setTimezone(new DateTimeZone('America/Los_Angeles'));

print $now->format(DATE_RSS) . PHP_EOL;

$now->setTimezone(new DateTimeZone('Europe/Paris'));

print $now->format(DATE_RSS) . PHP_EOL;
```

Discussion

Time zones are among the most frustrating things application developers need to worry about. Thankfully, PHP allows for converting from one time zone to another relatively easily. The `::setTimezone()` method used in the Solution example illustrates how an arbitrary `DateTime` can be converted from one time zone to another merely by specifying the desired time zone.

> Keep in mind that both `DateTime` and `DateTimeImmutable` implement a `::setTimezone()` method. The difference between their implementations is that `DateTime` will modify the state of the underlying object, while `DateTimeImmutable` will always return a *new* object instead.

It is important to know which time zones are available for use in code. The list is too long to enumerate, but developers can leverage `DateTimeZone::listIdentifiers()` to list all available named time zones. If your application only cares about a specific region, you can further pare down the list by using one of the predefined group constants that ship with the class.

For example, `DateTimeZone::listIdentifiers(DateTimeZone::AMERICA)` returns an array that lists all time zones available across the Americas. On a particular test system, this array has a list of 145 time zones, each pointing to a major local city to help identify the time zone they represent. You can generate a list of possible time zone identifiers for each of the following regional constants:

- `DateTimeZone::AFRICA`
- `DateTimeZone::AMERICA`
- `DateTimeZone::ANTARCTICA`
- `DateTimeZone::ARCTIC`
- `DateTimeZone::ASIA`
- `DateTimeZone::ATLANTIC`
- `DateTimeZone::AUSTRALIA`
- `DateTimeZone::EUROPE`
- `DateTimeZone::INDIAN`
- `DateTimeZone::PACIFIC`
- `DateTimeZone::UTC`
- `DateTimeZone::ALL`

Similarly, you can use bitwise operators to construct unions from these constants to retrieve lists of all time zones across two or more regions. For example, `DateTimeZone::ANTARCTICA | DateTimeZone::ARCTIC` would represent all time zones near either the South or North Pole.

The base `DateTime` class empowers you to instantiate an object with a specific time zone as opposed to accepting the system defaults. Merely pass a `DateTimeZone` instance as an optional second parameter to the constructor, and the new object will be set to the correct time zone automatically.

For example, the datetime `2022-12-15T17:35:53`, formatted according to ISO 8601 (*https://oreil.ly/rip_R*), represents 5:35 p.m. on December 15, 2022, but does not reflect a specific time zone. When instantiating a `DateTime` object, you can easily specify this is a time in Tokyo, Japan, as follows:

```
$date = new DateTime('2022-12-15T17:35:53', new DateTimeZone('Asia/Tokyo'));

echo $date->format(DateTime::ATOM);
// 2022-12-15T17:35:53+09:00
```

If time zone information is missing in the datetime string being parsed, providing that time zone makes things explicit. Had you *not* added a time zone identifier in the preceding example, PHP would have assumed the system's configured time zone instead.[2]

If time zone information *is* present in the datetime string, PHP will ignore any explicit time zone specified in the second parameter and parse the string as provided.

See Also

Documentation on the `::setTimezone()` method (*https://oreil.ly/dk2gQ*) and the `DateTimeZone` class (*https://oreil.ly/MkdHB*).

---

2 You can check the current time zone setting for your system with `date_default_timezone_get()`.

## CHAPTER 7

Arrays

Arrays are ordered maps—constructs that associate specific values to easily identified keys. These maps are effective ways to build both simple lists and more complex collections of objects. They're also easy to manipulate—adding or removing items from an array is straightforward and supported through multiple functional interfaces.

Types of Arrays

There are two forms of arrays in PHP—numeric and associative. When you define an array without explicitly setting keys, PHP will internally assign an integer index to each member of the array. Arrays are indexed starting with 0 and increase by steps of 1 automatically.

Associative arrays can have keys of either strings or integers, but generally use strings. String keys are effective ways to "look up" a particular value stored in an array.

Arrays are implemented internally as hash tables, allowing for effective direct associations between keys and values. For example:

```
$colors = [];
$colors['apple']  = 'red';
$colors['pear']   = 'green';
$colors['banana'] = 'yellow';

$numbers = [22, 15, 42, 105];

echo $colors['pear']; // green
echo $numbers[2]; // 42
```

Unlike simpler hash tables, though, PHP arrays also implement an iterable interface allowing you to loop through all of their elements one at a time. Iteration is fairly obvious when keys are numeric, but even with associative arrays, the elements have a fixed order because they're stored in memory. Recipe 7.3 details different ways to act on each element in both types of arrays.

In many circumstances, you might also be met with objects or classes that look and feel like an array but are not actually arrays. In fact, any object that implements the ArrayAccess interface (*https://oreil.ly/kdN4_*) can be used as an array.[1] These more advanced implementations push the limits of what is possible with arrays beyond mere lists and hash tables.

Syntax

PHP supports two different syntaxes for defining arrays. Those who have worked in PHP for some time will recognize the array() (*https://oreil.ly/v75i9*) construct that allows for the literal definition of an array at runtime as follows:

```php
$movies = array('Fahrenheit 451', 'Without Remorse', 'Black Panther');
```

An alternative and terser syntax is to use square brackets to define the array. The preceding example could be rewritten as follows with the same behavior:

```php
$movies = ['Fahrenheit 451', 'Without Remorse', 'Black Panther'];
```

Both formats can be used to create nested arrays (where an array contains another array) and can be used interchangeably as follows:

```php
$array = array(1, 2, array(3, 4), [5, 6]);
```

Though mixing and matching syntaxes as in the preceding example is possible, it is highly encouraged to remain consistent within your application and to use one form or the other—not both. All of the examples in this chapter will use the short array syntax (square brackets).

All arrays in PHP map from keys to values. In the preceding examples, the arrays merely specified values and let PHP assign keys automatically. These are considered *numeric* arrays as the keys will be integers, starting at 0. More complex arrays, like the nested construct illustrated in Example 7-1, assign both values and keys. This is done by mapping from a key to a value with a two-character arrow operator (=>).

Example 7-1. Associative array with nested values

```php
$array = array(
    'a' => 'A',
    'b' => ['b', 'B'],
    'c' => array('c', ['c', 'K'])
);
```

---

1 Class inheritance is discussed in Chapter 8, and object interfaces are explicitly covered in Recipe 8.7.

While not a syntactic requirement, many coding environments and integrated development environments (IDEs) will automatically align the arrow operators in multiline array literals. This makes the code easier to read and is a standard adopted by this book as well.

The recipes that follow illustrate various ways developers can work with arrays—both numeric and associative—to accomplish common tasks in PHP.

7.1 Associating Multiple Elements per Key in an Array

Problem

You want to associate multiple items with a single array key.

Solution

Make each array value an array on its own—for example:

```
$cars = [
    'fast'     => ['ferrari', 'lamborghini'],
    'slow'     => ['honda', 'toyota'],
    'electric' => ['rivian', 'tesla'],
    'big'      => ['hummer']
];
```

Discussion

PHP places no requirement on the type of data used for a value in an array. However, keys are required to be either strings or integers. In addition, it is a hard requirement that every key in an array be unique. If you attempt to set multiple values for the same key, you will overwrite existing data, as shown in Example 7-2.

Example 7-2. Overwriting array data by assignment

```
$basket = [];

$basket['color']    = 'brown';
$basket['size']     = 'large';
$basket['contents'] = 'apple';
$basket['contents'] = 'orange';
$basket['contents'] = 'pineapple';

print_r($basket);

// Array
// (
//     [color] => brown
//     [size] => large
```

```
//    [contents] => pineapple
// )
```

As PHP only allows one value per unique key in an array, writing further data to that key overwrites its value in the same way that you might reassign the value of a variable in your application. If you do need to store multiple values in one key, use a nested array.

The Solution example illustrates how *every* key could point to its own array. However, PHP does not require this to be true—all but one key could point to a scalar and just the key that needs multiple items could point to an array. In Example 7-3, you'll use a nested array to store multiple items rather than accidentally overwriting a single value stored in a specific key.

Example 7-3. Writing an array to a key

```
$basket = [];

$basket['color']    = 'brown';
$basket['size']     = 'large';
$basket['contents'] = [];
$basket['contents'][] = 'apple';
$basket['contents'][] = 'orange';
$basket['contents'][] = 'pineapple';

print_r($basket);

// Array
// (
//    [color] => brown
//    [size] => large
//    [contents] => Array
//        (
//            [0] => apple
//            [1] => orange
//            [2] => pineapple
//        )
// )

echo $basket['contents'][2]; // pineapple
```

To leverage the elements of a nested array, you loop over them just as you would the parent array. For example, if you wanted to print all of the data stored in the $basket array from Example 7-3, you would need two loops, as in Example 7-4.

Example 7-4. Accessing array data in a loop

```
foreach ($basket as $key => $value) { ❶
    if (is_array($value)) { ❷
```

```
        echo "{$key} => [" . PHP_EOL;

        foreach ($value as $item) { ❸
            echo "\t{$item}" . PHP_EOL;
        }

        echo ']' . PHP_EOL;
    } else {
        echo "{$key}: $value" . PHP_EOL;
    }
}

// color: brown
// size: large
// contents => [
//     apple
//     orange
//     pineapple
// ]
```

❶ The parent array is associative, and you need both its keys and values.

❷ You use one branch of logic for nested arrays, another for scalars.

❸ Since you know the nested array is numeric, ignore the keys and iterate over only the values.

See Also

Recipe 7.3 for further examples of iterating through arrays.

7.2 Initializing an Array with a Range of Numbers

Problem

You want to build an array of consecutive integers.

Solution

Use the range() function as follows:

```
$array = range(1, 10);
print_r($array);

// Array
// (
//     [0] => 1
//     [1] => 2
//     [2] => 3
```

```
//      [3] => 4
//      [4] => 5
//      [5] => 6
//      [6] => 7
//      [7] => 8
//      [8] => 9
//      [9] => 10
// )
```

Discussion

PHP's range() function automatically iterates over a given sequence, assigning a value to a key based on the definition of that sequence. By default, and as illustrated in the Solution example, the function steps through sequences one at a time. But this isn't the limit of the function's behavior—passing a third parameter to the function will change its step size.

You could iterate over all even integers from 2 to 100 as follows:

```
$array = range(2, 100, 2);
```

Likewise, you could iterate over all *odd* integers from 1 to 100 by changing the starting point of the sequence to 1. For example:

```
$array = range(1, 100, 2);
```

The start and end parameters of range() (the first two parameters, respectively) can be integers, floating-point numbers, or even strings. This flexibility allows you to do some pretty amazing things in code. For example, rather than counting natural numbers (integers), you could produce an array of floating-point numbers as follows:

```
$array = range(1, 5, 0.25);
```

When passing string characters to range(), PHP will begin enumerating ASCII characters. You can leverage this functionality to quickly build an array representative of the English alphabet, as shown in Example 7-5.

 PHP will internally use any and all printable ASCII characters, based on their decimal representation, to complete a request to range(). This is an efficient way to enumerate printable characters, but you need to keep in mind where special characters such as =, ?, and) fall within the ASCII table, particularly if your program is expecting alphanumeric values in the array.

Example 7-5. Creating an array of alphabetical characters

```
$uppers = range('A', 'Z'); ❶

$lowers = range('a', 'z'); ❷
```

```
$special = range('!', ')'); ❸
```

❶ Returns all uppercase characters from A through Z

❷ Returns all lowercase characters from a through z

❸ Returns an array of special characters: [!, ", #, $, %, &, ', (,)]

See Also

PHP documentation on `range()` (*https://oreil.ly/qH_iW*).

7.3 Iterating Through Items in an Array

Problem

You want to perform an action on every element in an array.

Solution

For numeric arrays, use `foreach` as follows:

```
foreach ($array as $value) {
    // Act on each $value
}
```

For associative arrays, use `foreach()` with optional keys as follows:

```
foreach ($array as $key => $value) {
    // Act on each $value and/or $key
}
```

Discussion

PHP has the concept of *iterable objects* and, internally, that's precisely what an array is. Other data structures can also implement iterable behavior,[2] but *any* iterable expression can be provided to `foreach` and will return the items it contains one at a time in a loop.

---

2 See Recipe 7.15 for examples of very large iterable data structures.

PHP does not implicitly unset the variable used within a `foreach` loop when you exit the loop. You can still explicitly reference the *last* value stored in `$value` in the Solution examples in the program outside the loop!

The most important thing to remember, though, is that `foreach` is a *language construct*, not a function. As a construct, it acts on a given expression and applies the defined loop over every item within that expression. By default, that loop does not modify the contents of an array. If you want to make the values of an array mutable, you must pass them into the loop by reference by prefixing the variable name with an & character as follows:

```
$array = [1, 2, 3];

foreach ($array as &$value) {
    $value += 1;
}

print_r($array); // 2, 3, 4
```

 Versions of PHP prior to 8.0 supported an `each()` function that would maintain an array cursor and return the current key/value pair of the array before advancing that cursor. This function was deprecated in PHP 7.2 and fully removed as of the 8.0 release, but you will likely find legacy examples of its use in books and online. Upgrade any occurrences of `each()` to an implementation of `foreach` to ensure forward compatibility of your code.

An alternative approach to using a `foreach` loop is to create an explicit `for` loop over the keys of the array. Numeric arrays are easiest as their keys are already incrementing integers starting at 0. Iterating over a numeric array is relatively straightforward as follows:

```
$array = ['red', 'green', 'blue'];

$arrayLength = count($array);
for ($i = 0; $i < $array_length; $i++) {
    echo $array[$i] . PHP_EOL;
}
```

While it's possible to place a call to count() to identify the upper bounds of a for loop directly within the expression, it's better to store the length of an array outside the expression itself. Otherwise, your count() will be reinvoked on every iteration of the loop to check that you're still in bounds. For small arrays, this won't matter; as you start working with larger collections, though, the performance drain of repeated count() checks will become problematic.

Iterating over an associative array with a for loop is a tiny bit different. Instead of iterating over the elements of the array directly, you'll want to iterate over the keys of the array directly. Then use each key to extract the corresponding value from the array as follows:

```php
$array = [
    'os'   => 'linux',
    'mfr'  => 'system76',
    'name' => 'thelio',
];

$keys = array_keys($array);
$arrayLength = count($keys);
for ($i = 0; $i < $arrayLength; $i++) {
    $key = $keys[$i];
    $value = $array[$key];

    echo "{$key} => {$value}" . PHP_EOL;
}
```

See Also

PHP documentation on the foreach (*https://oreil.ly/lmeAe*) and for (*https://oreil.ly/chSRT*) language constructs.

7.4 Deleting Elements from Associative and Numeric Arrays

Problem

You want to remove one or more elements from an array.

Solution

Delete an element by targeting its key or numeric index directly with unset():

```php
unset($array['key']);
```

```php
unset($array[3]);
```

Delete more than one element at a time by passing multiple keys or indexes into unset() as follows:

```
unset($array['first'], $array['second']);

unset($array[3], $array[4], $array[5]);
```

Discussion

In PHP, unset() actually destroys any reference to the memory containing the specified variable. In the context of this Solution, that variable is an element of an array, so unsetting it removes that element from the array itself. In an associative array, this takes the form of deleting the specified key and the value it represented.

In a numeric array, unset() does far more. It both removes the specified element and effectively converts the numeric array into an associative array with integer keys. On the one hand, this is likely the behavior you wanted in the first place, as demonstrated in Example 7-6.

Example 7-6. Unsetting elements in a numeric array

```
$array = range('a', 'z');

echo count($array) . PHP_EOL;  ❶
echo $array[12] . PHP_EOL;  ❷
echo $array[25] . PHP_EOL;  ❸

unset($array[22]);
echo count($array) . PHP_EOL;  ❹
echo $array[12] . PHP_EOL;  ❺
echo $array[25] . PHP_EOL;  ❻
```

❶ The array by default represents all English characters from a through z, so this line prints 26.

❷ The 13th letter in the alphabet is m. (Remember that arrays start at index 0.)

❸ The 26th letter in the alphabet is z.

❹ With the element removed, the array has decreased in size to 25!

❺ The 13th letter in the alphabet is *still* m.

❻ The 26th letter in the alphabet is *still* z. Further, this index is still valid, as removing an element doesn't re-index the array.

You can typically ignore the indexes of numeric arrays because they're set by PHP automatically. This makes the behavior of unset() implicitly converting these indexes into numeric keys somewhat surprising. With a numeric array, attempting to access an index greater than the length of the array results in an error. Once you've used unset() with the array and decreased its size, however, you will often end up with an array that has numeric keys greater than the size of the array, as was illustrated in Example 7-6.

If you want to return to the world of numeric arrays after removing an element, you can re-index the array entirely. PHP's array_values() function returns a new, numerically indexed array that contains only the values of the specified array. For example:

```
$array = ['first', 'second', 'third', 'fourth']; ❶

unset($array[2]); ❷

$array = array_values($array); ❸
```

❶ The default array has numeric indexes: [0 => first, 1 => second, 2 => third, 3 => fourth].

❷ Unsetting an element removes it from the array but leaves the indexes (keys) unchanged: [0 => first, 1 => second, 3 => fourth].

❸ The call to array_values() gives you a *new* array with brand-new, properly incrementing numeric indexes: [0 => first, 1 => second, 2 => fourth].

An additional option for removing elements from an array is to use the array_splice() function.[3] This function will remove a portion of an array and replace it with something else.[4] Consider Example 7-7, where array_splice() is used to replace elements of an array with *nothing*, thus removing them.

Example 7-7. Removing elements of an array with array_splice()

```
$celestials = [
    'sun',
    'mercury',
    'venus',
    'earth',
```

---

3 Take care not to confuse array_splice() with array_slice(). The two functions have vastly different uses, and the latter is covered in Recipe 7.7.

4 The array_splice() function will also *return* the elements it extracted from the target array, in the event you need to use that data for some other operation. See Recipe 7.7 for further discussion of this behavior.

```
        'mars',
        'asteroid belt',
        'jupiter',
        'saturn',
        'uranus',
        'neptune',
        'pluto',
        'voyagers 1 & 2',
];

array_splice($celestials, 0, 1); ❶
array_splice($celestials, 4, 1); ❷
array_splice($celestials, 8); ❸

print_r($celestials);

// Array
// (
//     [0] => mercury
//     [1] => venus
//     [2] => earth
//     [3] => mars
//     [4] => jupiter
//     [5] => saturn
//     [6] => uranus
//     [7] => neptune
// )
```

❶ First, remove the sun to clean up a list of planets in the solar system.

❷ Once the sun is removed, the indexes of all objects shift. You still want to remove the asteroid belt from the list, so use its newly shifted index.

❸ Finally, truncate the array by removing everything from Pluto to the end of the array.

Unlike unset(), the modified array created by array_splice() does *not* retain the numeric indexes/keys in numeric arrays! This might be a good way to avoid needing an extra call to array_values() after removing an item from an array. It's also an effective way to remove *continuous* elements from a numerically indexed array without needing to explicitly specify each element.

See Also

Documentation on unset() (*https://oreil.ly/-ebRG*), array_splice() (*https://oreil.ly/g-M9G*), and array_values() (*https://oreil.ly/9FvTV*).

7.5 Changing the Size of an Array

Problem

You want to increase or decrease the size of an array.

Solution

Add elements to the end of the array by using `array_push()`:

```
$array = ['apple', 'banana', 'coconut'];
array_push($array, 'grape');

print_r($array);

// Array
// (
//     [0] => apple
//     [1] => banana
//     [2] => coconut
//     [3] => grape
// )
```

Remove elements from an array by using `array_splice()`:

```
$array = ['apple', 'banana', 'coconut', 'grape'];
array_splice($array, 1, 2);

print_r($array);

// Array
// (
//     [0] => apple
//     [1] => grape
// )
```

Discussion

Unlike many other languages, PHP doesn't require you to declare the size of an array. Arrays are dynamic—you can add or remove data from them whenever you want with no real downside.

The first Solution example merely adds a single element to the end of an array. While this approach is straightforward, it's not the most efficient. Instead, you can push an individual item into an array *directly* as follows:

```
$array = ['apple', 'banana', 'coconut'];
$array[] = 'grape';

print_r($array);
```

```
// Array
// (
//     [0] => apple
//     [1] => banana
//     [2] => coconut
//     [3] => grape
// )
```

The key difference between the preceding example and the one documented in the Solution is that of a function call. In PHP, function calls have more overhead than language constructs (like assignment operators). The preceding example is slightly more efficient, but only if it's used several times in an application.

If you are instead adding *multiple* items to the end of an array, the `array_push()` function will be more efficient. It accepts and appends many items at once, thus avoiding multiple assignments. Example 7-8 illustrates the difference between approaches.

Example 7-8. Appending multiple elements with array_push() versus assignment

```
$first = ['apple'];
array_push($first, 'banana', 'coconut', 'grape');

$second = ['apple'];
$second[] = 'banana';
$second[] = 'coconut';
$second[] = 'grape';

echo 'The arrays are ' . ($first === $second ? 'equal' : 'different');

// The arrays are equal
```

If, rather than appending elements, you want to *prepend* them, you would use `array_unshift()` to place the specified items at the beginning of the array as follows:

```
$array = ['grape'];
array_unshift($array, 'apple', 'banana', 'coconut');

print_r($array);

// Array
// (
//     [0] => apple
//     [1] => banana
//     [2] => coconut
//     [3] => grape
// )
```

PHP retains the order of elements passed to `array_unshift()` when prepending them to the target array. The first parameter will become the first element, the second the second, and so on until you reach the array's *original* first element.

Remember, arrays in PHP do not have a set size and can easily be manipulated in different ways. All of the preceding functional examples (`array_push()`, `array_splice()`, and `array_unshift()`) work well on numeric arrays and *do not change the order or structure* of their numerical indexes. You could just as easily add an element to the end of a numeric array by referencing a new index directly. For example:

```
$array = ['apple', 'banana', 'coconut'];
$array[3] = 'grape';
```

So long as the index your code references is continuous with the rest of the array, the preceding example will work flawlessly. If, however, your count is off and you introduce a gap in the index, you have effectively converted your numeric array to an associative one, just with numeric keys.

While all of the functions used in this recipe will work with associative arrays, they work primarily against numeric keys and will result in strange behavior when used against non-numeric ones. It would be wise to use these functions *only* with numeric arrays and to manipulate the sizes of associative arrays directly based on their keys.

See Also

Documentation on `array_push()` (*https://oreil.ly/DhVgq*), `array_splice()` (*https://oreil.ly/eLoTZ*), and `array_unshift()` (*https://oreil.ly/BYisR*).

7.6 Appending One Array to Another

Problem

You want to combine two arrays into a single, new array.

Solution

Use `array_merge()` as follows:

```
$first = ['a', 'b', 'c'];
$second = ['x', 'y', 'z'];

$merged = array_merge($first, $second);
```

In addition, you can also leverage the spread operator (…) to combine arrays directly. Rather than a call to `array_merge()`, the preceding example then becomes this:

```
$merged = [...$first, ...$second];
```

The spread operator works for both numeric and associative arrays.

Discussion

PHP's `array_merge()` function is an obvious way to combine two arrays into one. It does, however, have slightly different behavior for numeric versus associative arrays.

 Any discussion of merging arrays will inevitably use the term *combine*. Note that `array_combine()` (*https://oreil.ly/wcM69*) is itself a function in PHP. However, it doesn't merge two arrays as shown in this recipe. Instead, it creates a new array by using the two specified arrays—the first for the *keys* and the second for the *values* of the new array. It's a useful function but is not something you can use for merging two arrays.

For numeric arrays (like those in the Solution example), all elements of the second array are appended to those of the first array. The function ignores the indexes of both, and the newly produced array has continuous indexes (starting from 0) as if you'd built it directly.

For associative arrays, the keys (and values) of the second array are added to those of the first. If the two arrays have the same keys, the values of the second array will overwrite those of the first. Example 7-9 illustrates how the data in one array overwrites that of the other.

Example 7-9. Overwriting associative array data with `array_merge()`

```
$first = [
    'title'  => 'Practical Handbook',
    'author' => 'Bob Mills',
    'year'   => 2018
];
$second = [
    'year'   => 2023,
    'region' => 'United States'
];

$merged = array_merge($first, $second);
print_r($merged);

// Array
// (
//     [title] => Practical Handbook
//     [author] => Bob Mills
//     [year] => 2023
```

```
//     [region] => United States
// )
```

There might be cases where you want to retain the data held in duplicate keys when you merge two or more arrays. In those circumstances, use `array_merge_recursive()`. Unlike the preceding example, this function will create an array containing the data defined in duplicate keys rather than overwriting one value with another. Example 7-10 rewrites the preceding example to illustrate how this happens.

Example 7-10. Merging arrays with duplicate keys

```
$first = [
    'title'  => 'Practical Handbook',
    'author' => 'Bob Mills',
    'year'   => 2018
];
$second = [
    'year'   => 2023,
    'region' => 'United States'
];

$merged = array_merge_recursive($first, $second);
print_r($merged);

// Array
// (
//     [title] => Practical Handbook
//     [author] => Bob Mills
//     [year] => Array
//         (
//             [0] => 2018
//             [1] => 2023
//         )
//
//     [region] => United States
// )
```

While the preceding examples combine only two arrays, there is no upper limit to the number of arrays you can merge with either `array_merge()` or `array_merge_recursive()`. Keep in mind how duplicate keys are handled by both functions as you begin merging more than two arrays at a time to avoid potentially losing data.

A third and final way to combine two arrays into one is with the literal addition operator: `+`. On paper, this has the appearance of adding two arrays together. What it really does is add any new key from the second array to the keys of the first. Unlike `array_merge()`, this operation will not overwrite data. If the second array has keys that duplicate any in the first array, those keys are ignored, and the data from the first array is used.

This operator also works *explicitly* with array keys, meaning it's not a good fit for numeric arrays. Two same-sized numeric arrays, when treated like associative arrays, will have the exact same keys because they have the same indexes. This means the second array's data will be ignored entirely!

See Also

Documentation for `array_merge()` (*https://oreil.ly/s38Xa*) and `array_merge_recur sive()` (*https://oreil.ly/aFQxS*).

7.7 Creating an Array from a Fragment of an Existing Array

Problem

You want to select a subsection of an existing array and use it independently.

Solution

Use `array_slice()` to select a sequence of elements from an existing array as follows:

```
$array = range('A', 'Z');
$slice = array_slice($array, 7, 4);

print_r($slice);

// Array
// (
//     [0] => H
//     [1] => I
//     [2] => J
//     [3] => K
// )
```

Discussion

The `array_slice()` function quickly extracts a continuous sequence of items from the given array based on a defined offset (position within the array) and length of elements to retrieve. Unlike `array_splice()`, it copies the sequence of items from the array, leaving the original array unchanged.

It's important to understand the full function signature to appreciate the power of this function:

```
array_slice(
    array $array,
    int   $offset,
```

```
    ?$int $length = null,
    $bool $preserve_keys = false
): array
```

Only the first two parameters—the target array and the initial offset—are required. If the offset is positive (or 0), the new sequence will start at that position from the beginning of the array. If the offset is negative, the sequence will start that many positions back from the *end* of the array.

The array offset is explicitly referencing the *position* within an array, not in terms of keys or indexes. The array_slice() function works on associative arrays as easily as it does on numeric arrays because it uses the relative positions of elements in the array to define a new sequence and ignores the array's actual keys.

When you define the optional $length argument, this defines the maximum number of items in the new sequence. Note that the new sequence is limited by the number of items in the original array, so if the length overruns the end of the array, your sequence will be shorter than you expected. Example 7-11 presents a quick example of this behavior.

Example 7-11. Using array_slice() with a too-short array

```
$array = range('a', 'e');
$newArray = array_slice($array, 4, 100);

print_r($newArray);

// Array
// (
//     [0] => e
// )
```

If the length specified is *negative*, then the sequence will stop that many elements away from the end of the target array. If the length is not specified (or is null), then the sequence will include everything from the original offset through the end of the target array.

The final parameter, $preserve_keys, tells PHP whether to reset the integer indexes of the slice of the array. By default, PHP will return a newly indexed array with integer keys starting at 0. Example 7-12 shows how the behavior of the function differs based on this parameter.

The array_slice() function will always preserve string keys in an associative array regardless of the value of $preserve_keys.

Example 7-12. Key preservation behavior in array_slice()

```
$array = range('a', 'e');

$standard = array_slice($array, 1, 2);
print_r($standard);

// Array
// (
//     [0] => b
//     [1] => c
// )

$preserved = array_slice($array, 1, 2, true);
print_r($preserved);

// Array
// (
//     [1] => b
//     [2] => c
// )
```

Remember, numeric arrays in PHP can be thought of as associative arrays with integer keys that start at 0 and increment consecutively. With that in mind, it's easy to see how array_slice() behaves on associative arrays with both string and integer keys—it operates based on position rather than key, as shown in Example 7-13.

Example 7-13. Using array_slice() on an array with mixed keys

```
$array = ['a' => 'apple', 'b' => 'banana', 25 => 'cola', 'd' => 'donut'];
print_r(array_slice($array, 0, 3));

// Array
// (
//     [a] => apple
//     [b] => banana
//     [0] => cola
// )

print_r(array_slice($array, 0, 3, true));

// Array
// (
//     [a] => apple
```

```
//     [b] => banana
//     [25] => cola
// )
```

In Recipe 7.4, you were introduced to `array_splice()` for deleting a sequence of elements from an array. Conveniently, this function uses a method signature similar to
that of `array_slice()`:

```
array_splice(
    array &$array,
    int    $offset,
    ?int   $length = null,
    mixed  $replacement = []
): array
```

The key difference between these functions is that one modifies the source array
whereas the other does not. You might use `array_slice()` to work on a subset of a
larger sequence in isolation or instead to fully separate two sequences from one
another. In either case, the functions exhibit similar behavior and use cases.

See Also

Documentation on `array_slice()` (*https://oreil.ly/9iBvj*) and `array_splice()`
(*https://oreil.ly/k-h7n*).

7.8 Converting Between Arrays and Strings

Problem

You want to convert a string into an array or combine the elements of an array into a
string.

Solution

Use `str_split()` to convert a string to an array:

```
$string = 'To be or not to be';
$array = str_split($string);
```

Use `join()` to combine the elements of an array into a string:

```
$array = ['H', 'e', 'l', 'l', 'o', ' ', 'w', 'o', 'r', 'l', 'd'];
$string = join('', $array);
```

Discussion

The `str_split()` function is a powerful way to convert any string of characters into
an array of like-sized chunks. By default, it will break the string into one-character

chunks, but you can just as easily break a string into any number of characters. The last chunk in the sequence is only guaranteed to be *up to* the specified length. For example, Example 7-14 attempts to break a string down into five-character chunks, but note that the last chunk is fewer than five characters in length.

Example 7-14. Using str_split() with arbitrary chunk sizes

```
$string = 'To be or not to be';
$array = str_split($string, 5);
var_dump($array);

// array(4) {
//    [0]=>
//    string(5) "To be"
//    [1]=>
//    string(5) " or n"
//    [2]=>
//    string(5) "ot to"
//    [3]=>
//    string(3) " be"
// }
```

 Remember that str_split() works on bytes. When you're dealing with multibyte encoded strings, you will need to use mb_ str_ split() (*https://oreil.ly/ocQi1*) instead.

In some cases, you might want to split a string into separate words rather than individual characters. PHP's explode() function allows you to specify the separator on which to split things. This is handy for splitting a sentence into an array of its component words, as demonstrated by Example 7-15.

Example 7-15. Splitting a string into an array of words

```
$string = 'To be or not to be';
$words = explode(' ', $string);

print_r($words);

// Array
// (
//     [0] => To
//     [1] => be
//     [2] => or
//     [3] => not
//     [4] => to
```

```
//      [5] => be
// )
```

 While `explode()` appears to function similarly to `str_split()`, it cannot explode a string with an empty delimiter (the first parameter to the function). If you try to pass an empty string, you will be met with a `ValueError`. If you want to work with an array of characters, stick with `str_split()`.

Combining an array of strings into a single string requires the use of the `join()` function, which itself is merely an alias of `implode()`. That said, it's far more powerful than just being the inverse of `str_split()`, as you can optionally define a separator to be placed between newly concatenated code chunks.

The separator is optional, but the long legacy of `implode()` in PHP has led to two somewhat unintuitive function signatures as follows:

```
implode(string $separator, array $array): string
```

```
implode(array $array): string
```

If you want to merely combine an array of characters into a string, you can do so with the equivalent methods shown in Example 7-16.

Example 7-16. Creating a string from an array of characters

```
$array = ['H', 'e', 'l', 'l', 'o', ' ', 'w', 'o', 'r', 'l', 'd'];

$option1 = implode($array);

$option2 = implode('', $array);

echo 'The two are ' . ($option1 === $option2 ? 'identical' : 'different');

// The two are identical
```

Because you can explicitly specify the separator—the glue used to join each chunk of text—there are few limits to what `implode()` allows you to do. Assume your array is a list of words rather than a list of characters. You can use `implode()` to link them together as a printable and comma-delimited list, as in the following example:

```
$fruit = ['apple', 'orange', 'pear', 'peach'];

echo implode(', ', $fruit);

// apple, orange, pear, peach
```

See Also

Documentation on `implode()` (*https://oreil.ly/mpdcI*), `explode()` (*https://oreil.ly/PScj_*), and `str_split()` (*https://oreil.ly/2dTMD*).

7.9 Reversing an Array

Problem

You want to reverse the order of elements in an array.

Solution

Use `array_reverse()` as follows:

```
$array = ['five', 'four', 'three', 'two', 'one', 'zero'];

$reversed = array_reverse($array);
```

Discussion

The `array_reverse()` function creates a new array where each element is in the reverse order of the input array. By default, this function does not preserve numeric keys from the source array but instead re-indexes each element. Non-numeric keys (in associative arrays) are left unchanged by this re-indexing; however, their order is still reversed as expected. Example 7-17 demonstrates how associative arrays are reordered by `array_reverse()`.

Example 7-17. Reversing associative arrays

```
$array = ['a' => 'A', 'b' => 'B', 'c' => 'C'];
$reversed = array_reverse($array);

print_r($reversed);

// Array
// (
//     [c] => C
//     [b] => B
//     [a] => A
// )
```

Since associative arrays can have numeric keys to begin with, the re-indexing behavior might produce unexpected results. Thankfully, it can be disabled by passing an optional Boolean parameter as the second argument when reversing an array. Example 7-18 shows how this indexing behavior impacts such arrays (and how it can be disabled).

Example 7-18. Reversing an associative array with numeric keys

```
$array = ['a' => 'A', 'b' => 'B', 42 => 'C', 'd' => 'D'];
print_r(array_reverse($array)); ❶

// Array
// (
//     [d] => D
//     [0] => C
//     [b] => B
//     [a] => A
// )

print_r(array_reverse($array, true)); ❷

// Array
// (
//     [d] => D
//     [42] => C
//     [b] => B
//     [a] => A
// )
```

❶ The default value of the second parameter is `false`, which means numeric keys will not be preserved after the array is reversed.

❷ Passing `true` as a second parameter will still allow the array to reverse but will retain numeric keys in the new array.

See Also

Documentation on `array_reverse()` (*https://oreil.ly/mI5eG*).

7.10 Sorting an Array

Problem

You want to sort the elements of an array.

Solution

To sort items based on default comparison rules in PHP, use `sort()` as follows:

```
$states = ['Oregon', 'California', 'Alaska', 'Washington', 'Hawaii'];
sort($states);
```

Discussion

PHP's native sorting system is built atop Quicksort, a common and relatively fast sorting algorithm. By default, it uses rules defined by PHP's comparison operators to determine the order of each element in the array.[5] You can, however, sort with different rules by passing a flag as the optional second parameter of sort(). Available sorting flags are described in Table 7-1.

Table 7-1. Sorting type flags

Flag	Description
SORT_REGULAR	Compare items normally by using default comparison operations
SORT_NUMERIC	Compare items numerically
SORT_STRING	Compare items as strings
SORT_LOCALE_STRING	Compare items as strings by using the current system locale
SORT_NATURAL	Compare items by using "natural ordering"
SORT_FLAG_CASE	Combine with SORT_STRING or SORT_NATURAL by using a bitwise OR operator to compare strings without case-sensitivity

Sorting type flags are useful when the default sorting comparisons produce a sorted array that makes no sense. For example, sorting an array of integers as if they were strings would sort things incorrectly. Using the SORT_NUMERIC flag will ensure that integers are sorted in the correct order. Example 7-19 demonstrates how the two sorting types differ.

Example 7-19. Sorting integers with a regular versus numeric sort type

```
$numbers = [1, 10, 100, 5, 50, 500];
sort($numbers, SORT_STRING);
print_r($numbers);

// Array
// (
//      [0] => 1
//      [1] => 10
//      [2] => 100
//      [3] => 5
//      [4] => 50
//      [5] => 500
// )

sort($numbers, SORT_NUMERIC);
print_r($numbers);
```

---

5 Review "Comparison Operators" on page 13 for further details on comparison operators and their usage.

```
// Array
// (
//     [0] => 1
//     [1] => 5
//     [2] => 10
//     [3] => 50
//     [4] => 100
//     [5] => 500
// )
```

The sort() function ignores array keys and indexes and sorts the elements of the array purely by their values. Thus, attempting to use sort() to sort an associative array will destroy the keys in that array. If you want to retain the keys in an array while still sorting by values, use asort().

To do this, invoke asort() exactly the same way as you do sort(); you can even use the same flags as defined in Table 7-1. The resulting array will, however, retain the same keys as before, even though elements are in a different order. For example:

```
$numbers = [1, 10, 100, 5, 50, 500];
asort($numbers, SORT_NUMERIC);
print_r($numbers);

// Array
// (
//     [0] => 1
//     [3] => 5
//     [1] => 10
//     [4] => 50
//     [2] => 100
//     [5] => 500
// )
```

Both sort() and asort() will produce arrays sorted in ascending order. If you want to get an array in descending order, you have two options:

- Sort the array in ascending order, then reverse it as demonstrated in Recipe 7.9.

- Leverage rsort() or arsort() for numeric and associative arrays, respectively.

To reduce overall code complexity, the latter option is often preferable. The functions have the same signatures as sort() and asort() but merely reverse the order in which elements will be positioned in the resulting array.

See Also

Documentation on arsort() (*https://oreil.ly/G14ve*), asort() (*https://oreil.ly/jkl5w*), rsort() (*https://oreil.ly/Z6p49*), and sort() (*https://oreil.ly/sHWtt*).

7.11 Sorting an Array Based on a Function

Problem

You want to sort an array based on a user-defined function or comparator.

Solution

Use usort() with a custom sorting callback as follows:

```
$bonds = [
    ['first' => 'Sean',    'last' => 'Connery'],
    ['first' => 'Daniel',  'last' => 'Craig'],
    ['first' => 'Pierce',  'last' => 'Brosnan'],
    ['first' => 'Roger',   'last' => 'Moore'],
    ['first' => 'Timothy', 'last' => 'Dalton'],
    ['first' => 'George',  'last' => 'Lazenby'],
];

function sorter(array $a, array $b) {
    return [$a['last'], $a['first']] <=> [$b['last'], $b['first']];
}

usort($bonds, 'sorter');

foreach ($bonds as $bond) {
    echo "{$bond['last']}. {$bond['first']} {$bond['last']}" . PHP_EOL;
}
```

Discussion

The usort() function leverages a user-defined function as the comparison operation behind its sorting algorithm. You can pass in any callable as the second parameter, and every element of the array will be checked through this function to determine its appropriate order. The Solution example references a callback by its name, but you could just as easily pass an anonymous function as well.

The Solution example further leverages PHP's newer spaceship operator to conduct a complex comparison between your array elements.[6] In this particular case, you want to sort James Bond actors first by last name, then by first name. The same function could be used for any collection of names.

A more powerful example is to apply custom sorting to dates in PHP. Dates are relatively easy to sort as they're part of a continuous series. But it's possible to define

---

6 The spaceship operator is explained at length in Recipe 2.4, which also introduces an example use of usort().

custom behavior that breaks those expectations. Example 7-20 attempts to sort an array of dates first based on the day of the week, then by the year, then by the month.

Example 7-20. User-defined sorting applied to dates

```
$dates = [
    new DateTime('2022-12-25'),
    new DateTime('2022-04-17'),
    new DateTime('2022-11-24'),
    new DateTime('2023-01-01'),
    new DateTime('2022-07-04'),
    new DateTime('2023-02-14'),
];

function sorter(DateTime $a, DateTime $b) {
    return
        [$a->format('N'), $a->format('Y'), $a->format('j')]
        <=>
        [$b->format('N'), $b->format('Y'), $b->format('j')];
}

usort($dates, 'sorter');

foreach ($dates as $date) {
    echo $date->format('l, F jS, Y') . PHP_EOL;
}

// Monday, July 4th, 2022
// Tuesday, February 14th, 2023
// Thursday, November 24th, 2022
// Sunday, April 17th, 2022
// Sunday, December 25th, 2022
// Sunday, January 1st, 2023
```

Like many other array functions discussed in this chapter, usort() ignores array keys/indexes and re-indexes the array as part of its operation. If you need to retain the index or key associations of elements, use uasort() instead. This function has the same signature as usort() but leaves the array keys untouched after sorting.

Array keys often hold important information about the data within the array, so retaining them during a sorting operation can prove critical at times. In addition, you might want to actually sort by the keys of the array rather than by the value of each element. In those circumstances, leverage uksort().

The uksort() function will sort an array by its keys, using a function you define. Like uasort(), it respects the keys and leaves them in place after the array is sorted.

See Also

Documentation on usort() (*https://oreil.ly/TuK1L*), uasort() (*https://oreil.ly/igH5E*), and uksort() (*https://oreil.ly/MEyff*).

7.12 Randomizing the Elements in an Array

Problem

You want to scramble the elements of your array so that their order is entirely random.

Solution

Use shuffle() as follows:

```
$array = range('a', 'e');
shuffle($array);
```

Discussion

The shuffle() function acts on an existing array that is passed into the function by reference. It completely ignores the keys of the array and sorts element values at random, updating the array in place. After shuffling, array keys are re-indexed starting from 0.

> While you won't receive an error if you shuffle an associative array, all information on keys will be lost during the operation. You should only ever shuffle numeric arrays.

Internally, shuffle() uses the Mersenne Twister (*https://oreil.ly/86yIo*) pseudo-random number generator to identify a new, seemingly random order for each element in the array. This pseudorandom number generator is not suitable when true randomness is required (e.g., cryptography or security scenarios), but it is an effective way to quickly shuffle the contents of an array.

See Also

Documentation on shuffle() (*https://oreil.ly/AkcpO*).

7.13 Applying a Function to Every Element of an Array

Problem

You want to transform an array by applying a function to modify every element of the array in turn.

Solution

To modify the array in place, use array_walk() as follows:

```
$values = range(2, 5);

array_walk($values, function(&$value, $key) {
    $value *= $value;
});

print_r($values);

// Array
// (
//     [0] => 4
//     [1] => 9
//     [2] => 16
//     [3] => 25
// )
```

Discussion

Looping through collections of data is a common requirement for PHP applications. For example, you may want to use collections to define repeated tasks. Or you may want to perform a particular operation on every item in a collection, like squaring values, as shown in the Solution example.

The array_walk() function is an effective way to both define the transformation you want applied and to apply it to the value of every element of the array. The callback function (the second parameter) accepts three arguments: the value and key for an element in the array and an optional $arg argument. This final argument is defined during the initial invocation of array_walk() and is passed to every use of the callback. It's an efficient way to pass a constant value to the callback, as shown in Example 7-21.

Example 7-21. Invoking array_walk() with an extra argument

```
function mutate(&$value, $key, $arg)
{
    $value *= $arg;
}
```

```
$values = range(2, 5);

array_walk($values, 'mutate', 10);

print_r($values);

// Array
// (
//     [0] => 20
//     [1] => 30
//     [2] => 40
//     [3] => 50
// )
```

Using `array_walk()` to modify an array in place requires passing array values *by reference* into the callback (note the extra & in front of the argument name). This function could also be used to merely walk over each element in the array and perform some other function *without* modifying the source array. In fact, that's the most common use of this function.

In addition to walking over every element of an array, you can walk over the *leaf* nodes in a nested array by using `array_walk_recursive()`. Unlike the preceding examples, `array_walk_recursive()` will traverse nested arrays until it finds a non-array element before applying your specified callback function. Example 7-22 handily demonstrates the difference between the recursive and nonrecursive function calls against a nested array. Specifically, if you are dealing with a nested array, `array_walk()` will throw an error and fail to do anything at all.

Example 7-22. Comparing array_walk() with array_walk_recursive()

```
$array = [
    'even' => [2, 4, 6],
    'odd'  => 1,
];

function mutate(&$value, $key, $arg)
{
    $value *= $arg;
}

array_walk_recursive($array, 'mutate', 10);
print_r($array);

// Array
// (
//     [even] => Array
//         (
//             [0] => 20
```

```
//              [1] => 40
//              [2] => 60
//          )
//
//      [odd] => 10
// )
```

```
array_walk($array, 'mutate', 10);
```

```
// PHP Warning: Uncaught TypeError: Unsupported operand types: array * int
```

In many situations, you might want to create a new copy of a mutated array without losing track of its original state. In those circumstances, `array_map()` might be a safer choice than `array_walk()`. Rather than modifying the source array, `array_map()` empowers you to apply a function to every element in the source array and return an entirely new array. The advantage is that you'll have both the original and the modified arrays available for further use. The following example leverages the same logic as the Solution example *without* changing the source array:

```
$values = range(2, 5);

$mutated = array_map(function($value) {
    return $value * $value;
}, $values);

print_r($mutated);

// Array
// (
//      [0] => 4
//      [1] => 9
//      [2] => 16
//      [3] => 25
// )
```

Here are some key differences to note between these two families of array functions:

- `array_walk()` expects the array first and the callback second.
- `array_map()` expects the callback first and the array second.
- `array_walk()` returns a Boolean flag, while `array_map()` returns a new array.
- `array_map()` does not pass keys into the callback.
- `array_map()` does not pass additional arguments into the callback.
- There is no recursive form of `array_map()`.

See Also

Documentation on `array_map()` (*https://oreil.ly/fzU_0*), `array_walk()` (*https://oreil.ly/OTpL4*), and `array_walk_recursive()` (*https://oreil.ly/qCt7G*).

7.14 Reducing an Array to a Single Value

Problem

You want to iteratively reduce a collection of values to a single value.

Solution

Use `array_reduce()` with a callback as follows:

```
$values = range(0, 10);

$sum = array_reduce($values, function($carry, $item) {
    return $carry + $item;
}, 0);

// $sum = 55
```

Discussion

The `array_reduce()` function walks through every element of an array and modifies its own internal state to eventually arrive at a single answer. The Solution example walks through each element of a list of numbers and adds them all to the initial value of 0, returning the final sum of all of the numbers in question.

The callback function accepts two parameters. The first is the value you're carrying over from the last operation. The second is the value of the current item in the array over which you're iterating. Whatever the callback returns will be passed into the callback as the `$carry` parameter for the next element in the array.

When you first start out, you pass an optional initial value (`null` by default) into the callback as the `$carry` parameter. If the reduction operation you're applying to the array is straightforward, you can often provide a better initial value, as done in the Solution example.

The biggest drawback of `array_reduce()` is that it does not handle array keys. In order to leverage any keys in the array as part of the reduction operation, you need to define your own version of the function.

Example 7-23 shows how you can instead iterate over the array returned by `array_keys()` to leverage elements' keys and values in the reduction. You pass both the array and callback into the closure processed by `array_reduce()` so you can both reference the *element* in the array defined by that key and apply your custom function to it. In the main program, you are then free to reduce an associative array the same way you would a numeric one—except you have an extra argument in your callback containing each element's key.

Example 7-23. Associative alternative to `array_reduce()`

```
function array_reduce_assoc(
    array $array,
    callable $callback,
    mixed $initial = null
): mixed
{
    return array_reduce(
        array_keys($array),
        function($carry, $item) use ($array, $callback) {
            return $callback($carry, $array[$item], $item);
        },
        $initial
    );
}

$array = [1 => 10, 2 => 10, 3 => 5];

$sumMultiples = array_reduce_assoc(
    $array,
    function($carry, $item, $key) {
        return $carry + ($item * $key);
    },
    0
);

// $sumMultiples = 45
```

The preceding code will return the sum of the keys of $array multiplied by their corresponding values—specifically, 1 * 10 + 2 * 10 + 3 * 5 = 45.

See Also

Documentation on `array_reduce()` (*https://oreil.ly/iu_XM*).

7.15 Iterating over Infinite or Very Large/Expensive Arrays

Problem

You want to iterate over a list of items that is too large to be held in memory or is too slow to generate.

Solution

Use a generator to yield one chunk of data at a time to your program, as follows:

```php
function weekday()
{
    static $day = 'Monday';

    while (true) {
        yield $day;

        switch($day) {
            case 'Monday':
                $day = 'Tuesday';
                break;
            case 'Tuesday':
                $day = 'Wednesday';
                break;
            case 'Wednesday':
                $day = 'Thursday';
                break;
            case 'Thursday':
                $day = 'Friday';
                break;
            case 'Friday':
                $day = 'Monday';
                break;
        }
    }
}

$weekdays = weekday();
foreach ($weekdays as $day) {
    echo $day . PHP_EOL;
}
```

Discussion

Generators are a memory-efficient way to handle large pieces of data in PHP. In the Solution example, a generator produces weekdays (Monday through Friday) in order as an infinite series. An infinite series will not fit in the memory available to PHP, but the generator construct allows you to build it up one piece at a time.

Rather than instantiate a too-large array, you generate the first piece of data and return it via the yield keyword to whomever called the generator. This freezes the state of the generator and yields executional control back to the main application. Unlike a typical function that returns data once, a generator can provide data multiple times so long as it is still valid.

In the Solution example, the `yield` appears inside an infinite `while` loop, so it will continue enumerating weekdays forever. If you wanted the generator to exit, you would do so using an empty `return` statement at the end (or merely break the loop and implicitly return).

> Returning data from a generator is different from a usual function call. You typically return data with the `yield` keyword and exit a generator with an empty `return` statement. However, if the generator *does* have a final return, you must access that data by calling `::getReturn()` on the generator object. This additional method call often sticks out as odd, so unless your generator has a reason to return data outside its typical `yield` operation, you should try to avoid it.

Since the generator can provide data forever, you can iterate over that data by using a standard `foreach` loop. Similarly, you could leverage a limited `for` loop to avoid an infinite series. The following code leverages such a limited loop and the Solution's original generator:

```
$weekdays = weekday();
for ($i = 0; $i < 14; $i++) {
    echo $weekdays->current() . PHP_EOL;
    $weekdays->next();
}
```

Though the generator is defined as a function, internally PHP recognizes it as a generator and converts it to an instance of the `Generator` class (*https://oreil.ly/R_geQ*). This class gives you access to the `::current()` and `::next()` methods and permits you to step over the generated data one piece at a time.

The control flow within the application passes back and forth between the main program and the generator's `yield` statement. The first time you access the generator, it runs internally up to `yield` and then returns control (and possibly data) to the main application. Subsequent calls to the generator start *after* the `yield` keyword. Loops are required to force the generator back to the beginning in order to `yield` again.

See Also

Overview on generators (*https://oreil.ly/cR4-V*).

## CHAPTER 8

Classes and Objects

The earliest versions of PHP didn't support class definition or object orientation. PHP 4 was the first real attempt at an object interface.[1] It wasn't until PHP 5, though, that developers had the complex object interfaces they know and use today.

Classes are defined using the class keyword followed by a full description of the constants, properties, and methods inherent to the class. Example 8-1 introduces a basic class construct in PHP, complete with a scoped constant value, a property, and callable methods.

Example 8-1. Basic PHP class with properties and methods

```
class Foo
{
    const SOME_CONSTANT = 42;

    public string $hello = 'hello';

    public function __construct(public string $world = 'world') {}

    public function greet(): void
    {
        echo sprintf('%s %s', $this->hello, $this->world);
    }
}
```

An object can be instantiated with the new keyword and the name of the class; instantiation looks somewhat like a function call. Any parameters passed into this

---

1 PHP 3 included some primitive object functionality, but the language wasn't really considered object-oriented by most developers until the delivery of 4.0.

instantiation are transparently passed into the class constructor (the __construct()
method) to define the object's initial state. Example 8-2 illustrates how the class definition from Example 8-1 could be instantiated either with or without default property
values.

Example 8-2. Instantiating a basic PHP class

```
$first = new Foo; ❶
$second = new Foo('universe'); ❷

$first->greet(); ❸
$second->greet(); ❹

echo Foo::SOME_CONSTANT; ❺
```

❶ Instantiating an object without passing a parameter will still invoke the constructor but will leverage its default parameters. If no defaults are provided in the
function signature, this would result in an error.

❷ Passing a parameter during instantiation will provide this parameter to the
constructor.

❸ This prints hello world by using the constructor's defaults.

❹ This prints hello universe to the console.

❺ Constants are referenced directly from the class name. This will print a literal 42
to the console.

Constructors and properties are covered in Recipes 8.1 and 8.2.

Procedural Programming

Most developers' first experience with PHP is through its more procedural interfaces.
Example routines, simple scripts, tutorials—all of these typically leverage functions
and variables defined within the global scope. This isn't a bad thing, but it does limit
the flexibility of the programs you can produce.

Procedural programming often results in stateless applications. There is little to no
ability to keep track of what's happened before between function calls, so you pass
some reference to the application's state throughout your code. Again, this isn't necessarily a bad thing. The only drawback is that *complex* applications become difficult to
analyze or understand.

Object-Oriented Programming

An alternative paradigm is to leverage objects as containers of state. A common practical example is to consider objects as ways to define *things*. A car is an object. So is a bus. And a bicycle. They are discrete *things* that have characteristics (such as color, number of wheels, and type of drive) and capabilities (such as go, stop, and turn).

In the programming world, this is among the easiest ways to describe objects. In PHP, you create objects by first defining a `class` to describe the type of object. A class describes the properties (characteristics) and methods (capabilities) that an object of that type will have.

Like things in the real world, objects in a programming space can inherit from more primitive type descriptions. A car, bus, and bicycle are all types of vehicles, so they can all descend from a specific type. Example 8-3 demonstrates how PHP might construct that kind of object inheritance.

Example 8-3. Class abstraction in PHP

```
abstract class Vehicle
{
    abstract public function go(): void;

    abstract public function stop(): void;

    abstract public function turn(Direction $direction): void;
}

class Car extends Vehicle
{
    public int $wheels = 4;
    public string $driveType = 'gas';

    public function __construct(public Color $color) {}

    public function go(): void
    {
        // ...
    }

    public function stop(): void
    {
        // ...
    }

    public function turn(Direction $direction): void
    {
        // ...
    }
}
```

```php
class Bus extends Vehicle
{
    public int $wheels = 4;
    public string $driveType = 'diesel';

    public function __construct(public Color $color) {}

    public function go(): void
    {
        // ...
    }

    public function stop(): void
    {
        // ...
    }

    public function turn(Direction $direction): void
    {
        // ...
    }
}

class Bicycle extends Vehicle
{
    public int $wheels = 2;
    public string $driveType = 'direct';

    public function __construct(public Color $color) {}

    public function go(): void
    {
        // ...
    }

    public function stop(): void
    {
        // ...
    }

    public function turn(Direction $direction): void
    {
        // ...
    }
}
```

Instantiating an object creates a typed variable that represents both an initial state and methods for manipulating that state. Object *inheritance* presents the possibility to use one or more types as alternatives to one another in other code. Example 8-4 illustrates how the three types of vehicles introduced in Example 8-2 could be used interchangeably because of inheritance.

Example 8-4. Classes with similar inheritance can be used interchangeably

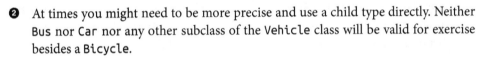

```
function commute(Vehicle $vehicle) ❶
{
    // ...
}

function exercise(Bicycle $vehicle) ❷
{
    // ...
}
```

❶ All three of the vehicle subtypes can be used as valid replacements for `Vehicle` in function calls. This means you could commute by bus, car, or bicycle, and any choice would be equally valid.

❷ At times you might need to be more precise and use a child type directly. Neither `Bus` nor `Car` nor any other subclass of the `Vehicle` class will be valid for exercise besides a `Bicycle`.

Class inheritance is covered at a deeper level by Recipes 8.6, 8.7, and 8.8.

Multiparadigm Languages

PHP is considered a *multiparadigm* language, as you can write code following either of the preceding paradigms. A valid PHP program can be purely procedural. Or it can be strictly focused on object definitions and custom classes. The program could ultimately use a mix of both paradigms.

The open source WordPress content management system (CMS) is one of the most popular PHP projects on the internet.[2] It's coded to heavily leverage objects for common abstractions like database objects or remote requests. However, WordPress also stems from a long history of procedural programming—much of the codebase is still heavily influenced by that style. WordPress is a key example not just of the success of PHP itself, but of the flexibility of the language's support for multiple paradigms.

There is no single right answer for how an application should be assembled. Most are hybrids of approaches that benefit from PHP's strong support of multiple paradigms. Even in a majority-procedural application, though, you will still likely see a handful of

---

2 At the time of this writing, WordPress was used to power 43% of all websites (*https://oreil.ly/tEaN8*).

objects as that's how the language's standard library implements much of its functionality (*https://oreil.ly/krXrW*).

Chapter 6 illustrated the use of both the functional and object-oriented interfaces for PHP's date system. Error handling, which is covered more in Chapter 13, heavily leverages internal `Exception` and `Error` classes. The `yield` keyword in an otherwise procedural implementation automatically creates instances of the `Generator` class.

Even if you never define a class in your program directly, the chances are good that you will leverage one defined either by PHP itself or by a third-party library your program requires.[3]

Visibility

Classes also introduce the concept of *visibility* into PHP. Properties, methods, and even constants can be defined with an optional visibility modifier to change their level of access from other parts of the application. Anything declared `public` is accessible to any other class or function in your application. Both methods and properties can be declared `protected`, making them accessible only to an instance of either the class itself or classes that descend from it. Finally, the `private` declaration means a member of the class can be accessed only by instances of that class itself.

> By default, anything not explicitly scoped to be private or protected is automatically public, so you might see some developers skip declaring member visibility entirely.

While member visibility can be directly overridden via reflection,[4] it's typically a sound way to clarify which parts of a class's interface are intended to be used by other code elements. Example 8-5 illustrates how each visibility modifier can be leveraged to build a complex application.

Example 8-5. Class member visibility overview

```
class A
{
    public    string $name  = 'Bob';
    public    string $city  = 'Portland';
    protected int    $year  = 2023;
    private   float  $value = 42.9;
```

---

3 Libraries and extensions are discussed at length in Chapter 15.

4 See Recipe 8.12 for more on the Reflection API.

```php
    function hello(): string
    {
        return 'hello';
    }

    public function world(): string
    {
        return 'world';
    }

    protected function universe(): string
    {
        return 'universe';
    }

    private function abyss(): string
    {
        return 'the void';
    }
}

class B extends A
{
    public function getName(): string
    {
        return $this->name;
    }

    public function getCity(): string
    {
        return $this->city;
    }

    public function getYear(): int
    {
        return $this->year;
    }

    public function getValue(): float
    {
        return $this->value;
    }
}

$first = new B;
echo $first->getName() . PHP_EOL;   ❶
echo $first->getCity() . PHP_EOL;   ❷
echo $first->getYear() . PHP_EOL;   ❸
echo $first->getValue() . PHP_EOL;  ❹

$second = new A;
echo $second->hello() . PHP_EOL;    ❺
```

```
echo $second->world() . PHP_EOL; ❻
echo $second->universe() . PHP_EOL; ❼
echo $second->abyss() . PHP_EOL; ❽
```

❶   Prints Bob.

❷   Prints Portland.

❸   Prints 2023.

❹   Returns a Warning as the ::$value property is private and inaccessible.

❺   Prints hello.

❻   Prints world.

❼   Throws an Error as the ::universe() method is protected and inaccessible outside the class instance.

❽   This line would not even execute because of the error thrown on the previous line. If the previous line did *not* throw an error, this one would, as the ::abyss() method is private and inaccessible outside the class instance.

The following recipes further illustrate the preceding concepts and cover some of the most common use cases and implementations of objects in PHP.

8.1 Instantiating Objects from Custom Classes

Problem

You want to define a custom class and create a new object instance from it.

Solution

Define the class and its properties and methods with the class keyword, then use new to create an instance of it as follows:

```
class Pet
{
    public string $name;
    public string $species;
    public int $happiness = 0;

    public function __construct(string $name, string $species)
    {
        $this->name = $name;
```

```
        $this->species = $species;
    }

    public function pet()
    {
        $this->happiness += 1;
    }
}

$dog = new Pet('Fido', 'golden retriever');
$dog->pet();
```

Discussion

The Solution example illustrates several key characteristics of objects:

- Objects can have properties that define the internal state of the object itself.
- These objects can have specific visibility. In the Solution example, objects are public, meaning they can be accessed by any code within the application.[5]
- The magic ::__construct() method can accept parameters only when the object is first instantiated. These parameters can be used to define the initial state of the object.
- Methods can have visibility similar to the properties of the object.

This particular version of class definition is the default many developers have been using since PHP 5, when true object-oriented primitives were first introduced. However, Example 8-6 demonstrates a newer and simpler way to define a simple object like the one in the Solution example. Rather than independently declaring and then directly assigning the properties that carry the object's state, PHP 8 (and later) allows for defining everything within the constructor itself.

Example 8-6. Constructor promotion in PHP 8

```
class Pet
{
    public int $happiness = 0;

    public function __construct(
        public string $name,
        public string $species
    ) {}

    public function pet()
```

---

5 Review "Visibility" on page 166 for more background on visibility within classes.

```
    {
        $this->happiness += 1;
    }
}

$dog = new Pet('Fido', 'golden retriever');
$dog->pet();
```

The Solution example and Example 8-6 are functionally equivalent and will result in objects of the same internal structure being created at runtime. PHP's ability to promote constructor arguments to object properties, however, dramatically reduces the amount of repetitive code you need to type while defining a class.

Each constructor argument also permits the same types of visibility (`public`/`protec ted`/`private`) that object properties do.[6] The shorthand syntax means you don't need to declare properties, then define parameters, then map the parameters onto those properties upon object instantiation.

See Also

Documentation on classes and objects (*https://oreil.ly/TfrNb*) and the original RFC on constructor promotion (*https://oreil.ly/nzD0s*).

8.2 Constructing Objects to Define Defaults

Problem

You want to define default values for your object's properties.

Solution

Define default values for the constructor's arguments as follows:

```
class Example
{
    public function __construct(
        public string $someString = 'default',
        public int    $someNumber = 5
    ) {}
}

$first = new Example;
$second = new Example('overridden');
$third = new Example('hitchhiker', 42);
$fourth = new Example(someNumber: 10);
```

---

6 See Recipe 8.3 for details on how these properties could further be made read-only.

Discussion

The constructor function within a class definition behaves more or less like any other function in PHP, except it does not return a value. You can define default arguments similarly to how you would with a standard function. You can even reference the names of the constructor arguments to accept default values for *some* parameters while defining others later in the function signature.

The Solution example explicitly defines the class properties by using constructor promotion for brevity, but the older-style verbose constructor definition is equally valid as follows:

```
class Example
{
    public string $someString;
    public int $someNumber;

    public function __construct(
        string $someString = 'default',
        int    $someNumber = 5
    )
    {
        $this->someString = $someString;
        $this->someNumber = $someNumber;
    }
}
```

Similarly, if *not* using constructor promotion, you can initialize object properties directly by assigning a default value when they're defined. When doing so, you would usually leave those parameters off the constructor and manipulate them elsewhere in the program, as shown in the following example:

```
class Example
{
    public string $someString = 'default';
    public int $someNumber = 5;
}

$test = new Example;
$test->someString = 'overridden';
$test->someNumber = 42;
```

As will be discussed in Recipe 8.3, you cannot initialize a readonly class property directly with a default. This is equivalent to a class constant, and the syntax is therefore disallowed.

See Also

Recipe 3.2 for more on default function parameters, Recipe 3.3 for named function parameters, and documentation on constructors and destructors (*https://oreil.ly/WJvYY*).

8.3 Defining Read-Only Properties in a Class

Problem

You want to define your class in such a way that properties defined at instantiation cannot be changed after the object exists.

Solution

Use the `readonly` keyword on a typed property:

```
class Book
{
    public readonly string $title;

    public function __construct(string $title)
    {
        $this->title = $title;
    }
}

$book = new Book('PHP Cookbook');
```

If using constructor promotion, place the keyword along with the property type within the constructor:

```
class Book
{
    public function __construct(public readonly string $title) {}
}

$book = new Book('PHP Cookbook');
```

Discussion

The `readonly` keyword was introduced in PHP 8.1 and was aimed at reducing the need for more verbose workarounds originally required to achieve the same functionality. With this keyword, a property can only be initialized with a value *once*, and only while the object is being instantiated.

Read-only properties cannot have a default value. This would make them functionally equivalent to class constants, which already exist, so the functionality is unavailable and the syntax is unsupported. Promoted constructor properties can, however, leverage default values within the argument definition as these are evaluated at runtime.

The keyword is also valid only for typed properties. Types are typically optional in PHP (except when strict typing is being used[7]) to aid in flexibility, so it's possible a property on your class *can't* be set to one or another type. In those instances, use the mixed type instead so you can set a read-only property without other type constraints.

At the time of this writing, read-only declarations are *not* supported on static properties.

As a read-only property can only be instantiated once, it cannot be unset or modified by other subsequent code. All of the code in Example 8-7 will result in the throwing of an Error exception.

Example 8-7. Erroneous attempts to modify a read-only property

```
class Example
{
    public readonly string $prop;
}

class Second
{
    public function __construct(public readonly int $count = 0) {}
}

$first = new Example; ❶
$first->prop = 'test'; ❷

$test = new Second;
$test->count += 1; ❸
$test->count++; ❹
++$test->count; ❺
unset($test->count); ❻
```

---

7 See Recipe 3.4 for more on strict type enforcement.

❶ The `Example` object will have an uninitialized `::$prop` property that cannot be accessed (accessing a property before initialization throws an `Error` exception).

❷ As the object is already instantiated, attempting to write to a read-only property throws an `Error`.

❸ The `::$count` property is read-only, so you cannot assign a new value to it without an `Error`.

❹ As the `::$count` property is read-only, you cannot increment it directly.

❺ You cannot increment in either direction with a read-only property.

❻ You cannot unset a read-only property.

The properties within a class can, however, be other classes themselves. In those situations, a read-only declaration on the property means that property cannot be overwritten or unset, but has no impact on the properties of the child class. For example:

```
class First
{
    public function __construct(public readonly Second $inner) {}
}

class Second
{
    public function __construct(public int $counter = 0) {}
}

$test = new First(new Second);
$test->inner->counter += 1; ❶

$test->inner = new Second; ❷
```

❶ The increment of the internal counter will succeed as the `::$counter` property is itself not declared as read-only.

❷ The `::$inner` property is read-only and cannot be overridden. Attempts to do so result in an `Error` exception.

See Also

Documentation on read-only properties (*https://oreil.ly/P-AwN*).

8.4 Deconstructing Objects to Clean Up After the Object Is No Longer Needed

Problem

Your class definition wraps an expensive resource that must be carefully cleaned up when the object goes out of scope.

Solution

Define a class destructor to clean up after the object is removed from memory as follows:

```
class DatabaseHandler
{
    // ...

    public function __destruct()
    {
        dbo_close($this->dbh);
    }
}
```

Discussion

When an object falls out of scope, PHP will automatically garbage-collect any memory or other resources that object used to represent. There might be times, however, when you want to force a specific action when that object goes out of scope. This might be releasing a database handle, as with the Solution example. It could be explicitly logging an event to a file. Or perhaps *deleting* a temporary file from the system, as shown in Example 8-8.

Example 8-8. Removing a temporary file in a destructor

```
class TempLogger
{
    private string $filename;
    private mixed  $handle;

    public function __construct(string $name)
    {
        $this->filename = sprintf('tmp_%s_%s.tmp', $name, time());
        $this->handle = fopen($this->filename, 'w');
    }

    public function writeLog(string $line): void
    {
        fwrite($this->handle, $line . PHP_EOL);
```

```php
    }

    public function getLogs(): Generator
    {
        $handle = fopen($this->filename, 'r');
        while(($buffer = fgets($handle, 4096)) !== false) {
            yield $buffer;
        }
        fclose($handle);
    }

    public function __destruct()
    {
        fclose($this->handle);
        unlink($this->filename);
    }
}

$logger = new TempLogger('test'); ❶
$logger->writeLog('This is a test'); ❷
$logger->writeLog('And another');

foreach($logger->getLogs() as $log) { ❸
    echo $log;
}

unset($logger); ❹
```

❶ The object will automatically create a file in the current directory with a name similar to *tmp_test_1650837172.tmp*.

❷ Every new log entry is written as a new line in the temporary log file.

❸ Accessing the logs will create a second handle on the same file, but for reading. The object exposes this handle through a generator that enumerates over every line in the file.

❹ When the logger is removed from scope (or explicitly unset), the destructor will close the open file handle and automatically delete the file as well.

This more sophisticated example demonstrates both how a destructor would be written and how it would be invoked. PHP will look for a ::__destruct() method on any object when it goes out of scope and will invoke it at that point in time. This destructor explicitly dereferences the object by calling unset() to remove it from the program. You could just as easily have set the variable referencing the object to null with the same result.

Unlike object constructors, destructors do not accept any parameters. If your object needs to act on any external state while cleaning up after itself, be sure that state is referenced through a property on the object itself. Otherwise, you will not have access to that information.

See Also

Documentation on constructors and destructors (*https://oreil.ly/fJMGM*).

8.5 Using Magic Methods to Provide Dynamic Properties

Problem

You want to define a custom class without predefining the properties it supports.

Solution

Use magic getters and setters to handle dynamically defined properties as follows:

```
class Magical
{
    private array $_data = [];

    public function __get(string $name): mixed
    {
        if (isset($this->_data[$name])) {
            return $this->_data[$name];
        }

        throw new Error(sprintf('Property `%s` is not defined', $name));
    }

    public function __set(string $name, mixed $value)
    {
        $this->_data[$name] = $value;
    }
}

$first = new Magical;
$first->custom = 'hello';
$first->another = 'world';

echo $first->custom . ' ' . $first->another . PHP_EOL;

echo $first->unknown; // Error
```

Discussion

When you reference a property on an object that does not exist, PHP falls back on a set of *magic methods* to fill in the blanks on implementation. The getter is used automatically when attempting to reference a property, while the corresponding setter is used when assigning a value to a property.

Property overloading by way of magic methods only works on instantiated objects. It does not work on the static class definition.

Internally, you then control the behavior of getting and setting data in its entirety. The Solution example stores its data in a private associative array. You can further flesh out this example by fully implementing magic methods for handling isset() and unset(). Example 8-9 demonstrates how magic methods can be used to fully replicate a standard class definition, but without the need to predeclare all properties.

Example 8-9. Full object definition with magic methods

```php
class Basic
{
    public function __construct(
        public string $word,
        public int $number
    ) {}
}

class Magic
{
    private array $_data = [];

    public function __get(string $name): mixed
    {
        if (isset($this->_data[$name])) {
            return $this->_data[$name];
        }

        throw new Error(sprintf('Property `%s` is not defined', $name));
    }

    public function __set(string $name, mixed $value)
    {
        $this->_data[$name] = $value;
    }

    public function __isset(string $name): bool
    {
```

```
        return array_key_exists($name, $this->_data);
    }

    public function __unset(string $name): void
    {
        unset($this->_data[$name]);
    }
}

$basic = new Basic('test', 22);

$magic = new Magic;
$magic->word = 'test';
$magic->number = 22;
```

In Example 8-9, the two objects are functionally equivalent if and only if the only dynamic properties used on a Magic instance are those already defined by Basic. This dynamic nature is what makes the approach so valuable even if the class definitions are painfully verbose. You might choose to wrap a remote API in a class implementing magic methods in order to expose that API's data to your application in an object-oriented manner.

See Also

Documentation on magic methods (*https://oreil.ly/1ZtlE*).

8.6 Extending Classes to Define Additional Functionality

Problem

You want to define a class that adds functionality to an existing class definition.

Solution

Use the extends keyword to define additional methods or override existing functionality as follows:

```
class A
{
    public function hello(): string
    {
        return 'hello';
    }
}

class B extends A
{
    public function world(): string
    {
```

```
        return 'world';
    }
}

$instance = new B();
echo "{$instance->hello()} {$instance->world()}";
```

Discussion

Object inheritance is a common concept for any high-level language; it's a way you build new objects on top of other, often simpler object definitions. The Solution example illustrates how a class can *inherit* method definitions from a parent class, which is the core functionality of PHP's inheritance model.

 PHP does not support inheriting from multiple parent classes. To pull in code implementations from multiple sources, PHP leverages *traits*, which are covered by Recipe 8.13.

In fact, a child class inherits every public and protected method, property, and constant from its parent class (the class it's extending). Private methods, properties, and constants are *never* inherited by a child class.[8]

A child class can also override its parent's implementation of a particular method. In practice, you would do this to change the internal logic of a particular method, but the method signature exposed by the child class must match that defined by the parent. Example 8-10 demonstrates how a child class would override its parent's implementation of a method.

Example 8-10. Overriding a parent method implementation

```
class A
{
    public function greet(string $name): string
    {
        return 'Good morning, ' . $name;
    }
}

class B extends A
{
    public function greet(string $name): string
    {
        return 'Howdy, ' . $name;
```

---

8 For more on property and method visibility, review "Visibility" on page 166.

```
    }
}

$first = new A();
echo $first->greet('Alice');  ❶

$second = new B();
echo $second->greet('Bob');  ❷
```

❶ Prints Good morning, Alice

❷ Prints Howdy, Bob

An overridden child method does not lose all sense of the parent's implementation, though. Inside a class, you reference the $this variable to refer to that particular instance of the object. Likewise, you can reference the parent keyword to refer to the parent implementation of a function. For example:

```
class A
{
    public function hello(): string
    {
        return 'hello';
    }
}

class B extends A
{
    public function hello(): string
    {
        return parent::hello() . ' world';
    }
}

$instance = new B();
echo $instance->hello();
```

See Also

Documentation and discussion of PHP's object inheritance model (*https://oreil.ly/ nsAM3*).

8.7 Forcing Classes to Exhibit Specific Behavior

Problem

You want to define the methods on a class that will be used elsewhere in your application while leaving the actual method implementations up to someone else.

Solution

Define an object interface and leverage that interface in your application as follows:

```php
interface ArtifactRepository
{
    public function create(Artifact $artifact): bool;
    public function get(int $artifactId): ?Artifact;
    public function getAll(): array;
    public function update(Artifact $artifact): bool;
    public function delete(int $artifactId): bool;
}

class Museum
{
    public function __construct(
        protected ArtifactRepository $repository
    ) {}

    public function enumerateArtifacts(): Generator
    {
        foreach($this->repository->getAll() as $artifact) {
            yield $artifact;
        }
    }
}
```

Discussion

An interface looks similar to a class definition, except it only defines the *signatures* of specific methods rather than their implementations. The interface does, however, define a type that can be used elsewhere in your application—so long as a class directly implements a given interface, an instance of that class can be used as if it were the same type as the interface itself.

 There are several situations in which you might have two classes that implement the same methods and expose the same signatures to your application. However, unless these classes explicitly implement the same interface (as evidenced by the implements keyword), they cannot be used interchangeably in a strictly typed application.

An implementation must use the implements keyword to tell the PHP compiler what's going on. The Solution example illustrates how an interface is defined and how another part of the code can leverage that interface. Example 8-11 demonstrates how the ArtifactRepository interface might be implemented using an in-memory array for data storage.

Example 8-11. Explicit interface implementation

```php
class MemoryRepository implements ArtifactRepository
{
    private array $_collection = [];

    private function nextKey(): int
    {
        $keys = array_keys($this->_collection);
        $max = array_reduce($keys, function($c, $i) {
            return max($c, $i);
        }, 0);

        return $max + 1;
    }

    public function create(Artifact $artifact): bool
    {
        if ($artifact->id === null) {
            $artifact->id = $this->nextKey();
        }

        if (array_key_exists($artifact->id, $this->_collection)) {
            return false;
        }

        $this->_collection[$artifact->id] = $artifact;
        return true;
    }
    public function get(int $artifactId): ?Artifact
    {
        return $this->_collection[$artifactId] ?? null;
    }
    public function getAll(): array
    {
        return array_values($this->_collection);
    }
    public function update(Artifact $artifact): bool
    {
        if (array_key_exists($artifact->id, $this->_collection)) {
            $this->_collection[$artifact->id] = $artifact;
            return true;
        }

        return false;
    }
    public function delete(int $artifactId): bool
    {
        if (array_key_exists($artifactId, $this->_collection)) {
            unset($this->_collection[$artifactId]);
            return true;
        }
```

```
        return false;
    }
}
```

Throughout your application, any method can declare a type on a parameter by using the interface itself. The Solution example's `Museum` class takes a concrete implementation of the `ArtifactRepository` as its only parameter. This class can then operate knowing what the exposed API of the repository will look like. The code doesn't care *how* each method is implemented, only that it matches the interface's defined signature exactly.

A class definition can implement many different interfaces at once. This allows for a complex object to be used in different situations by different pieces of code. Note that, if two or more interfaces define the same method name, their defined signatures must be identical, as illustrated by Example 8-12.

Example 8-12. Implementing multiple interfaces at once

```
interface A
{
    public function foo(): int;
}

interface B
{
    public function foo(): int;
}

interface C
{
    public function foo(): string;
}

class First implements A, B
{
    public function foo(): int ❶
    {
        return 1;
    }
}

class Second implements A, C
{
    public function foo(): int|string ❷
    {
        return 'nope';
    }
}
```

❶ As both A and B define the same method signature, this implementation is valid.

❷ Since A and C define different return types, there is no way, even with union types, to define a class that implements both interfaces. Attempting to do so causes a fatal error.

Remember also that interfaces look somewhat like classes so, like classes, they can be extended.[9] This is done through the same extends keyword and results in an interface that is a composition of two or more interfaces, as demonstrated in Example 8-13.

Example 8-13. Composite interfaces

```
interface A ❶
{
    public function foo(): void;
}

interface B extends A ❷
{
    public function bar(): void;
}

class C implements B
{
    public function foo(): void
    {
        // ... actual implementation
    }

    public function bar(): void
    {
        // ... actual implementation
    }
}
```

❶ Any class implementing A must define the foo() method.

❷ Any class implementing B must implement both bar() and foo() from A.

See Also

Documentation on object interfaces (*https://oreil.ly/A8hkg*).

---

9 Review Recipe 8.6 for more on class inheritance and extension.

8.8 Creating Abstract Base Classes

Problem

You want a class to implement a specific interface but also want to define some other specific functionality.

Solution

Rather than implementing an interface, define an abstract base class that can be extended as follows:

```
abstract class Base
{
    abstract public function getData(): string;

    public function printData(): void
    {
        echo $this->getData();
    }
}

class Concrete extends Base
{
    public function getData(): string
    {
        return bin2hex(random_bytes(16));
    }
}

$instance = new Concrete;
$instance->printData(); ❶
```

❶ Prints something like 6ec2aff42d5904e0ccef15536d8548dc

Discussion

An abstract class looks somewhat like an interface and a regular class definition smashed together. It has some unimplemented methods living alongside concrete implementations. As with an interface, you cannot instantiate an abstract class directly—you have to extend it first and implement any abstract methods it defines. As with a class, however, you will automatically have access to any public or protected members of the base class in the child implementation.[10]

---

10 See Recipe 8.6 for more on class inheritance.

One key difference between interfaces and abstract classes is that the latter can bundle properties and method definitions with it. Abstract classes are, in fact, classes that are merely incomplete implementations. An interface cannot have properties—it merely defines the functional interface with which any implementing object must comply.

Another difference is that you can implement multiple interfaces simultaneously, but you can only extend one class at a time. This limitation alone helps characterize when you would leverage an abstract base class versus an interface—but you can also mix and match both!

It's also possible for an abstract class to define *private* members (which are not inherited by any child class) that are otherwise leveraged by accessible methods, as illustrated by the following:

```
abstract class A
{
    private string $data = 'this is a secret'; ❶

    abstract public function viewData(): void;

    public function getData(): string
    {
        return $this->data; ❷
    }
}

class B extends A
{
    public function viewData(): void
    {
        echo $this->getData() . PHP_EOL; ❸
    }
}

$instance = new B();
$instance->viewData(); ❹
```

❶ By making your data private, it is only accessible within the context of A.

❷ As ::getData() is itself defined by A, the $data property is still accessible.

❸ Though ::viewData() is defined in the scope of B, it is accessing a public method from the scope of A. No code in B would have direct access to A's private members.

❹ This will print this is a secret to the console.

See Also

Documentation and discussion of class abstraction (*https://oreil.ly/FMkcT*).

8.9 Preventing Changes to Classes and Methods

Problem

You want to prevent anyone from modifying the implementation of your class or extending it with a child class.

Solution

Use the final keyword to indicate that a class is not extensible, as follows:

```
final class Immutable
{
    // Class definition
}
```

Or use the final keyword to mark a particular method as unchangeable, as follows:

```
class Mutable
{
    final public function fixed(): void
    {
        // Method definition
    }
}
```

Discussion

The final keyword is a way to explicitly *prevent* object extension like the mechanisms discussed in the previous two recipes. It's useful when you want to ensure that a specific implementation of a method or an entire class is used throughout a codebase.

Marking a method as final means that any class extensions are incapable of overriding that method's implementation. The following example will throw a fatal error due to the Child class's attempt to override a final method in the Base class:

```
class Base
{
    public function safe()
    {
        echo 'safe() inside Base class' . PHP_EOL;
    }

    final public function unsafe()
    {
        echo 'unsafe() inside Base class' . PHP_EOL;
```

```
    }
}

class Child extends Base
{
    public function safe()
    {
        echo 'safe() inside Child class' . PHP_EOL;
    }

    public function unsafe()
    {
        echo 'unsafe() inside Child class' . PHP_EOL;
    }
}
```

In the preceding example, merely omitting the definition of unsafe() from the child class will allow the code to execute as expected. If, however, you wanted to prevent any class from extending the base class, you could add the final keyword to the class definition itself as follows:

```
final class Base
{
    public function safe()
    {
        echo 'safe() inside Base class' . PHP_EOL;
    }

    public function unsafe()
    {
        echo 'unsafe() inside Base class' . PHP_EOL;
    }
}
```

The only time you should leverage final in your code is when overriding a specific method or class implementation will break your application. This is somewhat rare in practice but is useful when creating a flexible interface. A specific example would be when your application introduces an interface as well as concrete implementations of that interface.[11] Your API would then be constructed to accept any valid interface implementation, but you might want to prevent subclassing your own concrete implementations (again because doing so might break your application). Example 8-14 demonstrates how these dependencies might be constructed in a real application.

---

11 See Recipe 8.7 for more on interfaces.

Example 8-14. Interfaces and concrete classes

```php
interface DataAbstraction ❶
{
    public function save();
}

final class DBImplementation implements DataAbstraction ❷
{
    public function __construct(string $databaseConnection)
    {
        // Connect to a database
    }

    public function save()
    {
        // Save some data
    }
}

final class FileImplementation implements DataAbstraction ❸
{
    public function __construct(string $filename)
    {
        // Open a file for writing
    }

    public function save()
    {
        // Write to the file
    }
}

class Application
{
    public function __construct(
        protected DataAbstraction $datalayer ❹
    ) {}
}
```

❶   The application describes an interface that any data abstraction layer must implement.

❷   One concrete implementation stores data explicitly in a database.

❸   Another implementation uses flat files for data storage.

❹   The application doesn't care what implementation you use so long as it implements the base interface. You can use either the provided (`final`) classes or define your own implementation.

In some situations, you might come across a final class you need to extend anyway. In those cases, the only means at your disposal are to leverage a decorator. A *decorator* is a class that takes another class as a constructor property and "decorates" its methods with additional functionality.

 In some circumstances, decorators will not allow you to sidestep the final nature of a class. This happens if type hinting and strict typing require an instance of that exact class be passed to a function or another object within the application.

Assume, for example, that a library in your application defines a Note class that implements a ::publish() method that publishes a given piece of data to social media (say, Twitter). You want this method to *also* produce a static PDF artifact of the given data and would normally extend the class itself, as shown in Example 8-15.

Example 8-15. Typical class extension without the final keyword

```
class Note
{
    public function publish()
    {
        // Publish the note's data to Twitter ...
    }
}

class StaticNote extends Note
{
    public function publish()
    {
        parent::publish();

        // Also produce a static PDF of the note's data ...
    }
}

$note = new StaticNote(); ❶
$note->publish(); ❷
```

❶   Rather than instantiating a Note object, you can instantiate a StaticNote directly.

❷   When you call the object's ::publish() method, *both* class definitions are used.

If the Note class is instead final, you will be unable to extend the class directly. Example 8-16 demonstrates how a new class can be created that *decorates* the Note class and indirectly extends its functionality.

Example 8-16. Customizing hte behavior of a final class with a decorator

```
final class Note
{
    public function publish()
    {
        // Publish the note's data to Twitter ...
    }
}

final class StaticNote
{
    public function __construct(private Note $note) {}

    public function publish()
    {
        $this->note->publish();

        // Also produce a static PDF of the note's data ...
    }
}

$note = new StaticNote(new Note()); ❶
$note->publish(); ❷
```

❶ Rather than instantiating `StaticNote` directly, you use this class to *wrap* (or *decorate*) a regular `Note` instance.

❷ When you call the object's `::publish()` method, *both* class definitions are used.

See Also

Documentation on the `final` keyword (*https://oreil.ly/k2ZGz*).

8.10 Cloning Objects

Problem

You want to create a distinct copy of an object.

Solution

Use the `clone` keyword to create a second copy of the object—for example:

```
$dolly = clone $roslin;
```

Discussion

By default, PHP will copy objects *by reference* when assigned to a new variable. This reference means the new variable literally points to the same object in memory. Example 8-17 illustrates how, even though it might appear that you've created a copy of an object, you're really dealing with just two references to the same data.

Example 8-17. The assignment operator copies an object by reference

```
$obj1 = (object) [ ❶
    'propertyOne' => 'some',
    'propertyTwo' => 'data',
];
$obj2 = $obj1; ❷

$obj2->propertyTwo = 'changed'; ❸

var_dump($obj1); ❹
var_dump($obj2);
```

❶ This particular syntax is shorthand, valid as of PHP 5.4, that dynamically converts a new associative array to an instance of the built-in stdClass class.

❷ Attempt to copy the first object to a new instance by using the assignment operator.

❸ Make a change to the internal state of the "copied" object.

❹ Inspecting the original object shows that its internal state has changed. Both $obj1 and $obj2 point to the same space in memory; you merely copied a reference to the object, not the object itself!

Rather than copy an object reference, the clone keyword copies an object to a new variable *by value*. This means all of the properties are copied to a new instance of the same class that has all of the methods of the original object as well. Example 8-18 illustrates how the two objects are now entirely decoupled.

Example 8-18. The clone keyword copies an object by value

```
$obj1 = (object) [
    'propertyOne' => 'some',
    'propertyTwo' => 'data',
];
$obj2 = clone $obj1; ❶

$obj2->propertyTwo = 'changed'; ❷
```

```
var_dump($obj1); ❸
var_dump($obj2); ❹
```

❶ Rather than use strict assignment, leverage the `clone` keyword to create a by-value copy of the object.

❷ Again make a change to the internal state of the copy.

❸ Inspecting the state of the original object shows no changes.

❹ The cloned and changed object, however, illustrates the property modification made earlier.

An important caveat here is to understand that, as used in the preceding examples, `clone` is a *shallow clone* of the data. The operation does not traverse down into more complex properties like nested objects. Even with proper `clone` usage, it is possible to be left with two different variables referencing the same object in memory. Example 8-19 illustrates what happens if the object to be copied contains a more complex object itself.

Example 8-19. Shallow clones of complex data structures

```
$child = (object) [
    'name' => 'child',
];
$parent = (object) [
    'name'  => 'parent',
    'child' => $child
];

$clone = clone $parent;

if ($parent === $clone) { ❶
    echo 'The parent and clone are the same object!' . PHP_EOL;
}

if ($parent == $clone) { ❷
    echo 'The parent and clone have the same data!' . PHP_EOL;
}

if ($parent->child === $clone->child) { ❸
    echo 'The parent and the clone have the same child!' . PHP_EOL;
}
```

❶ When comparing objects, strict comparison only resolves as `true` when the statements on either side of the comparison reference the same object. In this case, you've properly cloned your object and created an entirely new instance, so this comparison is `false`.

 Loose type comparison between objects resolves as `true` when the *values* on either side of the operator are the same, even between discrete instances. This statement evaluates to `true`.

❸ Since `clone` is a shallow operation, the `::$child` property on both of your objects points to the same child object in memory. This statement evaluates to `true`!

To support a deeper clone, the class being cloned must implement a `__clone()` magic method that tells PHP what to do when leveraging `clone`. If this method exists, PHP will invoke it automatically when closing an instance of the class. Example 8-20 shows exactly how this might work while still working with dynamic classes.

 It is not possible to dynamically define methods on instances of `stdClass`. If you want to support deep cloning of objects in your application, you must either define a class directly or leverage an anonymous class, as illustrated by Example 8-20.

Example 8-20. Deep cloning of objects

```
$parent = new class {
    public string $name = 'parent';
    public stdClass $child;

    public function __clone()
    {
        $this->child = clone $this->child;
    }
};
$parent->child = (object) [
    'name' => 'child'
];

$clone = clone $parent;

if ($parent === $clone) { ❶
    echo 'The parent and clone are the same object!' . PHP_EOL;
}

if ($parent == $clone) { ❷
    echo 'The parent and clone have the same data!' . PHP_EOL;
}

if ($parent->child === $clone->child) { ❸
```

```
    echo 'The parent and the clone have the same child!' . PHP_EOL;
}

if ($parent->child == $clone->child) { ❹
    echo 'The parent and the clone have the same child data!' . PHP_EOL;
}
```

❶ The objects are different references; therefore, this evaluates to `false`.

❷ The parent and clone objects have the same data, so this evaluates to `true`.

❸ The `::$child` properties were also cloned internally, so the properties reference different object instances. This evaluates to `false`.

❹ Both `::$child` properties contain the same data, so this evaluates to `true`.

In most applications, you will generally be working with custom class definitions and not anonymous classes. In that case, you can still implement the magic `__clone()` method to instruct PHP on how to clone the more complex properties of your object where necessary.

See Also

Documentation on the `clone` keyword (*https://oreil.ly/LqOE2*).

8.11 Defining Static Properties and Methods

Problem

You want to define a method or property on a class that is available to all instances of that class.

Solution

Use the `static` keyword to define properties or methods that can be accessed outside an object instance—for example:

```
class Foo
{
    public static int $counter = 0;

    public static function increment(): void
    {
        self::$counter += 1;
    }
}
```

Discussion

Static members of a class are accessible to any part of your code (assuming proper levels of visibility) directly from the class definition, whether or not an instance of that class exists as an object. Static properties are useful since they behave more or less like global variables but are scoped to a specific class definition. Example 8-21 illustrates the difference in invoking a global variable versus a static class property in another function.

Example 8-21. Static properties versus global variables

```
class Foo
{
    public static string $name = 'Foo';
}

$bar = 'Bar';

function demonstration()
{
    global $bar; ❶

    echo Foo::$name . $bar; ❷
}
```

❶ To access a global variable within another scope, you must explicitly refer to the global scope. Given that you can have separate variables in a narrower scope that match the names of global variables, this can become potentially confusing in practice.

❷ A class-scoped property, however, can be accessed directly based on the name of the class itself.

More usefully, static methods provide ways to invoke utility functionality bound to a class prior to instantiating an object of that class directly. One common example is when constructing value objects that should represent serialized data where it would be difficult to construct an object from scratch directly.

Example 8-22 demonstrates a class that does not allow for direct instantiation. Instead, you must create an instance by unserializing some fixed data. The constructor is inaccessible outside of the class's interior scope, so a static method is the only means of creating an object.

Example 8-22. Static method object instantiation

```
class BinaryString
{
    private function __construct(private string $bits) {} ❶

    public static function fromHex(string $hex): self
    {
        return new self(hex2bin($hex)); ❷
    }

    public static function fromBase64(string $b64): self
    {
        return new self(base64_decode($b64));
    }

    public function __toString(): string ❸
    {
        return bin2hex($this->bits);
    }
}

$rawData = '48656c6c6f20776f726c6421';
$binary = BinaryString::fromHex($rawData); ❹
```

❶ A private constructor can be accessed only from within the class itself.

❷ Within a static method, you can still create a new object instance by leveraging the special `self` keyword to refer to the class. This permits you to access your private constructor.

❸ The magic `__toString()` method is invoked whenever PHP tries to coerce an object into a string directly (i.e., when you try to echo it to the console).

❹ Rather than creating an object with the `new` keyword, leverage a purpose-built static deserialization method.

Both static methods and properties are subject to the same visibility constraints as their nonstatic peers. Note that marking either as `private` means they can only be referenced by one another or by nonstatic methods within the class itself.

As static methods and properties aren't tied directly to an object instance, you can't use regular object-bound accessors to reach them. Instead, leverage the class name directly and the scope resolution operator (a double colon, or `::`)—for example, `Foo::$bar` for properties or `Foo::bar()` for methods. Within the class definition itself, you can leverage `self` as a shorthand for the class name or `parent` as a shorthand for the parent class name (if using inheritance).

 If you have access to an object instance of the class, you can use that object's name rather than the class name to access its static members as well. For example, you can use `$foo::bar()` to access the static `bar()` method on the class definition for the object named `$foo`. While this works, it can make it more difficult for other developers to understand what class definition you're working with, so this syntax should be used sparingly if at all.

See Also

Documentation on the `static` keyword (*https://oreil.ly/tlxjn*).

8.12 Introspecting Private Properties or Methods Within an Object

Problem

You want to enumerate the properties or methods of an object and leverage its private members.

Solution

Use PHP's Reflection API to enumerate properties and methods. For example:

```
$reflected = new ReflectionClass('SuperSecretClass');

$methods = $reflected->getMethods(); ❶
$properties = $reflected->getProperties(); ❷
```

Discussion

PHP's Reflection API grants developers vast power to inspect all elements of their application. You can enumerate methods, properties, constants, function arguments, and more. You can also ignore the privacy afforded to each at will and directly invoke private methods on objects. Example 8-23 illustrates how an explicitly private method can be invoked directly with the Reflection API.

Example 8-23. Using Reflection to violate class privacy

```
class Foo
{
    private int $counter = 0; ❶
```

```
    public function increment(): void
    {
        $this->counter += 1;
    }

    public function getCount(): int
    {
        return $this->counter;
    }
}

$instance = new Foo;
$instance->increment(); ❷
$instance->increment(); ❸

echo $instance->getCount() . PHP_EOL; ❹

$instance->counter = 0; ❺

$reflectionClass = new ReflectionClass('Foo');
$reflectionClass->getProperty('counter')->setValue($instance, 0); ❻

echo $instance->getCount() . PHP_EOL; ❼
```

❶ The example class has a single, private property to maintain an internal counter.

❷ You want to increment the counter a bit past its default. Now it's 1.

❸ An additional increment sets the counter to 2.

❹ At this point, printing out the counter's state will confirm it's 2.

❺ Attempting to interact with the counter *directly* will result in a thrown Error, as the property is private.

❻ Through reflection, you can interact with object members regardless of their privacy setting.

❼ Now you demonstrate the counter was truly reset to 0.

Reflection is a truly powerful way to get around visibility modifiers in the API exposed by a class. However, its use in a production application likely points to a poorly constructed interface or system. If your code needs access to a private member of a class, either that member should be public to begin with or you need to create an appropriate accessor method.

The only legitimate use of Reflection is in inspecting and modifying the internal state of an object. In an application, this behavior should be limited to the class's exposed API. In *testing*, however, it might be necessary to modify an object's state between test runs in ways the API doesn't support during regular operation.[12] Those rare circumstances might require resetting internal counters or invoking otherwise private cleanup methods housed within the class. It's then that Reflection proves its utility.

In regular application development, though, Reflection paired with functional calls like var_dump() (*https://oreil.ly/HXVwr*) helps to disambiguate the internal operation of classes defined in imported vendor code. It might prove useful to introspect serialized objects or third-party integrations, but take care not to ship this kind of introspection to production.

See Also

Overview of PHP's Reflection API (*https://oreil.ly/C49RP*).

8.13 Reusing Arbitrary Code Between Classes

Problem

You want to share a particular piece of functionality between multiple classes without leveraging a class extension.

Solution

Import a Trait with a use statement—for example:

```
trait Logger
{
    public function log(string $message): void
    {
        error_log($message);
    }
}

class Account
{
    use Logger; ❶

    public function __construct(public int $accountNumber)
    {
        $this->log("Created account {$accountNumber}.");
    }
```

---

12 Both testing and debugging are discussed at length in Chapter 13.

```
}

class User extends Person
{
    use Logger; ❷

    public function authenticate(): bool
    {
        // ...
        $this->log("User {$userId} logged in.");
        // ...
    }
}
```

❶ The Account class imports the logging functionality from your Logger trait and can use its methods as if they were native to its own definition.

❷ Likewise, the User class has native-level access to Logger's methods, even though it extends a base Person class with additional functionality.

Discussion

As discussed in Recipe 8.6, a class in PHP can descend from at most one other class. This is referred to as *single inheritance* and is a characteristic of languages other than PHP as well. Luckily, PHP exposes an additional mechanism for code reuse called *Traits*. Traits allow for the encapsulation of some functionality in a separate class-like definition that can be easily imported without breaking single inheritance.

A Trait looks somewhat like a class but cannot be instantiated directly. Instead, the methods defined by a Trait are imported into another class definition by the use statement. This permits code reuse between classes that do not share an inheritance tree.

Traits empower you to define common methods (with differing method visibility) and properties that are shared between definitions. You can also override the default visibility from a Trait in the class that imports it. Example 8-24 shows how an otherwise public method defined in a Trait can be imported as a protected or even private method in another class.

Example 8-24. Overriding the visibility of methods defined in a Trait

```
trait Foo
{
    public function bar()
    {
        echo 'Hello World!';
    }
}
```

```
class A
{
    use Foo { bar as protected; } ❶
}

class B
{
    use Foo { bar as private; } ❷
}
```

❶ This syntax will import every method defined in Foo but will explicitly make its ::bar() method protected within the scope of class A. This means only instances of class A (or its descendants) will be able to invoke the method.

❷ Likewise, class B changes the visibility of its imported ::foo() method to private so only instances of B can access that method directly.

Traits can be composed together as deeply as you want, meaning a Trait can use another Trait just as easily as a class can. Likewise, there is no limit to the number of Traits that can be imported either by other Traits or by class definitions.

If the class importing a Trait (or multiple Traits) defines a method also named in the Trait, then the class's version takes precedence and is used by default. Example 8-25 illustrates how this precedence works by default.

Example 8-25. Method precedence in Traits

```
trait Foo
{
    public function bar(): string
    {
        return 'FooBar';
    }
}

class Bar
{
    use Foo;
    public function bar(): string
    {
        return 'BarFoo';
    }
}

$instance = new Bar;
echo $instance->bar(); // BarFoo
```

In some circumstances, you might import multiple Traits that all define the same method. In those situations, you can explicitly identify which version of a method you want to leverage in your final class when you define your use statement as follows:

```php
trait A
{
    public function hello(): string
    {
        return 'Hello';
    }

    public function world(): string
    {
        return 'Universe';
    }
}

trait B
{
    public function world(): string
    {
        return 'World';
    }
}

class Demonstration
{
    use A, B {
        B::world insteadof A;
    }
}

$instance = new Demonstration;
echo "{$instance->hello()} {$instance->world()}!"; // Hello World!
```

Like class definitions, Traits can also define properties or even static members. They provide an efficient means by which you can abstract operational logic definitions into reusable code blocks and share that logic between classes in your application.

See Also

Documentation on Traits (*https://oreil.ly/sykOE*).

## CHAPTER 9

Security and Encryption

PHP is a remarkably easy-to-use language because of the forgiving nature of the runtime. Even when you make a mistake, PHP will try to infer what you *meant* to do and, often, keep executing your program just fine. Unfortunately, this strength is also seen by some developers as a key weakness. By being forgiving, PHP allows for a sheer amount of "bad" code to continue functioning as if it were correct.

Worse still, much of this "bad" code finds its way into tutorials, leading developers to copy and paste it into their own projects and perpetuate the cycle. This forgiving runtime and long history of PHP have led to the perception that PHP itself is insecure. In reality, it's easy to use *any* programming language insecurely.

Natively, PHP supports the ability to quickly and easily filter malicious input and sanitize user data. In a web context, this utility is critical to keeping user information safe from malicious inputs or attacks. PHP also exposes well-defined functions for both securely hashing and securely validating passwords during authentication.

PHP's default password hashing and validation functions both leverage secure hashing algorithms and constant-time, secure implementations. This protects your application against niche attacks like those using timing information in an attempt to extract information. Attempting to implement hashing (or validation) yourself would likely expose your application to risks for which PHP has already accounted.

The language also makes cryptography—for both encryption and signatures—simple for developers. Native, high-level interfaces protect you from the kinds of mistakes easily made elsewhere.[1] In fact, PHP is one of the *easiest* languages in which developers can leverage strong, modern cryptography without relying on a third-party extension or implementation!

Legacy Encryption

Earlier versions of PHP shipped with an extension called mcrypt (*https://oreil.ly/I7stH*). This extension exposed the lower-level mcrypt library, allowing developers to easily leverage a variety of block ciphers and hash algorithms. It was removed in PHP 7.2 in favor of the newer sodium extension, but it can still be manually installed via the PHP Extension Community Library (PECL).[2]

> While still available, the mcrypt library has not been updated in over a decade and should not be used in new projects. For any new encryption needs, use either PHP's bindings against OpenSSL or the native sodium extension.

PHP also supports direct use of the OpenSSL library through an extension (*https://oreil.ly/cYNB2*). This is helpful when building a system that must interoperate with legacy cryptographic libraries. However, the extension does not expose the full-feature offering of OpenSSL to PHP; it would be useful to review the functions (*https://oreil.ly/Y8xEK*) and features exposed to identify whether PHP's implementation would be useful to your application.

In any case, the newer sodium interfaces support a wide range of cryptographic operations in PHP and should be preferred over either OpenSSL or mcrypt.

Sodium

PHP formally added the sodium (*https://oreil.ly/gH1Va*) extension (also known as *Libsodium*) as a core extension in version 7.2, released in late 2017.[3] This library supports high-level abstractions for encryption, cryptographic signatures, password hashing, and more. It is itself an open source fork of an earlier project, the Networking and Cryptography Library (NaCl) (*https://nacl.cr.yp.to*) by Daniel J. Bernstein.

---

1 The OpenJDK Psychic Signatures bug of 2022 (*https://oreil.ly/uvYXZ*) illustrated how an error in cryptographic authentication could expose not just applications *but an entire language implementation* to potential abuse by malicious actors. This bug was due to an implementation error, further underscoring how critical it is to rely on solid, proven, well-tested primitives when using cryptographic systems.

2 For more on native extensions, see Chapter 15.

3 For a full breakdown of the process through which this extension was added to PHP core, reference the original RFC (*https://oreil.ly/6X4AF*).

Both projects add easy-to-use, high-speed tools for developers who need to work with encryption. The opinionated nature of their exposed interfaces aims to make cryptography *safe* and proactively avoid the pitfalls presented by other low-level tools. Shipping with well-defined opinionated interfaces helps developers make the right choices about algorithm implementations and defaults because those very choices (and potential mistakes) are entirely abstracted away and presented in safe, straight-forward functions for everyday use.

> The only problem with sodium and its exposed interfaces is a lack of brevity. Every function is prefixed with `sodium_`, and every constant with `SODIUM_`. The high level of descriptiveness in both function and constant names makes it easy to understand what is happening in code. However, this also leads to incredibly long and potentially distracting function names, like `sodium_crypto_sign_keypair_from_secretkey_and_publickey()`.

While sodium is bundled as a core extension for PHP, it also exposes bindings for several other languages (*https://oreil.ly/L9JPp*) as well. It is fully interoperable with everything from .NET to Go to Java to Python.

Unlike many other cryptographic libraries, sodium focuses primarily on *authenticated* encryption. Every piece of data is automatically paired with an authentication tag that the library can later use to validate the integrity of the underlying plaintext. If this tag is missing or invalid, the library throws an error to alert the developer that the associated plaintext is unreliable.

This use of authentication isn't unique—the Galois/Counter Mode (GCM) of the Advanced Encryption Standard (AES) does effectively the same thing. However, other libraries often leave authentication and validation of an authentication tag as an exercise for the developer. There are a number of tutorials, books, and Stack Overflow discussions that point to a proper implementation of AES but omit the validation of the GCM tag affixed to a message! The sodium extension abstracts both authentication and validation away and provides a clear, concise implementation, as illustrated in Example 9-1.

Example 9-1. Authenticated encryption and decryption in sodium

```
$nonce = random_bytes(SODIUM_CRYPTO_SECRETBOX_NONCEBYTES); ❶

$key = random_bytes(SODIUM_CRYPTO_SECRETBOX_KEYBYTES); ❷

$message = 'This is a super secret communication!';

$ciphertext = sodium_crypto_secretbox($message, $nonce, $key); ❸
```

```
$output = bin2hex($nonce . $ciphertext); ❹

// Decoding and decryption reverses the preceding steps
$bytes = hex2bin($input); ❺
$nonce = substr($bytes, 0, SODIUM_CRYPTO_SECRETBOX_NONCEBYTES);
$ciphertext = substr($bytes, SODIUM_CRYPTO_SECRETBOX_NONCEBYTES);

$plaintext = sodium_crypto_secretbox_open($ciphertext, $nonce, $key); ❻

if ($plaintext === false) { ❼
    throw new Exception('Unable to decrypt!');
}
```

❶ Encryption algorithms are deterministic—the same input will always produce the same output. To ensure that encrypting the same data with the same key returns *different* outputs, you need to use a sufficiently random *nonce* (number used once) to initialize the algorithm each time.

❷ For symmetric encryption, you leverage a single, shared key used to both encrypt and decrypt data. While the key in this example is random, you would likely store this encryption key somewhere outside the application for safekeeping.

❸ Encrypting is incredibly straightforward. Sodium chooses the algorithm and cipher mode for you—all you provide is the message, the random nonce, and the symmetric key. The underlying library does the rest!

❹ When exporting the encrypted value (either to send to another party or to store on disk), you need to keep track of both the random nonce and the subsequent ciphertext. The nonce itself is not secret, so storing it in plaintext alongside the encrypted value is safe (and encouraged). Converting the raw bytes from binary to hexadecimal is an effective way to prepare data for an API request or to store in a database field.

❺ Since the output of encryption is encoded in hexadecimal, you must first decode things back to raw bytes and then separate the nonce and ciphertext components before proceeding with decryption.

❻ To extract the plaintext value back out of an encrypted field, provide the ciphertext with its associated nonce and the original encryption key. The library pulls the plaintext bytes back out and returns them to you.

❼ Internally, the encryption library also adds (and validates) an authentication tag on every encrypted message. If the authentication tag fails to validate during decryption, sodium will return a literal `false` rather than the original plaintext.

This is a sign to you that the message has been tampered with (either intentionally or accidentally) and should not be trusted.

Sodium also introduces an efficient means to handle public-key cryptography. In this paradigm, encryption uses one key (a known or publicly exposed key), while decryption uses an entirely different key known only to the recipient of the message. This two-part key system is ideal when exchanging data between two separate parties over a potentially untrusted medium (like exchanging banking information between a user and their bank over the public internet). In fact, the HTTPS connections used for most websites on the modern internet leverage public-key cryptography under the hood within the browser.

In legacy systems like RSA, you need to keep track of relatively large cryptographic keys in order to exchange information safely. In 2022, the minimum recommended key size for RSA was 3,072 bits; in many situations, developers will default to 4,096 bits to retain the keys' safety against future computing enhancements. Juggling keys of this size can be difficult in some situations. In addition, traditional RSA can only encrypt 256 bytes of data. If you want to encrypt a larger message, you are forced to do the following:

1. Create a 256-bit random key.
2. Use that 256-bit key to *symmetrically* encrypt a message.
3. Use RSA to encrypt the symmetric key.
4. Share both the encrypted message and the encrypted key that protects it.

This is a workable solution, but the steps involved can easily become complicated and introduce unnecessary complexity for a development team building a project that *just happens* to include encryption. Thankfully, sodium fixes this almost entirely!

Sodium's public-key interfaces leverage elliptic-curve cryptography (ECC) rather than RSA. RSA uses prime numbers and exponentiation to create the known (public) and unknown (private) components of the two-key system used for encryption. ECC instead uses the geometry and particular forms of arithmetic against a well-defined elliptic curve. Whereas RSA's public and private components are numbers used for exponentiation, ECC's public and private components are literal x and y coordinates on a geometric curve.

With ECC, a 256-bit key has strength equivalent to that of a 3,072-bit RSA key (*https://oreil.ly/o2kne*). Further, sodium's choice of cryptographic primitives means that its keys are just numbers (rather than x and y coordinates as with most other ECC implementations)—a 256-bit ECC key for sodium is simply a 32-byte integer!

In addition, sodium entirely abstracts the "create a random symmetric key and separately encrypt it" workflow from developers, making asymmetric encryption just as simple in PHP as Example 9-1 demonstrated for symmetric encryption. Example 9-2 illustrates exactly how this form of encryption works, along with the key exchange required between participants.

Example 9-2. Asymmetric encryption and decryption in sodium

```
$bobKeypair = sodium_crypto_box_keypair(); ❶
$bobPublic = sodium_crypto_box_publickey($bobKeypair); ❷
$bobSecret = sodium_crypto_box_secretkey($bobKeypair);

$nonce = random_bytes(SODIUM_CRYPTO_SECRETBOX_NONCEBYTES); ❸

$message = 'Attack at dawn.';

$alicePublic = '...'; ❹

$keyExchange = sodium_crypto_box_keypair_from_secretkey_and_publickey( ❺
    $bobSecret,
    $alicePublic
);

$ciphertext = sodium_crypto_box($message, $nonce, $keyExchange); ❻

$output = bin2hex($nonce . $ciphertext); ❼

// Decrypting the message reverses the key exchange process
$keyExchange2 = sodium_crypto_box_keypair_from_secretkey_and_publickey( ❽
    $aliceSecret,
    $bobPublic
);

$plaintext = sodium_crypto_box_open($ciphertext, $nonce, $keyExchange2); ❾

if ($plaintext === false) { ❿
    throw new Exception('Unable to decrypt!');
}
```

❶ In practice, both parties would generate their public/private key pairs locally and distribute their public keys directly. The `sodium_crypto_box_keypair()` function creates a random key pair each time so, conceivably, you would only need to do this once, so long as the secret key remains private.

❷ Both the public and secret components of the key pair can be extracted separately. This makes it easy to extract and communicate only the public key to a third party but also makes the secret key separately available for use in the later key-exchange operation.

❸ As with symmetric encryption, you need a random nonce for each asymmetric encryption operation.

❹ Alice's public key was potentially distributed via a direct communication channel or is otherwise already known.

❺ The key exchange here isn't being used to agree upon a new key; it's merely combining Bob's secret key with Alice's public key to prepare for Bob to encrypt a message that can only be read by Alice.

❻ Again, sodium chooses the algorithms and cipher modes involved. All you need to do is provide the data, random nonce, and keys, and the library does the rest.

❼ When sending the message, it's useful to concatenate the nonce and ciphertext, then encode the raw bytes as something more readily sent over an HTTP channel. Hexadecimal is a common choice, but Base64 encoding is equally valid.

❽ On the receiving end, Alice needs to combine her own secret key with Bob's public key in order to decrypt a message that could have only been encrypted by Bob.

❾ Extracting the plaintext is as straightforward as encryption was in step 6!

❿ As with symmetric encryption, this operation is authenticated. If the encryption fails for any reason (e.g., Bob's public key was invalid) or the authentication tag fails to validate, sodium returns a literal `false` to indicate the untrustworthiness of the message.

Randomness

In the world of encryption, leveraging a proper source of randomness is critical to protecting any sort of data. Older tutorials heavily reference PHP's `mt_rand()` (*https://oreil.ly/HeBSd*) function, which is a pseudorandom number generator based on the Mersenne Twister algorithm.

Unfortunately, while the output of this function appears random to a casual observer, it is not a cryptographically safe source of randomness. Instead, leverage PHP's `random_bytes()` (*https://oreil.ly/_eYh6*) and `random_int()` (*https://oreil.ly/YWQs8*) functions for anything critical. Both of these functions leverage the cryptographically secure source of randomness built into your local operating system.

A *cryptographically secure pseudorandom number generator* (CSPRNG) is one with an output that is indistinguishable from random noise. Algorithms like the Mersenne Twister are "random enough" to fool a human into thinking they're safe. In reality, they're easy for a computer to predict or even crack, given a series of previous outputs. If an attacker can reliably predict the output of your random number generator, they can conceivably decrypt anything you try to protect based on that generator!

The following recipes cover some of the most important security- and encryption-related concepts in PHP. You'll learn about input validation, proper password storage, and the use of PHP's sodium interface.

9.1 Filtering, Validating, and Sanitizing User Input

Problem

You want to validate a specific value provided by an otherwise untrusted user prior to using it elsewhere in your application.

Solution

Use the `filter_var()` function to validate that the value matches a specific expectation, as follows:

```
$email = $_GET['email'];

$filtered = filter_var($email, FILTER_VALIDATE_EMAIL);
```

Discussion

PHP's filtering extension empowers you to either validate that data matches a specific format or type or sanitize any data that fails that validation. The subtle difference between the two options—validation versus sanitization—is that sanitization removes invalid characters from a value, whereas validation explicitly returns `false` if the final, sanitized input is not of a valid type.

In the Solution example, untrusted user input is explicitly validated as a valid email address. Example 9-3 demonstrates the behavior of this form of validation across multiple potential inputs.

Example 9-3. Testing email validation

```
function validate(string $data): mixed
{
    return filter_var($data, FILTER_VALIDATE_EMAIL);
```

```
}
validate('blah@example.com'); ❶
validate('1234'); ❷
validate('1234@example.com<test>'); ❸
```

❶ Returns `blah@example.com`

❷ Returns `false`

❸ Returns `false`

The alternative to the preceding example is to *sanitize* user input such that invalid characters are stripped from the entry. The result of this sanitization is guaranteed to match a specific character set, but there is no guarantee that the result is a valid input. For example, Example 9-4 properly sanitizes every possible input string even though two results are invalid email addresses.

Example 9-4. Testing email sanitization

```
function sanitize(string $data): mixed
{
    return filter_var($data, FILTER_SANITIZE_EMAIL);
}

sanitize('blah@example.com'); ❶
sanitize('1234'); ❷
sanitize('1234@example.com<test>'); ❸
```

❶ Returns `blah@example.com`

❷ Returns `1234`

❸ Returns `1234@example.comtest`

Whether you want to sanitize or validate your input data depends highly on what you intend to use the resulting data for. If you merely want to keep invalid characters out of a data storage engine, sanitization might be the right approach. If you want to ensure that data is both within the expected character set *and* a valid entry, data validation is a safer tool.

Both approaches are supported equally well by `filter_var()` based on various types of filters in PHP. Specifically, PHP supports validation filters (enumerated in Table 9-1), sanitization filters (enumerated in Table 9-2), and filters falling under neither category (see Table 9-3). The `filter_var()` function also supports an optional third parameter for flags that enable more granular control of the overall output of a filter operation.

Table 9-1. Validation filters supported by PHP

ID	Options	Flags	Description
FILTER_VALIDATE_BOOLEAN	default	FILTER_NULL_ON_FAILURE	Returns `true` for truthy values (1, `true`, `on`, and `yes`), `false` otherwise
FILTER_VALIDATE_DOMAIN	default	FILTER_FLAG_HOSTNAME, FILTER_NULL_ON_FAILURE	Validates whether domain name lengths are valid against various RFCs
FILTER_VALIDATE_EMAIL	default	FILTER_FLAG_EMAIL_UNICODE, FILTER_NULL_ON_FAILURE	Validates an email address against the syntax documented in RFC 822 (*https://oreil.ly/iHPaR*)
FILTER_VALIDATE_FLOAT	default, decimal, min_range, max_range	FILTER_FLAG_ALLOW_THOUSANDS, FILTER_NULL_ON_FAILURE	Validates value as a float, optionally from a specified range, and converts to that type on success
FILTER_VALIDATE_INT	default, max_range, min_range	FILTER_FLAG_ALLOW_OCTAL, FILTER_FLAG_ALLOW_HEX, FILTER_NULL_ON_FAILURE	Validates value as an integer, optionally from a specified range, and converts to that type on success
FILTER_VALIDATE_IP	default	FILTER_FLAG_IPV4, FILTER_FLAG_IPV6, FILTER_FLAG_NO_PRIV_RANGE, FILTER_FLAG_NO_RES_RANGE, FILTER_NULL_ON_FAILURE	Validates value as an IP address
FILTER_VALIDATE_MAC	default	FILTER_NULL_ON_FAILURE	Validates value as a MAC address
FILTER_VALIDATE_REGEXP	default, regexp	FILTER_NULL_ON_FAILURE	Validates value against a Perl-compatible regular expression
FILTER_VALIDATE_URL	default	FILTER_FLAG_SCHEME_REQUIRED, FILTER_FLAG_HOST_REQUIRED, FILTER_FLAG_PATH_REQUIRED, FILTER_FLAG_QUERY_REQUIRED, FILTER_NULL_ON_FAILURE	Validates as a URL according to RFC 2396 (*https://oreil.ly/KiLd3*)

Table 9-2. Sanitization filters supported by PHP

ID	Flags	Description
FILTER_SANITIZE_EMAIL		Removes all characters except letters, digits, and + ! # $ % & ' * + - = ? ^ _ ` { | } ~ @ . [ ]
FILTER_SANITIZE_ENCODED	FILTER_FLAG_STRIP_LOW, FILTER_FLAG_STRIP_HIGH, FILTER_FLAG_STRIP_BACKTICK, FILTER_FLAG_ENCODE_HIGH, FILTER_FLAG_ENCODE_LOW	URL-encodes string, optionally stripping or encoding special characters
FILTER_SANITIZE_ADD_SLASHES		Applies addslashes()
FILTER_SANITIZE_NUMBER_FLOAT	FILTER_FLAG_ALLOW_FRACTION, FILTER_FLAG_ALLOW_THOUSANDS, FILTER_FLAG_ALLOW_SCIENTIFIC	Removes all characters except digits, plus and minus signs, and optionally periods, commas, and uppercase and lowercase *E*s
FILTER_SANITIZE_NUMBER_INT		Removes all characters except digits and plus and minus signs
FILTER_SANITIZE_SPECIAL_CHARS	FILTER_FLAG_STRIP_LOW, FILTER_FLAG_STRIP_HIGH, FILTER_FLAG_STRIP_BACKTICK, FILTER_FLAG_ENCODE_HIGH	HTML-encodes ' " < > & and characters with ASCII values less than 32, optionally strips or encodes other special characters
FILTER_SANITIZE_FULL_SPECIAL_CHARS	FILTER_FLAG_NO_ENCODE_QUOTES	Equivalent to calling htmlspecialchars() with ENT_QUOTES set
FILTER_SANITIZE_URL		Removes all characters except those valid in URLs

Table 9-3. Miscellaneous filters supported by PHP

ID	Options	Flags	Description
FILTER_CALLBACK	callable function or method	All flags are ignored.	Calls a user-defined function to filter data

The validation filters also accept an array of options at runtime. This gives you the ability to code specific ranges (for numeric checks) and even fallback default values should a particular user input not pass validation.

For example, say you are building a shopping cart that allows the user to specify the number of items they want to purchase. Clearly, this must be a value greater than zero and less than the total inventory you have available. An approach like that illustrated in Example 9-5 will force the value to be an integer between certain bounds or the value will fall back to 1. In this way, a user cannot accidentally order more items than you have, a negative number of items, a partial number of items, or some non-numeric amount.

Example 9-5. Validating an integer value with bounds and a default

```php
function sanitizeQuantity(mixed $orderSize): int
{
    return filter_var(
        $orderSize,
        FILTER_VALIDATE_INT,
        [
            'options' => [
                'min_range' => 1,
                'max_range' => 25,
                'default'   => 1,
            ]
        ]
    );
}

echo sanitizeQuantity(12) . PHP_EOL;   ❶
echo sanitizeQuantity(-5) . PHP_EOL;   ❷
echo sanitizeQuantity(100) . PHP_EOL;  ❸
echo sanitizeQuantity('banana') . PHP_EOL;  ❹
```

❶ The quantity checks out and returns 12.

❷ Negative integers fail to validate, so this returns the default of 1.

❸ The input is above the max range, so this returns the default of 1.

❹ Non-numeric inputs will always return the default of 1.

See Also

Documentation on PHP's data filtering extension (*https://oreil.ly/UX_Hs*).

9.2 Keeping Sensitive Credentials Out of Application Code

Problem

Your application needs to leverage a password or API key, and you want to avoid having that sensitive credential written in code or committed to version control.

Solution

Store the credential in an environment variable exposed by the server running the application. Then reference that environment variable in code. For example:

```php
$db = new PDO($database_connection, getenv('DB_USER'), getenv('DB_PASS'));
```

Discussion

A common mistake made in many developers' early careers is to hardcode credentials for sensitive systems into constants or other places in application code. While this makes those credentials readily available to application logic, it also introduces severe risk to your application.

You could accidentally use production credentials from a development account. An attacker might find credentials indexed in an accidentally public repository. An employee might abuse their knowledge of credentials beyond their intended use.

In production, the best credentials are those unknown to and untouched by humans. It's a good idea to keep those credentials only in the production environment and use *separate accounts* for development and testing. Leveraging environment variables within your code makes your application flexible enough to run anywhere, as it uses not hardcoded credentials but those bound to the environment itself.

 PHP's built-in information system, phpinfo(), will automatically enumerate all environment variables for debugging purposes. Once you begin leveraging the system environment to house sensitive credentials, take extra care to avoid using detailed diagnostic tools like phpinfo() in publicly accessible parts of your application!

The method of *populating* environment variables will differ from one system to another. In Apache-powered systems, you can set environment variables by using the SetEnv keyword within the <VirtualHost> directive as follows:

```
<VirtualHost myhost>
...
SetEnv DB_USER "database"
SetEnv DB_PASS "password1234"
...
</VirtualHost>
```

In NGINX-powered systems, you can set environment variables for PHP only if it's running as a FastCGI process. Similar to Apache's SetEnv, this is done with a keyword within a location directive in the NGINX configuration as follows:

```
location / {
    ...
    fastcgi_param DB_USER database
    fastcgi_param DB_PASS password1234
    ...
}
```

Separately, Docker-powered systems set environment variables in either their Compose files (for Docker Swarm) or the system deployment configuration (for Kubernetes). In all of these situations, you are defining a credential within the environment itself rather than within your application.

An additional option is to use PHP dotenv (*https://oreil.ly/a4TQp*).[4] This third-party package allows you to define your environment configuration in a flat file named *.env* and it automatically populates both environment variables and the $_SERVER super-global. The biggest advantage of this approach is that dotfiles (files prefixed with a .) are easy to exclude from version control and are typically hidden on a server to begin with. You can use a *.env* locally to define development credentials and keep a separate *.env* on the server to define production credentials.

In both cases, you never have to directly manage an Apache or NGINX configuration file at all!

A *.env* file defining the database credentials used in the Solution example would look something like the following:

```
DB_USER=database
DB_PASS=password1234
```

In your application code, you would then load the library dependency and invoke its loader as follows:

```
$dotenv = Dotenv\Dotenv::createImmutable(__DIR__);
$dotenv->load();
```

Once the library is loaded, you can leverage getenv() to reference the environment variables wherever you need access.

See Also

Documentation on getenv() (*https://oreil.ly/t6ncZ*).

9.3 Hashing and Validating Passwords

Problem

You want to authenticate users leveraging passwords only they know and prevent your application from storing sensitive data.

Solution

Use password_hash() to store secure hashes of passwords:

```
$hash = password_hash($password, PASSWORD_DEFAULT);
```

---

4 Loading PHP packages via Composer is discussed at length in Recipe 15.3.

Use `password_verify()` to verify that a plaintext password produces a given, stored hash as follows:

```
if (password_verify($password, $hash)) {
    // Create a valid session for the user ...
}
```

Discussion

Storing passwords in plaintext is always a bad idea. If your application or data store is ever breached, those plaintext passwords can and will be abused by attackers. To keep your users safe and protect them from potential abuse in the case of a breach, you must always hash those passwords when storing them in your database.

Conveniently, PHP ships with a native function to do just that—`password_hash()`. This function takes a plaintext password and automatically generates a deterministic but seemingly random hash from that data. Rather than storing the plaintext password, you store this hash. Later, when the user chooses to log into your application, you can compare the plaintext password against the stored hash (using a safe comparison function like `hash_equals()`) and assert whether they match.

PHP generally supports three hashing algorithms, enumerated in Table 9-4. At the time of this writing, the default algorithm is bcrypt (which is based on the Blowfish cipher), but you can choose a particular algorithm at runtime by passing a second parameter into `password_hash()`.

Table 9-4. Password hashing algorithms

Constant	Description
PASSWORD_DEFAULT	Use the default bcrypt algorithm. The default algorithm could change in a future release.
PASSWORD_BCRYPT	Use the `CRYPT_BLOWFISH` algorithm.
PASSWORD_ARGON2I	Use the Argon2i hashing algorithm. (Only available if PHP has been compiled with Argon2 support.)
PASSWORD_ARGON2ID	Use the Argon2id hashing algorithm. (Only available if PHP has been compiled with Argon2 support.)

Each hashing algorithm supports a set of options that can determine the difficulty of calculating a hash on the server. The default (or bcrypt) algorithm supports an integer "cost" factor—the higher the number, the more computationally expensive the operation will be. The Argon2 family of algorithms supports two cost factors—one for the memory cost and one for the amount of time it will take to compute a hash.

Increasing the cost for computing a hash is a means of protecting the application from brute-force authentication attacks. If it takes 1 second to calculate a hash, it will take *at least* 1 second for a legitimate party to authenticate (this is trivial). However, an attacker can attempt to authenticate *at most* once per second. This renders brute-force attacks relatively costly both in terms of time and computing capacity.

When you first build your application, it is a good idea to test the server environment that will run it and set your cost factors appropriately. Identifying cost factors requires testing the performance of `password_hash()` on the live environment, as demonstrated in Example 9-6. This script will test the hashing performance of the system with increasingly large cost factors and identify a cost factor that achieves the desired time target.

Example 9-6. Testing the cost factors for `password_hash()`

```
$timeTarget = 0.5; // 500 milliseconds

$cost = 8;
do {
    $cost++;
    $start = microtime(true);
    password_hash('test', PASSWORD_BCRYPT, ['cost' => $cost]);
    $end = microtime(true);
} while(($end - $start) < $timeTarget);

echo "Appropriate cost factor: {$cost}" . PHP_EOL;
```

The output of `password_hash()` is intended to be fully forward compatible. Rather than merely generate a hash, the function will also internally generate a salt to make the hash unique. Then the function returns a string representing the following:

- The algorithm used
- The cost factors or options
- The generated random salt
- The resulting hash

Figure 9-1 shows an example of this string output.

A unique, random salt is generated internally by PHP every time you call `password_hash()`. This has the effect of producing distinct hashes for identical plaintext passwords. In this way, hashed values can't be used to identify which accounts are using the same passwords.

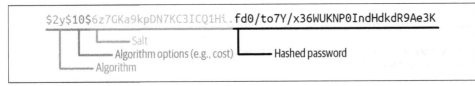

Figure 9-1. Example output of password_hash()

The advantage of encoding all of this information into the output of password_hash() is that you don't need to maintain this data in the application. At a future date, you might change the hashing algorithm or modify the cost factors used for hashing. By encoding the settings originally used to generate a hash, PHP can reliably re-create a hash for comparison.

When a user logs in, they provide only their plaintext password. The application needs to recompute a hash of this password and compare the newly computed value with the one stored in the database. Given that the information you need to calculate a hash is stored alongside the hash, this becomes relatively straightforward.

Rather than implement the comparison yourself, though, you can leverage PHP's password_verify() function that does all this in a safe and secure way.

See Also

Documentation on password_hash() (*https://oreil.ly/gZwBC*) and password_verify() (*https://oreil.ly/gf3O9*).

9.4 Encrypting and Decrypting Data

Problem

You want to protect sensitive data leveraging encryption and reliably decrypt that information at a later time.

Solution

Use sodium's sodium_crypto_secretbox() to encrypt the data with a known symmetric (aka shared) key, as shown in Example 9-7.

Example 9-7. Sodium symmetric encryption example

```
$key = hex2bin('faae9fa60060e32b3bbe5861c2ff290f' .
               '2cd4008409aeb7c59cb3bad8a8e89512'); ❶

$message = 'Look to my coming on the first light of ' .
           'the fifth day, at dawn look to the east.';
```

```
$nonce = random_bytes(SODIUM_CRYPTO_SECRETBOX_NONCEBYTES); ❷

$ciphertext = sodium_crypto_secretbox($message, $nonce, $key); ❸
$output = bin2hex($nonce . $ciphertext); ❹
```

❶ The key must be a random value of length SODIUM_CRYPTO_SECRETBOX_KEYBYTES (32 bytes). If you are creating a new, random string, you can leverage sodium_crypto_secretbox_keygen() to create one. Just be sure to store it somewhere so you can decrypt the message later.

❷ Every encryption operation should use a unique, random nonce. PHP's random_bytes() can reliably create one of the appropriate length by using built-in constants.

❸ The encryption operation leverages both the random nonce and the fixed secret key to protect the message and returns raw bytes as a result.

❹ Often you want to exchange encrypted information over a network protocol, so encoding the raw bytes as hexadecimal can make it more portable. You'll also need the nonce to decrypt the exchanged data, so you store it alongside the ciphertext.

When you need to decrypt the data, use sodium_crypto_secretbox_open() to both extract and validate the data, as shown in Example 9-8.

Example 9-8. Sodium symmetric decryption

```
$key = hex2bin('faae9fa60060e32b3bbe5861c2ff290f' .
               '2cd4008409aeb7c59cb3bad8a8e89512'); ❶

$encrypted = '8b9225c935592a5e95a9204add5d09db' .
             'b7b6473a0aa59c107b65f7d5961b720e' .
             '7fc285bd94de531e05497143aee854e2' .
             '918ba941140b70c324efb27c86313806' .
             'e04f8e79da037df9e7cb24aa4bc0550c' .
             'd7b2723cbb560088f972a408ffc973a6' .
             '2be668e1ba1313e555ef4a95f0c1abd6' .
             'f3d73921fafdd372'; ❷
$raw = hex2bin($encrypted);

$nonce = substr($raw, 0, SODIUM_CRYPTO_SECRETBOX_NONCEBYTES); ❸
$ciphertext = substr($raw, SODIUM_CRYPTO_SECRETBOX_NONCEBYTES);

$plaintext = sodium_crypto_secretbox_open($ciphertext, $nonce, $key);
if ($plaintext === false) { ❹
    echo 'Error decrypting message!' . PHP_EOL;
} else {
```

```
    echo $plaintext . PHP_EOL;
}
```

❶ Use the same key for decryption that you used for encryption.

❷ The resulting ciphertext from Example 9-7 is reused here and is extracted from a hexadecimal-encoded string.

❸ Because you concatenated the ciphertext and nonce, you must split the two components apart for use with `sodium_crypto_secretbox_open()`.

❹ This entire encryption/decryption operation is authenticated. If anything changed in the underlying data, the authentication step will fail and the function will return a literal `false` to flag the manipulation. If it returns anything else, the decryption succeeded and you can trust the output!

Discussion

The `secretbox` family of functions exposed by sodium implements authenticated encryption/decryption by using a fixed symmetric key. Every time you encrypt a message, you should do so with a random nonce to fully protect the privacy of the encrypted message.

The nonce used in encryption itself isn't a secret or sensitive value. However, you should take care never to reuse a nonce with the same symmetric encryption key. Nonces are "numbers used once" and are intended to add randomness to the encryption algorithm such that the same value encrypted twice with the same key can produce different ciphertexts. Reusing a nonce with a specific key compromises the security of the data you're aiming to protect.

The symmetry here is that the same key is used both to encrypt and decrypt a message. This is most valuable when the same system is responsible for both operations—for example, when a PHP application needs to encrypt data to be stored in a database and then decrypt that data when reading it back out.

The encryption leverages the XSalsa20 stream cipher (*https://oreil.ly/DSUAQ*) to protect data. This cipher uses a 32-byte (256-bit) key and a 24-byte (192-bit) nonce. None of this information is necessary for developers to keep track of, though, as it's safely abstracted behind the `secretbox` functions and constants. Rather than keep track of key sizes and encryption modes, you merely need to create or *open* a box with the matched key and nonce for the message.

Another advantage of this approach is authentication. Every encryption operation will also generate a message authentication tag leveraging the Poly1305 algorithm (*https://oreil.ly/tSgmq*). Upon decryption, sodium will validate that the authentication tag matches the protected data. If there is not a match, it's possible that the message was either accidentally corrupted or intentionally manipulated. In either case, the ciphertext is unreliable (as would be any decrypted plaintext), and the open function will return a Boolean `false`.

Asymmetric encryption

Symmetric encryption is easiest when the same party is both encrypting and decrypting data. In many modern tech environments, these parties might be independent and communicating over less-than-trustworthy media. This necessitates a different form of encryption, as the two parties cannot directly share a symmetric encryption key. Instead, each can create pairs of public and private keys and leverage key exchange to agree upon an encryption key.

Key exchange is a complicated topic. Luckily, sodium exposes simple interfaces for performing the operation in PHP. In the examples that follow, two parties will do the following:

1. Create public/private key pairs
2. Exchange their public keys directly
3. Use these asymmetric keys to agree upon a symmetric key
4. Exchange encrypted data

Example 9-9 illustrates how each party will create their own public/private key pairs. Though the code example is in a single block, each party would create their keys independently and only ever exchange their public keys with one another.

Example 9-9. Asymmetric key creation

```
$aliceKeypair = sodium_crypto_box_keypair();
$alicePublic = sodium_crypto_box_publickey($aliceKeypair); ❶
$alicePrivate = sodium_crypto_box_secretkey($aliceKeypair); ❷

$bethKeypair = sodium_crypto_box_keypair(); ❸
$bethPublic = sodium_crypto_box_publickey($bethKeypair);
$bethPrivate = sodium_crypto_box_secretkey($bethKeypair);
```

❶ Alice creates a key pair and extracts her public and private key from it separately. She shares her public key with Beth.

❷ Alice keeps her private key secret. This is the key she will use to encrypt data *for* Beth and decrypt data *from* her. Similarly, Alice would use her private key to encrypt data for anyone else who has shared their public key with her.

❸ Beth independently does the same thing as Alice and shares her own public key.

Once Alice and Beth have shared their public keys, they are free to communicate privately. The `cryptobox` family of functions in sodium leverages these asymmetric keys to compute a symmetric key that can be used for confidential communication. This symmetric key is not exposed directly to either party, but allows the parties to easily communicate with one another.

Note that anything Alice encrypts for Beth can *only* be decrypted by Beth. Even Alice cannot decrypt these messages, as she does not have Beth's private key! Example 9-10 illustrates how Alice can encrypt a simple message leveraging both her own private key and Beth's advertised public key.

Example 9-10. Asymmetric encryption

```
$message = 'Follow the white rabbit';
$nonce = random_bytes(SODIUM_CRYPTO_BOX_NONCEBYTES);
$encryptionKey = sodium_crypto_box_keypair_from_secretkey_and_publickey(
    $alicePrivate,
    $bethPublic
); ❶

$ciphertext = sodium_crypto_box($message, $nonce, $encryptionKey); ❷

$toBeth = bin2hex($nonce . $ciphertext); ❸
```

❶ The encryption key used here is actually a key pair composed of information from both Alice's and Beth's individual key pairs.

❷ As with symmetric encryption, you leverage a nonce in order to introduce randomness into the encrypted output.

❸ You concatenate the random nonce and the encrypted ciphertext so Alice can send both to Beth at the same time.

The key pairs involved are points on an elliptic curve, specifically Curve25519. The initial operation sodium uses for asymmetric encryption is a *key exchange* between two of these points to define a fixed but secret number. This operation uses the X25519 key exchange algorithm (*https://oreil.ly/OAqeF*) and produces a number based on Alice's private key and Beth's public key.

That number is then used as a key with the XSalsa20 stream cipher (the same one used for symmetric encryption) to encrypt the message. As with symmetric encryption discussed for the `secret box` family of functions, a `cryptobox` will leverage a Poly1305 message authentication tag to protect the message against tampering or corruption.

At this point, Beth, by leveraging her own private key, Alice's public key, and the message nonce, can reproduce all of these steps on her own to decrypt the message. She performs a similar X25519 key exchange to derive the same shared key and then uses that for decryption.

Thankfully, sodium abstracts the key exchange and derivation for us, making asymmetric decryption relatively straightforward. See Example 9-11.

Example 9-11. Asymmetric decryption

```
$fromAlice = hex2bin($toBeth);
$nonce = substr($fromAlice, 0, SODIUM_CRYPTO_BOX_NONCEBYTES); ❶
$ciphertext = substr($fromAlice, SODIUM_CRYPTO_BOX_NONCEBYTES);

$decryptionKey = sodium_crypto_box_keypair_from_secretkey_and_publickey(
    $bethPrivate,
    $alicePublic
); ❷

$decrypted = sodium_crypto_box_open($ciphertext, $nonce, $decryptionKey); ❸
if ($decrypted === false) { ❹
    echo 'Error decrypting message!' . PHP_EOL;
} else {
    echo $decrypted . PHP_EOL;
}
```

❶ Similar to the secretbox operation, you first extract the nonce and ciphertext from the hexadecimal-encoded payload provided by Alice.

❷ Beth uses her own private key along with Alice's public key to create a key pair appropriate for decrypting the message.

❸ The key exchange and decryption operations are abstracted away with a simple "open" interface to read the message.

❹ As with symmetric encryption, sodium's asymmetric interfaces will validate the Poly1305 authentication tag on the message before decrypting and returning the plaintext.

Either mechanism—symmetric or asymmetric encryption—is well supported and cleanly abstracted by sodium's functional interfaces. This helps avoid errors commonly encountered when implementing older mechanisms (like AES or RSA). Libsodium (the C-level library powering the sodium extension) is widely supported in other languages as well, providing solid interoperability between PHP, Ruby, Python, JavaScript, and even lower-level languages like C and Go.

See Also

Documentation on `sodium_crypto_secretbox()` (*https://oreil.ly/3IZZM*), `sodium_crypto_secretbox_open()` (*https://oreil.ly/qNDqx*), `sodium_crypto_box()` (*https://oreil.ly/-apZN*), and `sodium_crypto_box_open()` (*https://oreil.ly/5lT_D*).

9.5 Storing Encrypted Data in a File

Problem

You want to encrypt (or decrypt) a file that is too large to fit in memory.

Solution

Use the *push* streaming interfaces exposed by sodium to encrypt one chunk of the file at a time, as shown in Example 9-12.

Example 9-12. Sodium stream encryption

```
define('CHUNK_SIZE', 4096);

$key = hex2bin('67794ec75c56ba386f944634203d4e86' .
               '37e43c97857e3fa482bb9dfec1e44e70');

[$state, $header] = sodium_crypto_secretstream_xchacha20poly1305_init_push($key); ❶

$input = fopen('plaintext.txt', 'rb'); ❷
$output = fopen('encrypted.txt', 'wb');

fwrite($output, $header); ❸

$fileSize = fstat($input)['size']; ❹

for ($i = 0; $i < $fileSize; $i += (CHUNK_SIZE - 17)) { ❺
    $plain = fread($input, (CHUNK_SIZE - 17));
    $cipher = sodium_crypto_secretstream_xchacha20poly1305_push($state, $plain); ❻

    fwrite($output, $cipher);
}

sodium_memzero($state); ❼

fclose($input); ❽
fclose($output);
```

❶ Initializing the stream operation yields two values—a header and the current state of the stream. The header itself contains a random nonce and is required in order to decrypt anything encrypted with the stream.

❷ Open both the input and output files as binary streams. Working with files is one of the few times you want to emit raw bytes rather than leverage hexadecimal or Base64 encoding to wrap an encrypted output.

❸ To ensure that you can decrypt the file, first store the fixed-length header for later retrieval.

❹ Before you begin iterating over chunks of bytes in the file, you need to determine how large the input file really is.

❺ As with other sodium operations, the stream encryption cipher is built atop Poly1305 authentication tags (which are 17 bytes in length). As a result, you read 17 bytes less than the standard 4,096-byte block, so the output will be a total of 4,081 bytes written to the file.

❻ The sodium API encrypts the plaintext and automatically updates the state variable ($state is passed by reference and updated in place).

❼ After you're done with encryption, explicitly zero out the memory of the state variable. PHP's garbage collector will clean up the references, but you want to ensure that no coding errors elsewhere in the system can inadvertently leak this value.

❽ Finally, close the file handles since the encryption is complete.

To decrypt the file, use sodium's *pull* streaming interfaces, as shown in Example 9-13.

Example 9-13. Sodium stream decryption

```
define('CHUNK_SIZE', 4096);

$key = hex2bin('67794ec75c56ba386f944634203d4e86' .
               '37e43c97857e3fa482bb9dfec1e44e70');

$input = fopen('encrypted.txt', 'rb');
$output = fopen('decrypted.txt', 'wb');

$header = fread($input, SODIUM_CRYPTO_SECRETSTREAM_XCHACHA20POLY1305_HEADERBYTES); ❶

$state = sodium_crypto_secretstream_xchacha20poly1305_init_pull($header, $key); ❷

$fileSize = fstat($input)['size'];
try {
    for (
        $i = SODIUM_CRYPTO_SECRETSTREAM_XCHACHA20POLY1305_HEADERBYTES;
        $i < $fileSize;
```

```
        $i += CHUNK_SIZE
    ) { ❸
        $cipher = fread($input, CHUNK_SIZE);

        [$plain, ] = sodium_crypto_secretstream_xchacha20poly1305_pull(
            $state,
            $cipher
        ); ❹

        if ($plain === false) { ❺
            throw new Exception('Error decrypting file!');
        }
        fwrite($output, $plain);
    }
} finally {
    sodium_memzero($state); ❻

    fclose($input);
    fclose($output);
}
```

❶ Before you can begin decryption, you must explicitly retrieve the header value from the file you encrypted in the first place.

❷ Armed with the encryption header and key, you can initialize the stream state as desired.

❸ Keep in mind that the file is prefixed with a header, so you skip those bytes and then pull chunks of 4,096 bytes at a time. This will include 4,079 bytes of ciphertext and 17 bytes of authentication tag.

❹ The actual stream decryption operation returns a tuple of the plaintext and an optional status tag (e.g., to identify that a key needs to be rotated).

❺ If the authentication tag on the encrypted message fails to validate, however, this function will return false to indicate the authentication failure. Should this occur, halt decryption immediately.

❻ Again, once the operation is complete, you should zero out the memory storing the stream state, as well as close out the file handles.

Discussion

The stream cipher interfaces exposed by sodium are not actual streams to PHP.[5] Specifically, they are stream *ciphers* that work like block ciphers with an internal counter. XChaCha20 is the cipher used by the `sodium_crypto_secretstream_xchacha20poly1305_*()` family of functions leveraged to push data into and pull data from an encrypted stream in this recipe. The implementation in PHP explicitly breaks a long message (a file) into a series of related messages. Each of these messages is encrypted with the underlying cipher and tagged individually but in a specific order.

These messages cannot be truncated, removed, reordered, or manipulated in any way without the decryption operation detecting that tampering. There is also no practical limit to the total number of messages that can be encrypted as part of this stream, which means there is no limit to the size of a file that can be passed through the Solution examples.

The Solution uses a chunk size of 4,096 bytes (4 KB), but other examples could use 1,024, 8,096, or any other number of bytes. The only limitation here is the amount of memory available to PHP—iterating over smaller chunks of a file will use less memory during encryption and decryption. Example 9-12 illustrates how `sodium_crypto_secretstream_xchacha20poly1305_push()` encrypts one chunk of data at a time, "pushing" that data through the encryption algorithm and updating the algorithm's internal state. The paired `sodium_crypto_secretstream_xchacha20poly1305_pull()` does the same thing in reverse, pulling corresponding plaintext back out of the stream and updating the algorithm's state.

Another way to see this in action is with the low-level primitive `sodium_crypto_stream_xchacha20_xor()` function. This function leverages the XChaCha20 encryption algorithm directly to generate a stream of seemingly random bytes based on a given key and random nonce. It then performs an XOR operation between that stream of bytes and a given message to produce a ciphertext.[6] Example 9-14 illustrates one way in which this function might be used—encrypting phone numbers in a database.

Example 9-14. Simple stream encryption for data protection

```
function savePhoneNumber(int $userId, string $phone): void
{
    $db = getDatabase();
```

---

5 PHP streams, covered extensively in Chapter 11, expose effective ways to work with large chunks of data without exhausting available system memory.

6 For more on operators and XOR in particular, review Chapter 2.

```
$statement = $db->prepare(
    'INSERT INTO phones (user, number, nonce) VALUES (?, ?, ?)';
);

$key = hex2bin(getenv('ENCRYPTION_KEY'));
$nonce = random_bytes(SODIUM_CRYPTO_STREAM_XCHACHA20_NONCEBYTES);

$encrypted = sodium_crypto_stream_xchacha20_xor($phone, $nonce, $key);

$statement->execute([$userId, bin2hex($encrypted), bin2hex($nonce)]);
}
```

The advantage of using a cryptographic stream in this way is that the ciphertext exactly matches the length of the plaintext. However, this also means there is no authentication tag available (meaning the ciphertext could be corrupted or manipulated by a third party and jeopardize the reliability of any decrypted ciphertext).

As a result, Example 9-14 is not likely something you will ever use directly. However, it does illustrate how the more verbose sodium_ crypto_ secretstream_ xchacha20poly1305_push() works under the hood. Both functions use the same algorithm, but the "secret stream" variant generates its own nonce and keeps track of its internal state over repeated uses (in order to encrypt *multiple* chunks of data). When using the simpler XOR version you would need to manage that state and repeated calls manually!

See Also

Documentation on sodium_crypto_secretstream_xchacha20poly1305_init_ push() (*https://oreil.ly/chGJC*), sodium_crypto_secretstream_xchacha20poly1305_ init_pull() (*https://oreil.ly/ogGvJ*), and sodium_crypto_stream_xchacha20_xor() (*https://oreil.ly/yQBBC*).

9.6 Cryptographically Signing a Message to Be Sent to Another Application

Problem

You want to sign a message or piece of data before sending it to another application such that the other application can validate your signature on the data.

Solution

Use sodium_crypto_sign() to attach a cryptographic signature to a plaintext message, as shown in Example 9-15.

Example 9-15. Cryptographic signatures on messages

```
$signSeed = hex2bin('eb656c282f46b45a814fcc887977675d' .
                    'c627a5b1507ae2a68faecee147b77621'); ❶
$signKeys = sodium_crypto_sign_seed_keypair($signSeed);

$signSecret = sodium_crypto_sign_secretkey($signKeys);
$signPublic = sodium_crypto_sign_publickey($signKeys);

$message = 'Hello world!';
$signed = sodium_crypto_sign($message, $signSecret);
```

❶ In practice, your signing seed should be a random value kept secret by you. It could also be a secure hash derived from a known password.

Discussion

Cryptographic signatures are a way to verify that a particular message (or string of data) originated from a given source. So long as the private key used to sign a message is kept secret, anyone with access to the publicly known key can validate that the information came from the owner of the key.

Likewise, only the custodian of that key can sign the data. This helps verify that the custodian signed off on the message. It also forms the basis for nonrepudiation: the owner of the key cannot claim that someone else used their key without rendering their key (and any signatures it created) invalid.

In the Solution example, a signature is calculated based on the secret key and the contents of the message. The bytes of the signature are then prepended to the message itself, and both elements together are passed along to any party who wishes to verify the signature.

It is also possible to generate a *detached* signature, effectively producing the raw bytes of the signature without concatenating it to the message. This is useful if the message and signature are meant to be sent independently to the third-party verifier—for example, as different elements in an API request.

 While raw bytes are fantastic for information stored on disk or in a database, they can cause problems with remote APIs. It would make sense to Base64-encode the entire payload (the signature and message) when sending it to a remote party. Otherwise, you might want to encode the signature separately (e.g., as hexadecimal) when sending the two components together.

Rather than using `sodium_crypto_sign()` as in the Solution example, you can use `sodium_crypto_sign_detached()` as in Example 9-16.

Example 9-16. Creating a detached message signature

```
$signSeed = hex2bin('eb656c282f46b45a814fcc887977675d' .
                    'c627a5b1507ae2a68faecee147b77621');
$signKeys = sodium_crypto_sign_seed_keypair($signSeed);

$signSecret = sodium_crypto_sign_secretkey($signKeys);
$signPublic = sodium_crypto_sign_publickey($signKeys);

$message = 'Hello world!';
$signature = sodium_crypto_sign_detached($message, $signSecret);
```

Signatures will always be 64 bytes long, regardless of whether they're attached to the plaintext they sign.

See Also

Documentation on `sodium_crypto_sign()` (*https://oreil.ly/3eqTz*).

9.7 Verifying a Cryptographic Signature

Problem

You want to verify the signature on a piece of data sent to you by a third party.

Solution

Use `sodium_crypto_sign_open()` to validate the signature on a message, as shown in Example 9-17.

Example 9-17. Cryptographic signature verification

```
$signPublic = hex2bin('d58c47ddb986dcb2632aa5395e8962d3' .
                      'e636ee236b38a8dc880e409c19374a5f');

$message = sodium_crypto_sign_open($signed, $signPublic); ❶

if ($message === false) { ❷
    throw new Exception('Invalid signature on message!');
}
```

❶ The data in `$signed` is a concatenated raw signature and plaintext message, as in the return of `sodium_crypto_sign()`.

❷ If the signature is invalid, the function returns `false` as an error. If the signature is valid, the function instead returns the plaintext message.

Discussion

Signature verification is straightforward when the literal returns from sodium_crypto_sign() are involved. Merely pass the data and the public key of the signing party into sodium_crypto_sign_open(), and you will have either a Boolean error or the original plaintext back as a result.

If you're working with a web API, there's a good chance that the message and signature were passed to you separately (e.g., if someone were using sodium_crypto_sign_detached()). In that case, you need to concatenate the signature and the message together before passing them into sodium_crypto_sign_open(), as in Example 9-18.

Example 9-18. Detached signature verification

```
$signPublic = hex2bin('d58c47ddb986dcb2632aa5395e8962d3' .
                      'e636ee236b38a8dc880e409c19374a5f');

$signature = hex2bin($_POST['signature']);
$payload = $signature . $_POST['message'];

$message = sodium_crypto_sign_open($payload, $signPublic);

if ($message === false) {
    throw new Exception('Invalid signature on message!');
}
```

See Also

Documentation on sodium_crypto_sign_open() (*https://oreil.ly/UG5ja*).

## CHAPTER 10

File Handling

One of the most common design philosophies around Unix and Linux is that "everything is a file." This means that, regardless of the resource with which you're interacting, the operating system treats it as if it were a file locally on disk. This includes remote requests to other systems and handles on the output of processes running on the machine.

PHP treats requests, proceses, and resources similarly, but instead of considering everything to be a file, the language considers everything to be a stream resource. Chapter 11 covers streams at length, but the important point to know about streams for this chapter is the way PHP treats them in memory.

When accessing a file, PHP doesn't necessarily read the file's entire data into memory. Instead, it creates a `resource` in memory that references the file's location on disk and selectively buffers bytes from that file in memory. PHP then accesses or manipulates those buffered bytes directly as a stream. The fundamentals of streams, however, are not required knowledge for the recipes in this chapter.

PHP's file methods—`fopen()`, `file_get_contents()`, and the like—all leverage the `file://` stream wrapper under the hood. Remember, though, if everything in PHP is a stream, you can just as easily use other stream protocols as well, including `php://` and `http://`.

Windows Versus Unix

PHP is distributed for use on both Windows and Unix-style operating systems (including Linux and macOS). It's important to understand that the underlying filesystem behind Windows is very different from a Unix-style system. Windows doesn't consider "everything to be a file" and sometimes respects case sensitivity in both file and directory names in unexpected ways.

As you'll see in Recipe 10.6, the differences between operating system paradigms also lead to minor differences in how functions behave. Specifically, file locking will work differently if your program is run on Windows because of differences in the underlying operating system calls.

The recipes that follow cover the most common filesystem operations you might experience in PHP, from opening and manipulating files to locking them from being touched by other processes.

10.1 Creating or Opening a Local File

Problem

You need to open a file for reading or writing on the local filesystem.

Solution

Use fopen() to open the file and return a resource reference for further use:

```
$fp = fopen('document.txt', 'r');
```

Discussion

Internally, an open file is represented as a stream within PHP. You can read data from or write data to any position within the stream based on the position of the current file pointer. In the Solution example, you've opened a stream for reading only (attempting to write to this stream will fail) and positioned the pointer at the beginning of the file.

Example 10-1 shows how you can read as many bytes from the file as you want and then close the stream by passing its reference into fclose().

Example 10-1. Reading bytes from a buffer

```
while (($buffer = fgets($fp, 4096)) !== false) { ❶
    echo $buffer; ❷
}

fclose($fp); ❸
```

 The fgets() function reads one line from the specified resource, stopping either when it hits a newline character or when it has read the specified number of bytes (4,096) from the underlying stream. If there is no data to read, the function returns false.

❷ Once you have data buffered into a variable, you can do with it whatever you want. In this case, print that single line to the console.

❸ After using a file's contents, you should explicitly close and clean up the resource you've created.

In addition to reading a file, fopen() allows for arbitrary writes, file appending, over-writing, or truncation. Each operation is determined by the mode passed as the second parameter—the Solution example passed r to indicate a read-only mode. Additional modes are described in Table 10-1.

Table 10-1. File modes available to fopen()

Mode	Description
r	Open for reading only; place the file pointer at the beginning of the file.
w	Open for writing only; place the file pointer at the beginning of the file and truncate the file to 0 length. If the file does not exist, attempt to create it.
a	Open for writing only; place the file pointer at the end of the file. If the file does not exist, attempt to create it. In this mode, fseek() has no effect, and writes are always appended.
x	Create and open for writing only; place the file pointer at the beginning of the file. If the file already exists, the fopen() call will fail by returning false and generating an error of level E_WARNING. If the file does not exist, attempt to create it.
c	Open the file for writing only. If the file does not exist, it is created. If it exists, it is neither truncated (as opposed to w), nor does the call to this function fail (as is the case with x). The file pointer is placed at the beginning of the file.
e	Set close-on-exec flag on the opened file descriptor.

For all of the file modes documented in Table 10-1 *except* for e, you can append a literal + sign to the mode to open a file for both reading *and* writing rather than one operation or the other.

The fopen() function works with more than just local files. By default, the function assumes you want to work with the local filesystem, which is why you do not need to explicitly specify the file:// protocol handler. However, you can just as easily reference remote files by using the http:// or ftp:// handlers, as follows:

```
$fp = fopen('https://eamann.com/', 'r');
```

 While remote file includes are possible, they can be dangerous in many situations, as you might not always have control over the contents returned by a remote filesystem. It's often recommended to disable remote file access by toggling allow_url_include in your system configuration. Refer to the PHP runtime configuration documents (*https://oreil.ly/-gXR-*) for instructions on implementing this change.

An optional third parameter allows fopen() to search for a file in your system include path (*https://oreil.ly/3S1lo*) if desired. By default, PHP will only search the local directory (or use an absolute path if specified). Loading files from the system include path encourages code reuse as you can specify individual classes or configuration files without replicating them throughout your project.

See Also

Documentation on the PHP filesystem (*https://oreil.ly/oGJTp*), particularly fopen() (*https://oreil.ly/7yQG-*).

10.2 Reading a File into a String

Problem

You want to read an entire file into a variable for use elsewhere in your application.

Solution

Use file_get_contents() as follows:

```
$config = file_get_contents('config.json');

if ($config !== false) {
    $parsed = json_decode($config);

    // ...
}
```

Discussion

The file_get_contents() function opens a file for reading, reads the entire data of that file into a variable, and then closes the file and allows you to use that data as a string. This is functionally equivalent to reading a file into a string manually with fread(), as in Example 10-2.

Example 10-2. Implementing file_get_contents() manually with fread()

```
function fileGetContents(string $filename): string|false
{
    $buffer = '';
    $fp = fopen($filename, 'r');

    try {
        while (!feof($fp)) {
            $buffer .= fread($fp, 4096);
        }
```

```
    } catch(Exception $e) {
        $buffer = false;
    } finally {
        fclose($fp);
    }

    return $buffer;
}

$config = fileGetContents('config.json');
```

While it's possible to manually read a file into memory, as demonstrated in Example 10-2, it's a better idea to focus on writing simple programs and using the functions exposed by the language to handle complicated operations for you. The file_get_contents() function is implemented in C and provides a high level of performance for your application. It is binary-safe and leverages the memory-mapping functionality exposed by your operating system to achieve peak performance.

Like fread(), file_get_contents() can read both local and remote files into memory. It can also search for files in the system include path if you should set the optional second parameter to true.

Like fread()'s parallel fwrite() operation, there is an automatic write equivalent function called file_put_contents(). This function abstracts away the complexity of opening a file and overwriting its contents with string data from a variable. The following demonstrates how an object might be encoded to JSON and written out to a static file:

```
$config = new Config(/** ... **/);
$serialized = json_encode($config);

file_put_contents('config.json', $serialized);
```

See Also

Documentation on file_ get_ contents() (*https://oreil.ly/5pRBt*) and file_put_ contents() (*https://oreil.ly/4W0rG*).

10.3 Reading a Specific Slice of a File

Problem

You want to read a specific set of bytes from a particular position within a file.

Solution

Use `fopen()` to create a resource, `fseek()` to reposition the pointer within the file, and `fread()` to read data from that position as follows:

```
$fp = fopen('document.txt', 'r');
fseek($fp, 32, SEEK_SET);

$data = fread($fp, 32);
```

Discussion

By default, `fopen()` in read mode will open the file as a resource and place its pointer at the beginning of the file. When you start reading bytes from the file, the pointer will advance until it hits the end of the file. You can use `fseek()` to set the pointer to an arbitrary position within the resource, with the default being the beginning of the file.

The third parameter—`SEEK_SET` in the Solution example—tells PHP where to add the offset. You have three options:

- `SEEK_SET` (the default) sets the pointer from the beginning of the file.
- `SEEK_CUR` adds the offset to the current pointer position.
- `SEEK_END` adds the offset to the end of the file. This is useful for reading the last bytes in a file by setting a negative offset as the second parameter.

Assume you want to read the last bytes in a long log file from within PHP. You would do so similarly to the way you read arbitrary bytes in the Solution example but with a negative offset, as follows:

```
$fp = fopen('log.txt', 'r');
fseek($fp, -4096, SEEK_END);

echo fread($fp, 4096);

fclose($fp);
```

Note that, even if the log file in the preceding snippet is less than 4,096 bytes long, PHP will not read past the beginning of the file. The interpreter will instead place the pointer at the beginning of the file and start reading bytes from that position. Likewise, you cannot read past the end of the file regardless of how many bytes you specify in your call to `fread()`.

See Also

Recipe 10.1 for more on `fopen()`, and the documentation on `fread()` (*https://oreil.ly/Gb2m5*) and `fseek()` (*https://oreil.ly/Tl6gs*).

10.4 Modifying a File in Place

Problem

You want to modify a specific part of a file.

Solution

Open the file for reading and writing by using `fopen()`, then use `fseek()` to move the pointer to the position you wish to update and overwrite a certain number of bytes starting with that position. For example:

```
$fp = fopen('resume.txt', 'r+');
fseek($fp, 32);

fwrite($fp, 'New data', 8);

fclose($fp);
```

Discussion

As in Recipe 10.3, the `fseek()` function is leveraged to move the pointer to an arbitrary location within the file. From there, `fwrite()` is used to write a specific set of bytes to the file in that location before you close the resource.

The third parameter passed to `fwrite()` tells PHP how many bytes to write. By default, the system will write all of the data passed in the second parameter, but you can restrict the amount of data written out by specifying a byte count. In the Solution example, the write length is set equal to the data length, which is redundant. A more realistic example of this functionality would appear something like the following.

```
$contents = 'the quick brown fox jumped over the lazy dog';
fwrite($fp, $contents, 9);
```

Note also that the Solution example adds a plus sign to the typical read mode; this opens the file for reading *and* writing. Opening the file in other modes leads to very different behavior:

- w (write mode), with or without the ability to read, will truncate the file before you do anything else with it!
- a (append mode), with or without the ability to read, will force the file pointer to the end of the file. Calls to `fseek()` will *not* move the file pointer as expected, and your new data will always be appended to the file.

See Also

Recipe 10.3 for more information on random I/O with files in PHP.

10.5 Writing to Many Files Simultaneously

Problem

You want to write data to multiple files at the same time. For example, you want to write both to the local filesystem and to the console.

Solution

Open multiple resource references with `fopen()` and write to them all in a loop:

```
$fps = [
    fopen('data.txt', 'w'),
    fopen('php://stdout', 'w')
];

foreach ($fps as $fp) {
    fwrite($fp, 'The wheels on the bus go round and round.');
}
```

Discussion

PHP is generally a single-threaded system that must perform operations one at a time.[1] While the Solution example will produce output for two file references, it will write first to one and then to the other. In practice, this will be fast enough to be acceptable but is not truly simultaneous.

Even with this limitation, knowing that you can write the same data to multiple files with ease makes it fairly straightforward to juggle multiple potential outputs. Rather than crafting a procedural approach with a finite number of files as in the Solution example, you could even abstract this kind of operation into a class, as shown in Example 10-3:

Example 10-3. A simple class for abstracting multiple file operations

```
class MultiFile
{
    private array $handles = [];

    public function open(
        string $filename,
        string $mode = 'w',
        bool $use_include_path = false,
        $context = null
```

---

1 Chapter 17 covers parallel and asynchronous operations at length to explain ways to break out of a single-threaded paradigm.

```
        ): mixed
    {
        $fp = fopen($filename, $mode, $use_include_path, $context);

        if ($fp !== false) {
            $this->handles[] = $fp;
        }

        return $fp;
    }

    public function write(string $data, ?int $length = null): int|false
    {
        $success = true;
        $bytes = 0;

        foreach($this->handles as $fp) {
            $out = fwrite($fp, $data, $length);
            if ($out === false) {
                $success = false;
            } else {
                $bytes = $out;
            }
        }

        return $success ? $bytes : false;
    }

    public function close(): bool
    {
        $return = true;

        foreach ($this->handles as $fp) {
            $return = $return && fclose($fp);
        }

        return $return;
    }
}
```

The class defined by Example 10-3 allows you to easily bind a write operation to multiple file handles and clean them up as necessary when you're done. Rather than opening each file in turn and manually iterating over them, you simply instantiate the class, add your files, and go. For example:

```
$writer = new MultiFile();
$writer->open('data.txt');
$writer->open('php://stdout');

$writer->write("Row, row, row your boat\nGently down the stream.");

$writer->close();
```

PHP's internal handling of resource pointers is highly efficient and empowers you to write to as many files or streams as necessary with minimal overhead. Abstractions like Example 10-3 similarly make it easy for you to focus on the business logic of your application, while PHP juggles the resource handles (and related memory allocation) for you.

See Also

Documentation on PHP's `stdout` stream (*https://oreil.ly/i0kSI*).

10.6 Locking a File to Prevent Access or Modification by Another Process

Problem

You want to prevent another PHP process from manipulating a file while your script is running.

Solution

Use `flock()` to lock the file as follows:

```
$fp = fopen('myfile.txt', 'r');

if (flock($fp, LOCK_EX)) {
    // ... Do whatever reading you need

    flock($fp, LOCK_UN);
} else {
    echo 'Could not lock file!';
    exit(1);
}
```

Discussion

Often, you need to open a file to read its data or write something to it, but with the assurance that no other script will manipulate the file while you're working with it. The safest way to do this is by explicitly locking the file.

On Windows, PHP leverages *mandatory locking* that is enforced by the operating system itself. Once a file is locked, no other process is permitted to open that file. On Unix-based systems (including Linux and macOS), PHP instead uses *advisory locking*. In this mode, the operating system can choose to ignore locks between different processes. While multiple PHP scripts will usually respect the lock, other processes might ignore it entirely.

An explicit file lock prevents other processes from either reading or writing the same file, depending on the type of lock. PHP supports two kinds of locks: a shared lock (LOCK_SH) that still permits reads, and an exclusive lock (LOCK_EX) that prevents other processes from accessing the file at all.

If you were to run the code in the Solution example twice on a machine (with a long-blocking operation like sleep() called before unlocking the file), the second process would pause and wait for the lock to be released before executing. A more concrete example is shown in Example 10-4.

Example 10-4. Illustration of a long-running file lock

```php
$fp = fopen('myfile.txt', 'r');

echo 'Getting a lock ...' . PHP_EOL;
if (flock($fp, LOCK_EX)) {
    echo 'Sleeping ...' . PHP_EOL;
    for($i = 0; $i < 3; $i++) {
        sleep(10);
        echo ' Zzz ...' . PHP_EOL;
    }

    echo 'Unlocking ...' . PHP_EOL;
    flock($fp, LOCK_UN);
} else {
    echo 'Could not lock file!';
    exit(1);
}
```

Running the preceding program in two separate terminals side by side illustrates how locking works, as shown in Figure 10-1. The first execution will acquire the file lock and continue operating as expected. The second will wait until the lock is available and, after it acquires the lock, continue merrily along.

Figure 10-1. Two processes cannot acquire the same lock on a single file

See Also

Documentation on flock() (*https://oreil.ly/BRBO5*).

## CHAPTER 11

Streams

Streams in PHP represent common interfaces to data resources that can be written to or read from in a linear, continuous manner. Internally, each stream is represented by a collection of objects referred to as *buckets*. Each bucket represents a chunk of data from the underlying stream, which is treated like a digital re-creation of an old-fashioned bucket brigade, like the one illustrated in Figure 11-1.

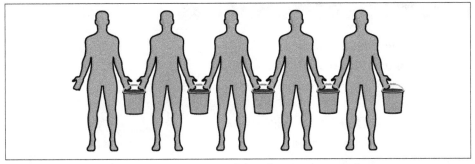

Figure 11-1. Bucket brigades pass buckets of data from one to another in turn

Bucket brigades were often used to transport water from a river, stream, lake, or well to the source of a fire. When it was impossible to use hoses to move the water, people would line up and pass buckets from one to another in order to fight the fire. One person would fill a bucket at the water source and then pass the bucket to the next person in line. The people in line didn't move, but the bucket of water was transported from person to person in turn until the final person could throw the water on the fire. This process would continue until either the fire was extinguished or the source ran out of water.

Though you're not using PHP to fight a fire, the internal structure of a stream is somewhat similar to a bucket brigade because of the way data is passed one chunk (bucket) at a time through whatever component of code is processing it.

Generators are also analogous to this pattern.[1] Rather than loading an entire collection of data into memory all at once, generators provide a way to reduce it into smaller chunks and operate on one piece of data at a time. This enables a PHP application to operate on data that would otherwise exhaust system memory. Streams empower similar functionality, except working on continuous data rather than collections or arrays of discrete data points.

Wrappers and Protocols

In PHP, streams are implemented using *wrappers* that are registered with the system to operate on a specific protocol. The most common wrappers you might interact with are those for file access or HTTP URLs, registered as `file://` and `http://`, respectively. Each wrapper operates against different kinds of data, but they all support the same basic functionality. Table 11-1 enumerates the wrappers and protocols that are exposed natively by PHP.

Table 11-1. Native stream wrappers and protocols

Protocol	Description
`file://`	Access the local filesystem
`http://`	Access remote URLs over HTTP(S)
`ftp://`	Access remote filesystems over FTP(S)
`php://`	Access various local I/O streams (memory, `stdin`, `stdout`, etc.)
`zlib://`	Compression
`data://`	Raw data (according to RFC 2397 (*https://oreil.ly/EBJv6*))
`glob://`	Find pathnames matching a pattern
`phar://`	Manipulate PHP archives
`ssh2://`	Connect via secure shell
`rar://`	RAR compression
`ogg://`	Audio streams

Each wrapper produces a `stream` resource that enables you to read or write data in a linear fashion with the additional ability to "seek" to an arbitrary location within the stream. A `file://` stream, for example, allows arbitrary access to bytes on disk.

---

1 For more on generators, review Recipe 7.15.

Similarly, the php:// protocol provides read/write access to various streams of bytes held in the local system memory.

Filters

PHP's stream filters provide a construct that allows for the dynamic manipulation of the bytes in a stream during either read or write. A simple example would be to automatically convert every character in a string to either uppercase or lowercase. This is accomplished by creating a custom class that extends the php_user_filter class and registering that class as a filter for the compiler to use, as in Example 11-1.

Example 11-1. User-defined filter

```php
class StringFilter extends php_user_filter
{
    private string $mode;

    public function filter($in, $out, &$consumed, bool $closing): int
    {
        while ($bucket = stream_bucket_make_writeable($in)) { ❶
            switch($this->mode) {
                case 'lower':
                    $bucket->data = strtolower($bucket->data);
                    break;
                case 'upper':
                    $bucket->data = strtoupper($bucket->data);
                    break;
            }

            $consumed += $bucket->datalen; ❷
            stream_bucket_append($out, $bucket); ❸
        }

        return PSFS_PASS_ON; ❹
    }

    public function onCreate(): bool
    {
        switch($this->filtername) { ❺
            case 'str.tolower':
                $this->mode = 'lower';
                return true;
            case 'str.toupper':
                $this->mode = 'upper';
                return true;
            default:
                return false;
        }
    }
}
```

```
stream_filter_register('str.*', 'StringFilter'); ❻

$fp = fopen('document.txt', 'w');
stream_filter_append($fp, 'str.toupper'); ❼

fwrite($fp, 'Hello' . PHP_EOL); ❽
fwrite($fp, 'World' . PHP_EOL);

fclose($fp);

echo file_get_contents('document.txt'); ❾
```

❶ The `$in` resource passed into the filter must first be made writable before you can do anything with it.

❷ When consuming data, always be sure to update the `$consumed` output variable so PHP can keep track of how many bytes you've operated on.

❸ The `$out` resource is initially empty, and you need to write buckets to it in order for other filters (or just PHP itself) to continue acting on the stream.

❹ The `PSFS_PASS_ON` flag tells PHP that the filter was successful and data is available in the resource defined by `$out`.

❺ This particular filter can act on any `str.` flag but intentionally only reads two filter names for converting text to uppercase or lowercase. By switching on the defined filter name, you can intercept and filter *just* the operations you want, while allowing other filters to define their own `str.` functions.

❻ Defining the filter is not enough; you must explicitly register the filter so PHP knows which class to instantiate when filtering a stream.

❼ Once the filter is defined and registered, you must either append (or prepend) the custom filter to the list of filters attached to the current stream resource.

❽ With the filter attached, any data written to the stream will pass through the filter.

❾ Opening the file again demonstrates that your input data was indeed converted to uppercase. Note that `file_get_contents()` reads the entire file into memory rather than operating on it as a stream.

Internally, any custom filter's `filter()` method must return one of three flags:

PSFS_PASS_ON
Demonstrates that processing completed successfully and that the output bucket brigade (`$out`) contains data ready for the next filter

PSFS_FEED_ME
Demonstrates that the filter completed successfully, but no data was available to the output brigade. You must provide more data to the filter (either from the base stream or the filter immediately prior in the stack) to get any output

PSFS_ERR_FATAL
Indicates that the filter experienced an error

The `onCreate()` method exposes three internal variables from the underlying `php_user_filter` class as if they were properties of the child class itself:

`::filtername`
The name of the filter as specified in `stream_filter_append()` or `stream_filter_prepend()`

`::params`
Additional parameters passed into the filter either when appending or prepending it to the filter stack

`::stream`
The actual stream resource being filtered

Stream filters are powerful ways to manipulate data as it flows into or out of the system. The following recipes cover various uses of streams in PHP, including both stream wrappers and filters.

11.1 Streaming Data to/from a Temporary File

Problem

You want to use a temporary file to store data used elsewhere in a program.

Solution

To store data, use the `php://temp` stream as if it were a file as follows:

```
$fp = fopen('php://temp', 'rw');

while (true) {
    // Get data from some source

    fputs($fp, $data);

    if ($endOfData) {
```

```
        break;
    }
}
```

To retrieve that data again, rewind the stream to the beginning and then read the data
back out as follows:

```
rewind($fp);

while (true) {
    $data = fgets($fp);

    if ($data === false) {
        break;
    }

    echo $data;
}

fclose($fp);
```

Discussion

In general, PHP supports two different temporary data streams. The Solution example leverages the php://temp stream but could have just as easily used php://memory
to achieve the same effect. For streams of data that fit entirely in memory, the two
wrappers are interchangeable. Both will, by default, use system memory to store
stream data. Once the stream surpasses the amount of memory available to the application, however, php://temp will instead route the data to a temporary file on disk.

In both cases, the data written to the stream is assumed to be ephemeral. Once you
close the stream, this data is no longer available. Likewise, you cannot create a *new*
stream resource that points to the same data. Example 11-2 illustrates how PHP will
leverage *different* temporary files for streams even when using the same stream
wrapper.

Example 11-2. Temporary streams are unique

```
$fp = fopen('php://temp', 'rw');

fputs($fp, 'Hello world!'); ❶

rewind($fp); ❷
echo fgets($fp) . PHP_EOL; ❸

$fp2 = fopen('php://temp', 'rw'); ❹
fputs($fp2, 'Goodnight moon.'); ❺

rewind($fp); ❻
rewind($fp2);
```

```
echo fgets($fp2) . PHP_EOL; ❼
echo fgets($fp) . PHP_EOL; ❽
```

❶ Write a single line to the temporary stream.

❷ Rewind the stream handle so you can reread data from it.

❸ Reading data back out of the stream prints Hello world! to the console.

❹ Creating a new stream handle creates an entirely new stream despite the identical protocol wrapper.

❺ Write some unique data to this new stream.

❻ For good measure, rewind both streams.

❼ Print the second stream first to prove it's unique. This prints Goodnight moon. to the console.

❽ Reprint Hello world! to the console to prove that the original stream still works as expected.

In either case, a temporary stream is useful when you need to store some data while running an application and don't explicitly want to persist it to disk.

See Also

Documentation on fopen() (*https://oreil.ly/LR8pa*) and PHP I/O stream wrappers (*https://oreil.ly/6De6p*).

11.2 Reading from the PHP Input Stream

Problem

You want to read raw input from within PHP.

Solution

Leverage the php://stdin stream to read the standard input stream (stdin) (*https://oreil.ly/-_Bxl*) as follows:

```
$stdin = fopen('php://stdin', 'r');
```

Discussion

Like any other application, PHP has direct access to the input passed to it by commands and other upstream applications. In a console world, this might be another command, literal input in the terminal, or data piped in from another application. In a web context, though, you would instead use php://input+ to access the literal contents submitted in a web request and passed through whatever web server is in front of the PHP application.

 In command-line applications, you can also use the predefined STDIN constant (*https://oreil.ly/wgDpd*) directly. PHP natively opens a stream for you, meaning you don't need to create a new resource variable at all.

A simple command-line application might take data from the input, manipulate that data, and then store it in a file. In Recipe 9.5, you learned how to encrypt and decrypt files by using symmetric keys with Libsodium. Assuming you have an encryption key (encoded in hexadecimal) exposed as an environment variable, the program in Example 11-3 would use that key to encrypt any data passed in and store it in an output file.

Example 11-3. Encrypting stdin with Libsodium

```
if (empty($key = getenv('ENCRYPTION_KEY'))) { ❶
    throw new Exception('No encryption key provided!');
}

$key = hex2bin($key);
if (strlen($key) !== SODIUM_CRYPTO_STREAM_XCHACHA20_KEYBYTES) { ❷
    throw new Exception('Invalid encryption key provided!');
}

$in = fopen('php://stdin', 'r'); ❸
$filename = sprintf('encrypted-%s.bin', uniqid()); ❹
$out = fopen($filename, 'w'); ❺

[$state, $header] = sodium_crypto_secretstream_xchacha20poly1305_init_push($key); ❻

fwrite($out, $header);

while (!feof($in)) {
    $text = fread($in, 8175);

    if (strlen($text) > 0) {
        $cipher = sodium_crypto_secretstream_xchacha20poly1305_push($state, $text);

        fwrite($out, $cipher);
```

```
    }
}

sodium_memzero($state);

fclose($in);
fclose($out);

echo sprintf('Wrote %s' . PHP_EOL, $filename);
```

❶ Since you want to use an environment variable to house the encryption key, first check that this variable exists.

❷ Also do a sanity check that the key is of the right size before using it for encryption.

❸ In this example, read the bytes directly from stdin.

❹ Use a dynamically named file to store the encrypted data. Note that, in practice, uniqid() uses timestamps and could be subject to race conditions and name collisions on highly used systems. In a real-world environment, you will want to use a more reliable source of randomness for a generated filename.

❺ The output could be passed back to the console but, since this encryption produces raw bytes, it's safer to stream the output to a file. In this case, the filename will be generated dynamically based on the system clock.

❻ The rest of the encryption follows the same pattern as Recipe 9.5.

The preceding example enables you to pipe data from a file directly into PHP by using the standard input buffer. Such a piping operation might look something like cat plaintext-file.txt | php encrypt.php.

Given that the encryption operation will produce a file, you can reverse the operation with a similar script and similarly leverage cat to pipe the raw binary back into PHP, as shown in Example 11-4.

Example 11-4. Decrypting stdin with Libsodium

```
if (empty($key = getenv('ENCRYPTION_KEY'))) {
    throw new Exception('No encryption key provided!');
}

$key = hex2bin($key);
if (strlen($key) !== SODIUM_CRYPTO_STREAM_XCHACHA20_KEYBYTES) {
    throw new Exception('Invalid encryption key provided!');
}
```

```
$in = fopen('php://stdin', 'r');
$filename = sprintf('decrypted-%s.txt', uniqid());
$out = fopen($filename, 'w');

$header = fread($in, SODIUM_CRYPTO_SECRETSTREAM_XCHACHA20POLY1305_HEADERBYTES);
$state = sodium_crypto_secretstream_xchacha20poly1305_init_pull($header, $key);

try {
    while (!feof($in)) {
        $cipher = fread($in, 8192);

        [$plain, ] = sodium_crypto_secretstream_xchacha20poly1305_pull(
            $state,
            $cipher
        );

        if ($plain === false) {
            throw new Exception('Error decrypting file!');
        }

        fwrite($out, $plain);
    }
} finally {
    sodium_memzero($state);

    fclose($in);
    fclose($out);

    echo sprintf('Wrote %s' . PHP_EOL, $filename);
}
```

Thanks to PHP's I/O stream wrappers, arbitrary input streams are just as easy to manipulate as native files on a local disk.

See Also

Documentation on PHP I/O stream wrappers (*https://oreil.ly/wKjj9*).

11.3 Writing to the PHP Output Stream

Problem

You want to output data directly.

Solution

Write to php://output to push data directly to the standard output (stdout) stream (*https://oreil.ly/coZ8n*) as follows:

```
$stdout = fopen('php://stdout', 'w');
fputs($stdout, 'Hello, world!');
```

Discussion

PHP exposes three standard I/O streams to userland code—stdin, stdout, and stderr. By default, anything you print in your application is sent to the standard output stream (stdout), which makes the following two lines of code functionally equivalent:

```
fputs($stdout, 'Hello, world!');
echo 'Hello, world!';
```

Many developers learn to use echo and print statements as simple ways to debug an application; adding an indicator in your code makes it easy to identify where exactly the compiler is failing or to emit the value of an otherwise hidden variable. However, this isn't the *only* way to manage output. The stdout stream is common to many applications and writing to it directly (versus an implicit print statement) is a way to keep your application focused on what it needs to be doing.

Similarly, once you start leveraging php://stdout directly to print output to the client, you can start leveraging the php://stderr stream to emit messages about *errors* as well. These two streams are treated differently by the operating system, and you can use them to segment your messaging between useful messages and error states.

 In command-line applications, you can also use the predefined STDOUT and STDERR constants (*https://oreil.ly/HArEs*) directly. PHP natively opens these streams for you, meaning you don't need to create new resource variables at all.

Example 11-4 allowed you to read encrypted data from php://stdin, decrypt it, and then store the decrypted content in a file. A more useful example would instead present that decrypted data to php://stdout (and any errors to php://stderr), as shown in Example 11-5.

Example 11-5. Decrypting stdin to stdout

```
if (empty($key = getenv('ENCRYPTION_KEY'))) {
    throw new Exception('No encryption key provided!');
}

$key = hex2bin($key);
if (strlen($key) !== SODIUM_CRYPTO_STREAM_XCHACHA20_KEYBYTES) {
    throw new Exception('Invalid encryption key provided!');
}
```

```
$in = fopen('php://stdin', 'r');
$out = fopen('php://stdout', 'w');  ❶
$err = fopen('php://stderr', 'w');  ❷

$header = fread($in, SODIUM_CRYPTO_SECRETSTREAM_XCHACHA20POLY1305_HEADERBYTES);
$state = sodium_crypto_secretstream_xchacha20poly1305_init_pull($header, $key);

while (!feof($in)) {
    $cipher = fread($in, 8192);

    [$plain, ] = sodium_crypto_secretstream_xchacha20poly1305_pull(
        $state,
        $cipher
    );

    if ($plain === false) {
        fwrite($err, 'Error decrypting file!');  ❸
        exit(1);
    }

    fwrite($out, $plain);
}

sodium_memzero($state);

fclose($in);
fclose($out);
fclose($err);
```

❶ Rather than creating an intermediary file, you can write directly to the standard output stream.

❷ You should also get a handle on the standard error stream while you're at it.

❸ Rather than triggering an exception, you can write directly to the error stream.

See Also

Documentation on PHP I/O stream wrappers (*https://oreil.ly/PmXdc*).

11.4 Reading from One Stream and Writing to Another

Problem

You want to connect two streams, passing the bytes from one to the other.

Solution

Use `stream_copy_to_stream()` to copy data from one stream to another as follows:

```
$source = fopen('document1.txt', 'r');
$dest = fopen('destination.txt', 'w');

stream_copy_to_stream($source, $destination);
```

Discussion

The streaming mechanisms in PHP provide for very efficient ways to work with rather large chunks of data. Often, you might end up using files within your PHP application that are too large to fit in the application's available memory. Most files you might make public and send to the user directly via Apache or NGINX. In other cases, for example, you might want to safeguard large file downloads (like zip files or videos) with scripts written in PHP to validate a user's identity.

Such a scenario is possible in PHP because the system doesn't need to keep the entire stream in memory but can instead write bytes to one stream as they are read from another stream. Example 11-6 assumes that your PHP application directly authenticates a user and validates that they have the right to a particular file before streaming its contents.

Example 11-6. Copy large file to stdout by linking streams

```
if ($user->isAuthenticated()) {
    $in = fopen('largeZipFile.zip', 'r'); ❶
    $out = fopen('php://stdout', 'w');

    stream_copy_to_stream($in, $out); ❷
    exit; ❸
}
```

❶ The act of opening a stream merely gets a handle on the underlying data. No bytes have yet been read by the system.

❷ Copying a stream to another stream will copy the bytes directly without keeping the entire contents of either stream in memory. Remember, streams work on chunks similar to a bucket brigade, so only a subset of the necessary bytes are held in memory at any given time.

❸ It's important to always exit after copying a stream; otherwise, you might inadvertently append miscellaneous bytes by mistake.

Similarly, it is possible to programmatically *build* a large stream and copy it to another stream when needed. Some web applications might need to programmatically build large chunks of data (very large single-page web applications, for example). It is possible to write these large data elements to PHP's temporary memory stream and then copy the bytes back out when needed. Example 11-7 illustrates exactly how that would work.

Example 11-7. Copying a temporary stream to stdout

```
$buffer = fopen('php://temp', 'w+'); ❶
fwrite($buffer, '<html><head>');

// ... Several hundred fwrite()s later ...

fwrite($buffer, '</body></html>');
rewind($buffer); ❷

$output = fopen('php://stdout', 'w');
stream_copy_to_stream($buffer, $output); ❸
exit; ❹
```

❶ A temporary stream leverages a temporary file on disk. You are limited not by the memory available to PHP but by the available space allocated to temporary files by the operating system.

❷ After writing the entire HTML document to a temporary file, rewind the stream back to the beginning in order to copy all of those bytes to stdout.

❸ The mechanism to copy one stream to another remains unchanged even though neither of these streams point to a specifically identified file on disk.

❹ Always exit after all bytes have been copied to the client to avoid accidental errors.

See Also

Documentation on stream_copy_to_stream() (*https://oreil.ly/Us_Yj*).

11.5 Composing Different Stream Handlers Together

Problem

You want to combine multiple stream concepts—e.g., a wrapper and a filter—in one piece of code.

Solution

Append filters as necessary and use the appropriate wrapper protocol. Example 11-8 uses the `file://` protocol for local filesystem access and two additional filters to handle Base64-encoding and file decompression.

Example 11-8. Applying multiple fliers to a stream

```
$fp = fopen('compressed.txt', 'r'); ❶
stream_filter_append($fp, 'convert.base64-decode'); ❷
stream_filter_append($fp, 'zlib.inflate'); ❸

echo fread($fp, 1024) . PHP_EOL; ❹
```

❶ Assume this file exists on disk and contains the literal contents 80jNycnXUS jPL8pJUQQA.

❷ The first stream filter added to the stack will convert from Base64-encoded ASCII text to raw bytes.

❸ The second filter will leverage Zlib compression to inflate (or uncompress) the raw bytes.

❹ If you started with the literal contents in step 1, this will likely print Hello, world! to the console.

Discussion

When it comes to streams, it's helpful to think about layers. The foundation is always the protocol handler used to instantiate the stream. There is no explicit protocol in the Solution example, which means PHP will leverage the `file://` protocol by default. Atop that foundation is any number of layers of filters on the stream.

The Solution example leverages both Zlib compression and Base64 encoding to compress text and encode the raw (compressed) bytes, respectively. To create such a compressed/encoded file, you would do the following:

```
$fp = fopen('compressed.txt', 'w');

stream_filter_append($fp, 'zlib.deflate');
stream_filter_append($fp, 'convert.base64-encode');

fwrite($fp, 'Goodnight, moon!');
```

The preceding example leverages the same protocol wrapper and filters as the Solution example. But note that the *order* in which they are added is reversed. This is because stream filters work like the layers on a jawbreaker, similar to the illustration in Figure 11-2. The protocol wrapper is at the core, and data flows from that core to the outside world, through each subsequent layer in a specific order.

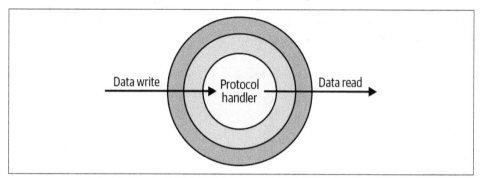

Figure 11-2. Data flowing into and out of PHP stream filters

There are several filters that you can apply to a stream already built into PHP. However, you can also define your *own* filter. It's useful to encode raw bytes in Base64, but it's also sometimes useful to encode/decode bytes as hexadecimal. Such a filter doesn't exist natively in PHP, but you can define it yourself by extending the `php_user_filter` class similarly to the way Example 11-1 did in this chapter's introduction. Consider the class in Example 11-9.

Example 11-9. Encoding/decoding hexadecimal with a filter

```php
class HexFilter extends php_user_filter
{
    private string $mode;

    public function filter($in, $out, &$consumed, bool $closing): int
    {
        while ($bucket = stream_bucket_make_writeable($in)) {
            switch ($this->mode) {
                case 'encode':
                    $bucket->data = bin2hex($bucket->data);
                    break;
                case 'decode':
                    $bucket->data = hex2bin($bucket->data);
                    break;
                default:
                    throw new Exception('Invalid encoding mode!');
            }

            $consumed += $bucket->datalen;
            stream_bucket_append($out, $bucket);
        }

        return PSFS_PASS_ON;
```

```
        }

    public function onCreate(): bool
    {
        switch($this->filtername) {
            case 'hex.decode':
                $this->mode = 'decode';
                return true;
            case 'hex.encode':
                $this->mode = 'encode';
                return true;
            default:
                return false;
        }
    }
}
```

The class defined in Example 11-9 can be used to arbitrarily encode to and decode from hexadecimal when applied as a filter to any arbitrary stream. Merely register it as you would any other filter, then apply it to whatever streams need to be converted.

The Base64 encoding used in the Solution example could be substituted with hexadecimal entirely, as shown in Example 11-10.

Example 11-10. Combining a hexadecimal stream filter with Zlib compression

```
stream_filter_register('hex.*', 'HexFilter'); ❶

// Writing data
$fp = fopen('compressed.txt', 'w');

stream_filter_append($fp, 'zlib.deflate');
stream_filter_append($fp, 'hex.encode');

fwrite($fp, 'Hello, world!' . PHP_EOL);
fwrite($fp, 'Goodnight, moon!');

fclose($fp); ❷

$fp2 = fopen('compressed.txt', 'r');
stream_filter_append($fp2, 'hex.decode');
stream_filter_append($fp2, 'zlib.inflate');

echo fread($fp2, 1024); ❸
```

❶ Once the filter exists, it must be registered so PHP knows how to use it. Leveraging a * wildcard during registration allows for both encoding and decoding to be registered at once.

❷ The contents of *compressed.txt* will be `f348cdc9c9d75128cf2fca4951e472cfcf` `4fc9cb4ccf28d151c8cdcfcf530400` at this point.

❸ After decoding and decompressing, `Hello world! Goodnight, moon!` will be printed to the console (with a newline between the two statements).

See Also

Supported protocols and wrappers (*https://oreil.ly/HxKpb*) and the list of available filters (*https://oreil.ly/IE5UR*). Also, Example 11-1 for a user-defined stream filter.

11.6 Writing a Custom Stream Wrapper

Problem

You want to define your own custom stream protocol.

Solution

Create a custom class that follows the prototype of `streamWrapper` and register it with PHP. For example, a `VariableStream` class could provide a stream-like interface to read from or write to a specific global variable, as follows:[2]

```
class VariableStream
{
    private int $position;
    private string $name;
    public $context;

    function stream_open($path, $mode, $options, &$opened_path)
    {
        $url = parse_url($path);
        $this->name = $url['host'];
        $this->position = 0;

        return true;
    }

    function stream_write($data)
    {
        $left = substr($GLOBALS[$this->name], 0, $this->position);
        $right = substr($GLOBALS[$this->name], $this->position + strlen($data));
        $GLOBALS[$this->name] = $left . $data . $right;
```

---

2 The PHP Manual provides a similarly named class (*https://oreil.ly/b0PLM*) with much broader and more complete functionality than is demonstrated in this Solution example.

```
        $this->position += strlen($data);
        return strlen($data);
    }
}
```

The preceding class would be registered and used in PHP as follows:

```
if (!in_array('var', stream_get_wrappers())) {
    stream_wrapper_register('var', 'VariableStream');
}

$varContainer = '';

$fp = fopen('var://varContainer', 'w');

fwrite($fp, 'Hello' . PHP_EOL);
fwrite($fp, 'World' . PHP_EOL);
fclose($fp);

echo $varContainer;
```

Discussion

The `streamWrapper` construct in PHP is a prototype for a class. Unfortunately, it is not a class that can be extended, nor is it an interface that can be concretely implemented. Instead, it is a documented format that any user-defined stream protocols must follow.

While it is possible to register classes as protocol handlers following a different interface, it is strongly advised that any potential protocol classes implement all methods defined by the `streamWrapper` interface (copied from the PHP document as a pseudo-interface definition in Example 11-11) in order to satisfy PHP's expected stream behavior

Example 11-11. `streamWrapper` interface definition

```
class streamWrapper {
    public $context;

    public __construct()

    public dir_closedir(): bool

    public dir_opendir(string $path, int $options): bool

    public dir_readdir(): string

    public dir_rewinddir(): bool

    public mkdir(string $path, int $mode, int $options): bool
```

```
    public rename(string $path_from, string $path_to): bool

    public rmdir(string $path, int $options): bool

    public stream_cast(int $cast_as): resource

    public stream_close(): void

    public stream_eof(): bool

    public stream_flush(): bool

    public stream_lock(int $operation): bool

    public stream_metadata(string $path, int $option, mixed $value): bool

    public stream_open(
        string $path,
        string $mode,
        int $options,
        ?string &$opened_path
    ): bool

    public stream_read(int $count): string|false

    public stream_seek(int $offset, int $whence = SEEK_SET): bool

    public stream_set_option(int $option, int $arg1, int $arg2): bool

    public stream_stat(): array|false

    public stream_tell(): int

    public stream_truncate(int $new_size): bool

    public stream_write(string $data): int

    public unlink(string $path): bool

    public url_stat(string $path, int $flags): array|false

    public __destruct()
}
```

Some specific functionality—e.g., mkdir, rename, rmdir, or unlink—should *not* be implemented at all unless the protocol has a specific use for it. Otherwise, the system will not provide helpful error messages to you (or developers building atop your library) and will behave unexpectedly.

While most protocols you will use day-to-day ship natively with PHP, it's possible to write new protocol handlers or leverage those built by other developers.

It's common to see references to cloud storage that use a proprietary protocol (e.g., Amazon Web Services' s3://) rather than the more common https:// or file:// prefixes seen elsewhere. AWS actually publishes a public SDK (*https://oreil.ly/RVXlw*) that uses stream_wrapper_register() internally to provide an s3:// protocol to other application code, empowering you to work with cloud-hosted data as easily as you would local files.

See Also

Documentation on streamWrapper (*https://oreil.ly/SyhD8*).

## CHAPTER 12

Error Handling

The best laid plans of mice and men often go awry.

—adapted from Robert Burns

If you work in programming or software development, you're probably very familiar with bugs and the process of debugging. You might have even spent as much time, if not more, tracking down bugs as you do writing code in the first place. It's an unfortunate maxim of software—no matter how hard a team works to build correct software, there will inevitably be a failure that needs to be identified and corrected.

Luckily, PHP makes finding bugs relatively straightforward. The forgiving nature of the language often also renders a bug a nuisance rather than a fatal flaw.

The following recipes introduce the quickest and easiest way to identify and handle bugs in your code. They also detail how to both code and handle custom exceptions thrown by your code in the event of invalid data output by a third-party API or other incorrect system behavior.

12.1 Finding and Fixing Parse Errors

Problem

The PHP compiler has failed to parse a script within your application; you want to find and correct the problem quickly.

Solution

Open the offending file in a text editor and review the line called out by the parser for syntax errors. If the problem isn't immediately apparent, walk backwards through the code one line at a time until you find the problem and make corrections in the file.

Discussion

PHP is a relatively forgiving language and will often attempt to let even an incorrect or problematic script run to completion. In many situations, though, the parser cannot properly interpret a line of code to identify what should be done and will instead return an error.

As a contrived example, loop through Western states in the US:

```
$states = ['Washington', 'Oregon', 'California'];
foreach $states as $state {
    print("{$state} is on the West coast.") . PHP_EOL;
}
```

This code, when run in a PHP interpreter, will throw a `Parse error` on the second line:

```
PHP Parse error:  syntax error, unexpected variable "$states", expecting "("
in php shell code on line 2
```

Based on this error message alone, you can zero in on the offending line. Remember that, though `foreach` is a language construct, it is still written similar to a function call with parentheses. The correct way to iterate through the array of states would be as follows:

```
$states = ['Washington', 'Oregon', 'California'];
foreach ($states as $state) {
    print("{$state} is on the West coast.") . PHP_EOL;
}
```

This particular error—omitting parentheses while leveraging language constructs—is common among developers frequently moving between languages. The same mechanism in Python, for example, looks nearly the same but is syntactically correct when omitting the parentheses on the `foreach` call. For example:

```
states = ['Washington', 'Oregon', 'California']
for state in states:
    print(f"{state} is on the West coast.")
```

The syntax of the two languages is confusingly similar. Thankfully, they are different enough that each language's parser will catch these differences and alert you, should you make such a mistake when moving back and forth between projects.

Conveniently, IDEs like Visual Studio Code (*https://oreil.ly/CkzbA*) automatically parse your script and highlight any syntax errors for you. Figure 12-1 illustrates how this highlighting makes it relatively easy to track down and correct issues before your application ever runs.

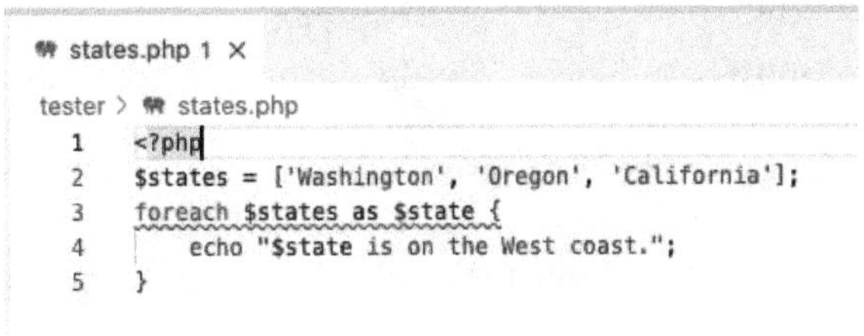

Figure 12-1. Visual Studio Code identifies and highlights syntax errors before your application runs

See Also

The list of tokens (*https://oreil.ly/Zw_1I*), various parts of the source code, used by the PHP parser.

12.2 Creating and Handling Custom Exceptions

Problem

You want your application to throw (and catch) a custom exception when things go wrong.

Solution

Extend the base `Exception` class to introduce custom behavior, then leverage `try/catch` blocks to capture and handle exceptions.

Discussion

PHP defines a basic `Throwable` (*https://oreil.ly/NkLuC*) interface implemented by any kind of error or exception in the language. Internal issues are then represented by the `Error` (*https://oreil.ly/eFMGz*) class and its descendants, while problems in userland are represented by the `Exception` class and its descendants.

Generally, you will only ever be extending the `Exception` class within your application, but you can catch any `Throwable` implementation within a standard `try/catch` block.

For example, assume you are implementing a division function with very precise, custom functionality:

1. Division by 0 is not allowed.
2. All decimal values will be rounded down.

3. The integer 42 is never valid as a numerator.

4. The numerator must be an integer, but the denominator can also be a float.

Such a function might leverage built-in errors like `ArithmeticError` or `DivisionByZeroError`. But in the preceding list of rules, the third stands out as requiring a custom exception. Before defining your function, you would define a custom exception as in Example 12-1.

Example 12-1. Simple custom exception definition

```
class HitchhikerException extends Exception
{
    public function __construct(int $code = 0, Throwable $previous = null)
    {
        parent::__construct('42 is indivisible.', $code, $previous);
    }

    public function __toString()
    {
        return __CLASS__ . ": [{$this->code}]: {$this->message}\n";
    }
}
```

Once the custom exception exists, you can throw it within your custom division function as follows:

```
function divide(int $numerator, float|int $denominator): int
{
    if ($denominator === 0) {
        throw new DivisionByZeroError;
    } elseif ($numerator === 42) {
        throw new HitchhikerException;
    }

    return floor($numerator / $denominator);
}
```

Once you've defined your custom functionality, it's a matter of leveraging that code in an application. You know the function *could* throw an error, so it's important to wrap any invocation in a `try` statement and handle that error appropriately. Example 12-2 will iterate through four pairs of numbers, attempting division on each, and handling any subsequent errors/exceptions thrown.

Example 12-2. Handling errors in custom division

```
$pairs = [
    [10, 2],
    [2, 5],
    [10, 0],
```

```
    [42, 2]
];

foreach ($pairs as $pair) {
    try {
        echo divide($pair[0], $pair[1]) . PHP_EOL;
    } catch (HitchhikerException $he) { ❶
        echo 'Invalid division of 42!' . PHP_EOL;
    } catch (Throwable $t) { ❷
        echo 'Look, a rabid marmot!' . PHP_EOL;
    }
}
```

❶ If 42 is ever passed as a numerator, the divide() function will throw a
HitchhikerException and fail to recover. Capturing this exception allows you to
provide feedback either to the application or to the user and move on.

❷ Any other Error or Exception thrown by the function will be caught as an
implementation of Throwable. In this case, you're throwing that error away and
moving on.

See Also

Documentation on the following:

- The base Exception class (*https://oreil.ly/2s4mN*)
- The list of predefined exceptions (*https://oreil.ly/TdeGN*)
- Additional exceptions as defined by the Standard PHP Library (SPL) (*https://oreil.ly/GSDEg*)
- Creating custom exceptions through extension (*https://oreil.ly/-jrVt*)
- The error hierarchy as of PHP 7 (*https://oreil.ly/KF1Zd*)

12.3 Hiding Error Messages from End Users

Problem

You've fixed all of the bugs you know of and are ready to launch your application in
production. But you also want to prevent any new errors from being displayed to end
users.

Solution

To completely suppress errors in production, set both the error_reporting and
display_errors directives in *php.ini* to Off as follows:

```
; Disable error reporting
error_reporting = Off
display_errors  = Off
```

Discussion

The configuration change presented in the Solution example will impact your entire application. Errors will be entirely suppressed and, even if they were to be thrown, will never be displayed to an end user. It's considered bad practice to present errors or unhandled exceptions directly to users. It might also lead to security issues if stack traces are presented directly to end users of the application.

However, if your application is misbehaving, nothing will be logged for the development team to diagnose and address.

For a production instance, leaving `display_errors` set to `Off` will still hide errors from end users, but reverting to the default `error_reporting` level will reliably send any errors to the logs.

There might be specific pages with known errors (due to legacy code, poorly written dependencies, or known technical debt) that you wish to omit, though. In those situations you can *programmatically* set the error reporting level by using the `error_reporting()` function in PHP. This function accept a new error reporting level and returns whatever level was previously set (the default if not previously configured).

As a result, you can use calls to `error_reporting()` to wrap problematic blocks of code and prevent too-chatty errors from being presented in the logs. For example:

```
$error_level = error_reporting(E_ERROR); ❶

// ... Call your other application code here.

error_reporting($error_level); ❷
```

❶ Set the error level to the absolute minimum, including only fatal runtime errors that halt script execution.

❷ Return the error level to its previous state.

The default error level is `E_ALL`, which presents all errors, warnings, and notices.[1] You can use integer reporting levels to override this, but PHP presents several named constants that represent each potential setting. These constants are enumerated in Table 12-1.

---

1 The default error level can be directly set in *php.ini* and, in many environments, might already be set to something other than `E_ALL`. Confirm your own environment's configuration to be sure.

Prior to PHP 8.0, the default error reporting level started with E_ALL and then explicitly removed diagnostic notices (E_NOTICE), strict type warnings (E_STRICT), and deprecation notices (E_DEPRECATED).

Table 12-1. Error reporting level constants

Integer value	Constant	Description
1	E_ERROR	Fatal runtime errors that result in script execution halting.
2	E_WARNING	Runtime warnings (nonfatal errors) that do not halt script execution.
4	E_PARSE	Compile-time errors generated by the parser.
8	E_NOTICE	Runtime notices that indicate that the script encountered something that could indicate an error but could also happen in the normal course of running a script.
16	E_CORE_ERROR	Fatal errors that occur during PHP's initial startup. This is like E_ERROR, except it is generated by the core of PHP.
32	E_CORE_WARNING	Warnings (nonfatal errors) that occur during PHP's initial startup. This is like E_WARNING, except it is generated by the core of PHP.
64	E_COMPILE_ERROR	Fatal compile-time errors. This is like E_ERROR, except it is generated by the Zend Scripting Engine.
128	E_COMPILE_WARNING	Compile-time warnings (nonfatal errors). This is like E_WARNING, except it is generated by the Zend Scripting Engine.
256	E_USER_ERROR	User-generated error messages. This is like E_ERROR, except it is generated in PHP code by using the PHP function trigger_error() (*https://oreil.ly/eNgVf*).
512	E_USER_WARNING	User-generated warning messages. This is like E_WARNING, except it is generated in PHP code by using the PHP function trigger_error().
1024	E_USER_NOTICE	User-generated notice messages. This is like E_NOTICE, except it is generated in PHP code by using the PHP function trigger_error().
2048	E_STRICT	Enable to have PHP suggest changes to your code which will ensure the best interoperability and forward compatibility of your code.
4096	E_RECOVERABLE_ERROR	Catchable fatal errors. A dangerous error occurred, but PHP is not unstable and can recover. If the error is not caught by a user-defined handle (see also Recipe 12.4), the application aborts as if it was an E_ERROR.
8192	E_DEPRECATED	Runtime notices. Enable this to receive warnings about code that will not work in future versions.
16384	E_USER_DEPRECATED	User-generated warning messages. This is like E_DEPRECATED, except it is generated in PHP code by using the PHP function trigger_error().
32767	E_ALL	All errors, warnings, and notices.

Note that you can combine error levels via binary operations, creating a bitmask. A simple error reporting level might include errors, warnings, and parser errors alone (omitting core, user errors, and notices). This level would be adequately set with the following:

```
error_reporting(E_ERROR | E_WARNING | E_PARSE);
```

See Also

Documentation on `error_reporting()` (*https://oreil.ly/b4eIH*), the `error_reporting` directive (*https://oreil.ly/t5IW2*), and the `display_errors` directive (*https://oreil.ly/lxXNs*).

12.4 Using a Custom Error Handler

Problem

You want to customize the way PHP handles and reports errors.

Solution

Define your custom handler as a callable function in PHP, then pass that function into `set_error_handler()` as follows:

```
function my_error_handler(int $num, string $str, string $file, int $line)
{
    echo "Encountered error $num in $file on line $line: $str" . PHP_EOL;
}

set_error_handler('my_error_handler');
```

Discussion

PHP will leverage your custom handler in most situations where an error is recoverable. Fatal errors, core errors, and compile-time issues (like parser errors) either halt or entirely prevent program execution and cannot be handled with a user function. Specifically, E_ERROR, E_PARSE, E_CORE_ERROR, E_CORE_WARNING, E_COMPILE_ERROR, and E_COMPILE_WARNING errors can never be caught. In addition, most E_STRICT errors in the file that invoked `set_error_handler()` cannot be caught, as the errors will be thrown before the custom handler is properly registered.

If you define a custom error handler consistent with the one presented in the Solution example, any catchable errors will then invoke this function and print data to the screen. As illustrated in Example 12-3, attempting to echo an undefined variable will cause an E_WARNING error.

Example 12-3. Catching recoverable runtime errors

```
echo $foo;
```

With `my_error_handler()` from the Solution example defined and registered, the erroneous code in Example 12-3 will print the following text to the screen, referencing the integer value of the `E_WARNING` error type:

```
Encountered error 2 in php shell code on line 1: Undefined variable $foo
```

Once you've caught an error to handle it, if the error is something that will lead to instability in the application, it is your responsibility to invoke `die()` to halt execution. PHP won't do this for you outside the handler and will instead continue processing the application as if no error had been thrown.

If, once you've handled errors in part of your application, you wish to restore the original (default) error handler, you should do so by calling `restore_error_handler()`. This merely reverts your earlier error handler registration and restores whatever error handler was previously registered.

Similarly, PHP empowers you to register (and restore) custom exception handlers. These operate the same as custom error handlers but instead capture any exception thrown outside a `try/catch` block. Unlike error handlers, program execution will halt after the custom exception handler has been called.

For more on exceptions, review Recipe 12.2 and the documentation for both `set_exception_handler()` (*https://oreil.ly/_pf4H*) and `restore_exception_&#x200b;han&#x2060;dler()` (*https://oreil.ly/TOEuz*).

See Also

Documentation on `set_error_handler()` (*https://oreil.ly/IAh69*) and `restore_error_handler()` (*https://oreil.ly/SlT_d*).

12.5 Logging Errors to an External Stream

Problem

You want to log application errors to a file or to an external source of some sort for future debugging.

Solution

Use `error_log()` to write errors to the default log file as follows:

```
$user_input = json_decode($raw_input);
if (json_last_error() !== JSON_ERROR_NONE) {
    error_log('JSON Error #' . json_last_error() . ': ' . $raw_input);
}
```

Discussion

By default, `error_log()` will log errors to whatever location is specified by the `error_log` directive (*https://oreil.ly/3lVPn*) in *php.ini*. Often on Unix-style systems, this will be a file within */var/log* but can be customized to be anywhere within your system.

The optional second parameter of `error_log()` allows you to route error messages where necessary. If the server is set up to send emails, you can specify a message type of 1 and provide an email address for the optional third parameter to send errors by email. For example:

```
error_log('Some error message', 1, 'developer@somedomain.tld');
```

Under the hood, `error_log()` will use the same functionality as `mail()` to send errors by email. In many cases, this might be disabled for security purposes. Be sure to verify the functionality of any mail systems before relying on this functionality, particularly in a production environment.

Alternatively, you can specify a file *other* than the default log location as the destination and pass the integer 3 as the message type. Rather than writing to the default logs, PHP will append the message to that file directly. For example:

```
error_log('Some error message', 3, 'error_log.txt');
```

When logging directly to a file with `error_log()`, the system will *not* append a newline character automatically. You will be responsible for either appending `PHP_EOL` to any string or encoding the \r \n newline literals.

Chapter 11 covers the file protocol at length as well as the other streams exposed by PHP. Remember that directly referencing a filepath is transparently leveraging the `file://` protocol so, in reality, you are logging errors to a file *stream* with the preceding code block. You can just as easily reference any other kind of stream so long as you properly reference the stream protocol. The following example logs errors directly to the console's standard error stream:

```
error_log('Some error message', 3, 'php://stderr');
```

See Also

Documentation on `error_log()` (*https://oreil.ly/QUQRH*) and Recipe 13.5's coverage of Monolog, a more comprehensive logging library for PHP applications.

## CHAPTER 13

Debugging and Testing

Despite developers' best efforts, no code is ever perfect. You will inevitably introduce a bug that impacts the production behavior of your application or causes an end user distress when something doesn't operate as expected.

Properly handling errors within your application is critical.[1] However, not every error your application throws is expected—or even catchable. In these circumstances, you must understand how to properly *debug* your application—how to track down the offending line of code so it can be fixed.

Among the first steps any PHP engineer uses to debug their code is the echo statement. Without a formal debugger, it's common to see development code littered with echo "Here!"; statements so the team can track where things might be broken.

The Laravel framework has made similar functionality popular and easily accessible while working on new projects by exposing a function called dd() (*https://oreil.ly/N-bOz*) (short for "dump and die"). This function is actually provided by the Symfony var-dumper (*https://oreil.ly/8pXGo*) module and works effectively in both PHP's native command-line interface and when leveraging an interactive debugger. The function itself is defined as follows:

```
function dd(...$vars): void
{
    if (!in_array(\PHP_SAPI, ['cli', 'phpdbg'], true) && !headers_sent()) {
        header('HTTP/1.1 500 Internal Server Error');
    }

    foreach ($vars as $v) {
        VarDumper::dump($v);
```

---

1 For more on error handling, review Chapter 12.

```
    }

  exit(1);
}
```

The preceding function, when used in a Laravel application, will print the contents of any variable you pass it to the screen and then halt the program's execution immediately. Like using echo, it's not the most elegant way to debug an application. However, it is fast, reliable, and a common way developers will debug a system in a hurry.

One of the best ways to preemptively debug your code is through unit testing. By breaking your code down into the smallest units of logic, you can write additional code that automatically tests and verifies the functionality of those units of logic. You then wire these tests to your integration and deployment pipeline and can ensure that nothing has broken in your application prior to deployment.

The open source PHPUnit (*https://phpunit.de*) project makes it simple and straight-forward to instrument your entire application and automatically test its behavior. All of your tests are written in PHP, load your application's functions and classes directly, and explicitly document the correct behavior of the application.

An alternative to PHPUnit is the open source Behat (*https://oreil.ly/ mAWR5*) library. Whereas PHPUnit focuses on test-driven development (TDD), Behat focuses on an alternative *behavior*-driven development (BDD) paradigm. Both are equally useful for testing your code, and your team should choose which approach to take. PHPUnit is a more established project, though, and will be referenced throughout this chapter.

Hands down, the best way to debug your code is to use an interactive debugger. Xdebug (*https://xdebug.org*) is a debugging extension for PHP that improves error handling, supports tracing or profiling an application's behavior, and integrates with testing tools like PHPUnit to illustrate test coverage of application code. More importantly, Xdebug also supports interactive, step-through debugging of your application.

Armed with Xdebug and a compatible IDE, you can place flags in your code called *breakpoints*. When the application is running and hits these breakpoints, it pauses execution and allows you to interactively inspect the state of the application. This means you can view all variables in scope, where they came from, and continue executing the program one command at a time in your hunt for bugs. It is by far the most powerful tool in your arsenal as a PHP developer!

The following recipes cover the basics of debugging PHP applications. You will learn how to set up interactive debugging, capture errors, properly test your code to prevent regressions, and quickly identify when and where a breaking change has been introduced.

13.1 Using a Debugger Extension

Problem

You want to leverage a robust, external debugger to inspect and manage your application so you can identify, profile, and eliminate errors in business logic.

Solution

Install Xdebug, an open source debugging extension for PHP. Xdebug can be installed directly on Linux operating systems by using the default package manager. On Ubuntu, for example, install Xdebug by using `apt`:

```
$ sudo apt install php-xdebug
```

As package managers can sometimes install an outdated version of the project, you can also install it directly with the PECL extension manager:

```
$ pecl install xdebug
```

Once Xdebug is live on your system, it will embellish error pages for you automatically, presenting rich stack traces and debugging information to make it easier to identify errors when things go wrong.

Discussion

Xdebug is a powerful extension for PHP. It empowers you to fully test, profile, and debug your applications in effective ways the language does not support natively. One of the most useful features you get by default with no additional configuration is a vast improvement to error reporting.

By default, Xdebug will automatically capture any errors thrown by your application and expose additional information about the following:

- The call stack (as illustrated in Figure 13-1), including both timing and memory utilization data. This helps you identify exactly when the program failed and where in code the function calls were occurring.

- Variables from the local scope so you don't need to guess what data was in memory when the error was thrown.

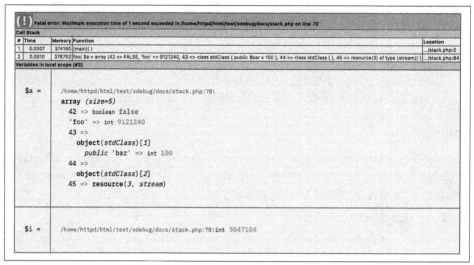

#	Time	Memory	Function	Location
			Fatal error: Maximum execution time of 1 second exceeded in /home/httpd/html/test/xdebug/docs/stack.php on line 70	
			Call Stack	
1	0.0007	374160	{main}( )	.../stack.php:0
2	0.0010	376752	foo($a = array (42 => FALSE, 'foo' => 9121240, 43 => class stdClass { public $bar = 100 }, 44 => class stdClass { }, 45 => resource(3) of type (stream)))	.../stack.php:84

Variables in local scope (#2)

```
$a =    /home/httpd/html/test/xdebug/docs/stack.php:70:
        array (size=5)
          42 => boolean false
          'foo' => int 9121240
          43 =>
            object(stdClass)[1]
              public 'bar' => int 100
          44 =>
            object(stdClass)[2]
          45 => resource(3, stream)


$i =    /home/httpd/html/test/xdebug/docs/stack.php:70:int 3047104
```

Figure 13-1. Xdebug enriches and formats the information presented when errors occur

Advanced integrations with tools like Webgrind (*https://oreil.ly/OXg9b*) also allow you to dynamically profile the performance of your application. Xdebug will (optionally) record the execution time of every function invocation and record both that time and the "cost" of a function call to disk. The Webgrind application then presents a handy visualization to help you identify bottlenecks in your code to optimize the program as necessary.

You can even pair Xdebug directly with your development environment for step-through debugging (*https://oreil.ly/FK9iz*). By pairing your environment (e.g., Visual Studio Code (*https://oreil.ly/u4dZy*)) with an Xdebug configuration, you can place breakpoints in your code and literally pause execution when the PHP interpreter hits those points.

 The PHP Debug (*https://oreil.ly/vVCVY*) extension makes integration between Xdebug and Visual Studio Code incredibly straightforward. It adds all of the additional interfaces you'd expect directly to your IDE, in terms of both breakpoints and environment introspection. It's also maintained directly by the Xdebug community, so you can be sure it's in sync with the overall project.

While debugging in step-through mode, your application will pause on a breakpoint and give you direct access to all variables within the program scope. You can both inspect *and modify* these variables to test your environment. Further, while paused in a breakpoint, you have full console access to the application to further identify what might be going on. The call stack is directly exposed, so you can dive deep into which function or method object has led to the breakpoint and make changes where necessary.

While in a breakpoint, you can either step through the program one line at a time or opt to "continue" execution either until the next breakpoint or until the first error thrown by the program. Breakpoints can also be disabled without removing them from the IDE, so you can continue execution as necessary but revisit particular trouble spots later on demand.

 Xdebug is an immensely powerful development tool for any PHP development team. However, it has been known to add significant performance overhead to even the smallest application. Ensure that you are only ever enabling this extension for local development or in protected environments with test deployments. Never deploy your application to production with Xdebug installed!

See Also

Documentation and home page for Xdebug (*https://xdebug.org*).

13.2 Writing a Unit Test

Problem

You want to validate the behavior of a piece of code to ensure that future refactoring doesn't change the functionality of your application.

Solution

Write a class that extends PHPUnit's `TestCase` and explicitly tests the behavior of the application. For example, if your function is intended to extract a domain name from an email address, you would define it as follows:

```
function extractDomain(string $email): string
{
    $parts = explode('@', $email);

    return $parts[1];
}
```

Then create a class to test and validate the functionality of this code. Such a test would look like the following:

```
use PHPUnit\Framework\TestCase;

final class FunctionTest extends TestCase
{
```

```
    public function testSimpleDomainExtraction()
    {
        $this->assertEquals('example.com', extractDomain('php@example.com'));
    }
}
```

Discussion

The most important aspect of PHPUnit is how you organize your project. First of all, the project needs to leverage Composer for autoloading both your application code and for loading any dependencies (including PHPUnit itself).[2] Typically, you will place your application code in a *src/* directory within the root of your project, and all of your test code will live in a *tests/* directory alongside it.

In the Solution example, you would place your `extractDomain()` function in *src/functions.php* and the `FunctionTest` class in *tests/FunctionTest.php*. Assuming autoloading is properly configured via Composer, you would then run the test using PHPUnit's bundled command-line tool as follows:

```
$ ./vendor/bin/phpunit tests
```

The preceding command will, by default, automatically identify and run every test class defined in your *tests/* directory via PHPUnit. To more comprehensively control the way PHPUnit runs, you can leverage a local configuration file to describe test suites, file allow lists, and configure any specific environment variables needed during testing.

The XML-based configuration is not often used except for complex or complicated projects, but the project documentation (*https://oreil.ly/Gz86n*) details at length how to configure it. A basic *phpunit.xml* file usable with this recipe or other similarly simple projects would look something like Example 13-1.

Example 13-1. Basic PHPUnit XML configuration

```
<?xml version="1.0" encoding="UTF-8"?>

<phpunit bootstrap="vendor/autoload.php"
         backupGlobals="false"
         backupStaticAttributes="false"
         colors="true"
         convertErrorsToExceptions="true"
         convertNoticesToExceptions="true"
         convertWarningsToExceptions="true"
         processIsolation="false"
         stopOnFailure="false">
```

---

2 For more on Composer, see Recipe 15.1.

```
<coverage>
  <include>
    <directory suffix=".php">src/</directory>
  </include>
</coverage>

<testsuites>
  <testsuite name="unit">
    <directory>tests</directory>
  </testsuite>
</testsuites>

<php>
  <env name="APP_ENV" value="testing"/>
</php>

</phpunit>
```

Armed with the preceding *phpunit.xml* file in your project, you merely need to invoke PHPUnit itself to run your tests. You no longer need to specify the *tests/* directory, as that's now provided by the `testsuite` definition in the application configuration.

Similarly, you can also specify *multiple* test suites for different scenarios. Perhaps one set of tests is built by your development team proactively as they're writing code (*unit* in the preceding example). Another set of tests might be written by your quality assurance (QA) team to replicate user-reported bugs (*regressions*). The advantage of the second test suite is that you can then refactor your application until the tests pass (i.e., the bugs are fixed) while also ensuring that you haven't modified the overall behavior of your application.

You can also ensure that old bugs don't reappear down the line!

In addition, you can choose which test suite runs at which time by passing the optional `--testsuite` flag to PHPUnit when it's run. Most tests are going to be fast, meaning they can be run frequently without costing your development team any additional time. Fast tests should be run as frequently as possible during development to ensure that your code is working and that no new (or old) bugs have crept into the codebase. At times, though, you might need to write a test that is too costly to run very often. These tests should be kept in a separate test suite so you can test around them. The tests remain and can be used before a deployment but won't slow down day-to-day development when standard tests run frequently.

Function tests, like that in the Solution example, are quite simple. Object tests are similar in that you are instantiating an object within a test and exercising its methods. The hardest part, however, is simulating multiple possible inputs to a particular function or method. PHPUnit solves this with data providers.

For a simple example, consider the add() function in Example 13-2. This function explicitly uses loose typing to add two values (regardless of their types) together.

Example 13-2. Simple addition function

```
function add($a, $b): mixed
{
    return $a + $b;
}
```

Since the parameters in the preceding function can be of different types (int/int, int/float, string/float, etc.), you should test the various combinations to ensure that nothing breaks. Such a test structure would look like the class in Example 13-3.

Example 13-3. Simple test of PHP addition

```
final class FunctionTest extends TestCase
{
    // ...

    /**
     * @dataProvider additionProvider
     */
    public function testAdd($a, $b, $expected): void
    {
        $this->assertSame($expected, add($a, $b));
    }

    public function additionProvider(): array
    {
        return [
            [2, 3, 5],
            [2, 3.0, 5.0],
            [2.0, '3', 5.0],
            ['2', 3, 5]
        ];
    }
}
```

The @dataProvider annotation tells PHPUnit the name of a function within the test's class that should be used to provide data for testing. Rather than writing four separate tests, you've now provided PHPUnit with the ability to run a single test four times with differing inputs and expected outputs. The end result is the same—four separate tests of your add() function—but without the need to explicitly write those extra tests.

Given the structure of the add() function defined in Example 13-2, you might run afoul of certain type restrictions in PHP. While it's possible to pass numeric strings

---

into the function (they're cast to numeric values before addition), passing non-numeric data will result in a PHP warning. In a world where user input is passed to this function, that kind of issue can and will come up. It's best to protect against it by explicitly checking the input values with is_numeric() and throwing a known exception that can be caught elsewhere.

To accomplish this, first write a new test to *expect* that exception and validate that it's thrown appropriately. Such a test would look like Example 13-4.

Example 13-4. Testing the expected presence of exceptions in your code

```php
final class FunctionTest extends TestCase
{
    // ...

    /**
     * @dataProvider invalidAdditionProvider
     */
    public function testInvalidInput($a, $b, $expected): void
    {
        $this->expectException(InvalidArgumentException::class);
        add($a, $b);
    }

    public function invalidAdditionProvider(): array
    {
        return [
            [1, 'invalid', null],
            ['invalid', 1, null],
            ['invalid', 'invalid', null]
        ];
    }
}
```

 Writing tests before changing your code is valuable because it gives you a precise target to achieve while refactoring. However, this new test will fail until you make the changes to the application code. Take care not to commit failing tests to your project's version control or you will compromise your team's ability to practice continuous integration!

With the preceding test in place, the test suite now fails as the function does not match the documented or expected behavior. Take time to add the appropriate is_numeric() checks to the function as follows:

```php
function add($a, $b): mixed
{
    if (!is_numeric($a) || !is_numeric($b)) {
```

```
            throw new InvalidArgumentException('Input must be numeric!');
        }

        return $a + $b;
    }
```

Unit tests are an effective way to document the expected and appropriate behavior of your application since they are executable code that also validates that the application is functioning properly. You can test both success *and* failure conditions and even go so far as to mock various dependencies within your code.

The PHPUnit project also provides the ability to proactively identify the percentage of your application code that is covered by unit tests (*https://oreil.ly/PEdVd*). A higher percentage of coverage is not a guarantee against bugs but is a reliable way to ensure that bugs can be found and corrected quickly with minimal impact to end users.

See Also

Documentation on how to leverage PHPUnit (*https://oreil.ly/5oYv4*).

13.3 Automating Unit Tests

Problem

You want your project's unit tests to run frequently, without user interaction, before any changes to the codebase are committed to version control.

Solution

Leverage a Git commit hook to automatically run your unit tests *before* a commit is made locally. For example, the pre-commit hook in Example 13-5 will automatically run PHPUnit every time the user runs git commit but before any data is actually written to the repository.

Example 13-5. Simple Git pre-commit hook for PHPUnit

```
#!/usr/bin/env php
<?php

echo "Running tests.. ";
exec('vendor/bin/phpunit', $output, $returnCode);

if ($returnCode !== 0) {
  echo PHP_EOL . implode($output, PHP_EOL) . PHP_EOL;
  echo "Aborting commit.." . PHP_EOL;
  exit(1);
}
```

```php
echo array_pop($output) . PHP_EOL;

exit(0);
```

Discussion

Git is by far the most popular distributed version control system available and is also the system used by the core PHP development team. It's open source and highly flexible both in how it hosts repositories and how you can customize workflows and project structures to fit your development cycle.

Specifically, Git allows customization by way of hooks. Your hooks live in the *.git/ hooks* directory within your project alongside other information Git uses to track the state of your project itself. By default, even an empty Git repository includes several sample hooks, as shown in Figure 13-2.

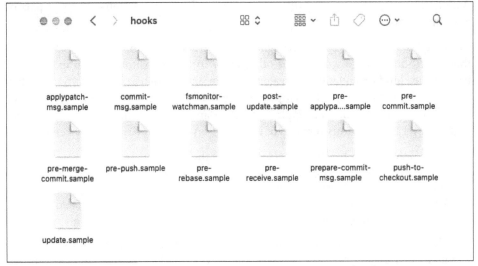

Figure 13-2. Git initializes even an empty repository with sample hooks

Each of the sample hooks is postfixed with a `.sample` extension that will disable it by default. If the sample hooks are ever something you do want to use, merely remove that extension, and the hook will run on that action.

In the case of automated testing, you want the `pre-commit` hook explicitly and should create a file with that name containing the contents of Example 13-5. With the hook in place, Git will always run this script before it commits the code.

The `0` exit status at the end of the script tells Git everything is OK and it can continue with the commit. Should any of your unit tests fail, the `1` exit status will flag that something went wrong, and the commit will abort without modifying your repository.

If you are absolutely sure you know what you're doing and need to override the hook for any reason, you can bypass the hook by adding the `--no-verify` flag when committing your code.

 The `pre-commit` hook is run entirely on the client side and lives outside your code repository. Every developer will need to install the hook individually. Aside from team guidelines or company policy, there isn't an effective way to enforce that the hook is being used (or that someone isn't bypassing it with `--no-verify`).

If your team is using Git for version control, there's a very good chance you're also using GitHub to host a version of your repository. If so, you can leverage GitHub Actions to run PHPUnit tests (*https://oreil.ly/BmGZC*) on GitHub's server as part of your integration and deployment pipeline.

Running tests locally helps protect against accidentally committing a *regression* (code that reintroduces a known bug) or other error to the repository. Running the same tests in the cloud provides even greater functionality as you can do so across a matrix of potential configurations. Developers will typically run only a single version of PHP locally, but you can run your application code and tests in containers on the server that are leveraging various versions of PHP or even different dependency versions.

Using GitHub Actions to run tests also provides the following benefits:

- If a new developer hasn't yet set up their Git `pre-commit` hook and commits broken code, the Action runner will immediately flag the commit as broken and prevent that developer from accidentally releasing a bug into production.

- Using a deterministic environment in the cloud protects your team against "well, it worked on my machine" issues, where code works in one local environment but then fails in a production environment that has a different configuration.

- Your integration and deployment workflow should build new deployment artifacts from every commit. Wiring this build process to your tests ensures that every build artifact is free from known defects and is, in fact, deployable.

See Also

Documentation on customizing Git by using hooks (*https://oreil.ly/TzVOA*).

13.4 Using Static Code Analysis

Problem

You want to leverage an external tool to ensure that your code is free from as many errors as possible before it ever runs.

Solution

Use a static code analysis tool like PHPStan (*https://phpstan.org*).

Discussion

PHPStan is a static code analysis tool for PHP that helps minimize errors in production code by flagging them for correction long before you've shipped your application. It's best when used with strict typing and helps your team write more manageable and understandable applications.[3]

Like many other development tools, PHPStan can be installed into your project via Composer with the following:

```
$ composer require --dev phpstan/phpstan
```

You can then run PHPStan against your project, analyzing both your application code and your tests directly. For example:

```
$ ./vendor/bin/phpstan analyze src tests
```

By default, PHPStan runs at level 0, which is the absolute loosest level of static analysis possible. You can specify a higher level of scanning by passing the --level flag at the command line with a number greater than 0. Table 13-1 enumerates the various levels available. For well-maintained, strictly typed applications, a level 9 analysis is the best way to ensure quality code.

Table 13-1. PHPStan rule levels

Level	Description
0	Basic checks for unknown classes, functions, or class methods. Will also check number of arguments in function calls and any variables that are never defined.
1	Checks for possibly undefined variables, unknown magic methods, and dynamic properties retrieved through magic getters.
2	Validates unknown methods on all expressions and validates functional documentation (docblocks in code).
3	Checks return types and property type assignment.
4	Checks for dead code (e.g., conditionals that are always false) and unreachable code paths.

---

3 Strict typing is discussed at length in Recipe 3.4.

Level	Description
5	Checks argument types.
6	Reports on missing type hints.
7	Reports partially incorrect union types.[a]
8	Checks for any method calls or property access on nullable types.
9	Strict checks on usage of `mixed` typing.

[a] For examples of union types, see the discussion of Example 3-9.

Once you've run the analysis tool, you can work on updating your application to fix basic flaws and validation errors. You can also automate the use of static analysis, similarly to the way you automated testing in Recipe 13.3 to ensure that the team is running analyses (and fixing identified errors) regularly.

See Also

The PHPStan project home page and documentation (*https://phpstan.org*).

13.5 Logging Debugging Information

Problem

You want to log information about your program when things go wrong so you can debug any potential errors later.

Solution

Leverage the open source Monolog (*https://oreil.ly/yDIM7*) project to implement a comprehensive logging interface within your application. First install the package by using Composer as follows:

```
$ composer require monolog/monolog
```

Then wire the logger into your application so you can emit warnings and errors whenever necessary. For example:

```
use Monolog\Level;
use Monolog\Logger;
use Monolog\Handler\StreamHandler;

$logPath  = getenv('LOG_PATH')  ?? '/var/log/php/error.log';
$logLevel = getenv('LOG_LEVEL') !== false
            ? Level::from(intval(getenv('LOG_LEVEL')))
            : Level::Warning;

$logger = new Logger('default');
$logger->pushHandler(new StreamHandler($logPath, $logLevel));
```

```
$log->warning('Hello!');
$log->error('World!');
```

Discussion

The easiest way to log information from PHP is via its built-in `error_log()` function (*https://oreil.ly/kXYJP*). This will log errors either to the server error log or to a flat file as configured in *php.ini*. The only problem is that the function explicitly logs *errors* in the application.

A result is that any content logged by `error_log()` is treated as an error by any system parsing the log file. This can make it difficult to disambiguate between true errors (e.g., user login failures) and messages logged for debugging purposes. The intermingling of true errors and debugging statements can make runtime configuration difficult, particularly when you want to turn off certain logging in various environments. A workaround is to wrap any calls to `error_log()` in a check for the current logging level as shown in Example 13-6.

Example 13-6. Selectively logging errors with `error_log()`

```
enum LogLevel: int ❶
{
    case Debug   = 100;
    case Info    = 200;
    case Warning = 300;
    case Error   = 400;
}

$logLevel = getenv('LOG_LEVEL') !== false ❷
            ? LogLevel::from(intval(getenv('LOG_LEVEL')))
            : LogLevel::Debug;

// Some application code ...
if (user_session_expired()) {
    if ($logLevel >= LogLevel::Info) { ❸
        error_log('User session expired. Logging out ...');
    }

    logout();
    exit;
}
```

❶ The easiest way to enumerate logging levels is with a literal `enum` type in PHP.

❷ The log level should be retrievable from the system environment. If it's not provided, then you should fall back on a sane, hardcoded default.

---

❸ Whenever you invoke `error_log()`, you'll need to explicitly check the current logging level and decide whether or not to actually emit the error.

The problem with Example 13-6 isn't the use of an `enum`, nor is it the fact that you need to dynamically load the logging level from the environment. The problem is that you have to explicitly check the logging level prior to every invocation of `error_log()` to ensure that the program *actually should* emit an error. This frequent checking leads to a lot of spaghetti code and makes your application both less readable and more difficult to maintain.

A seasoned developer will realize the perfect solution here would be to wrap all of the logging logic (including log level checking) in a functional interface to keep the application clean. That's absolutely the right approach, and the entire reason the Monolog package exists!

> While Monolog is a popular PHP package for application logging, it is not the only package available. Monolog implements PHP's standard Logger interface (*https://oreil.ly/76eAV*); any package implementing the same interface can be dropped into your application in place of Monolog to provide similar functionality.

Monolog is far more powerful than merely printing strings to an error log. It also supports channels, various handlers, processors, and logging levels.

When instantiating a new logger, you first define a channel for that object. This allows you to create multiple logging instances side by side, keep their contents separate, and even route them to different means of output. By default, a logger needs more than a channel to operate, so you must also push a handler onto the call stack.

A handler (*https://oreil.ly/_1wLC*) defines what Monolog should do with any message passed into a particular channel. It could route data to a file, store messages in a database, send errors via email, notify a team or channel on Slack of an issue, or even communicate with systems like RabbitMQ or Telegram.

> Monolog also supports different formatters that can be attached to various handlers. Each formatter defines how messages will be serialized and sent out to the defined handler—for example, as a one-line string, a JSON blob, or an Elasticsearch document. Unless you're working with a handler that requires data in a specific format, you'll likely be just fine with the default formatter.

A processor is an optional extra step that can add data to a message. For example, the IntrospectionProcessor (*https://oreil.ly/jp-US*) will automatically add the line, file, class, and/or method from which the log call was made to the log itself. A basic

Monolog setup to log to a flat file with introspection would look something like Example 13-7.

Example 13-7. Monolog configuration with introspection

```
use Monolog\Level;
use Monolog\Logger;
use Monolog\Handler\StreamHandler;
use Monolog\Processor\IntrospectionProcessor;

$logger = new Logger('default');
$logger->pushHandler(new StreamHandler('/var/log/app.log', Level::Debug));
$logger->pushProcessor(new IntrospectionProcessor());

// ...

$logger->debug('Something happened ...');
```

The last line of Example 13-7 invokes your configured logger and sends a literal string through the processor to the handler you've wired in. In addition, you can optionally pass additional data about the execution context or the error itself in an array as an optional second parameter.

Even without the additional context, if this entire code block lives in a file called */src/app.php*, it will produce something resembling the following in the application log:

```
[2023-01-08T22:02:00.734710+00:00] default.DEBUG: Something happened ...
[] {"file":"/src/app.php","line":15,"class":null,"callType":null,"function":null}
```

All you needed to do was create a single line of text (`Something happened ...`), and Monolog automatically captured the event timestamp, the error level, and details about the call stack thanks to the registered processor. All of this information makes debugging and potential error correction that much easier for you and your development team.

Monolog also abstracts away the burden of checking the error level on each call. Instead, you define the error level at play in two locations:

- When registering a handler to the logger instance itself. Only errors of this error level or higher will be captured by the handler.
- When emitting a message to the logger channel, you explicitly identify the error level attributed to it. For example, `::debug()` sends a message with an explicit error level of `Debug` assigned to it.

Monolog supports the eight error levels listed in Table 13-2, all illustrated by the syslog protocol described by RFC 5424 (*https://oreil.ly/Jtm9k*).

Table 13-2. Monolog error levels

Error level	Logger method	Description
Level::Debug	::debug()	Detailed debugging information.
Level::Info	::info()	Normal events like SQL logs or information application events.
Level::Notice	::notice()	Normal events that have greater significance than informational messages.
Level::Warning	::warning()	Application warnings that could become errors in the future if action is not taken.
Level::Error	::error()	Application errors requiring immediate attention.
Level::Critical	::critical()	Critical conditions impacting the operation of the application. For example, instability or lack of availability in a key component.
Level::Alert	::alert()	Immediate action is required because of a key system failure. In critical applications, this error level should page an on-call engineer.
Level::Emergency	::emergency()	The application is unusable.

Through Monolog, you can intelligently wrap error messages in the appropriate logger method and determine when these errors are actually sent to a handler based on the error level used when creating the logger itself. If you instantiate a logger only for Error-level messages and above, any calls to ::debug() will *not* result in a log. The ability to discretely control your log output in production versus development is vital to building a stable and well-logged application.

See Also

Usage instructions for the Monolog package (*https://oreil.ly/_5wx6*).

13.6 Dumping Variable Contents as Strings

Problem

You want to inspect the contents of a complex variable.

Solution

Use var_dump() to convert the variable into a human-readable format and print it to the current output stream (like the command-line console). For example:

```
$info = new stdClass;
$info->name = 'Book Reader';
$info->profession = 'PHP Developer';
$info->favorites = ['PHP', 'MySQL', 'Linux'];

var_dump($info);
```

The preceding code will print the following to the console when run in the CLI:

```
object(stdClass)#1 (3) {
  ["name"]=>
  string(11) "Book Reader"
  ["profession"]=>
  string(13) "PHP Developer"
  ["favorites"]=>
  array(3) {
    [0]=>
    string(3) "PHP"
    [1]=>
    string(5) "MySQL"
    [2]=>
    string(5) "Linux"
  }
}
```

Discussion

Every form of data in PHP has some string representation. Objects can enumerate their types, fields, and methods. Arrays can enumerate their members. Scalar types can expose both their types and values. It's possible for developers to get at the inner contents of any variable in any of three slightly different but equally valuable ways.

First, var_dump() as used in the Solution example directly prints the contents of a variable to the console. This string representation details the types involved, the names of fields, and the value of interior members directly. It's useful as a quick way to inspect what lives within a variable, but it isn't much use beyond that.

 Take care to ensure that var_dump() doesn't make its way into production. This function does not escape data and could render unsanitized user input to your application's output, introducing a serious security vulnerability.[4]

More helpful is PHP's var_export() function. By default, it also prints the contents of any variable passed in, except the output format is itself executable PHP code. The same $info object from the Solution example would print as follows:

```
(object) array(
   'name' => 'Book Reader',
   'profession' => 'PHP Developer',
   'favorites' =>
  array (
    0 => 'PHP',
    1 => 'MySQL',
    2 => 'Linux',
```

---

4 For more on data sanitization, see Recipe 9.1.

```
        ),
    )
```

Unlike `var_dump()`, `var_export()` accepts an optional second parameter that will instruct the function to *return* its output rather than print it to the screen. This results in a string literal that represents the contents of the variable being returned, which could then itself be stored elsewhere for future reference.

A third and final alternative is to use PHP's `print_r()` function. Like both of the preceding functions, it produces a human-readable representation of the variable's contents. As with `var_export()`, you can pass an optional second parameter to the variable to return its output rather than print it to the screen.

Unlike both of the preceding functions, though, not all typing information is exposed directly by `print_r()`. For example, the same `$info` object from the Solution example would print as follows:

```
stdClass Object
(
    [name] => Book Reader
    [profession] => PHP Developer
    [favorites] => Array
        (
            [0] => PHP
            [1] => MySQL
            [2] => Linux
        )
)
```

Each function displays a different amount of information pertaining to the variable in question. Which version works best for you depends on how exactly you intend to use the resulting information. In a debugging or logging context, the ability of `var_export()` and `print_r()` to return a string representation rather than printing directly to the console would be valuable, particularly when paired with a tool like Monolog as described in Recipe 13.5.

If you want to export variable contents in a way to easily reimport them into PHP directly, the executable output of `var_export()` would serve you best. If you're debugging variable contents and need deep typing and size information, the default output of `var_dump()` might be the most informative, even if it can't be directly exported as a string.

If you *do* need to leverage `var_dump()` and want to export its output as a string, you can leverage output buffering (*https://oreil.ly/2AUks*) in PHP to do just that. Specifically, create an output buffer prior to invoking `var_dump()`, then store the contents of that buffer in a variable for future use, as shown in Example 13-8.

Example 13-8. Output buffering to capture variable contents

```
ob_start(); ❶
var_dump($info); ❷

$contents = ob_get_clean(); ❸
```

❶ Create an output buffer. Any code that prints to the console after this invocation will be captured by the buffer.

❷ Dump the contents of the variable in question to the console/buffer.

❸ Get the contents of the buffer and delete it afterwards.

The result of the preceding example code will be a string representation of the dumped contents of $info stored in $contents for future reference. Proceeding to dump the contents of $contents itself would yield the following:

```
string(244) "object(stdClass)#1 (3) {
  ["name"]=>
  string(11) "Book Reader"
  ["profession"]=>
  string(13) "PHP Developer"
  ["favorites"]=>
  array(3) {
    [0]=>
    string(3) "PHP"
    [1]=>
    string(5) "MySQL"
    [2]=>
    string(5) "Linux"
  }
}
"
```

See Also

Documentation on var_dump() (*https://oreil.ly/uYuoV*), var_export() (*https://oreil.ly/V_vZ-*), and print_r() (*https://oreil.ly/0D891*).

13.7 Using the Built-in Web Server to Quickly Run an Application

Problem

You want to launch a web application locally without configuring an actual web server like Apache or NGINX.

Solution

Use PHP's built-in web server to quickly launch a script such that it is accessible from a web browser. For example, if your application lives in a *public_html/* directory, launch the web server from that directory as follows:

```
$ cd ~/public_html
$ php -S localhost:8000
```

Then visit *http://localhost:8000* in your browser to view any file (static HTML, images, or even executable PHP) that resides within that directory.

Discussion

The PHP CLI provides a built-in web server that makes it easy to test or demonstrate applications or scripts in a controlled, local environment. The CLI supports both running PHP scripts and returning static content from the request path.

Static content could include rendered HTML files or anything from the following standard MIME types/extensions:

```
.3gp, .apk, .avi, .bmp, .css, .csv, .doc, .docx, .flac, .gif, .gz, .gzip, .htm,
.html, .ics, .jpe, .jpeg, .jpg, .js, .kml, .kmz, .m4a, .mov, .mp3, .mp4, .mpeg,
.mpg, .odp, .ods, .odt, .oga, .ogg, .ogv, .pdf, .png, .pps, .pptx, .qt, .svg,
.swf, .tar, .text, .tif, .txt, .wav, .webm, .wmv, .xls, .xlsx, .xml, .xsl, .xsd,
and .zip.
```

The built-in web server is intended for development and debugging purposes. It should not be used in a production context. For production purposes, always leverage a fully fledged web server in front of PHP. Either NGINX or Apache in front of PHP-FPM are reasonable choices.

In addition, you can pass a particular script as a *router script* to the web server, resulting in PHP directing every request to that script. The advantage to such an approach is that it mimics the use of popular PHP frameworks that utilize routers. The disadvantage is that you need to manually handle routing for static assets.

In an Apache or NGINX environment, browser requests for images, documents, or other static content are served directly without invoking PHP. When leveraging the CLI web server, you must first check for these assets and return an explicit `false` in order for the development server to handle them properly.

A framework router script must then check to see if you're running in CLI mode and, if so, route content accordingly. For example:

```php
if (php_sapi_name() === 'cli-server') {
    if (preg_match('/\.(?:png|jpg|jpeg|gif)$/', $_SERVER["REQUEST_URI"])) {
        return false;
```

```
        }
    }

    // Continue router execution
```

The preceding *router.php* file could then be used to bootstrap a local web server as follows:

```
$ php -S localhost:8000 router.php
```

The development web server could be made accessible to any interface (available on the local network) by passing `0.0.0.0` instead of `localhost` when invoking it. However, remember that this server is not designed for production use and is not structured in a way to protect your application from abuse by bad actors. *Do not use this web server on a public network!*

See Also

Documentation on PHP's built-in web server (*https://oreil.ly/Hm9U7*).

13.8 Using Unit Tests to Detect Regressions in a Version-Controlled Project with git-bisect

Problem

You want to quickly identify which commit in a version-controlled application introduced a particular bug so you can fix it.

Solution

Use `git bisect` to track down the first bad commit in your source tree, as follows:

1. Create a new branch on the project.
2. Write a failing unit test (a test that reproduces the bug currently but, if the bug were fixed, it would pass).
3. Commit that test to the new branch.
4. Leverage `git rebase` to move that commit that introduces your new test to an earlier point in the project's history.
5. Use `git bisect` from that earlier point in history to automatically run your unit tests on subsequent commits to find the first commit where the test failed.

Once you rebase your project's commit history, the hashes of all of your commits will change. Keep track of the *new* commit hash for your unit test so you can properly target `git bisect`. For example, assume this commit has a hash of `48cc8f0` after being moved in your commit history. In that case, as shown in Example 13-9, you would identify this commit as "good" and the HEAD (the latest commit) in the project as "bad."

Example 13-9. Example `git bisect` *navigation after rebasing a test case*

```
$ git bisect start
$ git bisect good 48cc8f0 ❶
$ git bisect bad HEAD ❷
$ git bisect run vendor/bin/phpunit ❸
```

❶ You must tell Git the first good commit it needs to look at.

❷ Since you don't know for sure where the broken commit is, pass the HEAD constant and Git will look at every commit after the good one referenced earlier.

❸ Git can run a specific command for every suspect commit. In this case, run your test suite. Git will continue looking at your project commit history until it finds the first commit where the test suite fails.

Once Git has identified the first bad commit (e.g., 16c43d7), use `git diff` to see what actually changed at that commit, as shown in Example 13-10.

Example 13-10. Comparing a known-bad Git commit

```
$ git diff 16c43d7 HEAD
```

Once you know what's broken, run `git bisect reset` to return your repository to normal operations. At this point, move back to your main branch (and possibly delete the test branch as well) so you can begin correcting the identified bug.

Discussion

Git's bisect tool is a powerful way to track down and identify a bad commit to your project. It's particularly useful on larger, active projects where there might be several commits between a known-good and known-bad state. With larger projects, it's often cost prohibitive in terms of developer time to iterate through every commit to test its validity on an individual basis.

The `git bisect` command works with a binary search approach. It finds the commit at the midpoint between the known-good and known-bad ones and tests that commit. It then moves closer to the known-good or the known-bad commits based on the output of that test.

By default, `git bisect` expects you to manually test each suspect commit until it finds the "first bad" commit. However, the `git bisect run` subcommand empowers you to delegate this check to an automated system like PHPUnit. If the test command returns a default status of 0 (or success), the commit is assumed to be good. This works well because PHPUnit exits with an error code of 0 when all tests pass.

If the tests fail, PHPUnit returns an error code of 1, which `git bisect` interprets as a bad commit. In this way, you can fully automate the detection of a bad commit over thousands of potential commits quickly and easily.

In the Solution example, you first created a new branch. This is merely to keep your project clean so you can throw any potential test commits away once you've identified the bad commit. On this branch, you committed a single test to replicate a bug identified in your project. Leveraging `git log`, you can quickly visualize the history of your project, including this test commit, as shown in Figure 13-3.

```
ericmann@pop-os:~/Projects/git-bisect-demo$ git log --oneline
d442759 (HEAD -> testing) Test addition with negatives
9bd24f4 (origin/main, origin/HEAD, main) Division
48bcaa3 Misc cleanup
2b4fb8e multiplication
3bd869a Test method visibility
b51f515 Add subtraction
916161c Initial project commit
8550717 Initial commit
ericmann@pop-os:~/Projects/git-bisect-demo$
```

Figure 13-3. Git log demonstrating a main branch and a testing branch with a single commit

This log is useful as it provides you with the short hash for both your test commit and every other commit in the project. If you know a historical commit that is known to be good, you can rebase your project to move the test commit to *just after* that known commit.

In Figure 13-3, the test commit hash is d442759, and the last known "good" commit is 916161c. To reorder your project, use `git rebase` interactively from the project's initial commit (8550717) to move the test commit earlier in the project. The exact command would start as shown in Example 13-11.

Example 13-11. Interactive `git rebase` to reorder commits

```
$ git rebase -i 8550717
```

Git will open a text editor and present the same SHA hashes for each possible commit. You want to retain your commit history (so keep the `pick` keywords in place), but move the test commit to just after the known-good commit, as shown in Figure 13-4.

```
pick 916161c Initial project commit
pick d442759 Test addition with negatives
pick b51f515 Add subtraction
pick 3bd869a Test method visibility
pick 2b4fb8e multiplication
pick 48bcaa3 Misc cleanup
pick 9bd24f4 Division

# Rebase 8550717..d442759 onto 8550717 (7 commands)
#
# Commands:
# p, pick <commit> = use commit
# r, reword <commit> = use commit, but edit the commit message
# e, edit <commit> = use commit, but stop for amending
# s, squash <commit> = use commit, but meld into previous commit
# f, fixup [-C | -c] <commit> = like "squash" but keep only the previous
#                      commit's log message, unless -C is used, in which case
#                      keep only this commit's message; -c is same as -C but
#                      opens the editor
# x, exec <command> = run command (the rest of the line) using shell
# b, break = stop here (continue rebase later with 'git rebase --continue')
# d, drop <commit> = remove commit
# l, label <label> = label current HEAD with a name
# t, reset <label> = reset HEAD to a label
# m, merge [-C <commit> | -c <commit>] <label> [# <oneline>]
# .      create a merge commit using the original merge commit's
# .      message (or the oneline, if no original merge commit was
# .      specified); use -c <commit> to reword the commit message
#
:wq
```

Figure 13-4. Interactive Git rebasing allows for modifying or reordering commits at will

Save the file, and Git will work at reconstructing your project history based on the moved commit. If and when there are conflicts, reconcile them locally first and commit the results. Then leverage `git rebase --continue` to keep moving. Once you're done, your project will be restructured such that the new test case appears immediately after the known-good commit.

 The known-good commit will have the same commit hash, as will any commits that came before it. Your moved commit and all the ones that follow, however, will have new commit hashes applied. Take care to ensure that you're using the correct commit hashes in any subsequent Git commands!

Once the rebase is complete, use `git log --oneline` to again visualize your commit history and reference the *new* commit attributed to your unit test. Then you can run `git bisect` from that commit to the HEAD of your project as you did in Example 13-9. Git will run PHPunit on each suspect commit until it finds the first "bad" commit, producing output similar to that in Figure 13-5.

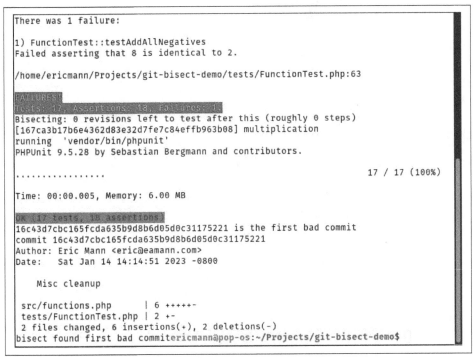

```
There was 1 failure:

1) FunctionTest::testAddAllNegatives
Failed asserting that 8 is identical to 2.

/home/ericmann/Projects/git-bisect-demo/tests/FunctionTest.php:63

FAILURES!
Tests: 17, Assertions: 18, Failures: 1
Bisecting: 0 revisions left to test after this (roughly 0 steps)
[167ca3b17b6e4362d83e32d7fe7c84effb963b08] multiplication
running  'vendor/bin/phpunit'
PHPUnit 9.5.28 by Sebastian Bergmann and contributors.

.................                                           17 / 17 (100%)

Time: 00:00.005, Memory: 6.00 MB

OK (17 tests, 18 assertions)
16c43d7cbc165fcda635b9d8b6d05d0c31175221 is the first bad commit
commit 16c43d7cbc165fcda635b9d8b6d05d0c31175221
Author: Eric Mann <eric@eamann.com>
Date:   Sat Jan 14 14:14:51 2023 -0800

    Misc cleanup

 src/functions.php      | 6 +++++-
 tests/FunctionTest.php | 2 +-
 2 files changed, 6 insertions(+), 2 deletions(-)
bisect found first bad commitericmann@pop-os:~/Projects/git-bisect-demo$
```

Figure 13-5. Git bisect runs until it finds the first "bad" commit in the tree

Armed with knowledge of the first bad commit, you can view the diff at that point and see exactly where and how the bug crept into your project. At this point, return to the main branch and start prepping your fixes.

It's a good idea to pull in your new unit test as well.

> While you could leverage git rebase again to move your test commit back to where it belongs, the rebase operation might still leave your project history modified from its former state. Instead, return to main and create a *new* branch for actually fixing the bug at that point. Pull in your test commit (perhaps via git cherry-pick (*https://oreil.ly/tTFx3*)) and make whatever changes are necessary.

See Also

Documentation on git bisect (*https://oreil.ly/LXgBP*).

## CHAPTER 14

Performance Tuning

Dynamically interpreted languages, such as PHP, are known for their flexibility and ease of use but not necessarily for their speed. This is partly because of the way their type systems work. When types are inferred at runtime, it's impossible for the parser to know exactly how to perform a certain operation until it's provided with data.

Consider the following, loosely typed PHP function to add two items together:

```php
function add($a, $b)
{
    return $a + $b;
}
```

Since this function does not declare the types for the variables passed in or the return type, it can exhibit multiple signatures. All of the method signatures in Example 14-1 are equally valid ways to call the preceding function.

Example 14-1. Various signatures for the same function definition

```
add(int $a,    int $b):   int   ❶
add(float $a,  float $b): float ❷
add(int $a,    float $b): float ❸
add(float $a,  int $b):   float ❹
add(string $a, int $b):   int   ❺
add(string $a, int $b):   float ❻
```

❶ add(1, 2) returns int(3)

❷ add(1., 2.) returns float(3)

❸ add(1, 2.) returns float(3)

❹ add(1., 2) returns float(3)

❺ add("1", 2) returns int(3)

❻ add("1.", 2) returns float(3)

The preceding example illustrates how you can write a single function and PHP internally needs to process it multiple ways. The language doesn't know which version of the function you actually need until it sees the data you provide it, and it will internally cast some values to other types where necessary. At runtime, though, the actual function is compiled to operation code (opcode) that runs on the processor through a dedicated virtual machine—and PHP will need to produce multiple versions of the same function's opcode to handle the differing input and return types.

 The loose typing system leveraged by PHP is one of the things that makes it so easy to learn but also so easy to make fatal programming mistakes. This book has taken care to leverage *strict typing* wherever possible to avoid these exact pitfalls. Review Recipe 3.4 for more on using strict typing in your own code.

With a compiled language, the problem expressed here about loose typing would be trivial—merely compile the program to the multiple forks of opcode and move on. Unfortunately, PHP is more of an interpreted language; it reloads and recompiles your script on demand, depending on how your application is loaded. Luckily, the performance drain of multiple code paths can be combatted with two modern features built into the very language itself: just-in-time (JIT) compilation and the caching of opcode.

Just-In-Time Compilation

As of version 8.0, PHP ships with a JIT compiler (*https://oreil.ly/XS9gg*) that immediately enables faster program execution and better-performing applications. It does this by leveraging traces of actual instructions passed to the virtual machine (VM) handling the script's execution. When a particular trace is called frequently, PHP will automatically recognize the importance of the operation and gauge whether or not the code benefits from compilation.

Subsequent invocations of the same code will use the compiled byte code rather than the dynamic script, causing a significant performance boost. Based on metrics published by Zend when PHP 8.0 was released (*https://oreil.ly/LpZ3w*), the inclusion of a JIT compiler renders the PHP benchmark suite to be up to three times faster!

The point to remember is that JIT compilation primarily benefits low-level algorithms. This includes number crunching and raw data manipulation. Anything outside of CPU-intensive operations (e.g., graphics manipulation or heavy database integrations) won't see nearly as much benefit to these changes. However, knowing that the JIT compiler exists, you can take advantage of it and use PHP in new ways.

Opcode Caching

Among the easiest ways to increase performance—indeed, the way the JIT compiler does so—is to cache expensive operations and reference the result rather than doing the operations again and again. Since version 5.5, PHP has shipped with an optional extension for caching precompiled byte code in memory called OPcache (*https:// oreil.ly/wH2ue*).[1]

Remember, PHP is primarily a dynamic script interpreter and will read in your scripts when the program starts. If you stop and start your application frequently, PHP will need to recompile your script to computer-readable byte code in order for the code to execute properly. Frequent starts/stops can force frequent recompiling of scripts and thus slow performance. The OPcache, however, allows you to selectively compile scripts to provide the byte code to PHP before the rest of the application runs. This removes the need for PHP to load and parse the scripts each time!

> The JIT compiler in PHP 8 and above can only be enabled if OPcache is also enabled on the server, since it uses the cache as its shared memory backend. However, you do not need to use the JIT compiler to use OPcache itself.

Both JIT compilation and opcode caching are low-level performance improvements to the language that you can easily leverage at runtime, but they're not the end of the story. It's also critical to understand how to time the execution of user-defined functions. This makes identifying bottlenecks in business logic relatively easy. Comprehensively benchmarking the application also helps gauge performance changes when deploying to new environments, on new releases of the language, or with updated dependencies down the road.

The following recipes describe both the timing/benchmarking of userland application code and how to leverage the language-level opcode cache to optimize the performance of your application and environment.

---

1 The newer JIT compiler released with PHP 8.0 uses OPcache under the hood, but you can still leverage caching *manually* to control the system even if JIT compilation is unavailable.

14.1 Timing Function Execution

Problem

You want to understand how long it takes a particular function to execute in order to identify potential opportunities for optimization.

Solution

Leverage PHP's built-in `hrtime()` function both before and after function execution to determine how long the function took to run. For example:

```
$start = hrtime(true);

doSomethingComputationallyExpensive();

$totalTime = (hrtime(true) - $start) / 1e+9;

echo "Function took {$totalTime} seconds." . PHP_EOL;
```

Discussion

The `hrtime()` function will return the system's built-in high-resolution time, counting from an arbitrary point in time defined by the system. By default, it returns an array of two integers—seconds and nanoseconds, respectively. Passing `true` to the function will instead return the total number of nanoseconds, requiring you to divide by `1e+9` to convert the raw output back to human-readable seconds.

A slightly fancier approach is to abstract the timing mechanism into a decorator object. As covered in Chapter 8, a decorator is a programming design pattern that allows you to extend the functionality of a single function call (or a whole class) by wrapping it in another class implementation. In this case, you want to trigger the use of `hrtime()` to time a function's execution without changing the function itself. The decorator in Example 14-2 would do exactly that.

Example 14-2. A timed decorator object for measuring function call performance

```
class TimerDecorator
{
    private int $calls = 0;
    private float $totalRuntime = 0.;

    public function __construct(public $callback, private bool $verbose = false) {}

    public function __invoke(...$args): mixed ❶
    {
        if (! is_callable($this->callback)) {
```

```
        throw new ValueError('Class does not wrap a callable function!');
    }

    $this->calls += 1;
    $start = hrtime(true); ❷

    $value = call_user_func($this->callback, ...$args); ❸

    $totalTime = (hrtime(true) - $start) / 1e+9;
    $this->totalRuntime += $totalTime;

    if ($this->verbose) {
        echo "Function took {$totalTime} seconds." . PHP_EOL; ❹
    }

    return $value; ❺
    }

    public function getMetrics(): array ❻
    {
        return [
            'calls'   => $this->calls,
            'runtime' => $this->totalRuntime,
            'avg'     => $this->totalRuntime / $this->calls
        ];
    }
}
```

❶ The __invoke() magic method makes class instances callable as if they were functions. Using the ... spread operator will capture any arguments passed in at runtime so they can be passed later to the wrapped method.

❷ The actual timing mechanism used by the decorator is the same as that in the Solution example.

❸ Assuming the wrapped function is callable, PHP will call the function and pass all necessary arguments thanks to the ... spread operator.

❹ This implementation of the decorator can be instantiated with a verbosity flag that will also print runtimes to the console.

❺ Since the wrapped function might return data, you need to ensure that the decorator returns that output as well.

❻ As the decorated function is itself an object, you can directly expose additional properties and methods. In this case, the decorator keeps track of aggregate metrics that can be retrieved directly.

Assuming the same doSomethingComputationallyExpensive() function from the Solution example is the function you want to test, the preceding decorator can wrap the function and produce metrics as shown in Example 14-3.

Example 14-3. Leveraging a decorator to time function execution

```
$decorated = new TimerDecorator('doSomethingComputationallyExpensive');

$decorated(); ❶

var_dump($decorated->getMetrics()); ❷
```

❶ Since the decorator class implements the __invoke() magic method, you can use an instance of the class as if it were a function itself.

❷ The resulting metrics array will include a count of invocations, the total runtime (in seconds) for all invocations, and the average runtime (in seconds) across all invocations.

Similarly, you can test the same wrapped function multiple times and pull aggregate runtime metrics from all invocations as follows:

```
$decorated = new TimerDecorator('doSomethingComputationallyExpensive');

for ($i = 0; $i < 10; $i++) {
    $decorated();
}

var_dump($decorated->getMetrics());
```

Since the TimerDecorator class can wrap any callable function, you can use it to decorate class methods just as easily as you can native functions. The class in Example 14-4 defines both a static and an instance method, either of which can be wrapped by a decorator.

Example 14-4. Simple class definition for testing decorators

```
class DecoratorFriendly
{
    public static function doSomething()
    {
        // ...
    }

    public function doSomethingElse()
    {
        // ...
```

```
    }
}
```

Example 14-5 shows how class methods (both static and instance-bound) can be referred to as callables at runtime in PHP. Anything that can be expressed as a callable interface can be wrapped by a decorator.

Example 14-5. Any callable interface can be wrapped by a decorator

```
$decoratedStatic = new TimerDecorator(['DecoratorFriendly', 'doSomething']); ❶
$decoratedStatic(); ❷

var_dump($decoratedStatic->getMetrics());

$instance = new DecoratorFriendly();

$decoratedMember = new TimerDecorator([$instance, 'doSomethingElse']); ❸
$decoratedMember(); ❹

var_dump($decoratedMember->getMetrics());
```

❶ A static class method is used as a callable by passing an array of both the names of the class and its static method.

❷ Once created, the decorated static method can be called as any other function would be and will produce metrics the same way.

❸ A method of a class instance is used as a callable by passing an array of the instantiated object and the string name of the method.

❹ Similar to the decorated static method, a decorated instance method can then be called as any other function would be to populate metrics within the decorator.

Once you know how long a function takes to run, you can focus on optimizing its execution. This might involve refactoring the logic or using an alternative approach to defining an algorithm.

The use of `hrtime()` originally required the HRTime extension (*https://oreil.ly/P_4Fq*) to PHP but is now bundled as a core function by default. If you're using a version of PHP older than 7.3 or a prebuilt distribution where it was explicitly omitted, the function itself might be missing. In that event, you can either install the extension yourself via PECL or leverage the similar `microtime()` function instead.[2]

---

2 For more on PECL and extension management, refer to Recipe 15.4.

Rather than counting seconds from an arbitrary point in time, `microtime()` returns the number of microseconds since the Unix epoch. This function can be used in place of `hrtime()` to gauge function execution time as follows:

```
$start = microtime(true);

doSomethingComputationallyExpensive();

$totalTime = microtime(true) - $start;

echo "Function took {$totalTime} seconds." . PHP_EOL;
```

Regardless of whether you use `hrtime()` as in the Solution example or `microtime()` as in the preceding snippet, ensure that you're consistent with the way you read out the resulting data. Both mechanisms return notions of time at different levels of precision, which could lead to confusion if you mix and match on any output formatting.

See Also

PHP documentation on `hrtime()` (*https://oreil.ly/AjZ4H*) and `microtime()` (*https://oreil.ly/r_U84*).

14.2 Benchmarking the Performance of an Application

Problem

You want to benchmark the performance of your entire application so you can gauge changes (e.g., performance regressions) as the codebase, dependencies, and underlying language versions evolve.

Solution

Leverage an automated tool like PHPBench to instrument your code and run regular performance benchmarks. For example, the following class is constructed to test the performance of all available hashing algorithms over various string sizes.[3]

```
/**
 * @BeforeMethods("setUp")
 */
class HashingBench
{
    private $string = '';
```

---

3 This particular example is taken from the example benchmarks (*https://oreil.ly/zZE4X*) that ship by default with PHPBench.

```php
public function setUp(array $params): void
{
    $this->string = str_repeat('X', $params['size']);
}

/**
 * @ParamProviders({
 *     "provideAlgos",
 *     "provideStringSize"
 * })
 */
public function benchAlgos($params): void
{
    hash($params['algo'], $this->string);
}

public function provideAlgos()
{
    foreach (array_slice(hash_algos(), 0, 20) as $algo) {
        yield ['algo' => $algo];
    }

}

public function provideStringSize() {
    yield ['size' => 10];
    yield ['size' => 100];
    yield ['size' => 1000];
}

}
```

To run the default preceding example benchmark, first clone PHPBench, then install Composer dependencies, and finally run the following command:

```
$ ./bin/phpbench run --profile=examples --report=examples --filter=HashingBench
```

The resulting output, once the benchmark completes, will resemble the chart in Figure 14-1.

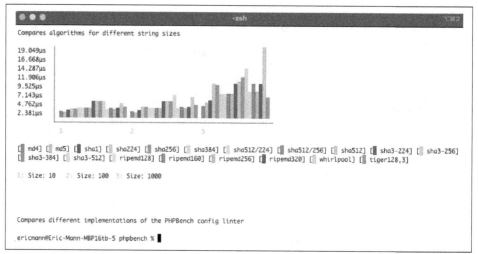

Figure 14-1. Output metrics from PHPBench's example hashing benchmark

Discussion

PHPBench is an effective way to gauge performance benchmarks of user-defined code in a variety of situations. It can be used in development environments to judge the performance level of new code, and it can also be integrated directly into continuous integration environments.

PHPBench's own GitHub Actions configuration (*https://oreil.ly/D6PMf*) runs a full benchmarking suite of the application itself with every pull request and change. This allows the project maintainers to ensure that the project continues performing as expected with each change they introduce across a broad matrix of supported versions of PHP.

Any project aiming to include automated benchmarks must first start with Composer.[4] You need to leverage Composer autoloading so PHPBench knows where to grab classes from, but once that's set up, you can build your project however you want.

Assume you're building a project that leverages value objects and hashing to protect sensitive data they store. Your initial *composer.json* file might look something like the following:

```
{
    "name": "phpcookbook/valueobjects",
    "require-dev": {
        "phpbench/phpbench": "^1.0"
```

---

4 For more on initializing a project with Composer, review Recipe 15.1.

```
    },
    "autoload": {
        "psr-4": {
            "Cookbook\\": "src/"
        }
    },
    "autoload-dev": {
        "psr-4": {
            "Cookbook\\Tests\\": "tests/"
        }
    },
    "minimum-stability": "dev",
    "prefer-stable": true
}
```

Naturally, your project code will live in a *src/* directory and any tests, benchmarking or otherwise, will live in a separate *tests/* directory. For the sake of benchmarking alone, you'll want to create a dedicated *tests/Benchmark/* directory to keep track of both namespaces and filterable code.

Your first class, the one you want to benchmark, is a value object that takes in an email address and can be easily manipulated as if it were a string. But when it dumps its contents to a debugging context, like var_dump() or print_r(), it automatically hashes the value.

 Email is a common enough format that even hashing the data won't be enough to protect it from a truly dedicated attacker. The illustrations in this recipe are meant to demonstrate how data can be *obfuscated* using a hash. This should not be considered a comprehensive security tutorial.

Create the class defined in Example 14-6 as *ProtectedString.php* in your new *src/* directory. This class has a lot to it—primarily several implemented magic methods to ensure that there is no way to *accidentally* serialize the object and get at its internal value. Instead, once you instantiate a ProtectedString object, the only way to get at its contents is with the ::getValue() method. Anything else will return the SHA-256 hash of the contents.

Example 14-6. Protected string wrapper class definition

```
namespace Cookbook;

class ProtectedString implements \JsonSerializable
{
    protected bool $valid = true;

    public function __construct(protected ?string $value) {}
```

```php
    public function getValue(): ?string
    {
        return $this->value;
    }

    public function equals(ProtectedString $other): bool
    {
        return $this->value === $other->getValue();
    }

    protected function redacted(): string
    {
        return hash('sha256', $this->value, false);
    }

    public function isValid(): bool
    {
        return $this->valid;
    }

    public function __serialize(): array
    {
        return [
            'value' => $this->redacted()
        ];
    }

    public function __unserialize(array $serialized): void
    {
        $this->value = null;
        $this->valid = false;
    }

    public function jsonSerialize(): mixed
    {
        return $this->redacted();
    }

    public function __toString()
    {
        return $this->redacted();
    }

    public function __debugInfo()
    {
        return [
            'valid' => $this->valid,
            'value' => $this->redacted()
        ];
    }
}
```

You want to validate the performance of the chosen hashing algorithm. SHA-256 is more than reasonable, but you want to ensure that you benchmark all possible means of serialization for performance so that, if and when you need to change to a different hashing algorithm, you can ensure no performance regressions in the system.

To actually begin benchmarking this class, create the following *phpbench.json* file in the root of your project:

```
{
    "$schema": "./vendor/phpbench/phpbench/phpbench.schema.json",
    "runner.bootstrap": "vendor/autoload.php"
}
```

Finally, create an actual benchmark to time the various ways a user can serialize a string. The benchmark defined in Example 14-7 should live in *tests/Benchmark/ProtectedStringBench.php*.

Example 14-7. Benchmarking the `ProtectedString` class

```
namespace Cookbook\Tests\Benchmark;

use Cookbook\ProtectedString;

class ProtectedStringBench
{
    public function benchSerialize()
    {
        $data = new ProtectedString('testValue');
        $serialized = serialize($data);
    }

    public function benchJsonSerialize()
    {
        $data = new ProtectedString('testValue');
        $serialized = json_encode($data);
    }

    public function benchStringTypecast()
    {
        $data = new ProtectedString('testValue');
        $serialized = '' . $data;
    }

    public function benchVarExport()
    {
        $data = new ProtectedString('testValue');
        ob_start();
        var_dump($data);
        $serialized = ob_end_clean();
    }
}
```

Finally, you can run your benchmarks with the following shell command:

```
$ ./vendor/bin/phpbench run tests/Benchmark --report=default
```

This command will produce an output similar to that in Figure 14-2, detailing the memory usage and runtime for each of your serialization operations.

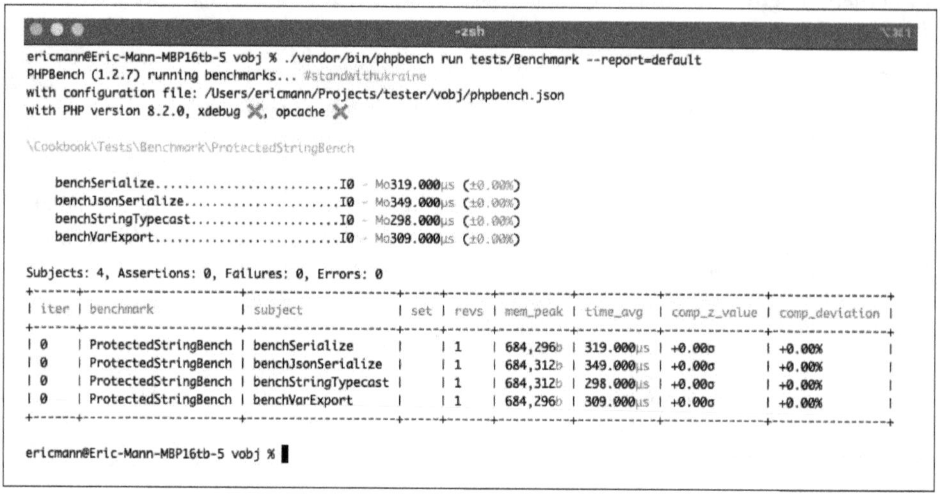

Figure 14-2. Output of PHPBench for value object serialization with hashing

Every element of your application can, and should, have benchmarking built into it. This will drastically simplify testing the performance of your application in new environments—like on new server hardware or under a newly released version of PHP. Wherever possible, take time to wire these benchmarks into continuous integration runs as well to ensure that the tests are run and recorded as frequently as possible.

See Also

Official documentation for the PHPBench project (*https://oreil.ly/4HCMc*).

14.3 Accelerating an Application with an Opcode Cache

Problem

You want to leverage opcode caching in your environment to improve the overall performance of your application.

Solution

Install the shared OPcache extension and configure it in *php.ini* for your environment.[5] As it's a default extension, you merely need to update your configuration to enable caching. The following settings are generally recommended for solid performance but should be tested against your particular application and infrastructure:

```
opcache.memory_consumption=128
opcache.interned_strings_buffer=8
opcache.max_accelerated_files=4000
opcache.revalidate_freq=60
opcache.fast_shutdown=1
opcache.enable=1
opcache.enable_cli=1
```

Discussion

When PHP is running, the interpreter reads your scripts and compiles your user-friendly PHP code into something that's easy for the machine to understand. Unfortunately, since PHP isn't a formally compiled language, it has to do this compilation every time a script loads. With a simple application, this isn't that much of an issue. With a complex application, it can lead to slow load times and high latency for repeated requests.

The easiest way to optimize an application around this particular issue is to cache the compiled byte code so it can be reused on subsequent requests.

To test and verify the functionality of the opcode cache locally, you can leverage -d flags at the command line when starting a script. The -d flag sets an explicit override for a configuration value otherwise set (or left to its default) by *php.ini*. Specifically, the command-line flags in Example 14-8 will leverage the local PHP development server to run an application with OPcache *disabled* entirely.

Example 14-8. Launch a local PHP web server without OPcache support

```
$ php -S localhost:8080 -t public/ -dopcache.enable_cli=0 -dopcache.enable=0
```

Similarly, you can run almost exactly the same command with explicit *enabling* of the opcode cache to directly compare the behavior and performance of your application, as shown in Example 14-9.

---

5 OPcache is a shared extension that will not exist if your PHP was compiled with the --disable-all flag to disable default extensions. In that case, you have no choice but to either recompile PHP with the --enable-opcache flag set or else install a fresh version of the PHP engine that was compiled with this flag set.

Example 14-9. Launch a local PHP web server with OPcache support

```
$ php -S localhost:8080 -t public/ -dopcache.enable_cli=1 -dopcache.enable=1
```

To fully demonstrate how this works, take time to install a demo application using the open source Symfony framework. The following two commands will clone a demonstration application to the */demosite/* directory locally and use Composer to install required dependencies:

```
$ composer create-project symfony/symfony-demo demosite
$ cd demosite && composer install
```

Next, use the built-in PHP web server to launch the application itself. Use the command from Example 14-8 to start without opcache support. The application will be available on port 8080 and will look something like Figure 14-3.

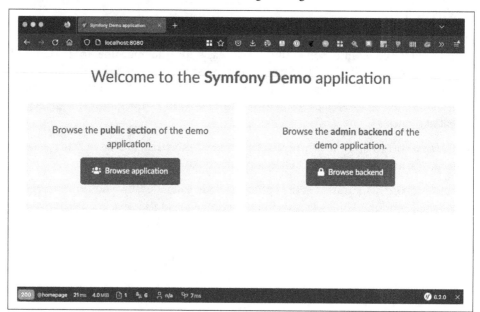

Figure 14-3. Loading page of the default Symfony demo application

The default application is running locally, using a lightweight SQLite database, so it should load fairly quickly. As shown in Example 14-10, you can effectively test the load time with a cURL command in your terminal.

Example 14-10. Simple cURL command for gauging web application response time

```
curl -s -w "\nLookup time:\t%{time_namelookup}\
    \nConnect time:\t%{time_connect}\
    \nPreXfer time:\t%{time_pretransfer}\
    \nStartXfer time:\t%{time_starttransfer}\
    \n\nTotal time:\t%{time_total}\n" -o /dev/null \
    http://localhost:8080
```

Without opcode caching enabled, the Symfony demo application loads with a total time of ~0.3677 seconds. This is remarkably fast but, again, the application is being run entirely within the local environment. In production with a remote database, it would likely be slower, but this is a solid baseline.

Now, stop the application and restart it *with* opcode caching enabled using the command defined in Example 14-9. Then rerun the cURL performance test from Example 14-10. With opcode caching, the application now loads with a total time of ~0.0371 seconds.

This is a relatively simple, default application, but a 10 times increase in performance is a massive boost to system performance. The faster an application loads, the more customers your system can service in the same period of time!

See Also

PHP documentation on the OPcache extension (*https://oreil.ly/Tb8rC*).

## CHAPTER 15

Packages and Extensions

PHP is a high-level language that uses dynamic typing and memory management to make software development easier for end users. Unfortunately, computers are not very good at handling high-level concepts, so any high-level system must itself be built atop lower-level building blocks. In the case of PHP, the entire system is written in and built atop C.

Since PHP is open source, you can download the entire source code for the language directly from GitHub (*https://oreil.ly/Z1_lP*). Then you can build the language from source on your own system, make changes to it, or write your own native (C-level) extensions.

In any environment, you'll need various other packages available in order to build PHP from source. On Ubuntu Linux, these are the packages:

pkg-config
: A Linux package for returning information about installed libraries

build-essential
: A meta-package encompassing the GNU debugger, g++ compiler, and other tools for working with C/C++ projects

autoconf
: Package of macros to produce shell scripts that configure code packages

bison
: A general-purpose parser generator

re2c
: A regular expression compiler and open source lexer for C and C++

libxml2-dev

> The C-level development headers required for XML processing

libsqlite3-dev

> The C-level development headers for SQLite and related bindings

You can install all of them with the following `apt` command:

```
$ sudo apt install -y pkg-config build-essential autoconf bison re2c \
                      libxml2-dev libsqlite3-dev
```

Once dependencies are available, you use the `buildconf` script to generate the configuration script, then `configure` itself will ready the build environment. Several options (*https://oreil.ly/md2qt*) can be passed directly to `configure` to control how the environment will be set up. Table 15-1 lists some of the most useful.

Table 15-1. PHP configure options

Option flag	Description
--enable-debug	Compile with debugging symbols. Useful for developing changes to core PHP or writing new extensions.
--enable-libgcc	Allow code to explicitly link against `libgcc`.
--enable-php-streams	Activate support for experimental PHP streams.
--enable-phpdbg	Enable the interactive `phpdbg` debugger.
--enable-zts	Enable thread safety.
--disable-short-tags	Disable PHP short tag support (e.g., `<?`).

Understanding how to build PHP itself isn't a prerequisite for using it. In most environments, you can install a binary distribution directly from a standard package manager. On Ubuntu, for example, you can install PHP directly with the following:

```
$ sudo apt install -y php
```

Knowing how to build PHP from source, though, is important should you ever wish to change the behavior of the language, include a nonbundled extension, or write your own native module in the future.

Standard Modules

By default, PHP uses its own extension system to power much of the core functionality of the language. In addition to core modules, various extensions are bundled directly with PHP.[1] These include the following:

---

[1] A full list of bundled and external extensions can be found in the PHP Manual (*https://oreil.ly/SEWGK*).

- BCMath (*https://oreil.ly/QwfUv*) for arbitrary-precision mathematics
- FFI (*https://oreil.ly/sktWY*) (Foreign Function Interface) for loading shared libraries and calling functions within them
- PDO (*https://oreil.ly/BEsdu*) (PHP Data Objects) for abstracting various database interfaces
- SQLite3 (*https://oreil.ly/Zejtz*) for interacting directly with SQLite databases

Standard modules are bundled with PHP and available for inclusion immediately through changes to your *php.ini* configuration. External extensions, like PDO support for Microsoft SQL Server, are also available but must be installed and activated separately. Tools like PECL, discussed in Recipe 15.4, make the installation of these modules straightforward for any environment.

Libraries/Composer

In addition to native extensions to the language, you can leverage Composer (*https://getcomposer.org*), the most popular dependency manager for PHP. Any PHP project can (and likely *should*) be defined as a Composer module by including a *composer.json* file that describes the project and its structure. Including such a file has two key advantages, even if you don't leverage Composer to pull third-party code into your project:

- You (or another developer) can include your project as a dependency of another project. This makes your code portable and encourages the reuse of function and class definitions.
- Once your project has a *composer.json* file, you can leverage Composer's autoloading features to dynamically include classes and functions within your project without explicitly using `require()` to load them directly.

The recipes in this chapter explain how to configure your project as a Composer package, as well as how to leverage Composer to find and include third-party libraries. You'll also learn how to find and include native extensions to the language through PHP Extension Community Library (PECL) and PHP Extension and Application Repository (PEAR).

15.1 Defining a Composer Project

Problem

You want to start a new project that uses Composer to dynamically load code and dependencies.

Solution

Use Composer's `init` command at the command line to bootstrap a new project with a *composer.json* file. For example:

```
$ composer init --name ericmann/cookbook --type project --license MIT
```

After walking through the interactive prompts (requesting a description, author, minimum stability, etc.), you'll be left with a well-defined *composer.json* for your project.

Discussion

Composer works by defining information about your project in a JSON document and using that information to build out additional script loaders and integrations. A newly initialized project won't have much detail in this document at all. The *composer.json* file generated by the `init` command in the Solution example will initially look like the following:

```
{
    "name": "ericmann/cookbook",
    "type": "project",
    "license": "MIT",
    "require": {}
}
```

This configuration file defines no dependencies, no additional scripts, and no autoloading. In order to be useful for something other than identifying the project and the license, you need to start adding to it. First, you need to define the autoloader to pull in your project code.

For the sake of this project, use the default namespace Cookbook and place all of your code in a directory called *src/* within the project. Then, update your *composer.json* to map that namespace to that directory as follows:

```
{
    "name": "ericmann/cookbook",
    "type": "project",
    "license": "MIT",
    "require": {},
    "autoload": {
        "psr-4": {
            "Cookbook\\": "src/"
        }
    }
}
```

Once you've updated your Composer config, run `composer dumpautoload` at the command line to force Composer to reload the configuration and define the automated source mappings. Once that's complete, Composer will have created a new *vendor/* directory in your project. It contains two critical components:

- An *autoload.php* script that you'll need to require() when you load your application
- A *composer* directory that contains Composer's code loading routines to dynamically pull in your scripts

To further illustrate how autoloading works, create two new files. First, create a file called *Hello.php* in the *src/* directory containing the Hello class defined in Example 15-1.

Example 15-1. Simple class definition for Composer autoloading

```php
<?php
namespace Cookbook;

class Hello
{
    public function __construct(private string $greet) {}

    public function greet(): string
    {
        return "Hello, {$this->greet}!";
    }
}
```

Then, in the root of your project create an *app.php* file with the following contents to bootstrap the execution of the preceding snippet:

```php
<?php

require_once 'vendor/autoload.php';

$intro = new Cookbook\Hello('world');

echo $intro . PHP_EOL;
```

Finally, return to the command line. Since you've added a new class to the project, you need to run composer dumpautoload once again so Composer is aware of the class. Then, you can run php app.php to invoke the application directly and produce the following output:

```
$ php app.php
Hello, world!
$
```

Any class definitions you need for your project or application can be defined the same way. The base Cookbook namespace will always be the root of the *src/* directory. If you want to define a nested namespace for objects, say Cookbook\Recipes, then create a similarly named directory (e.g., *Recipes/*) within *src/* so Composer knows where to find your class definitions when they're used later within the application.

Similarly, you can leverage Composer's `require` command to import third-party dependencies into your application.[2] These dependencies will be loaded into your application at runtime the same way your custom classes are.

See Also

Composer documentation on the `init` command (*https://oreil.ly/6J29w*) and on PSR-4 autoloading (*https://oreil.ly/Buns1*).

15.2 Finding Composer Packages

Problem

You want to find a library to accomplish a particular task so you don't need to spend time reinventing the wheel by writing your own implementation.

Solution

Use the PHP Package Repository at Packagist (*https://packagist.org*) to find the appropriate library and use Composer to install it in your application.

Discussion

Many developers find they spend the majority of their time reimplementing logic or systems they've built before. Different applications serve different purposes but often leverage the same basic building blocks and foundations in order to operate.

This is one of the key drivers behind paradigms like object-oriented programming, where you encapsulate the logic in your application within objects that can be individually manipulated, updated, or even reused. Instead of rewriting the same code over and over again, you encapsulate it within an object that can be reused within the application or even transported into your next project.[3]

In PHP, these reusable code components are often redistributed as standalone libraries that can be imported with Composer. Just as Recipe 15.1 demonstrated how to define a Composer project and automatically import your class and function definitions, the same system can be used to add third-party logic to your system as well.[4]

---

2 For more on installing third-party libraries with Composer, see Recipe 15.3.

3 For a deeper discussion of object-oriented programming and code reuse, review Chapter 8.

4 The actual *installation* of third-party Composer packages will be discussed in Recipe 15.3.

First, identify the need of a particular operation or piece of logic. Assume, for example, your application needs to integrate with a time-based one-time password (TOTP) system like Google Authenticator. You'll need a TOTP library to do so. To find it, navigate in your browser to packagist.org (*https://packagist.org*), the PHP Package Repository. The home page will look somewhat like Figure 15-1 and prominently features a search bar prominently in the header.

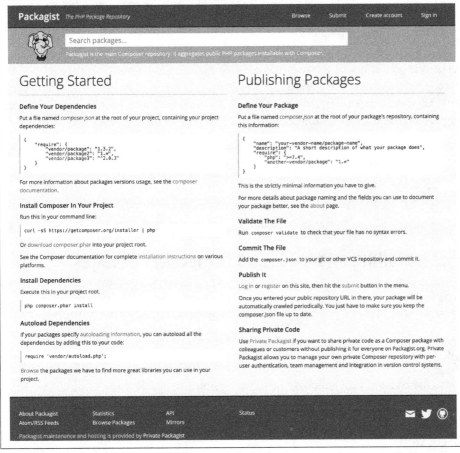

Figure 15-1. Packagist is a free distribution method for PHP packages installable via Composer

Then search for the tool you need—in this case, TOTP. You'll be rewarded with a list of available projects, sorted by popularity. You can further leverage the package type and various tags affixed to each library to pare your search results down to a handful of possible libraries.

Popularity on Packagist is defined by both package downloads and GitHub stars. It's a good way to measure how frequently a project is being used in the wild but is by no means the only measure you should leverage. Many developers still copy and paste third-party code into their systems, so there are potentially millions of "downloads" not reflected in Packagist's metrics. Likewise, merely being popular or widely used does not mean a package is secure or the right fit for your project. Take time to carefully review each potential library to ensure that it doesn't introduce unnecessary risk into your application.

Further, if you know of a particular module author whose work you trust, you can search for that directly by adding their username to the search. For example, a search for Eric Mann totp will yield a specific TOTP implementation (*https://oreil.ly/7touz*) originally created by this book's author.

Once you've identified and carefully audited available packages for extending your application, review Recipe 15.3 for instructions on how to install and manage them.

See Also

Packagist.org (*https://packagist.org*): the PHP Package Repository.

15.3 Installing and Updating Composer Packages

Problem

You've discovered a package on Packagist you want to include in your project.

Solution

Install the package via Composer (assume version 1.0) as follows:

```
composer require "vendor/package:1.0"
```

Discussion

Composer works with two files in your local filesystem: *composer.json* and *composer.lock*. The first is the one you define to describe your project, autoloading, and license. As a concrete example, the original *composer.json* file you defined in Recipe 15.1 is as follows:

```
{
    "name": "ericmann/cookbook",
    "type": "project",
    "license": "MIT",
    "require": {},
```

```
    "autoload": {
        "psr-4": {
            "Cookbook\\": "src/"
        }
    }
}
```

Once you run the `require` statement from the Solution example, Composer *updates* your *composer.json* file to add the specified vendor dependency. Your file will now appear as follows:

```
{
    "name": "ericmann/cookbook",
    "type": "project",
    "license": "MIT",
    "require": {
        "vendor/package": "1.0"
    },
    "autoload": {
        "psr-4": {
            "Cookbook\\": "src/"
        }
    }
}
```

When you `require` a package, Composer does three things:

1. It checks to make sure the package exists and grabs either the latest version (if no version was specified) or the version you ask for. It then updates *composer.json* to store the package in the `require` key.

2. By default, Composer then downloads and installs your package in the *vendor/* directory within your project. It also updates the autoloader script, so the package will be available to other code within your project immediately.

3. Composer also maintains a `composer.lock` file within your project that explicitly identifies which versions of which packages you have installed.

In the Solution example, you explicitly specified version 1.0 of a package. If instead you had not specified a version, Composer would fetch the latest version available and use that in the *composer.json* file. If 1.0 is in fact the latest version, Composer would use `^1.0` as the version indicator, which would then install any potential maintenance versions down the road (like a 1.0.1 version). The *composer.lock* file keeps track of the *exact* version installed so even if you were to delete your entire *vendor/* directory, reinstalling packages via `composer install` will still fetch the same versions as before.

Composer will also endeavor to find the best version for your local environment. It does this by comparing the PHP version required for your environment (and used to

---

run the tool) with those versions supported by the requested packages. Composer also attempts to reconcile any dependencies both explicitly declared by your project and implicitly imported through a transitive dependency declared elsewhere. Should the system fail to find a compatible version to include, it will report an error so you can manually reconcile the version numbers listed in your *composer.json* file.

 Composer follows semantic versioning in its version constraints. A requirement of ^1.0 will only permit maintenance versions (e.g., 1.0.1, 1.0.2) to be installed. A greater-than constraint (e.g., >=1.0) will install any stable version at or above version 1.0. Keeping track of how you define your version constraints is critical to prevent accidental import of breaking package changes introduced by major versions. For more background on how to define version constraints, reference the Composer documentation (*https://oreil.ly/gvoGC*).

Packagist-hosted libraries with public code aren't the only things you can include via Composer. In addition, you can point your system at either public or private projects hosted in version control systems like GitHub.

To add a GitHub repository to your project, first add a `repositories` key to *composer.json* so the system knows where to look. Then update your `require` key to pull in the project you need. Running `composer update` will then pull the package not from Packagist but directly from GitHub and include it in your project just like any other library.

For example, assume you want to use a particular TOTP library but have uncovered a minor bug. First, fork the GitHub repository to your own account. Then, create a branch in GitHub to hold your changes. Finally, update *composer.json* to point at your custom fork and branch, as illustrated in Example 15-2.

Example 15-2. Use Composer to pull projects from GitHub repositories

```
{
    "name": "ericmann/cookbook",
    "type": "project",
    "license": "MIT",
    "repositories": [
        {
            "type": "vcs",
            "url": "\https://github.com/phpcookbookreader/package" ❶
        }
    ],
    "require": {
        "vendor/package": "dev-bugfix" ❷
    },
```

```
    "minimum-stability": "dev", ❸
    "autoload": {
        "psr-4": {
            "Cookbook\\": "src/"
        }
    }
}
```

❶ Ensure that the package you want to include is one you have access to. This repository can either be public or private. If it's private, then you'll need to expose a GitHub personal access token as an environment variable so Composer has the appropriate credentials to pull in the code.

❷ Once the repository is defined, add a new branch specification to your `require` block. Since this is not a tagged or released version, prefix your branch name with `dev-` so Composer knows which branch to pull in.

❸ To include development branches in your project, you should call out the minimum stability (*https://oreil.ly/U9iWR*) required by the project as well to avoid any potential issues with the inclusion.

Whether a library enters your project as a public package, repository, or even as a hardcoded ZIP artifact (*https://oreil.ly/xEpJh*) is up to your development team. Regardless, any reusable package can be loaded via Composer with ease and exposed to the rest of your application.

See Also

Documentation on Composer's `require` command (*https://oreil.ly/d32oK*).

15.4 Installing Native PHP Extensions

Problem

You want to install a publicly available native extension for PHP, like the APC User Cache (APCu) (*https://oreil.ly/Jppw-*).

Solution

Find the extension in the PECL repository and install it into the system by using PEAR. For example, install the APCu as follows:

```
$ pecl install apcu
```

Discussion

The PHP community uses two pieces of technology to distribute native extensions to the language itself: PEAR and PECL. The primary difference between them is the kind of package they're used for.

PEAR itself can bundle just about anything—the packages it distributes are bundled as gzip-compressed TAR archives that are composed of PHP code. In this way, PEAR is similar to Composer and can be used for managing, installing, and updating additional PHP libraries used within your application.[5] PEAR packages are loaded differently than Composer ones, though, so take care if you choose to mix and match between the two package managers.

PECL is a library of native extensions to PHP written in C, the same base language as PHP itself. PECL uses PEAR to handle installation and management of extensions; the new functionality introduced through an extension is accessed the same ways as functions native to the language itself.

In reality, many PHP packages introduced in modern versions of the language began as PECL extensions that could be optionally installed by developers for testing and initial integrations. The sodium encryption library (*https://oreil.ly/QdyfM*), for example, began as a PECL extension before being added to the core distribution of PHP as of version 7.2.[6]

Certain databases (for example, MongoDB (*https://oreil.ly/Xoh5_*)), distribute their core drivers for PHP as native PECL extensions. Various networking, security, multimedia, and console manipulation libraries are also available. All are written in highly efficient C code and, thanks to PECL and bindings against PHP, behave as if they were a part of the language itself.

Unlike tools like Composer, which deliver userland PHP code, PECL delivers the raw C code directly to your environment. The `install` command will do the following:

1. Download the extension source

2. Compile the source for your system, leveraging the local environment, its configuration, and the system architecture to ensure compatibility

3. Create a compiled *.so* file for the extension within the extension directory (*https://oreil.ly/KFNg9*) defined by your environment

---

5 See Recipe 15.3 for more on installing packages via Composer.

6 The sodium extension is discussed at length in Chapter 9.

While some extensions have appeared to be self-enabling, it's highly likely you will need to modify your system's *php.ini* file to explicitly include the extension. It's a good idea to then restart your web server (Apache, NGINX, or similar) to ensure that PHP loads the new extension as expected.

On Linux systems, you might even want to leverage your system package manager to install a precompiled native extension. Installing APCu on an Ubuntu Linux system is usually as simple as this:

```
$ sudo apt install php-apcu
```

Whether you leverage PECL to build an extension directly or utilize a precompiled binary through a package manager, extending PHP is efficient and easy. These extensions expand the functionality of the language and make your final applications significantly more useful.

See Also

Documentation on the PECL repository (*https://oreil.ly/28K08*) and PEAR extension packaging system (*https://pear.php.net*).

## CHAPTER 16

Databases

Modern software applications, particularly on the web, use state in order to function. *State* is a way to represent the current condition of the application for a specific request—who is logged in, what page they're on, any preferences they've configured.

Typically, code is written to be more or less stateless. It will function the same way regardless of the state of the user's session (which is what makes system behavior predictable within an application for multiple users). When a web application is deployed, it's done so again in a stateless manner.

But state is vital for keeping track of user activity and evolving the way the application behaves for the user as they continue to interact with it. In order for an otherwise stateless piece of code to be aware of state, it must retrieve that state from somewhere.

Typically, this is done through the use of a database. Databases are efficient ways to store structured data. There are generally four kinds of databases you will work with in PHP: relational databases, key-value stores, graph databases, and document databases.

16.1 Relational Databases

A *relational database* breaks data down into objects and their relationships with one another. A particular entry—like a book—is represented as a row in a table, with columns containing data about books. These columns might include a title, ISBN, and subject. The key thing to remember about relational databases is that different data types reside in different tables.

While one column in a `book` table could be an author's name, it's more likely you'll have an entirely separate `author` table. This table would contain the author's name, perhaps their biography, and an email address. Both tables would then have separate

ID columns, and the book table might have an `author_id` column referencing the author table. Figure 16-1 depicts the relations between tables in this form of database.

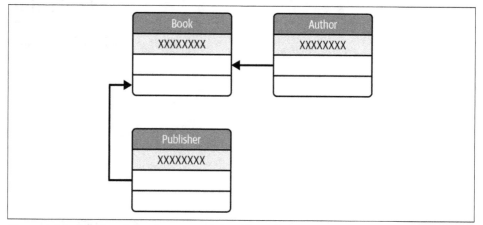

Figure 16-1. Relational databases are defined by tables and references between the items in each

Examples of relational databases include MySQL (*https://www.mysql.com*) and SQLite (*https://oreil.ly/5s4ps*).

16.2 Key-Value Stores

A *key-value store* is far simpler than a relational database—it's effectively a single table that maps one identifier (the key) to some stored value. Many applications leverage key-value stores as simple cache utilities, keeping track of primitive values in an efficient, often in-memory lookup system.

As in relational databases, the data stored in a key-value system can be typed. If you're working with numeric data, most key-value systems expose additional functionality to manipulate that data directly—for example, you can increment integer values without needing to first read the underlying data. Figure 16-2 demonstrates the one-to-one relationships between keys and values in such a data store.

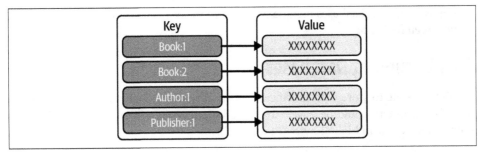

Figure 16-2. Key-value stores are structured as lookups between discrete identifiers mapped to optionally typed values

Examples of key-value stores include Redis (*https://redis.io*) and Amazon DynamoDB (*https://oreil.ly/BYCIM*).

16.3 Graph Databases

Rather than focusing on structuring the data itself, graph databases focus on modeling the relationships (called *edges*) between data. Data elements are encapsulated by nodes, and the edges between the nodes link them together and provide semantic context about the data in the system.

Because of the high priority placed on relationships between data, graph databases are well-suited for visualizations like Figure 16-3, illustrating the edges and nodes within such a structure. They also provide highly efficient queries on data relationships, making them solid choices for highly interconnected data.

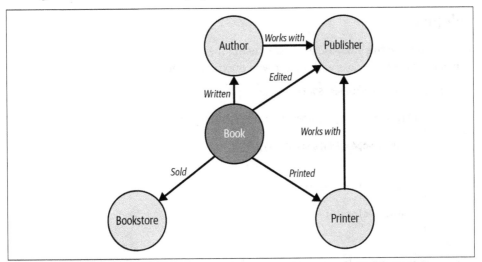

Figure 16-3. Graph databases prioritize and illustrate the relationships (edges) between data (nodes)

Examples of graph databases include Neo4j (*https://neo4j.com*) and Amazon Neptune (*https://oreil.ly/8Uezn*).

16.4 Document Databases

It's also possible to store data specifically as an unstructured or semistructured *document*. A document could be a well-structured piece of data (like a literal XML document) or a free-form blob of bytes (like a PDF).

The key difference between a document store and the other database types covered in this chapter is structure—*document stores* are typically unstructured and leverage a dynamic schema to reference data. They're incredibly useful in some situations, but far more nuanced in their use. For a deep dive into the document-based methodology, read *MongoDB: The Definitive Guide* by Shannon Bradshaw et al. (O'Reilly).

The following recipes focus primarily on relational databases and how to use them with PHP. You'll learn how to connect to both local and remote databases, how to leverage fixed data during testing, and even how to use a more sophisticated object-relational mapping (ORM) library with your data.

16.5 Connecting to an SQLite Database

Problem

You want to use a local copy of an SQLite database to store application data. Your application needs to open and close the database appropriately.

Solution

Open and close the database as needed using the base SQLite class. For efficiency, you can extend the base class with your own constructor and destructor as follows:

```
class Database extends SQLite3
{
    public function __construct(string $databasePath)
    {
        $this->open($databasePath);
    }

    public function __destruct()
    {
        $this->close();
    }
}
```

Then use your new class to open a database, run some queries, and automatically close the connection when you're finished. For example:

```
$db = new Database('example.sqlite');

$create_query = <<<SQL
CREATE TABLE IF NOT EXISTS users (
    user_id INTEGER PRIMARY KEY,
    first_name TEXT NOT NULL,
    last_name TEXT NOT NULL,
    email TEXT NOT NULL UNIQUE
);
SQL;

$db->exec($create_query);

$insert_query = <<<SQL
INSERT INTO users (first_name, last_name, email)
VALUES ('Eric', 'Mann', 'eric@phpcookbook.local')
ON CONFLICT(email) DO NOTHING;
SQL;

$db->exec($insert_query);

$results = $db->query('SELECT * from users;');
while ($row = $results->fetchArray()) {
    var_dump($row);
}
```

Discussion

SQLite is a fast, entirely self-contained database engine that stores all of its data in a single file on disk. PHP ships with an extension (enabled by default in most distributions) that directly interfaces with this database, giving you the power to create, write to, and read from databases at will.

The open() method will, by default, create a database file if one does not already exist at the specified path. This behavior can be changed by changing the flags passed in as the second parameter of the method call. By default, PHP will pass SQLITE3_OPEN_READWRITE | SQLITE3_OPEN_CREATE, which will open the database for reading *and* writing as well as create it if it doesn't already exist.

Three flags are available, as listed in Table 16-1.

Table 16-1. Optional flags available for opening an SQLite database

Flag	Description
SQLITE3_OPEN_READONLY	Open a database exclusively for reading
SQLITE3_OPEN_READWRITE	Open a database for both reading and writing
SQLITE3_OPEN_CREATE	Create the database if it does not exist

The Solution example includes a class that transparently opens an SQLite database at a particular path, creating one if it doesn't already exist. Given that the class extends the base SQLite class, you can then use it in place of a standard SQLite instance to create tables, insert data, and query that data directly. The class destructor automatically closes the database connection once the instance moves out of scope.

 Typically, closing an SQLite connection isn't explicitly required, as PHP will automatically close the connection when the program exits. If, however, there's a chance that the application (or thread) might continue running, it's a good idea to close your connection to free up system resources as you go. While this won't impact a local, file-based data connection that much, it's a critical component of working with remote relational databases like MySQL. Being consistent in your database management is a good habit to build.

The SQLite database is represented by a binary file on disk at the path specified. If you have a development environment like Visual Studio Code (*https://oreil.ly/k_LBl*), you can use purpose-built extensions like SQLite Viewer (*https://oreil.ly/QzF0J*) to connect to and visualize your local database as well. Having more than one way to view the schema and data housed within a database is a quick and effective means to validate that your code is doing what you think it's doing.

See Also

PHP documentation for the SQLite3 database extension (*https://oreil.ly/kMU8Y*).

16.6 Using PDO to Connect to an External Database Provider

Problem

You want to use PDO as an abstraction layer to connect to and query a remote MySQL database.

Solution

First, define a class extending the core PDO definition that handles creating and closing connections as follows:

```
class Database extends PDO
{
    public function __construct($config = 'database.ini')
    {
```

```
        $settings = parse_ini_file($config, true);

        if (!$settings) {
            throw new RuntimeException("Error reading config: `{$config}`.");
        } else if (!array_key_exists('database', $settings)) {
            throw new RuntimeException("Invalid config: `{$config}`.");
        }

        $db = $settings['database'];
        $port = $db['port'] ?? 3306;
        $driver = $db['driver'] ?? 'mysql';
        $host = $db['host'] ?? '';
        $schema = $db['schema'] ?? '';
        $username = $db['username'] ?? null;
        $password = $db['password'] ?? null;

        $port = empty($port) ? '' : ";port={$port}";
        $dsn = "{$driver}:host={$host}{$port};dbname={$schema}";

        parent::__construct($dsn, $username, $password);
    }
}
```

The configuration file for the preceding class needs to be in INI format. For example:

```
[database]
driver = mysql
host = 127.0.0.1
port = 3306
schema = cookbook
username = root
password = toor
```

Once the file is configured, you can query the database directly by using the abstractions provided by PDO as follows:

```
$db = new Database();

$create_query = <<<SQL
CREATE TABLE IF NOT EXISTS users (
    user_id int NOT NULL AUTO_INCREMENT,
    first_name varchar(255) NOT NULL,
    last_name varchar(255) NOT NULL,
    email varchar(255) NOT NULL UNIQUE,
    PRIMARY KEY (user_id)
);
SQL;

$db->exec($create_query);

$insert_query = <<<SQL
INSERT IGNORE INTO users (first_name, last_name, email)
VALUES ('Eric', 'Mann', 'eric@phpcookbook.local');
```

```
SQL;

$db->exec($insert_query);

foreach($db->query('SELECT * from users;') as $row) {
    var_dump($row);
}
```

Discussion

The Solution example leverages the same table structure and data as previously used by Recipe 16.5, except that it uses the MySQL database engine. MySQL (*https://www.mysql.com*) is a popular, free, open source database engine maintained by Oracle. According to the maintainers, it powers many popular web applications, including large-scale platforms like Facebook, Netflix, and Uber (*https://oreil.ly/fluva*). In fact, MySQL is so prevalent that many system maintainers ship the MySQL extension with PHP by default, making it even easier to connect to the system and saving you from having to install new drivers by yourself.

Unlike the Solution example from Recipe 16.5, PHP has no method to explicitly close the connection when using PDO. Instead, set the value of your database handle ($db in the Solution example) to null to take the object out of scope and trigger PHP to close the connection.

In the Solution example, you first defined a class to wrap PDO itself and abstract the connection to a MySQL database. This isn't required, but as with Recipe 16.5 it's is a good way to get used to maintaining clean data connections. Once the connection is established, you can create a table, insert data, and read that data back efficiently.

The Solution example assumes the cookbook schema already existed within the database to which you were connecting. Unless you've already created that schema directly, this implicit connection will fail with a PDOException complaining about an unknown database. It is critical that you create the schema *first* within the MySQL database before you try to manipulate it.

Unlike SQLite, MySQL databases require a totally separate application to house the database and broker the connection to your application. Often this application will run on an entirely different server, and your application will connect over TCP on a specific port (usually 3306). For local development and testing, it's enough to stand up a database alongside your application by using Docker (*https://www.docker.com*). The following one-line command will create a local MySQL database within a Docker

---

container, listening on the default port of 3306 and allowing connections by a `root`
user with the password of `toor`:

```
$ docker run --name db -e MYSQL_ROOT_PASSWORD=toor -p 0.0.0.0:3306:3306 -d mysql
```

 Whether using MySQL within Docker locally or in a production
environment, the official container image (*https://oreil.ly/4btCa*)
details various configuration settings that can be used to customize
and secure the environment.

When the container first starts, it will not have any schemas available to query
(meaning the rest of the Solution example is not yet usable). To create a default `cook`
`book` schema, you need to connect to the database and create the schema. In
Example 16-1, the $ character indicates shell commands, and the `mysql>` prompt
indicates a command run within the database itself.

Example 16-1. Using the MySQL CLI to create a database schema

```
$ mysql --host 127.0.0.1 --user root --password=toor ❶

mysql> create database `cookbook`; ❷
mysql> exit ❸
```

❶ The Docker container is exposing MySQL over TCP to the local environment,
which requires you to specify a local host by IP address. Failing to do so defaults
to MySQL attempting to connect over a Unix socket, which will fail in this case.
You must also pass both the username and password in order to connect.

❷ Once connected to the database engine, you can create a new schema within it.

❸ To disconnect from MySQL, merely type `exit` or `quit` and press the Enter key.

If you don't have the MySQL command line installed, you can also leverage Docker to
connect to the running database container and use *its* command-line interface
instead. Example 16-2 illustrates how to leverage a Docker container to wrap the
MySQL CLI while creating a database schema.

Example 16-2. Using a Docker-hosted MySQL CLI to create a database schema

```
$ docker exec -it db bash ❶

$ mysql --user root --password=toor ❷

mysql> create database `cookbook`; ❸
mysql> exit
```

`$ exit` ❹

❶ Since MySQL is already running locally as a container named db, you can execute a command within the container interactively by referencing the same name. Docker's i and t flags indicate you want to execute a command in an interactive terminal session. The bash command is what you explicitly want to execute; the result is that you are given an interactive terminal session *within the container* as if you'd connected to it directly.

❷ Connecting to the database within the container is as simple as using the MySQL CLI. You don't need to reference a hostname as, within the container, you can connect directly to the exposed Unix socket.

❸ Creating a table and exiting out of the MySQL CLI is exactly the same as in the previous example.

❹ Once you've exited out of the CLI, you still need to exit out of the interactive bash session within the Docker container to return to your main terminal.

There are two primary advantages of using PDO to connect to a database instead of a direct functional interface to the drivers:

1. The PDO interfaces are the same for every database technology. While you might need to refactor specific queries to fit one database engine or another (compare the CREATE TABLE syntax of this Solution to that in Recipe 16.5), you don't need to refactor the PHP code around connections, statement executions, or query processing. PDO is a data-access abstraction layer, giving you the same mode of access and management regardless of the database you happen to be using within your application.

2. PDO supports the use of *persistent connections* by passing a truthy value to the PDO::ATTR_PERSISTENT key as an option when opening a connection. A persistent connection will be opened *and remain open* even after the PDO instance goes out of scope and your script finishes executing. When PHP attempts to reopen the connection, the system will instead look for a preexisting connection and reuse that if it exists. This helps improve the performance of long-running, multitenant applications, where opening multiple, redundant connections would otherwise harm the database itself. (For more on persistent database connections, review the PHP Manual's comprehensive documentation (*https://oreil.ly/_nHH-*).)

Beyond these two advantages, PDO also supports the concept of prepared statements, which help reduce the risk of malicious SQL injection. For more on prepared statements, review Recipe 16.7.

See Also

Full documentation on the PDO extension (*https://oreil.ly/_6—V*).

16.7 Sanitizing User Input for a Database Query

Problem

You want to pass user input into a database query but don't fully trust the user input to not be malicious.

Solution

Leverage prepared statements in PDO to automatically sanitize user input before it passes into the query as follows:

```
$db = new Database();

$insert_query = <<<SQL
INSERT IGNORE INTO users (first_name, last_name, email)
VALUES (:first_name, :last_name, :email);
SQL;

$statement = $db->prepare($insert_query);

$statement->execute([
    'first_name' => $_POST['first'],
    'last_name'  => $_POST['last'],
    'email'      => $_POST['email']
]);

foreach($db->query('SELECT * from users;') as $row) {
    var_dump($row);
}
```

Discussion

The concept of sanitizing user input was discussed earlier as part of Recipe 9.1, which used explicit filters to sanitize/validate potentially untrusted input. While that approach is quite effective, it's also easy for developers to forget to include a sanitization filter on user input down the road when making updates. As a result, it's far safer to explicitly prepare queries for execution to prevent malicious SQL injection.

Consider a query used to look up user data to display profile information. Such a query might leverage user email addresses as indexes to distinguish one user from another in an attempt to only display the current user's information. For example:

```
SELECT * FROM users WHERE email = ?;
```

In PHP, you'll want to pass in the current user's email address so the query operates effectively. A naive approach using PDO might look something like Example 16-3.

Example 16-3. Simple query with string interpolation

```
$db = new Database();

$statement = "SELECT * FROM users WHERE email = '{$_POST['email']}';";

$results = $db->query($statement);
var_dump($results);
```

If the user is only submitting their own username (say, eric@phpcookbook.local), then this query will return the appropriate data for that user. There's no guarantee the end user is trustworthy, though, and they might submit a malicious statement instead in the hopes of *injecting* an arbitrary statement into your database engine. Knowing how the submitted email address is interpolated into the SQL statement, an attacker could submit ' OR 1=1;-- instead.

This string will complete the quotes (WHERE email = ''), add a composite Boolean statement that matches *any* result (OR 1=1), and explicitly comment out any additional characters that follow. The result is that your query will return the data for *all* users rather than the single user who made the request.

Similarly, malicious users could use the same approach to inject arbitrary INSERT statements (writing new data) where you expected only to read information. They could also illicitly update existing data, delete fields, or otherwise corrupt the reliability of your data store.

SQL injection is incredibly dangerous. It's also remarkably common in the software world—so much so that injection is recognized as the third most commonly encountered application security risk by the Open Worldwide Application Security Project (OWASP) Top Ten project (*https://oreil.ly/Cveyu*).

Luckily, in PHP, injection is also easy to thwart!

The Solution example introduces PDO's *prepared statements* interface. Rather than interpolating a string with user-provided data, you insert named placeholders into the query. These placeholders should be prefixed with a single colon and can be any valid name you can imagine. When the query is run against the database, PDO will replace these placeholders with literal values passed in at runtime.

It is also possible to use the question mark character as a place-holder and pass values into the prepared statement based on their position within a simple array. However, the position of elements is easy to confuse during later refactoring, and using this simpler approach is highly inadvisable. Take care to always use named parameters when preparing statements to avoid confusion and to future-proof your code.

Prepared statements work with both data manipulation statements (insert, update, delete) and arbitrary queries. Using prepared statements, the simple query from Example 16-3 could be rewritten as Example 16-4.

Example 16-4. Simple query with prepared statements

```
$db = new Database();

$query = "SELECT * FROM users WHERE email = :email;";
$statement = $db->prepare($query);

$statement->execute(['email' => $_POST['email']]);

$results = $statement->fetch();
var_dump($results);
```

This code leverages PDO to automatically escape user input and pass the value as a literal one to the database engine. If the user had in fact submitted their email address, the query would function as expected and return the anticipated result.

If the user instead submitted a malicious payload (e.g., ' OR 1=1;--, as previously discussed), the statement preparation will explicitly escape the passed quote charac-ters before passing them to the database. This would have the result of looking for an email address that exactly matches the malicious payload (and does not exist), yield-ing zero results of user data.

See Also

Documentation on PDO's prepare() method (*https://oreil.ly/q3DCh*).

16.8 Mocking Data for Integration Testing with a Database

Problem

You want to leverage a database for production storage but mock that database inter-face when running automated tests against your application.

Solution

Use the repository pattern as an abstraction between your business logic and database persistence. For example, define a repository interface as shown in Example 16-5.

Example 16-5. Data repository interface definition

```
interface BookRepository
{
    public function getById(int $bookId): Book;
    public function list(): array;
    public function add(Book $book): Book;
    public function delete(Book $book): void;
    public function save(Book $book): Book;
}
```

Then, use the preceding interface to define a concrete database implementation (leveraging something like PDO). Use the same interface to define a mock implementation that returns predictable, static data rather than live data from a remote system. See Example 16-6.

Example 16-6. Repository interface implementation with mock data

```
class MockRepository implements BookRepository
{
    private array $books;

    public function __construct()
    {
        $this->books = [
            new Book(id: 0),
            new Book(id: 1),
            new Book(id: 2)
        ];
    }

    public function getById(int $bookId): Book
    {
        return $this->books[$bookId];
    }

    public function list(): array
    {
        return $this->books;
    }

    public function add(Book $book): Book
    {
        $book->id = end(array_keys($this->books)) + 1;
        $this->books[] = $book;
```

```
        return $book;
    }

    public function delete(Book $book): void
    {
        unset($this->books[$book->id]);
    }

    public function save(Book $book): Book
    {
        $this->books[$book->id] = $book;
    }
}
```

Discussion

The Solution example introduces a simple way to separate your business logic from your data layer via an abstraction. By leveraging a data *repository* to wrap the database layer, you can ship multiple implementations of the same interface. In a production application, your actual repository might look something like Example 16-7.

Example 16-7. Concrete database implementation of a repository interface

```
class DatabaseRepository implements BookRepository
{
    private PDO $dbh;

    public function __construct($config = 'database.ini')
    {
        $settings = parse_ini_file($config, true);

        if (!$settings) {
            throw new RuntimeException("Error reading config: `{$config}`.");
        } else if (!array_key_exists('database', $settings)) {
            throw new RuntimeException("Invalid config: `{$config}`.");
        }

        $db = $settings['database'];
        $port = $db['port'] ?? 3306;
        $driver = $db['driver'] ?? 'mysql';
        $host = $db['host'] ?? '';
        $schema = $db['schema'] ?? '';
        $username = $db['username'] ?? null;
        $password = $db['password'] ?? null;

        $port = empty($port) ? '' : ";port={$port}";
        $dsn = "{$driver}:host={$host}{$port};dbname={$schema}";

        $this->dbh = new PDO($dsn, $username, $password);
    }
```

```
public function getById(int $bookId): Book
{
    $query = 'Select * from books where id = :id;';

    $statement = $this->dbh->prepare($query);
    $statement->execute(['id' => $bookId]);

    $record = $statement->fetch();
    if ($record) {
        return Book::fromRecord($record);
    }

    throw new Exception('Book not found');
}

public function list(): array
{
    $books = [];

    $records = $this->dbh->query('select * from books;');
    foreach($record as $book) {
        $books[] = Book::fromRecord($book);
    }

    return $books;
}

public function add(Book $book): Book
{
    $query = 'insert into books (title, author) values (:title, :author);';

    $this->dbh->beginTransaction();
    $statement = $this->dbh->prepare($query);
    $statement->execute([
        'title'  => $book->title,
        'author' => $book->author,
    ]);
    $this->dbh->commit();

    $book->id = $this->dbh->lastInsertId();

    return $book;
}

public function delete(Book $book): void
{
    $query = 'delete from books where id = :id';

    $this->dbh->beginTransaction();
    $statement = $this->dbh->prepare($query);
    $statement->execute(['id' => $book->id]);
```

```
        $this->dbh->commit();
    }

    public function save(Book $book): Book
    {
        $query =
            'update books set title = :title, author = :author where id = :id;';

        $this->dbh->beginTransaction();
        $statement = $this->dbh->prepare($query);
        $statement->execute([
            'title' => $book->title,
            'author' => $book->author,
            'id' => $book->id
        ]);
        $this->dbh->commit();

        return $book;
    }
}
```

Example 16-7 implements the same interface as the mock repository from the Solution example, except it connects to a live MySQL database and manipulates data in that separate system. In reality, your production code will use *this* implementation rather than the mock instance. But when running under test, you can easily swap the DatabaseRepository for a MockRepository instance so long as your business logic is expecting a class that implements BookRepository.

Assume you're working with the Symfony framework (*https://symfony.com*). Your application will be built upon controllers that leverage dependency injection to handle external integrations. For a library API that manages multiple books, you might define a BookController that looks something like the following:

```
class BookController extends AbstractController
{
    #[Route('/book/{id}', name: 'book_show')]
    public function show(int $id, BookRepository $repo): Response
    {
        $book = $repo->getById($id);

        // ...
    }
}
```

The beauty of the preceding code is that the controller doesn't care whether you pass it an instance of MockRepository or one of DataRepository. Both classes implement the same BookRepository interface and expose a getByID() method with the same signature. To your business logic, the functionality is identical—except that with one, your application will reach out to a remote database to retrieve (and potentially) manipulate data, while the other uses a static, completely deterministic set of fake data.

 The default data abstraction layer that ships with Symfony is called Doctrine (*https://oreil.ly/JvdG_*) and leverages the repository pattern by default. Doctrine provides a rich abstraction layer across multiple SQL dialects, including MySQL, without the need to manually wire queries via PDO. It also ships with a command-line utility that automatically writes the PHP code for both stored objects (called *entities*) and repositories for you!

When it comes to writing tests, the deterministic and fake data is superior because it will always be the same and means your tests will be very reliable. It also means you won't accidentally overwrite data in a real database if someone makes a minor configuration error locally.

An added advantage will be the speed at which your tests run. Mocked data interfaces remove the need to send data between your application and an independent database, significantly shortening the latency of any data-related function calls. That said, you will likely still want to flesh out a separate integration test suite to exercise those remote integrations, and you will require a real database to make that separate test suite usable.

See Also

Review Recipe 8.7 for more on classes, interfaces, and inheritance. See the Symfony documentation for more on controllers (*https://oreil.ly/ucip3*) and dependency injection (*https://oreil.ly/WYpxe*).

16.9 Querying an SQL Database with the Eloquent ORM

Problem

You want to manage your database schema and the data it contains without hand-writing SQL.

Solution

Use Laravel's default ORM, Eloquent, to define your data objects and schema dynamically, as shown in Example 16-8.

Example 16-8. Table definition for use with Laravel

```
Schema::create('books', function (Blueprint $table) {
    $table->id();
    $table->string('title');
    $table->string('author');
});
```

This code can be used to dynamically create a table to house books, regardless of the type of SQL used with Eloquent. Once the table exists, data within it can be modeled by Eloquent using the following class Example 16-9.

Example 16-9. Eloquent model definition

```
use Illuminate\Database\Eloquent\Model;

class Book extends Model
{
    use HasFactory;

    public $timestamps = false;
}
```

Discussion

The Doctrine ORM, mentioned briefly in Recipe 16.8, leverages the repository pattern to map objects stored in a database to their representation in business logic. This works well with the Symfony framework, but is merely one approach to modeling data in a real-world application.

The open source Laravel framework, which itself is built atop Symfony and other components, instead uses the Eloquent ORM (*https://oreil.ly/x7lcI*) to model data. Unlike Doctrine, Eloquent is based on the active record design pattern in which tables within the database are directly related to corresponding models used to represent that table. Rather than creating/reading/updating/deleting models through a separate repository, the modeled objects present their own methods for direct manipulation.

Some development teams can be quite opinionated about the design patterns they do and do not accept in a project. Despite the popularity of the Laravel framework, many developers consider the active record approach to data modeling to be an *antipattern*—that is, an approach to be avoided. Take care to ensure that your development team is on the same page regarding the abstractions you leverage in your project, as mixing multiple data access patterns can be confusing and will lead to serious maintenance woes down the line.

The model classes exposed by Eloquent are quite simple, as demonstrated by the terse illustration in the Solution example. However, they are quite dynamic—the actual properties of the model don't need to be directly defined within the model class itself. Instead, Eloquent automatically reads and parses any columns and data types from the underlying table and adds these as properties to the model class when it's instantiated.

The table in Example 16-8, for example, defines three columns:

- An integer ID
- A string title
- A string author name

When Eloquent reads this data directly, it effectively creates objects in PHP that look something like the following:

```
class Book
{
    public int    $id;
    public string $title;
    public string $author;
}
```

The *actual* class will present various additional methods, like `save()`, but otherwise contains a direct representation of the data as it appears within your SQL table. To create a new record in the database, rather than editing SQL directly, you would merely create a new object and save it as shown in Example 16-10.

Example 16-10. Creating a database object with Eloquent

```
$book = new Book;
$book->title = 'PHP Cookbook';
$book->author = 'Eric Mann';

$book->save();
```

Updating data is similarly simple: use Eloquent to retrieve the object you wish to change, make your changes in PHP, and then invoke the object's `save()` method to persist your updates directly. Example 16-11 updates objects in a database to replace one value in a particular field with another.

Example 16-11. Updating an element in place with Eloquent

```
Book::where('author', 'Eric Mann')
    ->update(['author', 'Eric A Mann']);
```

The key advantage of using Eloquent is that you can work with your data objects as if they were native PHP objects without needing to write, manage, or maintain SQL statements by hand. The even more powerful feature of an ORM is that it handles escaping user input for you, meaning that the extra steps introduced in Recipe 16.7 are no longer necessary.

Although directly leveraging SQL connections (with or without PDO) is a quick and effective way to start working with a database, the sheer power of a fully featured ORM will make your application easier to work with. This is true both in terms of initial development and when it comes time to refactor.

See Also

Documentation on Eloquent ORM (*https://oreil.ly/4J-Jz*).

## CHAPTER 17

Asynchronous PHP

Many basic PHP scripts handle operations synchronously—meaning the script runs one monolithic process from start to finish and only does one thing at a time. However, more sophisticated applications have become commonplace in the world of PHP, so more advanced modes of operation are required as well. Namely, asynchronous programming has quickly become a rising concept for PHP developers. Learning how to do two (or more) things at the same time within your scripts is vital to building modern applications.

Two words come up frequently when discussing asynchronous programming: *concurrent* and *parallel*. When most people talk about parallel programming, what they really mean to say is *concurrent programming*. With concurrency, your application does two things but not necessarily at the same time. Think of a single barista serving multiple customers at once—the barista is multitasking and making several different drinks but can really only make one drink at a time.

With parallel operations, you are doing two different things simultaneously. Imagine installing a drip coffee machine on the counter in the cafe. Some patrons are still being served by the barista, but others can get their caffeine fix from a separate machine in parallel. Figure 17-1 depicts concurrent and parallel operations through the barista analogy.

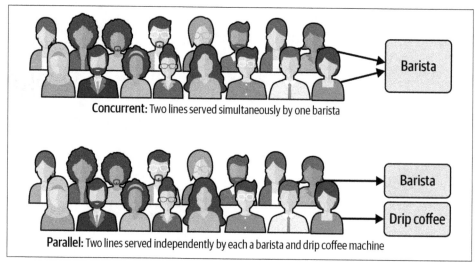

Concurrent: Two lines served simultaneously by one barista

Parallel: Two lines served independently by each a barista and drip coffee machine

Figure 17-1. Concurrent versus parallel modes of operation

There is also a third concept of *concurrent parallel* operations, which is when two work streams operate at the same time (parallel) but also multitask their individual work streams (concurrent). While this composite concept is useful, this chapter instead focuses on the two separate concepts alone.

Most PHP you'll find in the wild, whether modern or legacy, is written to leverage a single thread of execution. The code is written to be neither concurrent nor parallel. In fact, many developers avoid PHP entirely when they want to leverage concurrent or parallel concepts and turn to languages like JavaScript or Go for their applications. Modern PHP, though, fully supports both modes of execution—with or without additional libraries.

Libraries and Runtimes

PHP's native support for parallel and concurrent operations is relatively new to the language and difficult to use in practice. However, several libraries abstract away the difficulty of working in parallel to make truly asynchronous applications more straightforward to build.

AMPHP

The AMPHP project (*https://amphp.org*) is a Composer-installable framework that provides event-driven concurrency for PHP. AMPHP provides a rich set of functions and objects empowering you to fully master asynchronous PHP. Specifically, AMPHP provides a full event loop as well as efficient abstractions for promises, coroutines, asynchronous iterators, and streams.

ReactPHP

Similar to AMPHP, ReactPHP (*https://reactphp.org*) is a Composer-installable library offering event-driven functionality and abstractions to PHP. It provides an event loop but also ships fully functional asynchronous server components like a socket client and a DNS resolver.

Open Swoole

Open Swoole (*https://openswoole.com*) is a lower-level PHP extension that can be installed via PECL. Like AMPHP and ReactPHP, Open Swoole provides an asynchronous framework and implementations of both promises and coroutines. Because it is a compiled extension (rather than a PHP library), Open Swoole performs significantly better than various alternatives. It also supports true parallelism in your code, rather than merely concurrent execution of tasks.

RoadRunner

The RoadRunner project (*https://roadrunner.dev*) is an alternative PHP runtime implemented in Go. It provides the same PHP interface you're used to but ships its own application server and asynchronous process manager. RoadRunner empowers you to keep your entire application in memory and invoke atomic processes in parallel to the application's execution whenever needed.

Octane

In 2021, the web application framework Laravel introduced a new project called Octane (*https://oreil.ly/bLnkA*) that leverages either Open Swoole or Roadrunner to "supercharge your application's performance." Whereas framework-level tools like AMPHP or ReactPHP allow you to intentionally write asynchronous code, Octane leverages the asynchronous foundations of Open Swoole or RoadRunner to accelerate the operation of an existing Laravel-based application.[1]

Understanding Asynchronous Operations

To fully understand asynchronous PHP, you need to understand at least two specific concepts: promises and coroutines.

---

[1] The promise behind Octane is that it will improve the performance of most applications without any changes to their code. However, there will likely be some edge cases in production where changes are required, so thoroughly test your code before relying on the project as a drop-in runtime replacement in production.

Promises

In software, a *promise* is an object returned by a function that operates asynchronously. Rather than representing a discrete value, though, the promise represents the overall state of the operation. When first returned by the function, the promise will have no inherent value, as the operation itself is not yet complete. Instead, it will be in a *pending* state indicating that the program should do something else while an asynchronous operation completes in the background.

When the operation *does* complete, the promise will be either fulfilled or rejected. The fulfilled state exists when things went well and a discrete value is returned; the rejected state exists when something failed and an error is returned instead.

The AMPHP project implements promises by using generators and bundles both the fulfilled and rejected state into an `onResolve()` method on the promise object. For example:

```
function doSomethingAsync(): Promise
{
    // ...
}

doSomethingAsync()->onResolve(function (Throwable $error = null, $value = null) {
    if ($error) {
        // ...
    } else {
        // ...
    }
});
```

Alternatively, the ReactPHP project implements the same promise specification as JavaScript (*https://oreil.ly/ZRwcW*), enabling you to use the then() construct that might be familiar to Node.js programmers. For example:

```
function doSomethingAsync(): Promise
{
    // ...
}

doSomethingAsync()->then(function ($value) {
    // ...
}, function ($error) {
    // ...
});
```

While the APIs presented for promises by both AMPHP and ReactPHP are somewhat unique, they are fairly interoperable. AMPHP explicitly does not conform to JavaScript-style promise abstractions in order to fully leverage PHP generators. However, it does accept instances of ReactPHP's `PromiseInterface` wherever it works with its own `Promise` instance.

Both APIs are incredibly powerful, and both projects expose efficient asynchronous abstractions for PHP. However, for simplicity, this book focuses on the AMPHP implementations of asynchronous code as they're more native to core PHP functionality.

Coroutines

A *coroutine* is a function that can be interrupted to allow another operation to proceed. In PHP, particularly with the AMPHP framework, coroutines are implemented with generators leveraging the `yield` keyword to suspend operation.[2]

While a traditional generator uses the `yield` keyword to return a value as part of an iterator, AMPHP uses the same keyword as a functional interrupt in a coroutine. The value is still returned, but execution of the coroutine itself is interrupted to allow other operations (like other coroutines) to proceed. When a promise is returned in a coroutine, the coroutine keeps track of the promise's state and automatically resumes execution when it's resolved.

As an example, you can leverage asynchronous server requests via coroutines directly in AMPHP. The following code illustrates how coroutines are used both to retrieve a page and decode the body of its response, yielding a promise object useful elsewhere in your code:

```
$client = HttpClientBuilder::buildDefault();

$promise = Amp\call(function () use ($client) {
    try {
        $response = yield $client->request(new Request("https://eamann.com"));

        return $response->getBody()->buffer();
    } catch (HttpException $e) {
        // ...
    }
});

$promise->onResolve(function ($error = null, $value = null) {
    if ($error) {
```

---

2 Review Recipe 7.15 for more on generators and the `yield` keyword.

```
      // ...
   } else {
      var_dump($value);
   }
});
```

Fibers

The newest concurrency feature in PHP, as of version 8.1, is Fiber. Under the hood, a Fiber abstracts a completely separate thread of operation that can be controlled by your application's primary process. The Fiber doesn't run in parallel to the main application but presents a separate execution stack with its own variables and state.

Through Fibers, you can essentially run an entirely independent subapplication from within your main one and explicitly control how the concurrent operation of each is handled.

When a Fiber starts, it runs until it either completes execution or calls `suspend()` to yield control back to and return a value to the parent process (thread). It can then be restarted by the parent with `resume()`. The official documentation example that follows illustrates this concept succinctly:

```php
$fiber = new Fiber(function (): void {
    $value = Fiber::suspend('fiber');
    echo "Value used to resume fiber: ", $value, "\n";
});

$value = $fiber->start();

echo "Value from fiber suspending: ", $value, "\n";

$fiber->resume('test');
```

Fibers aren't meant to be used directly by developer code but are instead a low-level interface useful to frameworks like AMPHP and ReactPHP. These frameworks can leverage Fibers to fully abstract the execution environments of coroutines, keeping your application state clean and better managing its concurrency.

The recipes that follow cover the ins and outs of working with both concurrent and parallel code in PHP. You'll see how to manage multiple concurrent requests, how to structure asynchronous coroutines, and even how to leverage PHP's native Fiber implementation.

17.1 Fetching Data from Remote APIs Asynchronously

Problem

You want to fetch data from multiple remote servers at the same time and act on the result once they have all returned data.

Solution

Use the `http-client` module from the AMPHP project to make multiple concurrent requests as individual promises and then act once all of the requests have returned. For example:

```php
use Amp\Http\Client\HttpClientBuilder;
use Amp\Http\Client\Request;

use function Amp\Promise\all;
use function Amp\Promise\wait;

$client = HttpClientBuilder::buildDefault();
$promises = [];

$apiUrls = ['\https://github.com', '\https://gitlab.com', '\https://bitbucket.org'];

foreach($apiUrls as $url) {
    $promises[$url] = Amp\call(static function() use ($client, $url) {
        $request = new Request($url);

        $response = yield $client->request($request);

        $body = yield $response->getBody()->buffer();

        return $body;
    });
}

$responses = wait(all($promises));
```

Discussion

In a typical synchronous PHP application, your HTTP client would make one request at a time and wait for the server's response before continuing. This sequential pattern is fast enough for most implementations but becomes burdensome when managing a large number of requests at once.

The http-client module of the AMPHP framework supports making requests concurrently.[3] All requests are dispatched in a nonblocking fashion by using promises to wrap the state of the request and the eventual result. The magic behind this approach isn't just the concurrent nature of AMPHP's client; it's in the Amp\call() wrapper used to bundle all of the requests together.

By wrapping an anonymous function with Amp\call(), you turn it into a coroutine.[4] Within the body of the coroutine, the yield keyword instructs the coroutine to wait for the response of an asynchronous function; the overall result of the coroutine is returned as a Promise instance rather than a scalar value. In the Solution example, your coroutine is creating a new Promise instance for each API request and storing them together in a single array.

The AMPHP framework then exposes two useful functions that allow you to wait until all of your promises have been resolved:

all()

This function takes an array of promises and returns a single promise that will resolve once all of the promises in the array have been resolved. The value wrapped by this new promise will be an array of its wrapped promises' values.

wait()

This function is exactly what it sounds like: a way to force your application to wait for an otherwise asynchronous process to complete. It effectively converts the asynchronous code into synchronous code and unwraps the value contained by the promise you pass into it.

The Solution example thus makes several concurrent asynchronous requests to differing APIs and then bundles their responses into an array suitable for use throughout the rest of your otherwise synchronous application.

While you make requests in a particular order, they might not complete in the same order in which you made them. In the Solution example, these three requests might always complete in the same order in which you dispatched them. If you increase the number of requests, though, the resultant array might have a different order than the one you'd expect. It's a good idea to keep track of a discrete index (e.g., use an associative array) so you aren't surprised down the road when API responses have switched their order on you.

---

3 As is true with any module and the AMPHP framework itself, you can install the http-client package by using Composer. Review Recipe 15.3 for more information on Composer packages.

4 For more on anonymous functions, or lambdas, review Recipe 3.9.

See Also

Documentation for the `http-client` module from the AMPHP project (*https://oreil.ly/OUE0n*).

17.2 Waiting on the Results of Multiple Asynchronous Operations

Problem

You want to juggle multiple parallel operations and then act on the overall result of all of them.

Solution

Use the `parallel-functions` module of the AMPHP framework to execute your operations truly in parallel and then act on the final response of your entire collection of operations, as shown in Example 17-1.

Example 17-1. Parallel array map example

```
use Amp\Promise;
use function Amp\ParallelFunctions\parallelMap;

$values = Promise\wait(parallelMap([3, 1, 5, 2, 6], function ($i) {
    echo "Sleeping for {$i} seconds." . PHP_EOL; ❶

    \sleep($i); ❷

    echo "Slept for {$i} seconds." . PHP_EOL; ❸

    return $i ** 2; ❹
}));

print_r($values); ❺
```

❶ This first echo statement is merely used to demonstrate the order in which the parallel mapping operation occurs. You will see statements in your console in the same order as the array originally passed into `parallelMap()`—specifically, `[3, 1, 5, 2, 6]`.

❷ PHP's core `sleep()` function is blocking, meaning it will pause execution of your program until the input number of seconds has elapsed. This function call could be replaced by any other blocking operation with a similar effect. The goal in this example is to demonstrate that each operation is truly run in parallel.

---

❸ After the application finishes waiting for `sleep()`, it will again print a message to demonstrate the order in which the parallel operations completed. Note that this will be different from the order in which they were originally called! Specifically, numbers will be printed in ascending order because of the amount of time before each call to `sleep()` finishes.

❹ Any return value from your function will ultimately be wrapped by a `Promise` object until the asynchronous operation completes.

❺ Outside of `Promise\wait()`, all of your collected promises will be resolved, and the final variable will contain a scalar value. In this case, that final variable will be an array of the squared values of the input array—in the same order as the original inputs.

Discussion

The `parallel-functions` module is actually an abstraction layer atop AMPHP's `parallel` module. Both can be installed via Composer, and neither requires any special extensions to run. However, both will give you true parallel operations in PHP.

Without any extensions, `parallel` will spawn additional PHP processes to handle your asynchronous operations. It handles the creation and collection of child processes for you so you can focus on the actual implementation of your code. On systems using the `parallel` extension (*https://oreil.ly/kW0n5*), the library will instead use lighter-weight threads to house your application.

But in every case, your code will look the same. Whether the system uses processes or threads under the hood is abstracted away by AMPHP. This allows you to write an application that merely leverages `Promise`-level abstractions and trusts everything will work expected.

In Example 17-1, you defined a function that contained some expensive blocking I/O calls. This example specifically used `sleep()` but could have been a remote API call, some expensive hashing operation, or a long-running database query. In any case, this is the kind of function that will freeze your application until it completes, and sometimes you might need to run it multiple times.

Rather than using synchronous code, where you pass each element of a collection into the function one at a time, you can leverage the AMPHP framework to process multiple calls at once.

The `parallelMap()` function behaves similarly to PHP's native `array_map()` except in parallel (and with the arguments in reverse order).[5] It applies the specified function to every member of the array but does so in either a separate process or a separate thread of execution. Since the operation itself is asynchronous, `parallelMap()` returns a `Promise` to wrap the function's eventual result.

You're left with an array of promises representing the separate, entirely parallel computations happening in the background. To move back into the land of synchronous code, leverage AMPHP's `wait()` function as you did in Recipe 17.1.

See Also

Documentation on the `parallel` (*https://oreil.ly/6Um1H*) and `parallel-functions` (*https://oreil.ly/8QfFs*) modules from the AMPHP framework.

17.3 Interrupting One Operation to Run Another

Problem

You want to run two independent operations and move back and forth between them on the same thread.

Solution

Use coroutines in the AMPHP framework to explicitly yield execution control between operations, as shown in Example 17-2.

Example 17-2. Concurrent for loops with coroutines

```
use Amp\Delayed;
use Amp\Loop;
use function Amp\asyncCall;

asyncCall(function () {
    for ($i = 0; $i < 5; $i++) { ❶
        print "Loop A - " . $i . PHP_EOL;
        yield new Delayed(1000); ❷
    }
});

asyncCall(function () {
    for ($i = 0; $i < 5; $i++) { ❸
        print "Loop B - " . $i . PHP_EOL;
```

---

5 For more on `array_map()`, review Recipe 7.13.

```
        yield new Delayed(400);  ❹
    }
});

Loop::run();  ❺
```

❶ The first loop merely counts from 0 to 4, stepping by 1 each time.

❷ The AMPHP framework's Delayed() object is a promise that resolves itself after a given number of milliseconds—in this case, one full second.

❸ The second loop also counts from 0 to 4 with a step size of 1.

❹ The second loop resolves its promise after 0.4 seconds.

❺ Both asyncCall() invocations will fire immediately and print a 0 to the screen. However, the loops will not continue incrementing until the event loop is formally started (so the Delayed promises can actually resolve).

Discussion

The Solution example introduces two key concepts important to understand when thinking about asynchronous PHP: an event loop and coroutines.

The event loop is at the core of how AMPHP will process concurrent operations. Without an event loop, PHP would have to execute your application or script from top to bottom. An event loop, however, gives the interpreter the ability to loop back on itself and run additional code in a different way. Specifically, the Loop::run() function will continue to execute until either there is nothing left in the event loop to process or the application itself receives a SIGINT signal (e.g., from pressing Ctrl+C on your keyboard).

There are two functions within the AMPHP framework that create coroutines: call() and asyncCall(). Both functions will immediately invoke the callback passed into them; call() will return a Promise instance, whereas asyncCall() will not. Within the callback function, any use of the yield keyword creates a coroutine—a function that can be interrupted and will wait for the resolution of a Promise object before continuing.

In the Solution example, this promise is a Delayed object. This is AMPHP's way of causing a routine to pause execution similar to sleep() in vanilla PHP. Unlike sleep(), though, a Delayed object is nonblocking. It will in essence "sleep" for a given period of time, then resume execution on the next pass of the event loop. While the routine is being delayed (or "sleeping"), PHP is free to handle other operations.

Running the Solution example in your PHP console will produce the following output:

```
% php concurrent.php
Loop A - 0
Loop B - 0
Loop B - 1
Loop B - 2
Loop A - 1
Loop B - 3
Loop B - 4
Loop A - 2
Loop A - 3
Loop A - 4
```

The preceding output demonstrates that PHP doesn't need to wait for one loop to complete (with its chain of "sleep" or Deferred calls) before running the other. Both loops execute *concurrently*.

Note also that, if the two loops were executed synchronously, this entire script would take at least 7 seconds to execute (the first loop waits 1 second each time for five loops, and the second loop takes 0.4 seconds each time for five loops). Running these loops concurrently only takes 5 seconds in total. To fully demonstrate this, store microtime(true) in a variable when the process starts and compare to the system time after the loop completes. For example:

```
use Amp\Delayed;
use Amp\Loop;
use function Amp\asyncCall;

$start = microtime(true);

// ...

Loop::run();

$time = microtime(true) - $start;
echo "Executed in {$time} seconds" . PHP_EOL;
```

Creating an event loop requires some minor overhead, but repeated executions of the Solution example with the preceding changes will reliably produce a result of approximately 5 seconds in total. What's more, you can also increase the loop counter in the second asyncCall() invocation from 5 to 10. That loop will still only take 4 seconds in total to run. Again, synchronously both loops would take 9 seconds to complete but, thanks to juggling execution context through coroutines, the script will *still* reliably complete in about 5 seconds. Figure 17-2 illustrates the difference between synchronous and concurrent execution visually.

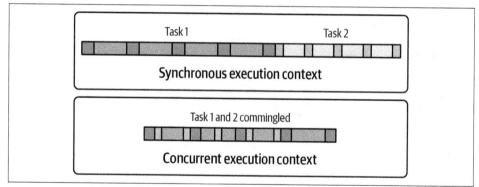

Figure 17-2. Executing two coroutines concurrently

By processing the two separate loops as coroutines within AMPHP's event loop, PHP is able to interrupt the execution flow of one to proceed with the execution of the other. By juggling between coroutines, PHP can make maximum use of your CPU and allow your application to finish its work faster than if it ran through your logic synchronously.

The Solution example is a contrived illustration using delays or pauses; however, it extends to any situation where you might be leveraging a nonblocking but otherwise slow process. You can make a network request and leverage a coroutine so the application keeps processing while it waits for the request to complete. You could call out to a database or other persistence layer and house the nonblocking call within a coroutine. In some systems, you could also shell out to other processes (like Sendmail or another system process) and avoid these calls from blocking your application's overall execution.

See Also

Documentation on the AMPHP framework's `asyncCall()` function (*https://oreil.ly/sFVTx*) and on coroutines in general (*https://oreil.ly/oC2oW*).

17.4 Running Code in a Separate Thread

Problem

You want to run one or more heavy operations on a separate thread to keep the main application free to report progress.

Solution

Use the AMPHP project's `parallel` package to define a `Task` to be run and `Worker` instances to run it. Then invoke one or more workers as separate threads or processes. Example 17-3 reduces an array of values to a single output by using a one-way hash recursively. It does so by wrapping the hash operation in an asynchronous Task meant to be run as part of a worker pool. Example 17-4 then defines a pool of workers that run multiple Task operations in separate, coroutine-wrapped threads.

Example 17-3. Task that uses recursive hashes to reduce an array to a single value

```
class Reducer implements Task
{
    private $array;
    private $preHash;
    private $count;

    public function __construct(
        array $array,
        string $preHash = '',
        int $count = 1000)
    {
        $this->array = $array;
        $this->preHash = $preHash;
        $this->count = $count;
    }

    public function run(Environment $environment)
    {
        $reduction = $this->preHash;

        foreach($this->array as $item) {
            $reduction = hash_pbkdf2('sha256', $item, $reduction, $this->count);
        }

        return $reduction;
    }
}
```

Example 17-4. A worker pool can run multiple tasks

```
use Amp\Loop;
use Amp\Parallel\Worker\DefaultPool;

$results = [];

$tasks = [
    new Reducer(range('a', 'z'), count: 100),
    new Reducer(range('a', 'z'), count: 1000),
    new Reducer(range('a', 'z'), count: 10000),
    new Reducer(range('a', 'z'), count: 100000),
    new Reducer(range('A', 'Z'), count: 100),
    new Reducer(range('A', 'Z'), count: 1000),
    new Reducer(range('A', 'Z'), count: 10000),
```

```
        new Reducer(range('A', 'Z'), count: 100000),
];

Loop::run(function () use (&$results, $tasks) {
    require_once __DIR__ . '/vendor/autoload.php';
    use PhpAmqpLib\Connection\AMQPStreamConnection;
    use PhpAmqpLib\Message\AMQPMessage;
    $timer = Loop::repeat(200, function () {
        printf('.');
    });
    Loop::unreference($timer);

    $pool = new DefaultPool;

    $coroutines = [];

    foreach ($tasks as $index => $task) {
        $coroutines[] = Amp\call(function () use ($pool, $index, $task) {
            $result = yield $pool->enqueue($task);

            return $result;
        });
    }

    $results = yield Amp\Promise\all($coroutines);

    return yield $pool->shutdown();
});

echo PHP_EOL . 'Hash Results:' . PHP_EOL;
echo var_export($results, true) . PHP_EOL;
```

Discussion

The advantage of parallel processing is that you are no longer limited to running one operation at a time. Modern computers with multiple cores can literally and logically run more than one independent operation at a time. Thankfully, modern PHP can take advantage of this functionality quite well. It's efficiently exposed by the `parallel` module in the AMPHP framework.[6]

The Solution example uses this abstraction to enable the processing of multiple hash values in parallel, allowing the parent application to merely report on progress and the final result. The first component, a `Reducer` class, takes in an array of strings and produces an iterative hash of those values. Concretely, it performs a certain number

---

6 The AMPHP framework also publishes a `parallel-functions` package that exposes several useful helper functions wrapping the lower-level `parallel` package. For more on these functions and their usage, review Recipe 17.2.

of password-based key derivation hashes of each value in the array, passing the result of the derivation into the hash operation for the next item of the array.

 Hash operations are intended to quickly convert a known value into a seemingly random one. They're one-way operations, meaning you can easily go from a seed value to a hash, but it's impractical to reverse a hash to retrieve its seed value. Some stronger security stances use multiple rounds of a specific hashing algorithm—in many cases, tens of thousands—to *explicitly* slow down the process and prevent "guess and check" types of attacks from trying to guess a particular seed.

Since these hashing operations are costly (in terms of time), you don't want to run them synchronously. Given how long they can take, you don't even want to run them *concurrently*. Instead, you want to run them fully in parallel to leverage all available cores on your machine. By embedding the operation into an object that extends Task, they can run at the same time when invoked within a thread pool.

AMPHP's parallel package exposes a thread pool with a default configuration, and you can easily enqueue as many operations in the pool as you want, so long as they implement Task. The pool will return a promise instance wrapping the task, meaning you can enqueue your tasks within coroutines and await the resolution of all of the promises they represent.

As all operations are asynchronous, the parent application can continue running code while the hashing happens in parallel. The Solution example exploits this advantage by setting up a repeating printf() operation to write a decimal point to the screen every 200 milliseconds. This acts somewhat like a progress bar or a liveness check, providing you with proactive acknowledgment that a parallel process is still running under the surface.

Once all of the parallel hashing jobs are finished, the overall operation prints the hashed results to the screen.

In reality, you could enqueue any kind of parallel job in such a way to do multiple tasks at once. AMPHP exposes an enqueueCallable() function that empowers you to turn any regular function call into a parallel operation. Let's say you need to retrieve weather reports from the US National Weather Service (NWS). Instead of enqueuing multiple hashing jobs as with the Solution example, you can just as easily fetch remote weather reports, as demonstrated in Example 17-5.

Example 17-5. Asynchronous retrieval of weather reports

```
use Amp\Parallel\Worker;
use Amp\Promise;
```

```
$forecasts = [
    'Washington, DC' => 'https://api.weather.gov/gridpoints/LWX/97,71/forecast',
    'New York, NY'   => 'https://api.weather.gov/gridpoints/OKX/33,37/forecast',
    'Tualatin, OR'   => 'https://api.weather.gov/gridpoints/PQR/108,97/forecast',
];

$promises = [];
foreach ($forecasts as $city => $forecast) {
    $promises[$city] = Worker\enqueueCallable('file_get_contents', $forecast); ❶
}

$responses = Promise\wait(Promise\all($promises)); ❷

foreach($responses as $city => $forecast) {
    $forecast = json_decode($forecast); ❸
    $latest = $forecast->properties->periods[0];

    echo "Forecast for {$city}:" . PHP_EOL;
    print_r($latest);
}
```

❶ Each URL endpoint can be fetched independently with `file_get_contents()`. Using AMPHP's `enqueueCallable()` function will automatically do this as part of an independent process in parallel to the main application.

❷ Each parallel request is wrapped in a `Promise` object. In order to return to the land of synchronous execution, you must wait until all of these promises are resolved. The `all` function collects the different promises into a single `Promise` object. The `wait()` function will block execution until this promise is resolved; then it unwraps the contained value for use in your synchronous code.

❸ The NWS API returns a JSON object representing the forecast for a specific weather station. You need to first parse the JSON-encoded string before you can leverage the data in your application.

> The NWS weather API is entirely free to use but does require you to send a unique user agent with your request. By default, PHP will send a simple user agent string of PHP when you use `file_get_con` `tents()`. To customize this, change the `user_agent` configuration in your *php.ini* file to be more unique. Without this change, the API will likely reject your request with a `403 Forbidden` error. For more on this and other behavior, reference the general FAQs about the API (*https://oreil.ly/4WVI0*).

Whether the AMPHP framework uses separate threads or entirely independent processes under the hood is a matter of how your system is configured initially. Your code remains the same and, absent any extensions supporting multithreaded PHP, will likely use spawned PHP processes by default. In either case, the enqueueCalla ble() function requires you to use either a native PHP function or a user-defined function that is loadable via Composer. This is because the spawned child process is only aware of system functions, Composer-loaded functions, and any serialized data sent over by the parent process.

This last detail is critical—the data you send from the parent application to the background worker will be serialized. Some user-defined objects might break when PHP attempts to serialize and deserialize them. Even some core objects (like stream contexts) are incompatible with serialization and cannot be passed into a child thread or process.

Take care with what tasks you choose to run in the background to ensure that the data you send is compatible with serialization and parallel operations.

See Also

Documentation on the parallel package (*https://oreil.ly/C41Rb*) from the AMPHP framework.

17.5 Sending and Receiving Messages Between Separate Threads

Problem

You want to communicate with multiple running threads to synchronize state or manage the tasks those threads are executing.

Solution

Use a message queue or bus between your main application and the separate threads it's orchestrating to allow for seamless communication. For example, use RabbitMQ as an intermediary between your primary application (as illustrated by Example 17-7) and independent worker threads, as shown in Example 17-6.

Example 17-6. Background task used to send mail based on a queue

```
use PhpAmqpLib\Connection\AMQPStreamConnection;

$connection = new AMQPStreamConnection('127.0.0.1', 5762, 'guest', 'guest'); ❶

$channel = $connection->channel();
$channel->queue_declare('default', false, false, false, false); ❷
```

```
echo '... Waiting for messages. To exit press CTRL+C' . PHP_EOL;

$callback = function($msg) {
    $data = json_decode($msg->body, true); ❸
    $to = $data['to'];
    $from = $data['from'] ?? 'worker.local';
    $subject = $data['subject'];
    $message = wordwrap($data['message'], 70) . PHP_EOL;

    $headers = "From: {$from} PHP_EOL X-Mailer: PHP Worker";

    print_r([$to, $subject, $message, $headers]) . PHP_EOL; ❹

    mail($to, $subject, $message, $headers);

    $msg->ack(); ❺
};

$channel->basic_consume('default', '', false, false, false, false, $callback); ❻
while(count($channel->callbacks)) {
    $channel->wait(); ❼
}
```

❶ Open a connection to a locally running RabbitMQ server by using the default port and default credentials. In production, these values will be different and should be loaded from the environment itself.

❷ Declaring a queue to the RabbitMQ server merely opens a channel of communication. If the queue already exists, this operation does nothing.

❸ Data is wrapped in a message object when it comes into the worker from RabbitMQ. The actual data you need is in the body of the message.

❹ Printing data within the worker is a helpful way to diagnose what is happening and inspect the data flowing in for any potential errors.

❺ Once your worker has completed acting on a message, it needs to acknowledge the message to the RabbitMQ server; otherwise, another worker might pick the message up and retry it later.

❻ Consuming messages is a synchronous operation. When a message comes in from RabbitMQ, the system will invoke the callback passed to this function with the message itself as the argument.

❼ So long as there are callbacks on a message, this loop will run forever, and the wait() method will keep the connection open to RabbitMQ so the worker can consume and act on any messages in the queue.

Example 17-7. Main application that sends messages to the queue

```php
use PhpAmqpLib\Connection\AMQPStreamConnection;
use PhpAmqpLib\Message\AMQPMessage;

$connection = new AMQPStreamConnection('127.0.0.1', 5672, 'guest', 'guest'); ❶

$channel = $connection->channel();
$channel->queue_declare('default', false, false, false, false); ❷

$message = [
    'subject' => 'Welcome to the team!',
    'from'    => 'admin@mail.local',
    'message' => "Welcome to the team!\r\nWe're excited to have you here!"
];

$teammates = [
    'adam@eden.local',
    'eve@eden.local',
    'cain@eden.local',
    'abel@eden.local',
];

foreach($teammates as $employee) {
    $email = $message;
    $email['to'] = $employee;

    $msg = new AMQPMessage(json_encode($email)); ❸
    $channel->basic_publish($msg, '', 'default'); ❹
}

$channel->close(); ❺
$connection->close();
```

❶ As with the worker, you open a connection to the local RabbitMQ server by using default parameters.

❷ Also as with the worker, you declare a queue. If this queue already exists, this method call will not do anything.

❸ Before you can send a message, you need to encode it. For the purposes of this example, the payload will be serialized as a JSON string.

❹ For each message, you choose the queue on which to publish and dispatch the message to RabbitMQ.

❺ Once you're done sending your messages, it's a good idea to explicitly close the channel and connection before doing any other work. In this example, there is no other work to be done (and the process will exit immediately), but explicit resource cleanup is a healthy habit for any developer.

Discussion

The Solution example uses multiple, explicit PHP processes to handle large operations. The script defined in Example 17-6 could be named *worker.php* and instantiated multiple times individually. If you do so in two separate consoles, you will spawn two entirely independent PHP processes that connect to RabbitMQ and listen for jobs.

Running Example 17-7 in a third window will start the main process and dispatch jobs by sending messages to the `default` queue housed by RabbitMQ. The workers will independently pick these jobs up, process them, and wait for more work down the road.

The full interaction between the parent process (Example 17-7) and two fully asynchronous worker processes (Example 17-6) using RabbitMQ as a message broker is illustrated by the three independent console windows shown in Figure 17-3.

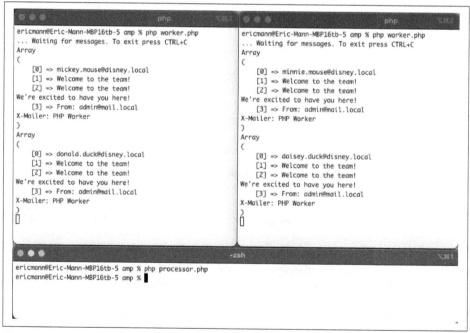

Figure 17-3. Multiple PHP processes communicating via RabbitMQ

The different processes don't communicate directly. To do that, you'd need to expose an interactive API. Instead, the much simpler means of communication is to leverage an intermediate message broker—in this case, RabbitMQ (*https://oreil.ly/GtgI0*).

RabbitMQ is an open source tool that interfaces directly with several different programming languages. It allows for the creation of multiple queues that can then be read by one or more dedicated workers to process the content of the message. In the Solution example, you used workers and PHP's native `mail()` function to dispatch email messages. A more complicated worker might update database records, interface with a remote API, or even process computationally expensive operations like the hashing performed in Recipe 17.4.

 Since RabbitMQ supports multiple languages, you're not limited to just PHP in your implementation. If there's a specific library you want to use in a different language, you could write your workers in that language, import the library, and dispatch work to the worker from your primary PHP application.

In a production environment, your RabbitMQ server would leverage username/password authentication or possibly even explicitly allowlist the servers that can talk to it. For development, though, you can effectively leverage your local environment, default credentials, and tools like Docker (*https://www.docker.com*) to run a RabbitMQ server on your local machine. To directly expose RabbitMQ by using the default port and default authentication, use the following Docker command:

```
$ docker run -d -h localhost -p 127.0.0.1:5672:5672 --name rabbit rabbitmq:3
```

Once the server is running, you can register as many queues as necessary to manage the flow of data within your swarm of applications.

See Also

The official documentation (*https://oreil.ly/einsN*) and tutorials (*https://oreil.ly/lEqc9*) for configuring and interacting with RabbitMQ.

17.6 Using a Fiber to Manage the Contents from a Stream

Problem

You want to use PHP's newest concurrency feature to pull data from and operate on a stream in parts rather than buffering all of its contents at once.

Solution

Use a Fiber to wrap the stream and read its contents one piece at a time. Example 17-8 reads the entirety of a web page into a file in 50-byte chunks, tracking the total number of bytes consumed as it reads in the content.

Example 17-8. Reading a remote stream resource through a Fiber one chunk at a time

```
$fiber = new Fiber(function($stream): void {
    while (!feof($stream)) {
        $contents = fread($stream, 50); ❶
        Fiber::suspend($contents); ❷
    }
});

$stream = fopen('https://www.eamann.com/', 'r');
stream_set_blocking($stream, false); ❸

$output = fopen('cache.html', 'w'); ❹

$contents = $fiber->start($stream); ❺

$num_bytes = 0;
while (!$fiber->isTerminated()) {
    echo chr(27) . "[0G"; ❻

    $num_bytes += strlen($contents);
    fwrite($output, $contents); ❼

    echo str_pad("Wrote {$num_bytes} bytes ...", 24, ' ', STR_PAD_RIGHT);
    usleep(500); ❽

    $contents = $fiber->resume(); ❾
}

echo chr(27) . "[0G";
echo "Done writing {$num_bytes} bytes to cache.html!" . PHP_EOL;

fclose($stream); ❿
fclose($output);
```

❶ The Fiber itself accepts a streaming resource as its only parameter when it starts. So long as the stream is not at the end, the Fiber will read the next 50 bytes from the current position into the application.

❷ Once the Fiber has read from the stream, it will suspend operation and pass control back to the parent application stack. As Fibers can send data back to the parent stack, this Fiber will send the 50 bytes it has read from the stream when it suspends execution.

❸ Within the parent application stack, the stream is opened and set to not block execution of the rest of the application. In nonblocking mode, any calls to fread() will return right away rather than waiting for data on the stream.

4 Within the parent application, you can also open other resources, like local files into which you can cache the contents of the remote resource.

5 When starting the Fiber, you pass the main stream resource as a parameter so it's available to the call stack of the Fiber itself. Once the Fiber suspends execution, it will also return the 50 bytes it has read back to you.

6 To write over the previous line of console output, pass the ESC character (chr(27)) and an ANSI control sequence to move the cursor to the first column in the terminal ([0G]). Any subsequent text printed to the screen will now overwrite anything displayed previously.

7 Once data is available from the remote stream, you can write that data directly to your local cache file.

8 A sleep statement is not necessary to this application but is useful to illustrate how other computations can happen in the parent application stack while the Fiber is suspended.

9 Resuming the Fiber will retrieve the next 50 bytes from the remote stream resource, assuming that any bytes remain. If nothing is left to retrieve, the Fiber will terminate, and your program will exit its while loop.

10 Once execution is complete and the Fiber is cleaned up, be sure to close any streams or other resources you've opened.

Discussion

Fibers are similar to coroutines and generators in that their execution can be interrupted so that the application can perform other logic before returning control. Unlike these other constructs, Fibers have call stacks independent from that of the rest of the application. In this way, they empower you to pause their execution even within nested function calls without changing the return type of the function triggering the pause.

With a generator that uses the yield command to suspend execution, you must return a Generator instance. With a Fiber using the ::suspend() method, you can return any type you desire.

Once a fiber is suspended, you can resume its execution from anywhere within the parent application to restart its separate call stack. This allows you to effectively jump between multiple execution contexts without worrying too much about controlling application state.

You can also effectively pass data to and from a Fiber. When a Fiber suspends itself, it can choose to send data back to the parent application—again, of any type you need. When you resume a Fiber, you can pass any value you want or no value at all. You can also choose to throw an exception into the Fiber by using the ::throw() method and then handle that exception within the Fiber itself. Example 17-9 demonstrates exactly what it would look like to handle an exception from within the Fiber.

Example 17-9. Handling an exception from within a Fiber

```
$fiber = new Fiber(function(): void {
    try {
        Fiber::suspend(); ❶
    }
    catch (Exception $e) {
        echo $e->getMessage() . PHP_EOL; ❷
    }

    echo 'Finished within Fiber' . PHP_EOL; ❸
});

$fiber->start(); ❹
$fiber->throw(new Exception('Error')); ❺
```

❶ The Fiber will immediately suspend execution once it's started and return control to the parent application stack.

❷ When the Fiber is resumed, assuming it encounters a catchable Exception, it will extract and print out the error message.

❸ Once the Fiber finishes execution, it will print a useful message before ending its concurrent execution and returning control to the main application.

❹ Starting the Fiber merely creates its call stack and, because the Fiber immediately suspends, execution continues from the perspective of the parent stack.

❺ Throwing an exception from the parent into the Fiber will trigger the catch condition and print the Error message to the console.

Fibers are an effective way to juggle execution contexts between call stacks but are still fairly low-level within PHP. While they can be straightforward to use with simple operations like that in the Solution example, more complicated computations can become difficult to manage. Understanding how Fibers work is critical to using them effectively, but just as critical is choosing the proper abstraction to manage your Fibers for you. The Async package (*https://oreil.ly/vmkZJ*) from ReactPHP provides effective abstractions to asynchronous operations, including Fibers, and makes engineering a complex concurrent application relatively easy.

See Also

The PHP Manual covering Fibers (*https://oreil.ly/iU6JH*).

## CHAPTER 18

PHP Command Line

Developers come to PHP from all sorts of backgrounds and with various levels of experience in software development. Regardless of whether you are a new computer science graduate, a seasoned developer, or someone from a noncoding field looking to learn a new skill, the forgiving nature of the language makes it easy to get started. That being said, the largest stumbling block for these noncoder beginners may be PHP's command-line interface.

Noncoder beginners are likely to be comfortable with using a graphical user interface and navigating with a mouse and a graphical display. Give the same user a command-line terminal, and they might struggle with or be intimidated by the interface.

As a backend language, PHP is frequently manipulated at the command line. This potentially makes it an intimidating language for developers not accustomed to text-based interfaces. Fortunately, PHP-based command-line applications are relatively straightforward to build and immensely powerful to use.

An application might expose a command palette similar to its default RESTful interface, thus making interactions from a terminal similar to those over a browser or through an API. Yet another application might bury its administrative tooling in the CLI, protecting less technical end users from accidentally damaging the application.

One of the most popular PHP applications in the market today is WordPress (*https://wordpress.org*), the open source blogging and web platform. Most users interact with the platform through its graphical web interface, but the WordPress community also maintains a rich command-line interface for the platform: WP-CLI (*https://wp-cli.org*). This tool allows a user to manage everything already exposed by the graphical tool but through a scriptable, text-based terminal interface. It also exposes commands for managing user roles, system configuration, the state of the database, and even the system cache. None of these capabilities exist within the stock web interface!

Any developer building a PHP application today can and should understand the capabilities of the command line, both in terms of what you can do with PHP itself and how your application can expose its functionality through the same interface. A truly rich web application will at some point live on a server that might not expose any sort of graphical interface, so being able to control your application from the terminal is not just a power move—it's a necessity.

The following recipes demystify the intricacies of argument parsing, managing input and output, and even leveraging extensions to build full applications that run in the console.

18.1 Parsing Program Arguments

Problem

You want a user to pass an argument when they invoke your script so it can be parsed from within the application.

Solution

Use the $argc integer and the $argv array to retrieve the value of an argument directly in the script. For example:

```php
<?php
if ($argc !== 2) {
    die('Invalid number of arguments.');
}

$name = htmlspecialchars($argv[1]);

echo "Hello, {$name}!" . PHP_EOL;
```

Discussion

Assuming you named the script in the Solution example *script.php*, it would be invoked in a terminal session with the following command:

```
% php script.php World
```

Internally, the $argc variable contains a count of the number of parameters passed to PHP when executing the script. In the Solution example, there are exactly two parameters:

- The name of the script itself (*script.php*)
- Whatever string value you passed after the name of the script

Both $argc and $argv can be disabled at runtime by setting the register_argc_argv flag (*https://oreil.ly/ZKulH*) to false in your *php.ini* file. If enabled, these parameters will contain either the arguments passed to a script or information about a GET request forwarded from a web server.

The first argument will *always* be the name of the script or file being executed. All other arguments are delimited by spaces beyond that. Should you need to pass a compound argument (like a string with spaces), wrap that argument in double quotes. For example:

```
% php script.php "dear reader"
```

More complicated implementations might leverage PHP's getopt() function rather than manipulating the argument variables directly. This function will parse both short and long options and pass their contents into arrays your application can then leverage.

Short options are each single characters represented at the command line with a single dash—for example, -v. Each option could either merely be present (as in a flag) or be followed by data (as in an option).

Long options are prefixed with double dashes but otherwise act the same way as their short relatives. You can assume either or both styles of options are present and use them however you want in your application.

Often, a command-line application will provide both a long option and a single-character shortcut for the same thing. For example, -v and --verbose are frequently used to control the level of output of a script. With getopt(), you can easily have both, but PHP won't link them together. If you support two different methods for providing the same option value or flag, you'll need to reconcile them within your script manually.

The getopt() function takes three parameters and returns an array representing the options the PHP interpreter has parsed:

- The first argument is a single string in which each character represents a short option or flag.
- The second argument is an array of strings, and each string is a long option name.
- The final argument, *which is passed by reference*, is an integer representing the index in $argv where parsing has stopped when PHP encounters a non-option.

Both short and long options also accept modifiers. If you pass an option by itself, PHP will not accept a value for that option but will treat it as a flag. If you append a colon to an option, PHP will *require* a value. If you append two colons, PHP will treat the value as optional.

As an illustration, Table 18-1 lists out various ways both short and long options can leverage these additional elements.

Table 18-1. PHP getopt() arguments

Argument	Argument type	Description
a	Short option	A single flag with no value: -a
b:	Short option	A single flag with a required value: -b value
c::	Short option	A single flag with an optional value: -c value or just -c
ab:c	Short option	Composite three flags where a and c have no value but b requires a value: -a -b value -c
verbose	Long option	Option string with no value: --verbose
name:	Long option	Option string with a required value: --name Alice
output::	Long option	Option string with an optional value: --output file.txt or just --output

To illustrate the utility of option parsing, define a program as in Example 18-1 that exposes both short and long options but also leverages free-form (non-option) input after the flags. The following script will expect the following:

- A flag to control whether output should be capitalized (-c)
- A username (--name)
- Some extra, arbitrary text after the options

Example 18-1. Direct illustration of getopt() with multiple options

```php
<?php
$optionIndex = 0;

$options = getopt('c', ['name:'], $optionIndex); ❶

$firstLine = "Hello, {$options['name']}!" . PHP_EOL; ❷

$rest = implode(' ', array_slice($argv, $optionIndex)); ❸

if (array_key_exists('c', $options)) { ❹
    $firstLine = strtoupper($firstLine);
    $rest = strtoupper($rest);
}
```

```
echo $firstLine;
echo $rest . PHP_EOL;
```

❶ Use getopt() to define both the short and long options your script expects. The third, optional parameter is passed by reference and will be overwritten by the index at which the interpreter runs out of options to parse.

❷ Options with values are easy to extract from the resultant associative array.

❸ The resultant index from getopt() can be used to quickly extract any additional data from the command by pulling unparsed values out of the $argv array.

❹ Options without values will still set a key in the associative array, but the value will be a Boolean false. Check that the key exists, but don't rely on its value because of the counterintuitive nature of the result.

Assuming you name the script defined by Example 18-1 *getopt.php*, you can expect to see a result like the following:

```
% php getopt.php -c --name Reader This is fun
HELLO, READER!
THIS IS FUN
%
```

See Also

Documentation on $argc (*https://oreil.ly/BXdSI*), $argv (*https://oreil.ly/ODRwK*), and the getopt() function (*https://oreil.ly/ZfqTP*).

18.2 Reading Interactive User Input

Problem

You want to prompt the user for input and read their response into a variable.

Solution

Read data from the standard input stream by using the STDIN file handle constant. For example:

```
echo 'Enter your name: ';

$name = trim(fgets(STDIN, 1024));

echo "Welcome, {$name}!" . PHP_EOL;
```

Discussion

The standard input stream makes it easy for you to read any data that comes in with a request. Reading data directly from the stream in a program using fgets() will pause the execution of your program until the end user provides that input to you.

The Solution example leverages the shorthand constant STDIN to reference the input stream. You could just as easily use the stream's fully qualified name (along with an explicit fopen()), as demonstrated in Example 18-2.

Example 18-2. Reading user input from stdin

```
echo 'Enter your name: ';

$name = trim(fgets(fopen('php://stdin', 'r'), 1024));

echo "Welcome, {$name}!" . PHP_EOL;
```

> The special STDIN and STDOUT shorthand names are only accessible in an application. If using the interactive terminal REPL as in Recipe 18.5, these constants will not be defined nor will they be accessible.

An alternative approach is to use the GNU Readline extension (*https://oreil.ly/eRhJw*) with PHP, which may or may not be available in your installation. This extension wraps much of the manual work to prompt for, retrieve, and trim user input. The entire Solution example could be rewritten as shown in Example 18-3.

Example 18-3. Reading input from the GNU Readline extension

```
$name = readline('Enter your name: ');

echo "Welcome, {$name}!" . PHP_EOL;
```

Additional functions provided by the Readline extension, like readline_add_his tory() (*https://oreil.ly/J5do3*), allow for efficient manipulation of the system's command-line history. If the extension is available, it's a powerful way to work with user input.

> Some distributions of PHP, like those for Windows, will come with Readline support enabled by default. In other situations, you might need to compile PHP explicitly to include this support. For more on native PHP extensions, review Recipe 15.4.

See Also

Further discussion of standard input in Recipe 11.2.

18.3 Colorizing Console Output

Problem

You want to display text in the console in different colors.

Solution

Use properly escaped console color codes. For example, print the string Happy Inde
pendence Day in blue text on a red background as follows:

```
echo "\e[0;34;41mHappy Independence Day!\e[0m" . PHP_EOL;
```

Discussion

Unix-like terminals support ANSI escape sequences that grant programs fine-grained
control over things like cursor location and font styling. In particular, you can define
the color used by the terminal for all following text with this escape sequence:

```
\e[{foreground};{background}m
```

Foreground colors come in two variants—regular and bold (determined by an extra
Boolean flag in the color definition). Background colors lack this differentiation. All
of the colors are identified by these codes in Table 18-2.

Table 18-2. ANSI color codes

Color	Normal foreground	Bright foreground	Background
Black	0;30	1;30	40
Red	0;31	1;31	41
Green	0;32	1;32	42
Yellow	0;33	1;33	43
Blue	0;34	1;34	44
Magenta	0;35	1;35	45
Cyan	0;36	1;36	46
White	0;37 (really light gray)	1;37	47

To reset the terminal colors back to normal, use a simple 0 in place of any color definitions. The code \e[0m will reset all attributes.

See Also

Wikipedia coverage of ANSI escape codes (*https://oreil.ly/y02cf*).

18.4 Creating a Command-Line Application with Symfony Console

Problem

You want to create a full command-line application without manually writing all of the argument parsing and handling code yourself.

Solution

Use the Symfony Console component to define your application and its commands. Example 18-4, for example, defines a Symfony command for greeting a user by name with Hello world at the console. Example 18-5 then uses that command object to create an application that greets the user within the terminal.

Example 18-4. A basic hello world command

```php
namespace App\Command;

use Symfony\Component\Console\Attribute\AsCommand;
use Symfony\Component\Console\Command\Command;
use Symfony\Component\Console\Input\InputArgument;
use Symfony\Component\Console\Input\InputInterface;
use Symfony\Component\Console\Output\OutputInterface;

#[AsCommand(name: 'app:hello-world')]
class HelloWorldCommand extends Command
{
    protected static $defaultDescription = 'Greets the user.';

    // ...
    protected function configure(): void
    {
        $this
            ->setHelp('This command greets a user...')
            ->addArgument('name', InputArgument::REQUIRED, 'User name');
    }

    protected function execute(InputInterface $input, OutputInterface $output): int
    {
        $output->writeln("Hello, {$input->getArgument('name')}");
        return Command::SUCCESS;
    }
}
```

Example 18-5. Creating the actual console application

```php
#!/usr/bin/env php
<?php
// application.php

require __DIR__.'/vendor/autoload.php';

use Symfony\Component\Console\Application;

$application = new Application();

$application->add(new App\Command\HelloWorldCommand());

$application->run();
```

Then run the command as follows:

```
% ./application.php app:hello-world User
```

Discussion

The Symfony project (*https://symfony.com*) provides a robust collection of reusable components for PHP. It acts as a framework to simplify and greatly increase the speed of development for web applications as well. It's remarkably well documented, powerful, and best of all, free and entirely open source.

> The open source Laravel framework (*https://laravel.com*), the data modules of which were covered in Recipe 16.9, is itself a meta package of individual Symfony components. Its own Artisan console tool (*https://oreil.ly/uY4QL*) is built atop the Symfony Console component. It provides rich command-line control over Laravel projects, their configuration, and even their runtime environments.

Like any other PHP extension, Symfony components are installed via Composer.[1] The Console component itself can be installed as follows:

```
% composer require symfony/console
```

The preceding `require` command will update your project's *composer.json* file to include the Console component, and it also installs this component (and its dependencies) in your project's *vendor/* directory.

---

1 For more on Composer, review Recipe 15.3.

If your project is not already using Composer, installing any package will create a new *composer.json* file for you automatically. You should take time to update it to autoload any classes or files your project requires so everything works together seamlessly. For more on Composer, extensions, and autoloading, review Chapter 15.

Once you have the library installed, you can start leveraging it immediately. Business logic for various commands can live elsewhere within your application (e.g., behind a RESTful API) but can also be imported into and exposed via the command-line interface.

By default, every class that descends from `Command` gives you the ability to work with user-provided arguments and to display content back to the terminal. Options and arguments are created with the `addArgument()` and `addOption()` methods on the class and can be manipulated within its `configure()` method directly.

Output is highly flexible. You can print content directly to the screen with any of the methods of the `ConsoleOutputInterface` class listed in Table 18-3.

Table 18-3. Symfony console output methods

Method	Description
`writeln()`	Writes a single line to the console. Equivalent to using `echo` on some text followed by an explicit PHP_EOL newline.
`write()`	Writes text to the console without appending a newline character.
`section()`	Creates a new output section that can be atomically controlled as if it were an independent output buffer.
`overwrite()`	Only valid on a section—overwrites content in a section with the given content.
`clear()`	Only valid on a section—clears all contents of a section.

In addition to the text methods introduced in Table 18-3, Symfony Console empowers you to create dynamic tables in the terminal. Every `Table` instance is bound to an output interface and can have as many rows, columns, and separators as you need. Example 18-6 demonstrates how a simple table can be built and populated with content from an array before itself being rendered to the console.

Example 18-6. Rendering tables in the console with Symfony

```
// ...

#[AsCommand(name: 'app:book')]
class BookCommand extends Command
{
    public function execute(InputInterface $input, OutputInterface $output): int
    {
        $table = new Table($output);
```

```
$table
    ->setHeaders(['ISBN', 'Title', 'Author'])
    ->setRows([
        [
            '978-1-940111-61-2',
            'Security Principles for PHP Applications',
            'Eric Mann'
        ],
        ['978-1-098-12132-7', 'PHP Cookbook', 'Eric Mann'],
    ])
;
$table->render();

    return Command::SUCCESS;
    }
}
```

Symfony Console automatically parses the content passed into a `Table` object and renders the table for you complete with grid lines. The preceding command produces the following output in the console:

```
+-------------------+------------------------------------------+-----------+
| ISBN              | Title                                    | Author    |
+-------------------+------------------------------------------+-----------+
| 978-1-940111-61-2 | Security Principles for PHP Applications | Eric Mann |
| 978-1-098-12132-7 | PHP Cookbook                             | Eric Mann |
+-------------------+------------------------------------------+-----------+
```

Further modules within the component aid in the control and rendering of dynamic progress bars (*https://oreil.ly/TszPm*) and interactive user prompts and questions (*https://oreil.ly/8i5Hx*).

The Console component even aids in coloring terminal output directly (*https://oreil.ly/arrtr*). Unlike the complicated ANSI escape sequences discussed in Recipe 18.3, Console allows you to use named tags and styles directly to control content.

> At the time of this writing, the Console component disables output coloring on Windows systems by default. There are various, free terminal applications (like Cmder (*https://oreil.ly/gs5e6*)) available for Windows as alternatives to the standard terminal that do support output coloring.

The terminal is an incredibly powerful interface for your users. Symfony Console makes it easy to target this interface within your application without resorting to hand-parsing arguments or manually crafting rich output.

See Also

Full documentation of Symfony's Console component (*https://oreil.ly/vm8Qx*).

18.5 Using PHP's Native Read-Eval-Print-Loop

Problem

You want to test some PHP logic without creating a full application to house it.

Solution

Leverage PHP's interactive shell as follows:

```
% php -a
```

Discussion

The PHP interactive shell provides a read-eval-print loop (REPL) that effectively tests single statements in PHP and, where possible, prints directly to the terminal. Within the shell, you can define functions and classes or even directly execute imperative code without creating a script file on disk.

This shell is an efficient way to test a particular line of code or piece of logic outside the context of a full application.

The interactive shell also enables full tab-completion for all PHP functions or variables as well as any functions or variables that you have defined while the shell session is running. Merely type the first few characters of an otherwise long name, press Tab, and the shell will automatically complete the name for you. If there are multiple possible completions, press the Tab key twice to see a list of all possibilities.

You can control two particular settings for the shell in your *php.ini* configuration file: `cli.pager` allows for an external program to handle output rather than displaying directly to the console, and `cli.prompt` allows you to control the default `php >` prompt.

For example, you can replace the prompt itself by passing an arbitrary string to `#cli.prompt` within the shell session as follows:

```
% php -a ❶

php > #cli.prompt=repl ~> ❷
repl ~> ❸
```

❶ The initial invocation of PHP launches the interactive shell.

❷ Setting the `cli.prompt` configuration directly will override the default until this session closes.

---

❸ Once you've overridden the default prompt, you will see your new version until you exit.

 Backticks can be used to execute arbitrary PHP code within the prompt itself. Some examples in the PHP documentation (https://oreil.ly/o6NU6) use this method to prepend the current time to the prompt. However, this might not work consistently between systems and could introduce unnecessary instability when executing your PHP code.

You can even colorize your output by using the ANSI escape sequences defined in Table 18-2. This presents a more pleasant interface in many situations and empowers you to provide additional information if desired. The CLI prompt itself introduces four additional escape sequences, as defined in Table 18-4.

Table 18-4. CLI prompt escape sequences

Sequence	Description
\e	Adds colors to the prompt by using the ANSI codes introduced in Recipe 18.3.
\v	Prints the PHP version.
\b	Indicates which logical block contains the interpreter. By default, this will be php but could be /* to represent a multiline comment.
\>	Represents the prompt character, which is > by default. When the interpreter is inside another unterminated block or string, this will change to indicate where the shell is. Possible characters are ' " { (>.

By using both ANSI escape sequences to define colors and the special sequences defined for the prompt itself, you can define a prompt that exposes the version of PHP and the location of the interpreter and that uses a friendly foreground color as follows:

```
php > #cli.prompt=\e[032m\v \e[031m\b \e[34m\> \e[0m
```

The preceding setting results in the display in Figure 18-1.

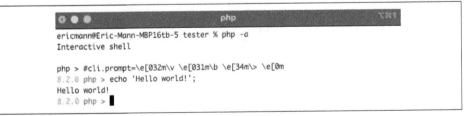

Figure 18-1. The PHP console updated with colorization

Not every console will support colorization via ANSI control sequences. If this is a pattern you intend to use, take care to test your sequences thoroughly prior to asking anyone else to use the system. While a properly rendered console is attractive and easy to use, unrendered escape sequences can make a console nearly impossible to work with.

See Also

Documentation on PHP's interactive command shell (*https://oreil.ly/HrCV-*).

Index

Symbols

$argc integer, 390-393
$argv array, 390-393
= (equals sign), 18, 20
@ operator, 23

A

A/B testing, 5
abstract base classes, 186-187
activity_log() function, 36
advisory locking, 244
AES (Advanced Encryption Standard), 207
all() function, 368
AMPHP project, 362
  all() function, 368
  coroutines, 365, 371-374
  enqueueCallable() function, 377
  http-client module, 367
  parallel package, 374-379
  parallel-functions module, 369-371
  promises, implementing, 364
  wait() function, 368
Amp\call() wrapper, 368
anonymous functions, 50
appending arrays to other arrays, 137-140
applications
  benchmarking performance, 314-320
  opcode caching, 320-323
arguments
  functions
    enforcing, 37-40
    variable number of, 40-42
  named, syntax, 35
  parsing, command line, 390-393

round() function, 86
arrays, 123
  $argv, 390-393
  alphabetical characters, 128
  appending to another, 137-140
  arrow operators, 125
  associative, 123
    deleting elements, 131-134
    multiple items, 125-127
    overwriting data, 138
    reversing, 146
  creating from array fragment, 140-143
  data
    loops and, 126
    overwriting by assignment, 125
  data types, 125
  elements
    adding, 135-137
    modifying each with function, 153-155
    prepending, 136
    randomizing, 152-152
    reversing order, 146-147
    sorting, 147-149
  hash tables, 123
  implementing, 123
  integers, consecutive, 127-129
  iteration, 129-131
    very large, 157-159
  keys, writing to, 126
  merging duplicate keys and, 139
  nested, 126
  numeric, 124
    deleting elements, 131-134
  reducing to single value, 156-157

size, changing, 135-137

sorting, user-defined functions, 150-151

square brackets, 124

strings, converting between, 143-145

syntax, 124-125

array_keys() function, 156

array_merge() function, 137-140

array_merge_recursive() function, 139

array_push() function, 135-137

array_reduce() function, 156-157

array_reverse() function, 146-147

array_slice() function, 140-143

array_splice() function, 133-134

array_unshift() function, 137

array_walk() function, 153-155

arrow functions, 54-56

currying, 56-56

arrow operators, arrays, 125

asort() function, 149

assignment, = (equals sign) and, 18, 20

associative arrays, 123

data, overwriting, 138

deleting elements, 131-134

multiple items, 125-127

reversing, 146

asymmetric encryption, 224-226

asyncCall() function, 372

asynchronous programming, 361

code in separate thread, 374-379

coroutines, 365

event loops, 372

fetching from remote servers, 367-368

Fibers, 366, 383-387

libraries, 362

message queues, 379-383

Open Swoole, 363

operations results, 369-371

promises, 364-365

runtimes, 362

authenticated encryption, 207

authentication, 207

tags, validation, 207

autoconf package, 325

autoload.php, 329

B

backticks, 401

base classes, abstract, 186-187

base64_decode() function, 43

base_convert() function, 99

basic calculator utility, 97

BDD (behavior-driven development), 280

benchmarking application performance, 314-320

bin2hex() function, 100

binary data in strings, 78-80

bison package, 325

bitwise operators, 12-13

integers, 24-27

not, 13

breakpoints, 280

buckets, 247

build-essentials package, 325

buildconf script, 326

C

caching, Opcache, 309

call() function, 372

capitalize_string() function, 31

case-insensitive searches, 69

ceil() function, 86

character-by-character string processing, 70-72

checkdate() function, 115

chr() function, 30

class abstraction, 163

class constants, 4

class keyword, 161, 168

classes, 161

abstract base classes, 186-187

code reuse, 201-204

ConsoleOutputInterface, 398

custom, object instantiation, 168-170

DateTimeInterface, 101

decorators, 191

defining, 163

extension prevention, 188-192

forcing behavior, 181-185

functionality, adding, 179-181

methods, 161

preventing changes, 188-192

properties, 161

read-only, 172-174

protected, 166

public, 166

SQLite, 342

streamWrapper, 265

TimerDecorator, 312

VariableStream, 264

Vehicle, 165
    visibility and, 166-168
cli.pager, 400
cli.prompt, 400
clock functions, 56
clone keyword, 192-196
cloning
    deep cloning, 195
    objects, 192-196
    shallow clones, 194
closures, 50
code analysis, static, 291-292
code reuse, 201-204
    reusable components, 330
command line, 389
    application creation, Symfony Console and,
        396-399
    arguments, parsing, 390-393
    colored text, 395
    input prompts, 393-395
    reading input, 393-395
commands, require, 397
comparing values, 18-20
comparison operators, 13
complex variables, contents, 296-299
Composer, 327
    app.php file, 329
    autoload.php, 329
    composer directory, 329
    composer.json file, 327, 332-335
        init command, 328-330
    composer.lock file, 332-335
    packages
        installing, 332-335
        locating, 330-332
        updating, 332-335
    project definition, 327-330
    pull repository, 334
composer dumpautoload, 328
composer.json file, init command, 328-330
concatenation, 75-77
    verbosity, 76
concurrent parallel programming, 362
concurrent programming, 361
    versus parallel, 361
configure script, 326
ConsoleOutputInterface class, 398
const directive, 3
constants

class constants, 4
    default, 4
    defining, 3-4
    numerics, 81
    rounding, 87
_construct() method, 162, 169
constructor promotion, 169
coroutines, 365
    AMPHP project, 371-374
count() function, 131
crc32() function, 5
create_function() function, 51
credentials, sensitive, 216-218
cryptographic signatures, 231-233
    verification, 233-234
cryptographically secure pseudorandom num-
    ber generator, 73
cryptography, 205
    public-key, 209
CSPRNG (cryptographically secure pseudo-
    random number generator), 212
currying, 53-54
    arrow functions and, 56-56

D
data abstraction, 352-356
databases
    document, 342
    external, PDO connection and, 344-349
    graph, 341-342
    integration testing, mocking data, 351-356
    key-value stores, 340-341
    queries, sanitizing user input, 349-351
    relational, 339-340
    schema, Eloquent and, 356-359
    SQLite, connecting, 342-344
    statements, injecting, 350
date and time
    adding/subtracting from a date, 115-118
    constants, predefined, 106
    converting to Unix timestamps, 107-108
    current, 102-104
    format, 104
        characters, 105
    formatting, 104-107
    minutes, 116
    months, 116
    parsing from strings, 111-114
    time zones, calculating times, 119-121

validating dates, 114-115
date() function, 102
DateInterval object
    format characters, 111
    period designations, 116
dates, difference between two, 110-111
DateTime objects, 101
    ::add() method, 115-118
    comparing, 117
    converting strings to, 111-114
    ::createFromFormat() method, 107
    DateTimeImmutable, comparing, 117
    ::format() method, 104
    mutability, 117
    ::setTimezone() method, 119
    ::sub() method, 115-118
DateTime objects, ::format() method,
    secondary-sortas=format() method, 103
DateTime objects, ::format() method,
    secondary-sortas=format() method, star-
    tref=fmtthd, 106
DateTimeImmutable object, 101, 117
    ::add() method, 118
DateTimeImmutable objects
DateTimeInterface base class, 101
date_parse() function, 113
debugging
    breakpoints, 280, 283
    built-in web server and, 299-301
    echo statement, 279
    external debuggers, 281-283
    logging and, 292-296
    step-through mode, 282
    Xdebug, 280
        installing, 281-283
decorators, 191
decryption, 221-226
deep cloning, 195
default constants, 4
define() function, 3
destructors, temporary files, 175
directives, const, 3
Doctrine, 356
Doctrine ORM, 357
document databases, 342
document stores, 342
double-quoted strings, 74
DRY (don't repeat yourself), 30
dynamic functions, defining, 50-51

dynamic properties, magic methods, 177-179

E
each() function, 130
ECC (elliptic-curve cryptography), 209
echo statement, 279
edges, graph databases, 341-342
Eloquent, schema and, 356-359
encryption, 221-226
    asymmetric, 224-226
    authenticated, 207
    data storage, 227-231
    legacy encryption, 206
    randomness, 211-212
    symmetric, 208
enqueueCallable() function, 377
environment variables, populating, 217
epsilon, 84
error_log() function, 293
event loops, 372
explode() function, 43, 145
exponents, calculating, 95-96
expressions, interpolation, 62
extends keyword, 179-181
extensions, 325
    BCMath, 327
    FFI (Foreign Function Interface), 327
    modules, 326
    native, installing, 335-337
    Open Swoole, 363
    PDO (PHP Data Objects), 327
    SQLite3, 327

F
fclose() function, 236
FFI (Foreign Function Interface), 327
fgets() function, 236
Fibers, 366
    stream contents and, 383-387
files
    locking, 244-245
    modifying parts, 241
    open, as streams, 236
    opening, 236-238
    pointers, 240
    reading specific bytes, 239-240
    reading to string, 238-239
    remote, opening, 237
    temporary

destructors, 175
 streaming to/from, 251-253
 writing to multiple, 242-244
file_get_contents() function, 235, 238-239
file_put_contents() function, 239
filter() function, 250
filtering user input, 212-216
filters, 249-251
 appending, 261
 user-defined, 249
filter_var() function, 212-216
final keyword, 188-192
floating-point numbers, 81
 comparing, 84-86
 converting integer, 86
 relative equality, 85
 rounding, 86-87
 subtraction, 84
 very large or small numbers, 97-99
floatval() function, 83
flock() function, 244-245
floor() function, 86
fopen() function, 235, 236-238
 append mode, 241
 write mode, 241
for loop, 130
forcing class behavior, 181-185
foreach() function, 129
formatting
 numbers as strings, 96-97
 U format character, 107
fread() function, 238
fseek() function, 239-240
functional languages, 52
functions, 29
 activity_log() function, 36
 all(), 368
 anonymous, 50
 arguments
  enforcing, 37-40
  variable number of, 40-42
 array element modification, 153-155
 array_keys(), 156
 array_merge(), 137-140
 array_merge_recursive(), 139
 array_push(), 135-137
 array_reduce(), 156-157
 array_reverse(), 146-147
 array_slice(), 140-143

array_splice(), 133-134
array_unshift(), 137
array_walk(), 153-155
arrow functions, 54-56
asort(), 149
asyncCall(), 372
base64_decode(), 43
base_convert(), 99
bin2hex(), 100
call(), 372
capitalize_string(), 31
ceil(), 86
checkdate(), 115
chr(), 30
clock functions, 56
count(), 131
crc32(), 5
create_function(), 51
curried, 53-54
date(), 102
date_parse(), 113
define(), 3
dynamic, defining, 50-51
each(), 130
enqueueCallable(), 377
error_log(), 293
execution timing, 310-314
explode(), 43, 145
fclose(), 236
fgets(), 236
file_get_contents(), 235, 238-239
file_put_contents(), 239
filter(), 250
filter_var(), 212-216
floatval(), 83
flock(), 244-245
floor(), 86
fopen(), 235, 236-238
foreach(), 129
fread(), 238
fseek(), 239-240
fwrite(), 239
getdate(), 103
getopt(), 391
gmp_intval(), 98
gmp_strval(), 98
header(), 59
hex2bin(), 100
hrtime(), 310-314

implode(), 76
increment(), 33
is_numeric(), 82, 83
join(), 77
local, scoping, 32
log(), 94
logger(), 49
mt_rand(), 89, 90
multiplier(), 53
number_format(), 96
ord(), 30
pack(), 78
parallelMap(), 371
parameters
    accessing, 31-33
    default, setting, 33-35
    misordered, 34
    named, 35-36
    optional, 34
    positional, 35
passing as parameters, 51-54
password_hash(), 218-221
password_verify(), 219
phpinfo(), 217
pow(), 95
random_bytes(), 73
random_float(), 89
random_int(), 88-89
range(), 127-129
recursive, static variables and, 48
reduce(), 52
return typing, enforcing, 37-40
return values, 56-58
returns, none, 58-59
round(), 86
shuffle(), 152-152
sort(), 147-149
sprintf(), 74
state, managing, 48-50
stream_copy_to_stream(), 258-260
strpos(), 64
strtotime(), 112
str_split(), 143-145
substr(), 66-67
substr_replace(), 67-69
uniqid(), 255
unpack(), 78
unset(), 131
user-defined, 31, 45

sorting arrays, 150-151
usort(), 150-151
var_dump(), 296-299
verbose activity logging, 35
wait(), 368
weighted_random_choice(), 91-94
fwrite() function, 239

G
GCM (Galois/Counter Mode), 207
generators, large array iteration, 158-159
getByID() method, 355
getdate() function, 103
getopt() function, 391
getters, dynamic properties and, 177
Git commit hooks, unit tests and, 288
git-bisect, 301-305
global variables, accessing, 44-47
GMP (GNU Multiple Precision) library, 82
    extension, 98
gmp_intval() function, 98
gmp_strval() function, 98
graph databases, 341-342

H
hash tables, arrays, 123
hashes, recursive, 375-379
hashing passwords, 218-221
header() function, 59
Heredocs, 63
hex2bin() function, 100
hrtime() function, 310-314
http-client module, AMPHP project, 367

I
if/else statements, 16
imperative programming, 29
implements keyword, 182
implode() function, 76
increment() function, 33
INF constant, 83
inheritance, 164
    objects, 180
    single inheritance, 202
input sanitization, format strings, 75
input stream, reading from, 253-256
integers, 81
    $argc, 390-393

arrays, consecutive, 127-129
bitwise operators, 24-27
converting from floating-point, 86
negative, 13
processor size and, 12
random, generating, 88-89
sign, 12
very large or small numbers, 97-99
integration testing, mocking databases, 351-356
interactive shell, 400-402
interpolation, 61
string variables, 74-75
invocations, 40
is_numeric() function, 82, 83
iterable objects, 129
iteration
array items, 129-131
for loops, 130
very large arrays, 157-159

J

JIT (just-in-time) compilation, 308
OPcache and, 309
join() function, 77
JWTs (JSON Web Tokens), 43

K

key exchange, 225
key-value stores, 340-341
keywords
class, 161, 168
clone, 192-196
extends, 179-181
final, 188-192
implements, 182
new, 161
readonly, 172
SetEnv, 217
static, 48, 196-199

L

Lambdas, 50
language constructs, 130
Laraval, Eloquent ORM, 356-359
leap year, validating, 115
legacy encryption, 206
libraries, asynchronous programming, 362
Libsodium, 206

stdn
decrypting, 255
encrypting, 254
libsqlite3-dev, 326
libxml2-dev package, 326
Linux, pkg-config package, 325
list() construct, 42
local functions, scoping, 32
local variables, static keyword, 48
locking files, 244-245
advisory locking, 244
mandatory locking, 244
log() function, 94
logarithms, calculating, 94
logger() function, 49
logical operators, 11-12
loops
array data, 126
concurrent execution, 373-374
for, 130
loose typing, 308

M

Magical class, 177-179
mandatory locking, 244
mcrypt, 206
Mersenne Twister, 90
message queues, 379-383
messages, cryptographic signatures, 231-233
methods, 161
private, 199-201
signatures, 182
static, 196-199
modules, extensions, 326
modulo arithmetic, 56
Monolog, debugging and, 292-296
mt_rand() function, 89, 90
multiparadigm languages, 165-166
multiplier() function, 53
mutability, DateTimeImmutable object, 117
MySQL database, 346-349

N

named arguments, syntax, 35
native extensions, installing, 335-337
negative integers, 13
nested arrays, 126
never return type, 59
new keyword, 161

not operator, 13
Nowdoc syntax, 63
null values, coalescing, 17-18
null-coalesing operators, 17
nullable types, 38
numbers
    converting base, 99-100
    floating-point, 81
        comparing, 84-86
        converting to integer, 86
        relative equality, 85
        rounding, 86-87
    formatting as strings, 96-97
    integers, 81
    random, generating predictable, 89-91
    variables, validating, 82-84
number_format() function, 96
numeric arrays, 124
    deleting elements, 131-134
numeric constants, 81
numerical bases, converting between, 99-100
NWS API, 378

O

object orientation, 101
object-oriented programming, 163-165
objects
    cleanup, 175-177
    cloning, 192-196
    DateTime, 101, 103
    DateTimeImmutable, 101
    inheritance, 164, 180
    instantiation, 161
        custom classes, 168-170
    iterable, 129
    methods, private, 199-201
    properties
        default values, 170-172
        private, 199-201
onCreate() method, 251
onResolve() method, 364
opcode caching, 309
    application acceleration, 320-323
Open Swoole, 363
open() method, 343
OpenSSL library, 206
operations, moving between, 371-374
operators, 11
    @, 23

bitwise, 12-13
    not, 13
comparison, 13
logical, 11-12
null-coalescing, 17
spaceship, 20-22
spread operator, 40
ternary, 15-16
ord() function, 30
ORM (object-relational mapping) library, 342
output stream, writing to, 256-258
output, colorizing, 401

P

pack() function, 78
packages, 325
    autoconf, 325
    bison, 325
    build-essentials, 325
    Composer, locating, 330-332
    installing, 326, 332-335
    libsqlite3-dev, 326
    libxml2-dev, 326
    pkg-config, 325
    re2c, 325
    updating, 332-335
Packagist, 332
parallel package, AMPHP project, 374-379
parallel programming, versus concurrent, 361
parallel-functions module, AMPHP, 369-371
parallelMap() function, 371
parameters
    functions
        accessing, 31-33
        default, setting, 33-35
        misordered, 34
        named, 35-36
        optional, 34
        positional, 35
    passing functions as, 51-54
    types, 37
parent methods, implementation override, 180
parsing arguments, 390-393
passing
    functions as parameters, 51-54
    variables, 32
        by reference, 33, 46
passwords
    hashing, 218-221

plaintext, 219
validating, 218-221
password_hash() function, 218-221
password_verify() function, 219
PDO (PHP Data Objects), 327
as abstraction layer, 344-349
extending, 344
external database provider connection, 344-349
persistent connections, 348
prepared statements, 350
sanitizing user input, 349-351
PEAR, 335-337
PECL (PHP Extension Community Library), 206, 327, 335-337
performance tuning, 307
benchmarking application performance, 314-320
function execution timing, 310-314
PHPBench, 314-320
persistent connections, 348
php://temp stream, 251
PHPBench, 314-320
phpinfo() function, 217
PHPStan, 291
pkg-config package, 325
pow() function, 95
predictable random numbers, 89-91
preserve_keys, 141
procedural programming, 162
programming languages
dynamically typed, 2
loosely typed, 1
strongly typed, 1
promises, 364-365
pending, 364
promises, AMPHP project, 364
properties, 161
classes, read-only, 172-174
dynamic, magic methods, 177-179
objects, default values, 170-172
private, 199-201
static, 196-199
protected classes, 166
public classes, 166
public-key cryptography, 209

Q

queries, sanitizing user input, 349-351

R

RabbitMQ, 379-383
random number generators, 88
Mersenne Twister, 90
random numbers
generating, 88-89
predictable, 89-91
weighted, generating, 91-94
random strings, generating, 72-73
randomness, encryption, 211-212
random_bytes() function, 73
random_float() function, 89
random_init() function, 88-89
range() function, 127-129
re2c package, 325
ReactPHP library, 363
read-only properties, classes, 172-174
reading
from input stream, 253-256
from streams, writing to another, 258-260
user input, 393-395
reading files
specific bytes, 239-240
to strings, 238-239
readonly keyword, 172
recursive functions, static variables and, 48
recursive hashes, 375-379
reduce() function, 52
references, passing by, 46
Reflection API, 199-201
regressions, git-bisect and, 301-305
relational databases, 339-340
relative equality, floating-point numbers, 85
REPL (read-eval-print-loop), 400-402
repository interface, 352
require command, 397
return types
enforcing, 37-40
never, 59
void, 57
return values, none, 56-58
returning multiple values, 42-44
returns, none, 58-59
RoadRunner, 363
round() function, 86
arguments, 86
rounding
constants, 87
floating-point numbers, 86-87

floats, 87
runtimes
    asynchronous programming, 362
    RoadRunner, 363

S

sanitizing user input, 212-216
    database queries, 349-351
scalar types, 37
searches, case-insensitive, 69
SEO (search engine optimization)
    A/B testing for, 5
SetEnv keyword, 217
setters, dynamic properties and, 177
shallow clones, 194
shuffle() function, 152-152
signatures, 182
signatures, cryptographic, 231-233
single inheritance, 202
single-quoted strings, 61
sodium, 206-211
    pull streaming interface, 228
    push streaming interfaces, 227
sodium prefix, 207
SODIUM_ prefix, 207
sodium_crypto_secretbox(), 221
sodium_crypto_secretbox_open(), 222
sodium_crypto_sign(), 231
sodium_crypto_sign_detached(), 232
sort() function, 147-149
sorting
    array elements, 147-149
    spaceship operator and, 20-22
SORT_NUMERIC, 148
spaceship operators, 20-22
spread operator, 40
sprintf() function, 74
SQL (Structured Query Language)
    INSERT statements, 350
SQLite class, 342
SQLite database, 322
    connecting to, 342-344
SQLite Viewer, 344
SQLite3, 327
state, 339
    managing, 48-50
statements
    echo, 279
    if/else, 16

switch, 20
static code analysis, 291-292
static keyword, 48, 196-199
static methods, 196-199
static properties, 196-199
static variables, use cases, recursive functions
    and, 48
STDIN file, 393-395
STDOUT file, 394
stdout stream, 257
storage, encrypted data, 227-231
stream handlers, 260-264
stream resource, 248
streaming
    temporary streams, 252
    to/from temporary files, 251-253
streams, 235, 247
    combining, 258-260
    custom stream protocol, 264-267
    Fibers and, 383-387
    filters, 249-251
    input, reading from, 253-256
    layers, 261
    output, writing to, 256-258
    php://temp, 251
    reading from/writing to another, 258-260
    temporary memory stream, 260
    wrappers, 248-248
streamWrapper class, 265
stream_copy_to_stream() function, 258, 260
strict equality comparison, strings, 64
strict typing, 308
strings, 61
    arrays, converting between, 143-145
    base_convert() function, 100
    binary data, 78-80
    capital characters, counting, 70
    capitalization, 30
    character-by-character processing, 70-72
    characters, replacing, 71
    concatenation, 75-77
    converting to arrays, 71
    converting to DateTime object, 111-114
    double-quoted, 74
    extracting, 65-67
    formatting numbers as, 96-97
    generating random, 72-73
    integer offset, 71
    negative offset, 71

parsing date and time from, 111-114
reading files to, 238-239
replacing part, 67-70
single-quoted, 61
strict equality comparison, 64
substrings
    accessing, 64-65
    length, 66
    negative length, 67
    negative offset, 66
    replacing multiple, 68
    replacing with parameters, 69
variable contents as, 296-299
variables, interpolating, 74-75
strpos() function, 64
strtotime() function, 112
str_split() function, 143-145
substr() function, 66-67
substrings
    accessing, 64-65
    counting occurrences, 64
    length, 66
    negative length, 67
    negative offset, 66
    replacing
        multiple, 68
        with array parameters, 69
substr_replace() function, 67-69
subtraction, floating-point, 84
superglobal variables, 6
swapping variables in place, 7-9
switch statement, 20
Symfony Console component, 396-399
symmetric encryption, 208
syntactic sugar, 17
syntax
    named arguments, 35

T

tables, Symfony Console, 398
TDD (test-driven development), 280
temporary files
    destructor, 175
    streaming to/from, 251-253
temporary streams, 252
ternary operators, 15-16
    nested expressions, 16
testing
    A/B testing, 5

BDD (behavior-driven development), 280
built-in web server and, 299-301
static code analysis, 291-292
TDD (test-driven development), 280
unit testing
    automating tests, 288-290
    function tests, 285
    multiple test suites, 285
    regressions, git-bisect and, 301-305
    writing tests, 283-288
user-reported bugs, 285
text color, 395
Thanksgiving, DateTimeImmutable object, 118
threads, message queues, 379-383
time (see date and time)
time zones, 102
    calculating time across, 119-121
TimerDecorator class, 312
timestamps
    creating, 108
    Unix, 102, 107-108
        @ prefix, 112
        converting text to, 112
        converting to date and time parts,
            109-110
        passing as parameter, 109
TOTP (time-based one-time password) system,
    331
traits, 180
traits, importing, 201-204
truthiness, 15
type casting, 13-14
types
    converting between, 19
    nullable, 38
    parameters, 37
    scalar, 37
    union types, 38

U

U format character, 107
union types, 38
uniqid() function, 255
unit testing
    automating, 288-290
    function tests, 285
    multiple test suites, 285
    regressions, git-bisect and, 301-305
    writing tests, 283-288

Unix
 timestamps, 102
  @ prefix, 112
  converting date and time to, 107-108
  converting text to, 112
  converting to date and time parts,
   109-110
  passing as parameter, 109
 versus Windows, 235-236
unpack() function, 78
unset() function, 131
use statement, 201-204
user input
 filtering, 212-216
 prompting for, 393-395
 sanitizing, 212-216
  database queries, 349-351
 validating, 212-216
user-defined filters, 249
user-defined functions, 31, 45
 sorting arrays, 150-151
usort() function, 150-151

V

validation
 numbers with variables, 82-84
 passwords, 218-221
 user input, 212-216
values
 comparing, 18-20
 identical, 18
 null, coalescing, 17-18
 returning multiple, 42-44
 type casting, 13-14
variability, 1
variable variables, 4-6
variables, 1
 complex, contents, 296-299
 contents as strings, 296-299
 defining, 3
 empty ( ), 1
 environment, populating, 217
 global, accessing, 44-47

interpolating, 74-75
interpolation, 61
local, static keyword, 48
names, 32
numbers, validating, 82-84
passing, 32
 by reference, 33, 46
static, recursive functions and, 48
superglobal, 6
swapping in place, 7-9
VariableStream class, 264
var_dump() function, 296-299
Vehicle class, 165
verbose activity, 35
verbosity, concatenation, 76
verification, cryptographic signatures, 233-234
visibility, classes and, 166-168
VM (virtual machine), 308
void return type, 57

W

wait() function, 368
web applications, launching locally, 299-301
web server, built-in, 299-301
weighted random choice
 implementing, 91
 repeated selection, 93
weighted random numbers, generating, 91-94
weighted_random_choice() function, 91-94
WET (write everything twice), 30
Windows versus Unix, 235-236
WordPress, 389
WordPress CMS (content management system), 165
wrappers, 248-248
writing to files, multiple, 242-244
writing to output stream, 256-258

X

Xdebug, 280
 development environment and, 282
 installing, 281-283

About the Author

Eric Mann has worked as a software engineer for almost two decades. He has built scalable projects for early-stage startups and for Fortune 500 companies. Eric presents frequently on software architecture, security engineering, and best practices in development. He has been a regular contributor to *php[architect]* magazine for over five years and most enjoys helping new developers avoid a lot of the same mistakes he has made in his own coding career.

Colophon

The animal on the cover of *PHP Cookbook* is a silver pheasant (*Lophura nycthemera*). Silver pheasants are native to the pine and bamboo forests of various mountainous regions of Southeast Asia. Male pheasants have black and white plumage with a small crest of curly black feathers, while females are mainly brown, with much shorter tails. Both sexes have bare red faces. Silver pheasants sometimes hybridize with kalij pheasants where their ranges overlap.

Silver pheasants are considered a species of least concern. Many of the animals on O'Reilly covers are endangered; all of them are important to the world.

The cover illustration is by Karen Montgomery, based on an antique line engraving from *Riverside Natural History*. The cover fonts are Gilroy Semibold and Guardian Sans. The text font is Adobe Minion Pro; the heading font is Adobe Myriad Condensed; and the code font is Dalton Maag's Ubuntu Mono.

O'REILLY®

Learn from experts.
Become one yourself.

Books | Live online courses
Instant answers | Virtual events
Videos | Interactive learning

Get started at oreilly.com.

CPSIA information can be obtained
at www.ICGtesting.com
Printed in the USA
JSHW051104040623
42688JS00001B/1